3.2
FINANCIAL MANAGEMENT

First edition 1988
Second edition 1989
Third edition 1990
Fourth edition July 1991

ISBN 0 86277 461 6 (previous edition 0 86277 402 0)

British Library Cataloguing-in-Publication Data

A catalogue record for this book is available from the British Library

Published by

BPP Publishing Limited
Aldine House, Aldine Place
London W12 8AW

Printed in Great Britain by
Ashford Colour Press, Gosport, Hampshire

We are grateful to the Chartered Association of Certified Accountants, the Chartered Institute of Management Accountants and the Institute of Chartered Accountants in England and Wales, for permission to reproduce past examination questions. The suggested solutions have been prepared by BPP Publishing Limited.

CONTENTS

CONTENTS

PREFACE

The examinations of the Chartered Association of Certified Accountants are a demanding test of students' ability to master the wide range of financial, commercial and legal knowledge required of the modern accountant. The Association's rapid response to the pace of change is shown both in the content of the syllabuses and in the style of examination questions set.

BPP's experience in producing study material for the Association's examinations is unparalleled. Over the years, BPP's *Study Texts* and *Practice and Revision Kits*, now supplemented by the *Password* series of multiple choice (objective test) question books, have helped thousands of students attain the examination success that is a prerequisite of career development in finance and management.

This study text is designed to prepare students for Paper 3.2 *Financial Management*. It provides comprehensive and targeted coverage of the syllabus (page (vii)) in the light of the Association's study guide (pages (viii) to (xi)) and recent examination questions (described on pages (xi) and (xii)).

BPP's Study Texts are noted for their clarity of explanation and their use of worked examples as essential aids to learning. They are reviewed and updated each year. BPP's study material, at once comprehensive and up to date, is thus the ideal investment that the aspiring accountant can make for examination success.

The July 1991 edition of this text

This text has been reviewed and updated in the light of recent developments in the subject and in the examination. The most significant amendments are outlined below.

- The text has been updated for recent developments in sources of finance.
- The material has been rearranged for easier learning.
- Extra quizzes and illustrative questions have been added for student practice.

BPP Publishing
July 1991

For details of other BPP titles relevant to your studies for this examination, please turn to page 503. Should you wish to send in your comments on this text please turn to page 504.

INTRODUCTION

Syllabus

Section 1: Financial objectives

The financial objectives of various types of organisations
The relationship between financial and other objectives

Section 2: Securities markets

The role and nature of the capital markets

Section 3: Sources of finance and capital structures

Sources of finance. Raising long and short-term finance
The costs of different sources of finance
The cost of capital
Capital structure
Problems of small businesses and unlisted companies

Section 4: The firm's investment decision

Long-term financial planning and corporate models
Capital budgeting
External growth and divestment strategies

Section 5: Financial structuring and control and reporting

The use and deployment of financial resources within groups of companies
Financial control and reporting systems appropriate to groups of companies
Schemes of capitalisation and financial restructuring
Methods of financing overseas operations

Section 6: The management of working capital

Role of working capital in the financial structure of the company
The management of working capital: stocks, debtors, creditors, cash and liquid resources
Special problems.

BPP note

The structure of this text follows that of the syllabus. However, certain topics in Section 3 of the syllabus use techniques covered in Section 4. If you are unfamiliar with discounted cash flow techniques, you should read Chapter 12, Sections 4, 5 and 6 before reading Chapters 7 and 8.

INTRODUCTION

Study guide

Objectives of the syllabus

The objectives of the syllabus are to ensure a student:

has a thorough understanding of the current practical methods used in making financial management decisions;

understands the concepts behind available theoretical models and can assess the relevance of developments in financial management theory to an enterprise;

can select the techniques most appropriate to optimise the employment of resources including the most effective method of financing the acquisition of an expensive piece of equipment;

understands the workings of the financial system and can evaluate alternative sources of finance and assess investment possibilities;

appreciates the treasury management function, in particular the working capital aspects and international considerations;

can communicate the consequences of financial management decisions to accountants or non-accountants.

Format and standard of the examination paper

1. Students will be required to answer four questions out of six. The paper is an introduction to current practice and theories of financial management, and to the financial resources available to organisations.

2. The abilities tested in the Paper will, therefore, range from knowledge of a particular factual topic (eg sources of finance available to a small business) to analysis and evaluation of a situation which is based on Level 2 subject matter (eg on management of working capital or cash budgets) or a basic appreciation of an area of theory with significant implications for practice.

3. The Paper may include both essay and data handling questions, but students will not be required to undertake detailed computations on advanced theoretical topics. Students will be expected to have a thorough understanding of the contents of Papers 2.4 Cost and Management Accounting II, of mathematical techniques studied in Paper 2.6 Quantitative Analysis and of Papers 2.8 The Regulatory Framework of Accounting and 2.9 Advanced Accounting Practice. In addition, students should have a comprehensive knowledge of the subject matter of the other Level 3 papers. Students must, for example, appreciate the way in which the financing of a project, ie by loan or equity capital is reflected in the profit and loss account and balance sheet; they will also be expected to demonstrate that they understand the influence that taxation has on financial decisions.

Knowledge levels

Each topic in the syllabus is given a level of knowledge which defines the depth at which it needs to be studied.

The three levels are:

I *Introductory*
Basic understanding of principles, concepts, theories and techniques

B *Broad*
Application of principles, concepts, theories and techniques in the solution of straightforward problems.

F *Full*
Identification and solution of more complex problems through the selection and application of principles, concepts, theories and techniques.

Content	*Knowledge level*
Section 1: Financial objectives	
The financial objectives of various types of organisations:	B
profit seeking organisations;	
not-for-profit organisations.	
The relationship between financial and other objectives:	B
financial objectives: long-term (discounted cash flow), and short-term;	
constraints, eg environmental, social, non-financial performance indicators (output per employee, per service unit).	
The relationships between an organisation's:	B
shareholders;	
management;	
lenders;	
customers, suppliers; and employees.	
Section 2: Securities markets	
The role of the capital markets:	B
securities markets including The Stock Exchange, the Unlisted Securities Market and over the counter markets;	
evaluation of corporate securities;	
the efficient market hypothesis (in particular the role of accounting information);	
takeovers, mergers and reconstructions, including general provisions of the City Code.	
Section 3: Sources of finance and capital structures	
Sources of finance:	
capital markets: new issues and rights issues, loan capital;	F
retained earnings and dividend policy;	F
bank borrowings (long, medium and various types of short-term);	F
government sources: regional and selective assistance;	I
business expansion scheme;	I
venture capital;	B
international money and capital markets.	I

	Knowledge level
Raising long and short-term finance:	F
long-term capital requirements: replacement and growth;	
debt/equity ratios; borrowing capacity;	
working capital requirements;	
treasury management and the use of short-term money markets.	
The costs of different sources of finance:	F
equity finance: retained profits, new issues;	
debt finance and gearing: debentures, convertibles;	
other financial instruments.	
The cost of capital (including the impact of inflation and taxation):	B
weighted average cost of capital;	
Modigliani and Miller: the effect of capital structure;	
Portfolio Theory and beta as a measure of risk: use of beta values;	
the Capital Asset Pricing Model.	
Particular problems associated with small businesses and unlisted companies.	B

Section 4: The firm's investment decision

Long-term financial planning and corporate models.	B
Capital budgeting:	
project acceptance criteria: payback, accounting rate of return, discounted cash flow;	
internal rate of return versus net present value;	F
relevant cost of capital;	B
treatment of risk and uncertainty: sensitivity analysis, expected values, variability of returns, certainty equivalents, simulation, portfolio considerations;	B
effects and treatment of inflation;	B
impact of taxation (simple calculations only and tax rates will be specified in questions when necessary);	B
capital rationing and project ranking;	I
asset replacement and lease or buy decisions.	B
External growth and divestment strategies:	
amalgamations, mergers and takeovers;	B
valuation of listed and unlisted companies;	B
management buyouts.	I

Section 5: Financial structuring and control and reporting

The use and deployment of financial resources within groups of companies.	B
Financial control and reporting systems appropriate to groups of companies.	B
Schemes of capitalisation and financial restructuring:	B
debt;	
equity;	
rights issues;	
tenders;	
term loans.	
Methods of financing overseas operations.	I

	Knowledge level
Section 6: The management of working capital	
Role of working capital in the financial structure of the company.	F
The management of working capital including: stocks; debtors; creditors; cash and liquid resources.	B
Special problems including: debt factoring; cash management and planning; short-term investment opportunities; foreign exchange markets; minimising foreign exchange risk.	B

General notes

In questions involving an assessment of the impact of taxation, any assumptions used will be specified.

Students should, where possible, be introduced to the software packages used in financial modelling, and to the computerised data bases which are available, eg Extel, Datastream.

Teachers should keep students up to date with new securities markets, as these develop.

Analysis of past papers

Apart from the syllabus and study guide above, the best guide to the kind of questions which may appear in the examination must be the recent papers set. The contents of these papers are therefore listed here. In each case, candidates had to answer any four of the six questions.

December 1990

1 Expected net present value calculations. A discussion of their limitations.
2 Redemption yields of securities. A discussion of Eurobonds.
3 The application of stock control techniques to borrowings. The selection of a mix of finance.
4 Portfolio theory and CAPM
5 Traded options. The valuation of a takeover target. The effects of a takeover.
6 The finance of foreign trade. Hedging foreign currency transactions.

June 1990

1 Discounted cash flow appraisal of a project for which expenses are in sterling and receipts in a foreign currency.
2 Disintermediation, securitisation, interest rate swaps and short-term investments.
3 The appraisal of a proposal for a leveraged management buyout.
4 Cost of capital computations and a discussion of their usefulness.
5 The appraisal of the strategic objectives and financial management of an expanding company.
6 Any two of:
   (a) types of flotation;
   (b) remuneration schemes for senior management;
   (c) the choice between fixed interest and variable interest borrowings.

December 1989

1 The appraisal of a new project. A discussion of Monte Carlo simulation.
2 The effect of a stock market crash on the cost of capital. The capital asset pricing model.
3 The appraisal of a scheme of capital reconstruction.
4 A discussion of different views on dividend policy.
5 The appraisal of alternative ways of raising new finance.
6 The choice of a method of hedging foreign exchange risk.

June 1989

1 Calculation of the internal rate of return. Finding an appropriate discount rate. The effect of taxation.
2 Cash budget. Ways to alleviate a cash shortage. Computerised cash management.
3 Computations and importance of financial gearing. The choice between debt and equity finance.
4 The assessment of a company's health. Deep discount bonds.
5 Diversification into a new industry. Asset and equity betas.
6 Any two of:
   (a) forms of market listing;
   (b) objectives of nationalised and private businesses;
   (c) efficient market hypothesis.

December 1988

1 DCF and mutually exclusive projects, including cash inflows in foreign currency.
2 (a) Centralising the finance functions of a group of companies.
   (b) Using financial ratios to monitor, evaluate and control the activities of a group of companies.
3 Methods of raising new capital for a major new project, and their relative merits and drawbacks.
4 Modigliani and Miller theory (with corporate taxes) and arbitrage.
5 (a) A bonus issue, a scrip dividend and a share split.
   (b) Reasons why a company might decide to purchase its own shares.
6 Any two of:
   (a) Eurocurrency, eurobond and euroequity markets.
   (b) Objectives of a company other than maximising the wealth of shareholders.
   (c) Credit management. The use of a credit scoring system and other methods of customer credit evaluation.

Types of question

You should expect a number of questions to require a lot of writing. Computational work will be an important feature of the paper, but the examiner has stated that:

(a) a 25 mark question that is *entirely* computational will not be set. Students are expected to be aware of the practical and theoretical merits and disadvantages of models and rules used, and not merely to be proficient at their basic numerical application without understanding what the numbers indicate;

(b) a 25 mark question that is *entirely* written is a possibility, but likely to be rare. Students should not be able to pass the exam on 'waffle' alone, and some ability to handle numbers will be required.

Where written work is required, you must plan your answer before you start to write. If (say) 12 marks are available for the relevant part of a question, five minutes of planning followed by 15 minutes of writing might earn eight marks, while 20 minutes of writing might earn only four marks.

It is likely that one question will involve a lengthy DCF project appraisal, probably involving inflation and/or taxation. When answering such questions, it is important to prepare clear, neat workings, so that you can be given credit for method even if your final answer is wrong.

Present value table

Present value of £1 = $(1 + r)^{-n}$ where r = discount rate, n = years until payment.

Discount rates (r)

Periods (n)	*1%*	*2%*	*3%*	*4%*	*5%*	*6%*	*7%*	*8%*	*9%*	*10%*	
1	0.990	0.980	0.971	0.962	0.952	0.943	0.935	0.926	0.917	0.909	1
2	0.980	0.961	0.943	0.925	0.907	0.890	0.873	0.857	0.842	0.826	2
3	0.971	0.942	0.915	0.889	0.864	0.840	0.816	0.794	0.772	0.751	3
4	0.961	0.924	0.888	0.855	0.823	0.792	0.763	0.735	0.708	0.683	4
5	0.951	0.906	0.863	0.822	0.784	0.747	0.713	0.681	0.650	0.621	5
6	0.942	0.888	0.837	0.790	0.746	0.705	0.666	0.630	0.596	0.564	6
7	0.933	0.871	0.813	0.760	0.711	0.665	0.623	0.583	0.547	0.513	7
8	0.923	0.853	0.789	0.731	0.677	0.627	0.582	0.540	0.502	0.467	8
9	0.914	0.837	0.766	0.703	0.645	0.592	0.544	0.500	0.460	0.424	9
10	0.905	0.820	0.744	0.676	0.614	0.558	0.508	0.463	0.422	0.386	10
11	0.896	0.804	0.722	0.650	0.585	0.527	0.475	0.429	0.388	0.350	11
12	0.887	0.788	0.702	0.625	0.557	0.497	0.444	0.397	0.356	0.319	12
13	0.879	0.773	0.681	0.601	0.530	0.469	0.415	0.368	0.326	0.290	13
14	0.870	0.758	0.661	0.577	0.505	0.442	0.388	0.340	0.299	0.263	14
15	0.861	0.743	0.642	0.555	0.481	0.417	0.362	0.315	0.275	0.239	15

	11%	*12%*	*13%*	*14%*	*15%*	*16%*	*17%*	*18%*	*19%*	*20%*	
1	0.901	0.893	0.885	0.877	0.870	0.862	0.855	0.847	0.840	0.833	1
2	0.812	0.797	0.783	0.769	0.756	0.743	0.731	0.718	0.706	0.694	2
3	0.731	0.712	0.693	0.675	0.658	0.641	0.624	0.609	0.593	0.579	3
4	0.659	0.636	0.613	0.592	0.572	0.552	0.534	0.516	0.499	0.482	4
5	0.593	0.567	0.543	0.519	0.497	0.476	0.456	0.437	0.419	0.402	5
6	0.535	0.507	0.480	0.456	0.432	0.410	0.390	0.370	0.352	0.335	6
7	0.482	0.452	0.425	0.400	0.376	0.354	0.333	0.314	0.296	0.279	7
8	0.434	0.404	0.376	0.351	0.327	0.305	0.285	0.266	0.249	0.233	8
9	0.391	0.361	0.333	0.308	0.284	0.263	0.243	0.225	0.209	0.194	9
10	0.352	0.322	0.295	0.270	0.247	0.227	0.208	0.191	0.176	0.162	10
11	0.317	0.287	0.261	0.237	0.215	0.195	0.178	0.162	0.148	0.135	11
12	0.286	0.257	0.231	0.208	0.187	0.168	0.152	0.137	0.124	0.112	12
13	0.258	0.229	0.204	0.182	0.163	0.145	0.130	0.116	0.104	0.093	13
14	0.232	0.205	0.181	0.160	0.141	0.125	0.111	0.099	0.088	0.078	14
15	0.209	0.183	0.160	0.140	0.123	0.108	0.095	0.084	0.074	0.065	15

Annuity table

Present value of an annuity of £1 = $\frac{1 - (1 + r)^{-n}}{r}$ where r = discount rate, n = years.

Discount rates (r)

Periods (n)	*1%*	*2%*	*3%*	*4%*	*5%*	*6%*	*7%*	*8%*	*9%*	*10%*	
1	0.990	0.980	0.971	0.962	0.952	0.943	0.935	0.926	0.917	0.909	1
2	1.970	1.942	1.913	1.886	1.859	1.833	1.808	1.783	1.759	1.736	2
3	2.941	2.884	2.829	2.775	2.723	2.673	2.624	2.577	2.531	2.487	3
4	3.902	3.808	3.717	3.630	3.546	3.465	3.387	3.312	3.240	3.170	4
5	4.853	4.713	4.580	4.452	4.329	4.212	4.100	3.993	3.890	3.791	5
6	5.795	5.601	5.417	5.242	5.076	4.917	4.767	4.623	4.486	4.355	6
7	6.728	6.472	6.230	6.002	5.786	5.582	5.389	5.206	5.033	4.868	7
8	7.652	7.325	7.020	6.733	6.463	6.210	5.971	5.747	5.535	5.335	8
9	8.566	8.162	7.786	7.435	7.108	6.802	6.515	6.247	5.995	5.759	9
10	9.471	8.983	8.530	8.111	7.722	7.360	7.024	6.710	6.418	6.145	10
11	10.37	9.787	9.253	8.760	8.306	7.887	7.499	7.139	6.805	6.495	11
12	11.26	10.58	9.954	9.385	8.863	8.384	7.943	7.536	7.161	6.814	12
13	12.13	11.35	10.63	9.986	9.394	8.853	8.358	7.904	7.487	7.103	13
14	13.00	12.11	11.30	10.56	9.899	9.295	8.745	8.244	7.786	7.367	14
15	13.87	12.85	11.94	11.12	10.38	9.712	9.108	8.559	8.061	7.606	15

	11%	*12%*	*13%*	*14%*	*15%*	*16%*	*17%*	*18%*	*19%*	*20%*	
1	0.901	0.893	0.885	0.877	0.870	0.862	0.855	0.847	0.840	0.833	1
2	1.713	1.690	1.668	1.647	1.626	1.605	1.585	1.566	1.547	1.528	2
3	2.444	2.402	2.361	2.322	2.283	2.246	2.210	2.174	2.140	2.106	3
4	3.102	3.037	2.974	2.914	2.855	2.798	2.743	2.690	2.639	2.589	4
5	3.696	3.605	3.517	3.433	3.352	3.274	3.199	3.127	3.058	2.991	5
6	4.231	4.111	3.998	3.889	3.784	3.685	3.589	3.498	3.410	3.326	6
7	4.712	4.564	4.423	4.288	4.160	4.039	3.922	3.812	3.706	3.605	7
8	5.146	4.968	4.799	4.639	4.487	4.344	4.207	4.078	3.954	3.837	8
9	5.537	5.328	5.132	4.946	4.772	4.607	4.451	4.303	4.163	4.031	9
10	5.889	5.650	5.426	5.216	5.019	4.833	4.659	4.494	4.339	4.192	10
11	6.207	5.938	5.687	5.453	5.234	5.209	4.836	4.656	4.486	4.327	11
12	6.492	6.194	5.918	5.660	5.421	5.197	4.988	4.793	4.611	4.439	12
13	6.750	6.424	6.122	5.842	5.583	5.342	5.118	4.910	4.715	4.533	13
14	6.982	6.628	6.302	6.002	5.724	5.468	5.229	5.008	4.802	4.611	14
15	7.191	6.811	6.462	6.142	5.847	5.575	5.324	5.092	4.876	4.675	15

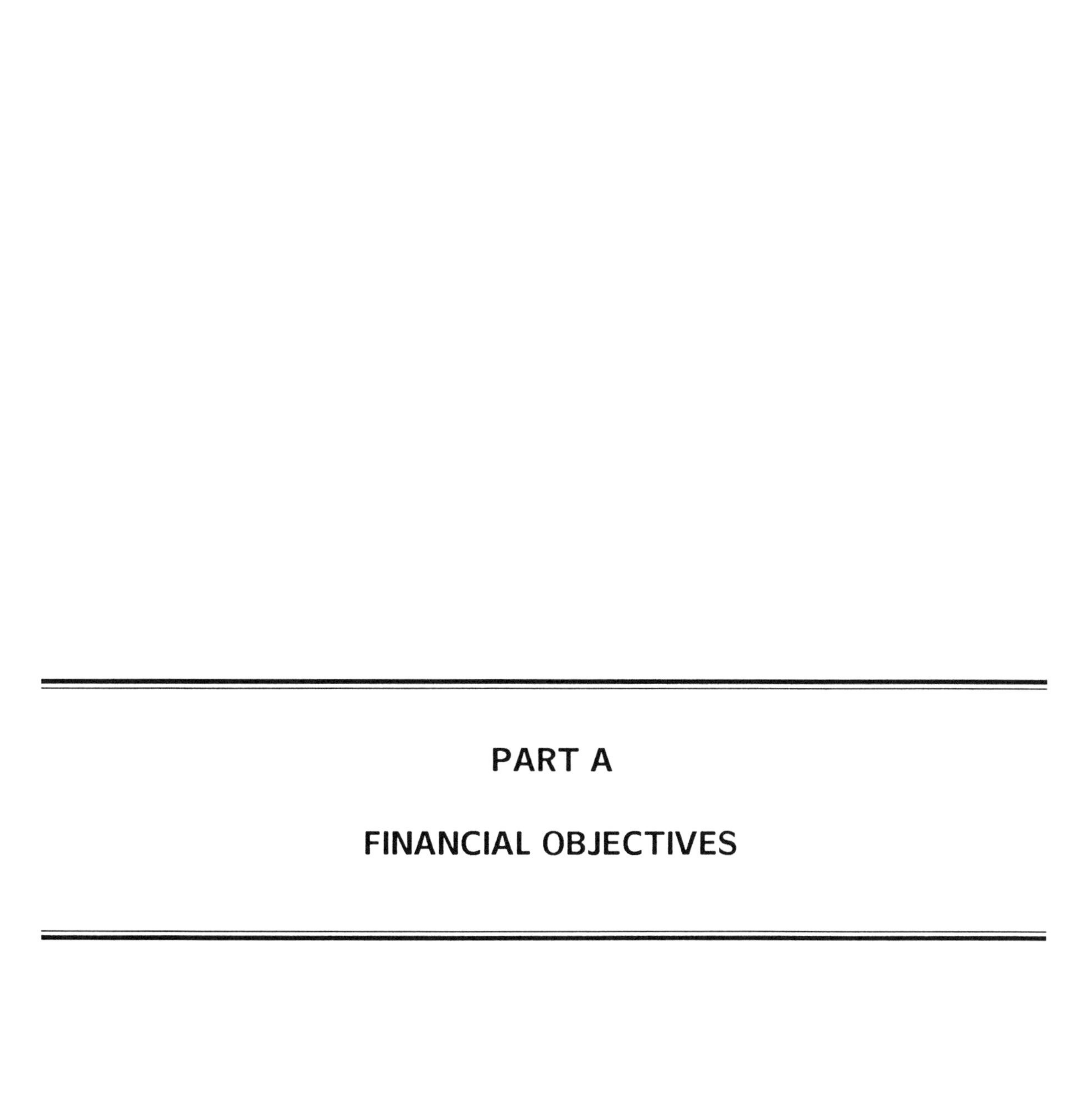

PART A

FINANCIAL OBJECTIVES

Chapter 1

FINANCIAL OBJECTIVES

This chapter covers the following topics.

1. Financial objectives of companies
2. Non-financial objectives
3. Shareholders and management
4. Bodies which are not purely commercial

1. FINANCIAL OBJECTIVES OF COMPANIES

1.1 Financial management is the management of the finances of a business; that is, financial planning and financial control in order to achieve the financial objectives of the business.

The prime financial objective of a company

1.2 The theory of company finance is based on the assumption that the objective of management is to maximise the market value of the company. Specifically, the main objective of a company should be to maximise the wealth of its ordinary shareholders.

1.3 A company is financed by ordinary shareholders, preference shareholders, loan stock holders and other long-term and short-term creditors. All surplus funds, however, belong to the legal owners of the company, its ordinary shareholders. Any retained profits are undistributed wealth of these equity shareholders.

How are the wealth of shareholders and the value of a company measured?

1.4 If the financial objective of a company is to maximise the value of the company, and in particular the value of its ordinary shares, we need to be able to put values on a company and its shares. How do we do it?

1.5 Three possible methods of valuation might occur to us.

(a) A *balance sheet valuation, with assets valued on a going concern basis*. Certainly, investors will look at a company's balance sheet. If retained profits rise every year, the company will be a profitable one. Balance sheet values are not a measure of 'market value', although retained profits might give some indication of what the company could pay as dividends to shareholders.

(b) The *valuation of a company's assets on a break-up basis.* This method of valuing a business is only of interest when the business is threatened with liquidation, or when its management is thinking about selling off individual assets (rather than a complete business) to raise cash.

(c) *Market values.* The market value is the price at which buyers and sellers will trade stocks and shares in a company. This is the method of valuation which is most relevant to the financial objectives of a company.

(i) When shares are traded on a recognised stock market, such as the Stock Exchange, the market value of a company can be measured by the price at which shares are currently being traded.

(ii) When shares are in a private company, and are not traded on any stock market, there is no easy way to measure their market value. Even so, the financial objective of these companies should be to maximise the wealth of their ordinary shareholders.

1.6 The *wealth* of the shareholders in a company comes from dividends received and the market value of the shares.

A shareholder's *return* on investment is obtained in the form of dividends received and capital gains from increases in the market value of his or her shares.

1.7 Dividends are paid just twice a year at most (interim and final dividends), whereas a current market value is (for quoted shares) always known from share prices. There is also a theory, supported by much empirical evidence (and common sense) that market prices are influenced strongly by expectations of what future dividends will be. So we might conclude that the wealth of shareholders in quoted companies can be measured by the market value of the shares.

How is the value of a business increased?

1.8 If a company's shares are traded on a stock market, the wealth of shareholders is increased when the share price goes up. Ignoring day-to-day fluctuations in price caused by patterns of supply and demand, and ignoring fluctuations caused by 'environmental' factors such as changes in interest rates, the price of a company's shares will go up when the company makes attractive profits, which it pays out as dividends or re-invests in the business to achieve future profit growth and dividend growth. However, to increase the share price the company should achieve its attractive profits without taking business risks and financial risks which worry shareholders.

1.9 If there is an increase in earnings and dividends, management can hope for an increase in the share price too, so that shareholders benefit from both higher revenue (dividends) and also capital gains (higher share prices).

Management should set targets for factors which they can influence directly, such as profits and dividend growth. And so a financial objective might be expressed as the aim of increasing profits, earnings per share and dividend per share by, say, 10% a year for each of the next five years.

1.10 Earnings are the after-tax profits attributable to equity (that is, to ordinary shareholders) excluding extraordinary gains or losses, which are non-recurring items. Earnings per share (EPS) are the earnings attributable to each equity share.

1.11 Dividends are the direct reward to shareholders that a company pays out, and so dividends are evidence of a company's ability to provide a return for its shareholders. Companies might therefore set targets for growth in dividend per share.

Other financial targets

1.12 In addition to targets for earnings, EPS, and dividend per share, a company might set other financial targets, such as:

(a) a restriction on the company's level of gearing, or debt. For example, a company's management might decide that:

(i) the ratio of long-term debt capital to equity capital should never exceed, say, 1:1;

(ii) the cost of interest payments should never be higher than, say, 25% of total profits before interest and tax;

(b) a target for profit retentions. For example, management might set a target that dividend cover (the ratio of distributable profits to dividends actually distributed) should not be less than, say, 2.5 times;

(c) a target for operating profitability. For example, management might set a target for the profit/sales ratio (say, a minimum of 10%) or for a return on capital employed (say, a minimum ROCE of 20%).

1.13 These financial targets are not primary financial objectives, but they can act as subsidiary targets or constraints which should help a company to achieve its main financial objective without incurring excessive risks.

1.14 However, these targets are usually measured over a year rather than over the long term, and it is the maximisation of shareholder wealth in the long term that ought to be the corporate objective.

Short-term measures of return can encourage a company to pursue short-term objectives at the expense of long-term ones, for example by deferring new capital investments, or spending only small amounts on research and development and on training.

Multiple financial targets

1.15 A major problem with setting a number of different financial targets, either primary targets or supporting secondary targets, is that they might not all be consistent with each other, and so might not all be achievable at the same time. When this happens, some compromises will have to be accepted.

Example

1.16 Lion Grange Ltd has recently introduced a formal scheme of long range planning. At a meeting called to discuss the first draft plans, the following estimates emerged.

(a) Sales in the current year reached £10,000,000, and forecasts for the next five years are £10,600,000, £11,400,000, £12,400,000, £13,600,000 and £15,000,000.
(b) The ratio of net profit after tax to sales is 10%, and this is expected to continue throughout the planning period.
(c) Net asset turnover, currently 0.8 times, will remain more or less constant.

1.17 It was also suggested that:

(a) if profits rise, dividends should rise by at least the same percentage;
(b) an earnings retention rate of 50% should be maintained;
(c) the ratio of long term borrowing to long term funds (debt plus equity) is limited (by the market) to 30%, which happens also to be the current gearing level of the company.

Prepare a financial analysis of the draft long range plan and suggested policies for dividends, retained earnings and gearing.

Solution

1.18 The draft financial plan, for profits, dividends, assets required and funding, can be drawn up in a table, as follows.

	Current Year	*Year 1*	*Year 2*	*Year 3*	*Year 4*	*Year 5*
	£m	£m	£m	£m	£m	£m
Sales	10.0	10.6	11.4	12.4	13.6	15.0
Net profit after tax	1.00	1.06	1.14	1.24	1.36	1.50
Dividends (50% of profit after tax)	0.50	0.53	0.57	0.62	0.68	0.75
Net assets (125% of sales)	12.50	13.25	14.25	15.50	17.00	18.75
Equity (increased by retained earnings)	8.75 *	9.28	9.85	10.47	11.15	11.90
Maximum debt (30% of assets)	3.75	3.97	4.27	4.65	5.10	5.62
Funds available	12.50	13.25	14.12	15.12	16.25	17.52
(Shortfalls) in funds, given maximum gearing of 30% and no new issue of shares = funds available minus net assets required	0	0	(0.13)	(0.38)	(0.75)	(1.23)

* The current year equity figure is a balancing figure, equal to the difference between net assets and long term debt, which is currently at the maximum level of 30% of net assets.

1.19 These figures show that the financial objectives of the company are not compatible with each other, and adjustments will have to be made.

(a) Given the assumptions about sales, profits, dividends and net assets required, there will be an increasing shortfall of funds from year 2 onwards, unless new shares are issued or the gearing level rises above 30%.

(b) In years 2 and 3, the shortfall can be eliminated by retaining a greater percentage of profits, but this may have a serious adverse effect on the share price. In year 4 and year 5, the shortfall in funds cannot be removed even if dividend payments are reduced to nothing.

(c) The net asset turnover appears to be low. The situation would be eased if investments were able to generate a higher volume of sales, so that fewer fixed assets and less working capital would be required to support the projected level of sales.

(d) If asset turnover cannot be improved, it may be possible to increase the profit to sales ratio by reducing costs or increasing selling prices.

(e) If a new issue of shares is proposed to make up the shortfall in funds, the amount of funds required must be considered very carefully. Total dividends would have to be increased in order to pay dividends on the new shares. The company seems unable to offer prospects of suitable dividend payments, and so raising new equity might be difficult.

(f) It is conceivable that extra funds could be raised by issuing new debt capital, so that the level of gearing would be over 30%. It is uncertain whether investors would be prepared to lend money so as to increase gearing. If more funds were borrowed, profits after interest and tax would fall so that the share price might also be reduced.

2. NON-FINANCIAL OBJECTIVES

2.1 A company will have important non-financial objectives, which will limit the achievement of financial objectives.

Examples of non-financial objectives are as follows.

(a) *The welfare of employees*
A company might try to provide good wages and salaries, comfortable and safe working conditions, good training and career development, and good pensions. If redundancies are necessary, many companies will provide generous redundancy payments, or spend money trying to find alternative employment for redundant staff.

(b) *The welfare of management*
Managers will often take decisions to improve their own circumstances, even though their decisions will incur expenditure and so reduce profits. High salaries, company cars and other perks are all examples of managers promoting their own interests.

(c) *The welfare of society as a whole*
The management of some companies are aware of the role that their company has to play in providing for the well-being of society. As an example, oil companies are aware of their role as providers of energy for society, faced with the problems of protecting the environment and preserving the Earth's dwindling energy resources.

(d) *The provision of a service*
The major objectives of some companies will include the provision of a service to the public. Examples are the privatised British Telecom and British Gas.

(e) *The fulfilment of responsibilities towards customers and suppliers*

(i) Responsibilities towards customers include providing a product or service of a quality that customers expect, and dealing honestly and fairly with customers.

(ii) Responsibilities towards suppliers are expressed mainly in terms of trading relationships. A company's size could give it considerable power as a buyer. The company should not use its power unscrupulously. Suppliers might rely on getting prompt payment, in accordance with the agreed terms of trade.

The relationship between financial and non-financial objectives

2.2 Non-financial objectives do not negate financial objectives, but they do mean that the simple theory of company finance, that the objective of a firm is to maximise the wealth of ordinary shareholders, is too simplistic. Financial objectives may have to be compromised in order to satisfy non-financial objectives.

3. SHAREHOLDERS AND MANAGEMENT

3.1 Although ordinary shareholders (equity shareholders) are the owners of the company to whom the board of directors are accountable, the actual powers of shareholders tend to be restricted, except in companies where the shareholders are also the directors.

3.2 The day-to-day running of a company is the responsibility of the management, and although the company's results are submitted for shareholders' approval at the annual general meeting (AGM), there is often apathy and acquiescence in directors' recommendations. AGMs are often very poorly attended.

3.3 Shareholders are often ignorant about their company's current situation and future prospects. They have no right to inspect the books of account, and their forecasts of future prospects are gleaned from the annual report and accounts, stockbrokers, investment journals and daily newspapers.

The problems in the relationship between management and shareholders

3.4 The relationship between management and shareholders is sometimes referred to as an *agency relationship*, in which managers act as agents for the shareholders, using delegated powers to run the affairs of the company in the shareholders' best interests.

3.5 However, if managers hold none or very little of the equity shares of the company they work for, what is to stop them from:

(a) working inefficiently?
(b) not bothering to look for profitable new investment opportunities?
(c) giving themselves high salaries and perks?

3.6 One power that shareholders possess is the right to remove the directors from office. But shareholders have to take the initiative to do this, and in many companies, the shareholders lack the energy and organisation to take such a step. Even so, directors will want the company's report and accounts, and the proposed final dividend, to meet with shareholders' approval at the AGM.

3.7 For management below director level, it is the responsibility of the directors to ensure that they perform well. Getting the best out of subordinates is one of the functions of management, and directors should be expected to do it as well as they can.

3.8 Another reason why managers might do their best to improve the financial performance of their company is that managers' pay is often related to the size or profitability of the company. Managers in very big companies, or in very profitable companies, will normally expect to earn higher salaries than managers in smaller or less successful companies.

3.9 There is an argument for giving managers some profit-related pay, or providing incentives which are related to profits or share price. Examples of such remuneration incentives are:

(a) bonuses related to the size of profits;

(b) rewarding managers with shares. This might be done when a private company 'goes public' and managers are invited to subscribe for shares in the company at an attractive offer price;

(c) rewarding managers with *share options*. In a share option scheme, selected employees are given a number of share options, each of which gives the holder the right after a certain date to subscribe for shares in the company at a fixed price. The value of an option will increase if the company is successful and its share price goes up. For example, an employee might be given 10,000 options to subscribe for shares in the company at a price of £2.00 per share. If the share price goes up to, say, £5 per share by the time that the exercise date for the options arrives, the employee will be able to profit by £30,000 (by buying £50,000 worth of shares for £20,000).

Why should managers bother to know who their shareholders are?

3.10 A company's senior management should remain aware of who its major shareholders are, and it will often help to retain shareholders' support if the chairman or the managing director meets occasionally with the major shareholders, to exchange views.

3.11 The advantages of knowing who the company's shareholders are can be listed as follows.

(a) The company's management might learn about shareholders' preferences for either high dividends or high retained earnings for profit growth and capital gain.

(b) For public companies, changes in shareholdings might help to explain recent share price movements.

(c) The company's management should be able to learn about shareholders' attitudes to both risk and gearing. If a company is planning a new investment, its management might have to consider the relative merits of seeking equity finance or debt finance, and shareholders' attitudes would be worth knowing about before the decision is taken.

(d) Management might need to know its shareholders in the event of an unwelcome takeover bid from another company, in order to identify key shareholders whose views on the takeover bid might be crucial to the final outcome.

3.12 The advantages of having a wide range of shareholders include the following.

(a) There is likely to be greater activity in the market in the firm's shares.
(b) There is less likelihood of one shareholder having a controlling interest.
(c) Since shareholdings are smaller on average, there is likely to be less effect on the share price if one shareholder sells his holding.
(d) There is a greater likelihood of a takeover bid being frustrated.

Disadvantages of a large number of shareholders include the following.

(a) Administrative costs will be high. These include the costs of sending out copies of the annual report and accounts, counting proxy votes, registering new shareholders and paying dividends.

(b) Shareholders will have varying tax rates and objectives in holding the firm's shares, which makes a dividend/retention policy more difficult for the management to decide upon.

Shareholders, managers and the company's long-term creditors

3.13 The relationship between *long-term* creditors of a company, the management and the shareholders of a company encompasses the following factors.

(a) Management may decide to raise finance for a company by taking out long-term or medium-term loans. They might well be taking risky investment decisions using outsiders' money to finance them.

(b) Investors who provide debt finance will rely on the company's management to generate enough net cash inflows to make interest payments on time, and eventually to repay loans.

However, long-term creditors will often take *security* for their loan, perhaps in the form of a fixed charge over an asset (such as a mortgage on a building). Debentures are also often subject to certain restrictive covenants, which restrict the company's rights to borrow more money until the debentures have been repaid.

If a company is unable to pay what it owes its creditors, the creditors may decide to:

(i) exercise their security; or
(ii) apply for the company to be wound up.

(c) The money that is provided by long-term creditors will be invested to earn profits, and the profits (in excess of what is needed to pay interest on the borrowing) will provide extra dividends or retained profits for the shareholders of the company. In other words, shareholders will expect to increase their wealth using creditors' money.

Shareholders, managers and government

3.14 The government does not have a direct interest in companies (except for those in which it actually holds shares). However, the government does often have a strong indirect interest in companies' affairs.

(a) *Tax revenue.* The government raises taxes on sales and profits and on shareholders' dividends. It also expects companies to act as tax collectors for income tax and VAT.

The *tax structure* might influence investors' preferences for either dividends or capital growth.

(b) *Encouraging new investments.* The government might provide funds towards the cost of some investment projects. It might also encourage private investment by offering tax incentives such as the business expansion scheme.

(c) *Encouraging a wider spread of share ownership.* In the UK, the government has made some attempts to encourage more private individuals to become company shareholders, by means of attractive privatisation issues (such as the electricity industry) and tax incentives, such as PEPs (personal equity plans) to encourage individuals to invest in shares.

(d) *Legislation.* The government also influences companies, and the relationships between shareholders, creditors, management, employees and the general public, through legislation, including the Companies Acts, legislation on employment, health and safety regulations, legislation on consumer protection and consumer rights and environmental legislation.

(e) *Economic policy.* A government's economic policy will affect business activity. For example, exchange rate policy will have implications for the revenues of exporting firms and purchase costs of importing firms. Policies on economic growth, inflation, employment, interest rates and so on are all relevant to business activities.

4. BODIES WHICH ARE NOT PURELY COMMERCIAL

Nationalised industries

4.1 In the context of financial management, nationalised industries are different from, but still show strong similarities to, companies.

(a) They borrow money, mainly from the government, but sometimes on the national or international money markets.

(b) They must invest funds so as to achieve their financial targets and required rates of return.

4.2 The framework of financial management in nationalised industries consists of:

(a) strategic objectives;
(b) rules about investment plans and their appraisal;
(c) corporate plans, targets and aims;
(d) external financing limits.

I: FINANCIAL OBJECTIVES

Strategic objectives for the nationalised industries

4.3 Nationalised industries are financed by government loans, and some borrowing from the capital markets. They do not have equity capital, and there is no stock exchange to give a continuous valuation of the business.

The financial objective cannot be to maximise the wealth of its owners, the government or the general public, because this is not a concept which can be applied in practice. Nevertheless, there will be a financial objective, to contribute in a certain way to the national economy. This objective may be varied according to the political views of the government.

(a) There may be an objective to earn enough profits for the industry to provide for a certain proportion of its investment needs from its own resources.

(b) A very profitable industry may be expected to lend surplus funds to the government.

4.4 Even so, the *principal* objective of a nationalised industry will in most cases *not* be a financial one at all.

The financial objectives will therefore be subordinated to a number of political and social considerations.

(a) A nationalised industry may be expected to provide a certain standard of service to all customers, regardless of the fact that some individuals will receive a service at a charge well below its cost. For example, the postal service must deliver letters to remote locations for the price of an ordinary first or second class stamp.

(b) The need to provide a service may be of such overriding social and political importance that the government is prepared to subsidise the industry. There is a strong body of opinion, for example, which argues that public transport is a social necessity and a certain level of service must be provided, with losses made up by government subsidies.

Investment plans and investment appraisal in nationalised industries

4.5 Nationalised industries in the UK are required to aim at a rate of return (before interest and tax) on their new investment programmes of 5% *in real terms*. This is required so that the industries do not divert resources away from those areas where they could be used to best effect.

Corporate plans, targets and aims for nationalised industries

4.6 Each nationalised industry has financial targets and a series of performance aims. These targets and performance aims are currently set for a period of three to five years ahead, and may be included within a broader corporate plan.

4.7 Financial targets vary from industry to industry, depending on how profitable or unprofitable it is expected to be. For profitable industries, the financial target has so far been set in terms of achieving a target rate of return. The return is measured as a current cost operating profit on the net replacement cost of assets employed.

4.8 Performance aims are intended to back up the financial targets, and may be expressed in terms of target cost reductions or efficiency improvements. Achieving cost reduction through efficiency improvements has been a prime target of nationalised industries in the UK in recent years. The Post Office, for example, has in the past had a target to reduce real unit costs in its mails business and in its counters business.

External financing limits (EFLs) for nationalised industries

4.9 External financing limits (EFLs) control the flow of finance to and from nationalised industries.

They set a limit on the amount of finance the industry can obtain from the government, and in the case of very profitable industries, they set requirements for the net repayment of finance to the government.

Not-for-profit organisations

4.10 Some organisations are set up with a prime objective which is not related to making profits. Charities and government organisations are examples.

4.11 These organisations exist to pursue non-financial aims, such as providing a service to the community. However, there will be financial constraints which limit what any such organisation can do.

(a) A not-for-profit organisation needs finance to pay for its operations, and the major financial constraint is the amount of funds that it can obtain.

(b) Having obtained funds, a not-for-profit organisation should seek to use the funds:
   (i) economically: not spending £2 when the same thing can be bought for £1;
   (ii) efficiently: getting the best use out of what money is spent on;
   (iii) effectively: spending funds so as to achieve the organisation's objectives.

4.12 The nature of financial objectives in a not-for-profit organisation can be explained in more detail, using government organisations in the UK as an illustration.

Government organisations

4.13 Financial management in government is substantially different from financial management in an industrial or commercial company, for some fairly obvious reasons.

(a) Government departments do not operate to make a profit, and the objectives of a department or of a programme of spending cannot be expressed in terms of maximising the return on capital employed.

(b) Government services are provided without the commercial pressure of competition. There are no competitive reasons for controlling costs, being efficient or, when services are charged for (such as medical prescriptions), keeping prices down.

(c) Government departments have full-time professional civil servants as their managers, but decisions are also taken by politicians.

(d) The government gets its money for spending from taxes, other sources of income and borrowing (such as issuing gilts) and the nature of its fund-raising differs substantially from fund-raising by companies.

(i) The financial markets regard the government as a totally secure borrower, and so the government can usually borrow whatever it likes, provided it is prepared to pay a suitable rate of interest.

(ii) Central government borrowing is co-ordinated centrally by the Treasury and the Bank of England. Individual departments of government do not have to borrow funds themselves.

(iii) Local governments raise some taxes locally and can do some borrowing in the financial markets, but they also rely for some of their funds on central government.

(iv) Companies rely heavily on retained profits as a source of funds. Government departments cannot rely on any such source, because they do not make profits. Some government services must be paid for by customers, for example medical prescriptions and school meals, although the price that is charged might not cover the costs in full.

4.14 Since managing government is different from managing a company, a different framework is needed for planning and control. This is achieved by:

(a) setting objectives for each department;
(b) careful planning of public expenditure proposals;
(c) emphasis on getting *value for money*.

4.15 A recent development has been the creation of agencies to carry out specific functions (such as vehicle licensing). These agencies are answerable to the government for providing a certain level of service, but are independently managed on business principles.

5. CONCLUSION

5.1 This chapter has set the scene for the study of financial management. We have identified the objectives of companies (and other bodies), and we will go on to study both the resources available to achieve these objectives and the methods for doing so.

TEST YOUR KNOWLEDGE

The numbers in brackets refer to paragraphs of this chapter

1. What are the main factors which contribute to an increase in a company's equity share price? (1.8, 1.9)

2. How are a company's financial objectives usually expressed? (1.9) What subsidiary financial targets might a company try to achieve? (1.12)

3. What non-financial objectives might a company have? (2.1) Do non-financial objectives invalidate the assumption of shareholder wealth maximisation as the prime objective of companies? (2.2)

4. What are the problems in the relationship between shareholders and management? (3.5)

5. What are the main elements in the relationship between a company and its long-term creditors? (3.13)

6. What might be the principal objective of a nationalised industry? (4.3, 4.4)

7. In what ways does financial management in government differ from financial management in a large public company? (4.13)

Now try question 1 at the end of the text

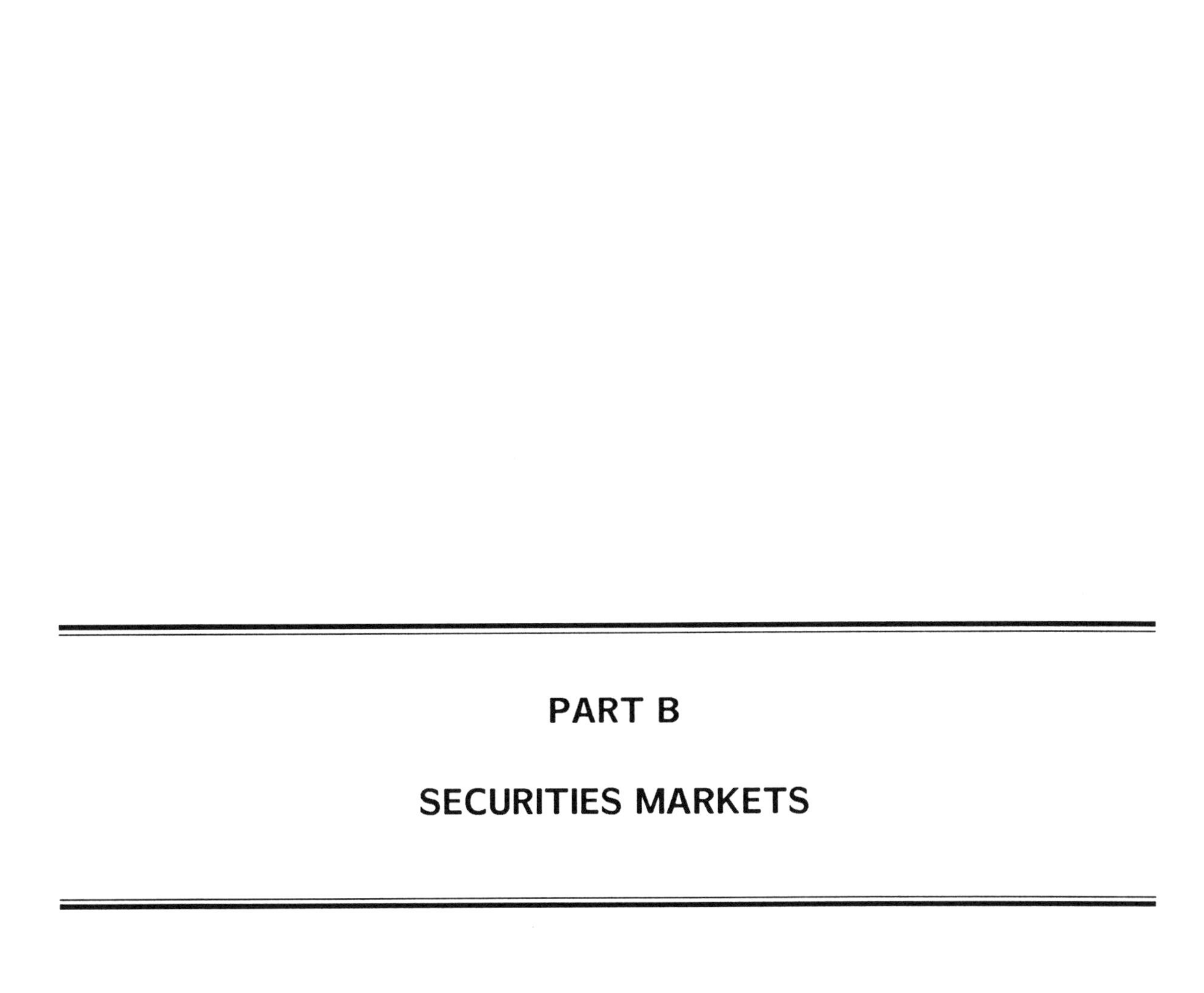

PART B

SECURITIES MARKETS

Chapter 2

THE ROLE AND NATURE OF THE CAPITAL MARKETS

This chapter covers the following topics.

1. The definition and the role of the capital markets
2. Capital markets in the UK

1. THE DEFINITION AND THE ROLE OF THE CAPITAL MARKETS

1.1 Capital markets are markets for trading in long-term finance, in the form of long-term financial instruments such as equities and debentures.

In the UK, the capital markets include the Stock Exchange (full title: the International Stock Exchange), the Unlisted Securities Market (USM) and the over-the-counter (OTC) markets. Large companies might also borrow long-term funds in a foreign currency, on the eurobond market.

1.2 The capital markets are distinguished from the money markets, which are markets for (i) trading short-term financial instruments such as bills of exchange and certificates of deposit and (ii) short-term lending and borrowing.

1.3 (a) By short-term capital, we mean capital that is lent or borrowed for a period which might range from as short as overnight up to about one year, and sometimes longer.

(b) By long-term capital, we mean capital invested or lent and borrowed for a period of five years or more.

1.4 There is a 'grey area' between long-term and short-term capital, which is lending and borrowing for a period from about a year up to about five years, which is not surprisingly sometimes referred to as medium-term capital. In the UK, the bulk of medium-term borrowing by firms is done through banks.

1.5 *Firms* obtain long-term or medium-term capital in one of the following ways.

(a) They may raise *share capital*. Most new issues of share capital are in the form of ordinary share capital (as distinct from preference share capital) and shareholders are the owners or members of the company. Firms that issue ordinary share capital are inviting investors to take an equity stake in the business, or to increase their existing equity stake.

(b) They may raise *loan capital.* Long-term loan capital might be raised in the form of a mortgage or debenture. The lender will usually want some security for the loan, and the mortgage deed or debenture deed will specify the security. Most loans have a fixed term to maturity. Debenture stock, like shares, can be issued on the Stock Market and then bought and sold in 'secondhand' trading. Interest is paid on the stock and the loan is repaid when the stock reaches its maturity date.

The role of the capital markets

1.6 The capital markets serve two main purposes.

(a) They enable organisations to raise new finance, by issuing new shares or new debentures. In the UK, a company must have public company status (be a plc) to be allowed to raise finance from the public on a capital market.

Capital markets make it easier for companies to raise new long-term finance than if they had to raise funds privately by contacting investors individually.

(b) They enable existing investors to sell their investments, should they wish to do so. A shareholder in a 'listed' company can sell his shares whenever he wants to on the Stock Exchange. The marketability of securities is a very important feature of the capital markets, because investors are more willing to buy stocks and shares if they know that they could sell them easily, should they wish to.

Most trading of stocks and shares on the capital markets is in secondhand securities, rather than new issues.

1.7 These are the main functions of a stock market, but we can add two more important ones.

(a) When a company comes to the stock market for the first time, and 'floats' its shares on the market, the owners of the company can realise some of the value of their shares in cash, because they will offer a proportion of their personally-held shares for sale to new investors.

(b) When one company wants to take over another, it is common to do so by issuing shares to finance the takeover. For example, if ABC plc wants to take over XYZ plc, it might offer XYZ plc shareholders three new shares in ABC plc for every two shares held in XYZ plc. Takeovers by means of a share exchange are only feasible if the shares that are offered can be readily traded on a stock market, and so have an identifiable market value.

2. CAPITAL MARKETS IN THE UK

2.1 There are several capital markets in the UK.

(a) *The Stock Exchange* is the market for stocks and shares in 'listed' companies (large public limited companies whose shares are listed in the Stock Exchange's Official List).

(b) *The 'gilts' or gilt-edged market* is the market for the government's long term debt securities. The government can raise new funds by issuing gilt-edged loan stock, and issued gilts are also traded secondhand.

(c) *The Unlisted Securities Market or USM* is a market for shares in com... enough to obtain a full listing on the Stock Exchange. The USM ... Exchange.

...oans or ... operating in ...pecially to well-

2.2 The *lenders* of capital include private individuals who buy stocks and shares directly on the Stock Exchange. However, there are some important *institutional investors*, such as institutions which specialise in lending capital in order to make a return. These include:

(a) pension funds;
(b) insurance companies;
(c) investment trust companies;
(d) unit trust companies;
(e) venture capital organisations.

The Stock Exchange

2.3 The Stock Exchange is a primary capital market in which companies and other institutions can raise funds by issuing shares or loan stock , but it is more important as a secondary market for buying and selling *existing* securities. The Stock Exchange governs and regulates two markets, the 'full market' or 'prime market' and the USM.

The Stock Exchange is also the market for dealings in government securities (gilts).

The main or 'full' market

2.4 A company wishing to have some or all of its shares listed on the Stock Exchange must agree to obey the Stock Exchange rules. For companies with a listing on the main market, these rules are contained in the so-called Yellow Book 'Admission of Securities to Listing'. (There is a different book of rules for companies on the USM, called the Green Book 'The Unlisted Securities Market').

2.5 Some of the rules in the Yellow Book are as follows.

(a) To obtain a full listing, the company should have traded successfully for at least three years.

(b) Enough shares should be made available to the investing public so that a ready market exists, and there is no shortage of supply for would-be investors.

(c) Enough shares must be available on the Stock Exchange launch to create a free market.

Thus it is more appropriate to issue 2,000,000 shares with a nominal value of £1 each than to issue only 2,000 shares with a nominal value of £1,000 each.

(d) The company's listed securities would be expected to have a minimum total value. Although the Stock Exchange will accept shares of a company valued at this minimum, currently under £1,000,000, for quotation, except in very special circumstances a prospective market capitalisation of £6,000,000 is considered to be a reasonable minimum. This would normally mean minimum annual profits before tax of between £750,000 and £1,200,000. In addition to the size qualification, a company must have a satisfactory trading record and be in a financially stable position.

(e) The company must undertake to obey the rules of the Stock Exchange, for example about the provision of information such as the announcement of half-year (interim) results. When an application is made for a listing, the board of directors must adopt as a resolution the terms and conditions of the Stock Exchange Listing Agreement.

(f) Shares in the company must be traded on the Stock Exchange by *market makers.*

The advantages and disadvantages of flotation on the main market

2.6 Flotation is the process of making shares available to the general public by obtaining a quotation on the Stock Exchange. Flotation is sometimes referred to as 'going public' or 'obtaining a Stock Exchange listing'. Why should a company want to be floated on the stock market?

2.7 The advantages of flotation to *the existing shareholders* are as follows.

(a) They can sell some of their shares.

(b) A wider market is created for their remaining shares.

(c) The mere fact of flotation may lead to the shares being perceived as a less risky investment.

(d) A quotation provides a ready share price, which lessens the uncertainties of inheritance tax by avoiding the problems of valuing unquoted shares.

2.8 The advantages of flotation to *the company* are as follows.

(a) New funds are obtained if the flotation involves the issue of new shares.

(b) A better credit standing is obtained, so that it may be easier to borrow money.

(c) Buying another company with a new issue of shares is much more practicable for a quoted company than for an unquoted company.

(d) Shares can be issued more easily at a later date. It is difficult for companies to expand beyond a certain size without getting a quotation, because of the difficulty of raising enough funds.

(e) The reduction in the perceived risk for shareholders and the greater marketability of shares may lead to a lower cost of equity.

(f) The extra status and prominence given to public companies might help the company to [illegible]

[illegible]

(b) The company must comply with the stringent Stock Exchange regulations.

(c) A dilution of control will result from the wider holding of the company's shares.

(d) Other ways of raising finance might be better.

(e) The company may not be big enough, or growing fast enough, for its shares to perform well on the stock market.

(f) Listed company status will put extra administrative burdens on to the management.

(g) The profits and performance of a listed company are much more in the public eye and the company cannot afford to show poor results without attracting considerable criticism.

(h) The company's share price may become vulnerable to campaigns to drive it down by selling shares. Several companies have been victims of such 'bear raids'.

In practice, a private company which goes public will often first seek a listing on the Unlisted Securities Market (USM) and may later progress to a full Stock Exchange listing after a few more years of growth.

The Unlisted Securities Market (USM)

2.10 The Unlisted Securities Market is a market in shares of companies which do not have a full listing.

2.11 The rules of this market include the following.

(a) To get into the market, a company must offer at least 10% of its equity for sale (compared to a minimum of 25% for the full market).

(b) There is no lower limit to the size of companies allowed to enter the market, although they should normally have traded for at least two years.

(c) Shares can be sold by placing or by an offer for sale, but only brief particulars of the company need be advertised (compared with full page advertisements for a main market quotation).

(d) An annual fee is levied by the Stock Exchange, but it is less than the fee for companies with a full listing.

(e) Shares in USM companies must be traded by market makers.

2.12 The USM was originally seen as a stepping stone for companies on the way to obtaining a full listing, and some companies have indeed made this jump already, going on to a full listing from the USM within a few years.

The advantages and disadvantages of going on to the USM

2.13 The major attractions of joining the USM are similar to the advantages of a listing on the main market, with the main difference being that a company does not need to be so big or to have traded for so long to obtain USM status.

(a) A USM quotation gives better access to capital markets, to raise extra finance.

(b) Becoming a quoted company will increase the marketability of the company's shares, although the shares of a USM company are most unlikely to be as marketable as the shares of a company with a full listing.

(c) A USM quotation will probably enhance a company's public image.

(d) Once a company has obtained a stock market quotation, it is easier to operate a worthwhile share incentive scheme for employees. Employees can be rewarded with shares or share options in their company, which have a recognisable money value and give both participation in ownership and financial rewards to the employees.

(e) Once it has obtained a USM quotation, a company can issue more shares to finance takeovers of other companies. Takeovers financed by share exchange deals are not easy to arrange unless the company making the acquisition has a market value for its shares.

(f) The owners of a company get a chance to cash in on its achievements so far, by selling some of their shares to the public.

2.14 The disadvantages of having a USM quotation, compared with being a private company, are as follows.

(a) There is greater public scrutiny, so more time must be spent on public relations.

(b) The market's expectations about profits, earnings, dividends and capital growth must be satisfied.

(c) The company will have a higher public profile, which might make it more likely to become the target of a takeover bid.

(d) The company must meet stringent disclosure requirements.

2.15 Progress to a full listing is by no means a guarantee of success. Poorly performing companies are likely to fare just as badly and to be as unattractive to investors if they have a full listing as if they are on the USM. However, successful USM companies are likely to progress to a full listing as they get bigger.

buy or sell. Most of them will be tied up in large blocks of shares, which are held by the previous owners of the company before it came to the USM, or by institutional investors. Not many shares will be held by small shareholders, and regularly bought and sold.

2.18 This fear that USM shares might not be readily marketable is accentuated by:

(a) the small number of market makers in shares of any USM company. USM companies might have two or three market makers, but of these, only one might be actively making a market in the shares;

(b) the relatively small number of shareholders. The shares are in danger of becoming illiquid because there is not enough interest in buying them, so when shareholders want to sell their shares, they cannot find a ready market.

The dealing mechanism on the Stock Exchange

2.19 Dealers on the Stock Exchange are of two types.

(a) *Market makers* are dealers in the shares of selected companies, whose responsibility is to 'make a market' in the shares of each of those companies.

(i) A market maker must be a member of the Stock Exchange.
(ii) Market makers announce which companies' shares they are prepared to market.
(iii) A market maker *must* undertake to make two-way prices (for selling and for buying) in the securities for which they are registered as market makers, under *any* trading conditions.
(iv) Market makers decide the share price.
(v) Another role of a market maker is to bring 'new' companies to the market. If a company wants to become a listed company, or a USM company, it must find a market maker to sponsor it, and to set up an initial market in its shares.

(b) *Stockbrokers* act on behalf of individual clients, who wish to buy or sell some of their shares or debentures.

(i) Stockbrokers, acting on behalf of a client, will deal with one of the market makers to buy or sell the shares.
(ii) Alternatively, market makers act as stockbrokers too, dealing directly with individual investors, buying or selling shares.

2.20 Stockbrokers earn a commission for their services, payable by the client. Market makers, in contrast, earn a profit (or suffer a loss) on the difference between their buying price and selling price for the shares they trade in.

2.21 The term *dual capacity trading* refers to the role of market makers as both brokers for clients and traders in companies' shares on their own account. Market makers can therefore earn a broker's commission and also a profit on buying and selling the shares.

Example

2.22 Alfred, a private investor, decides to buy 1,000 shares in NBG plc. He will ask his broker to obtain the shares on his behalf. The broker will then check share prices of NBG and select the best price for a deal. The best price for NBG might be 90 95.

The broker will contact the market maker to buy 1,000 shares at 95p each. The higher price is the price at which the market maker will sell NBG shares.

If the market maker then decides that he needs to restore his holding of shares in NBG plc, he may raise his prices to, say, 91 - 96, in the hope of attracting investors into selling shares by offering a higher price, 91p.

2.23 When a deal is reached between a broker and a market maker to buy shares for a client, a contract note will be sent the following day to the broker's client (the investor) giving details of:

(a) the securities bought and the buying price;

(b) transaction costs payable;

(c) *settlement day*, the day on which the purchase price and the transaction costs must be paid.

The regulatory framework

2.24 The Financial Services Act 1986 has established regulations for firms in the investment services industry, including the buying and selling of stocks and shares.

Regulatory powers under the Act are given to the Secretary of State for the Department of Trade, but these powers have been transferred to the Securities and Investment Board (SIB). The SIB has laid down three levels of rules: principles, core rules and detailed rules.

2.25 Under the terms of the Act, only 'authorised persons' are allowed to carry on investment business. Authorisation will be granted by the SIB, and methods by which the SIB can grant authorisation include:

(a) direct authorisation of individual firms, which are subject to all the SIB's rules;
(b) authorisation for all members of a recognised self-regulatory organisation (SRO) or a recognised professional body (RPB). This is an organisation which is approved by the SIB, and issues a code of regulations to its members. SRO members are also subject to the SIB's principles and core rules, and RPB members to its principles.

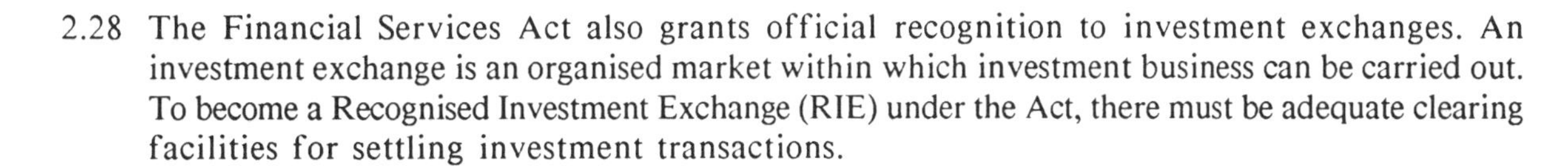

2.28 The Financial Services Act also grants official recognition to investment exchanges. An investment exchange is an organised market within which investment business can be carried out. To become a Recognised Investment Exchange (RIE) under the Act, there must be adequate clearing facilities for settling investment transactions.

The Stock Exchange is an RIE and its Yellow Book Rules are now its regulations as an RIE for listed companies.

Licensed securities dealers

2.29 Not every dealer in shares is a member of the Stock Exchange. Market makers in shares of companies on the Over the counter markets are not members of the Stock Exchange, although they must be licensed dealers, under the requirements of the Financial Services Act.

Licensed securities dealers (dealers who are not members of the Stock Exchange, but must still be licensed to deal in stocks and shares) are usually members of FIMBRA.

Over the counter (OTC) markets

2.30 This term covers markets in the shares of smaller unlisted public companies. There is no single OTC market in the UK. The OTC market is a collective term to describe a number of market makers in OTC shares, working in different locations and doing their business according to their own procedures and rules, not a single set of market rules.

2.31 If a company wants to raise capital, but cannot get a full listing on the Stock Exchange or a USM listing, it might approach an OTC market maker and ask him to sponsor the company on to the OTC.

2.32 If the market maker is willing to consider the company's request, he will screen the company, its financial accounts and its prospects.

If he is then willing to act as sponsor, he will:

(a) introduce the company's shares on to the OTC by means of:
  (i) a placing; or
  (ii) an offer for sale.

  This raises capital for the company (or its current owners). Only a small percentage of the company's shares, sometimes less than 5%, need be made available for the market;

(b) monitor the company's subsequent performance;

(c) provide a mechanism for secondhand dealing in shares, by:

  (i) finding a buyer for shares which the owner wishes to sell. This is *bargain-matching* and the dealer merely acts as a go-between for the seller and buyer. Often, it is difficult to find a willing buyer, or

  (ii) acting as a market maker in the shares, ie undertaking to buy and sell shares at certain prices, which means that the dealer runs a risk of acquiring shares that he cannot then sell.

Takeover bids

2.33 Whenever a company's shares are traded on a market, a takeover bid is a possibility. The conduct of such bids is regulated, and details are given in Chapter 17.

3. CONCLUSION

3.1 Recent years have seen very big changes in the capital markets of the world.

Some of the most important changes have been the following.

(a) *Globalisation*
The capital markets of separate countries have become internationally integrated. Securities issued in one country can now be traded in capital markets around the world. For example, shares in UK companies are traded in the USA. The shares are bought by US banks, which then issue ADRs (American depository receipts) which are a form in which foreign shares can be traded in US markets without a local listing.

(b) *Securitisation of debt*
Securitisation of debt refers to international borrowing by large companies, not from a bank, but by issuing securities instead. This has been possible because of the deregulation of capital markets, and the opening of overseas markets to borrowers since the abolition of exchange controls in the UK in 1979. Securitisation of debt has been popular with borrowers because this form of borrowing is cheaper and more flexible than a bank loan. Examples of securitised debt are Eurobonds and Eurocommercial paper.

(c) *Risk management (and risk assessment)*
Various techniques have been developed for companies to manage their financial risk. These techniques include off balance sheet transactions, such as swaps and options. The existence of these transactions, which are harder to monitor because they are off balance sheet, make it difficult for banks and other would-be lenders to assess the financial risk of a company that is asking to borrow more money.

(d) *Competition*
There is fierce competition between financial institutions for business. Building societies are emerging as competitors to the banks. Foreign banks have competed successfully in the UK with the big clearing banks. The Big Bang in the City of London in October 1986 brought greater competition between Stock Exchange firms.

4. What is a self-regulatory organisation? (2.25)

5. What are the over-the-counter markets? (2.30)

Now try question 2 at the end of the text

Chapter 3

PUTTING A VALUE TO SECURITIES. THE EFFICIENT MARKET HYPOTHESIS

This chapter covers the following topics.

1. Share price behaviour
2. The fundamental analysis theory of share values
3. Charting or technical analysis
4. Random walk theory
5. The efficient market hypothesis

1. SHARE PRICE BEHAVIOUR

1.1 Investors will buy shares to obtain an income from dividends and/or to make a capital gain from an increase in share prices.

1.2 If the purpose of investing is to earn dividend income, an investor will try to buy shares which are expected to provide a satisfactory dividend in relation to their market value. The *movement* in share prices, which occurs from day to day on the stock market, means that an investor can improve his return by *buying at the right time*. For example, if the share price is £1.50 on day 1, rising to £1.55 on day, falling to £1.48 on day 3 and rising to £1.50 on day 4, the investor will obtain the best return if he buys shares on day 3. However, if he predicts that the share price will fall even lower than £1.48 in one or two weeks time, he will prefer to wait until then before buying.

1.3 Similarly, the prediction of share price movements may help an investor to maximise his capital gain from buying and selling shares. Shares should be bought when prices are at their lowest and sold when they are at their highest. Since stockbrokers and investment advisers give advice to clients about when to buy and sell shares, they need a method of foretelling which way share prices will move, up or down, and when. It is therefore useful to consider the extent to which share prices and share price movements can be predicted.

Theories of share price behaviour

1.4 There are differing views about share price movements, which may be broadly classified as:

(a) the fundamental analysis theory;
(b) technical analysis (chartist theory);
(c) random walk theory.

These different theories about how share prices are reached in the market, especially fundamental analysis, have important consequences for financial management.

2. THE FUNDAMENTAL ANALYSIS THEORY OF SHARE VALUES

2.1. The fundamental theory of share values is based on the theory that the 'realistic' market price of a share can be derived from a valuation of estimated future dividends. The value of a share will be the discounted present value of all future expected dividends on the share, discounted at the shareholders' cost of capital.

You must learn the two formulae given below.

2.2 (a) When the company is expected to pay constant dividends every year into the future, 'in perpetuity':

$$MV = \frac{d}{r}$$

where MV is the market price of the share ex div, that is, excluding any current dividend that might be payable
d is the expected annual dividend per share in the future
r is the shareholders' cost of capital (the required rate of return).

(b) When the company is expected to pay a dividend which increases at a constant rate, g, every year into the future:

$$MV = \frac{d_0(1 + g)}{(r - g)} = \frac{d_1}{(r - g)}$$

where d_0 is the dividend in the current year (year 0) and so $d_0(1 + g)$ is the expected future dividend in year 1 (d_1). Again, MV is the market value of the share ex div.

Example

2.3 Hocus plc expects to pay a constant dividend of £450,000 at the end of every year for ever (in perpetuity). Assuming that a dividend has just been paid, calculate what the market value of Hocus plc's shares ought to be if its shareholders' cost of capital is 15%.

Solution

2.4 $$MV = \frac{£450{,}000}{(1.15)} + \frac{£450{,}000}{(1.15)^2} + \frac{£450{,}000}{(1.15)^3} + \ldots$$ and so on, in perpetuity.

The present value of £1 a year for ever at a rate of interest r% (r expressed as a proportion) is 1/r.

Therefore, the present value of £450,000 a year at a rate of interest of 15%

is $£450{,}000 \times \frac{1}{0.15} = £3{,}000{,}000$.

The value of Hocus plc's shares will be £3,000,000.

Example

2.5 Pocus plc paid a dividend this year of £3,000,000. The company expects the dividend to rise by 2% a year in perpetuity. This expectation is shared by the investors in the stock market. The current return expected by investors from shares in the same industry as Pocus plc is 11%.

(a) What would you expect the total market value of the shares of Pocus plc to be?

(b) If it is now rumoured in the stock market that interest rates are about to rise and so shareholders will want to earn an extra 1% on their shares. What change would you expect in the value of the shares of Pocus plc?

(c) What conclusion do you draw from this example?

Solution

2.6 $$MV = \frac{d_0(1 + g)}{(r - g)}$$

(a) Predicted share value (return of 11%) $= \frac{£3,000,000\ (1.02)}{(0.11 - 0.02)} = £34,000,000$

(b) Predicted share value (return of 12%) $= \frac{£3,000,000\ (1.02)}{(0.12 - 0.02)} = £30,600,000$

The value of the company's shares would fall by £3,400,000.

(c) When interest rates are expected to go up, there may well be a fall in share prices. Similarly, expectations of a fall in interest rates may well result in an increase in share prices. This is because the required return on shares is likely to move approximately in step with changes in rates of interest on other investments.

Exercise 1

The management of Crocus plc are trying to decide on the dividend policy of the company.

There are two options that are being considered.

(a) The company could pay a constant annual dividend of 8p per share.

(b) The company could pay a dividend of 6p per share next year, and use the retained earnings to achieve an annual growth of 3% in dividends for each year after that.

The shareholders' cost of capital is thought to be 18%. Which dividend policy would maximise the wealth of shareholders, by maximising the share price?

Solution

(a) *With a constant annual dividend*

$$\text{Share price} = \frac{8p}{0.18} = 44.4p$$

(b) *With dividend growth*

$$\text{Share price} = \frac{6p\ (1.03)}{(0.18-0.03)} = \frac{6.18}{0.15} = 41.2p$$

The constant annual dividend would be preferable.

Exercise 2

Lupin plc has paid a constant annual dividend of 8.4p a share for some years, and is expected to go on doing so in the future. The current dividend of 8.4p is about to be paid.

The return expected by shareholders is currently 14%.

(a) What would you expect the share price cum div for Lupin plc shares to be?

(b) What should the share price cum div move to if the return required by shareholders falls to 12%?

(c) Can you see a simplifying assumption about the payment of the annual dividend that is being made in the computations you make?

Note. The market value (MV) cum div is the market value including the value of the dividend that is soon to be paid out. The MV cum div equals the MV ex div plus the dividend.

Solution

(a) MV ex div $= \frac{8.4}{0.14} = 60p$

MV cum div = MV ex div + current dividend
= 60p + 8.4p
= 68.4p

(b) MV ex div $= \frac{8.4}{0.12} = 70p$

MV cum div = 70p + 8.4p
= 78.4p

Since the shareholders' required rate of return will go down, the share price will go up.

(c) The simplifying assumption is that the annual dividend will be paid in full all in one go. In practice, companies (especially public companies) will probably pay the dividend in two parts:

(i) an interim dividend part way through the year;
(ii) a final dividend after the end of the year.

In general, however, this simplifying assumption is accepted as giving a sufficiently accurate estimate of share values.

The value of debentures

2.7 The same valuation principle can be applied to the valuation of debentures and other loan stock. However, the future income from fixed interest debentures is predictable, which should make the process of valuation more straightforward.

(a) For irredeemable debentures or loan stock, where the company will go on paying interest every year in perpetuity, without ever having to redeem the loan:

$$MV = \frac{i}{r}$$

where MV is the market price of the stock ex interest, that is, excluding any interest payment that might soon be due
i is the annual interest payment on the stock
r is the return required by the loan stock investors.

(b) For redeemable debentures or loan stock, the market value is the discounted present value of future interest receivable, up to the year of redemption, *plus* the discounted present value of the redemption payment.

Example

2.8 A company has issued some 9% debentures, which are now redeemable at par in three years time. Investors now require an interest yield of 10%. What will be the current market value of £100 of debentures?

Solution

2.9

Year		*Cash flow*	*Discount factor at 10%*	*Present value*
		£		£
1	Interest	9	0.909	8.18
2	Interest	9	0.826	7.43
3	Interest	9	0.751	6.76
3	Redemption value	100	0.751	75.10
				97.47

£100 of debentures will have a market value of £97.47.

The importance of the fundamental theory of share values

2.10 If the fundamental analysis theory of share values is correct, the price of any share will be predictable, provided that all investors have:

(a) the same information about a company's expected future profits and dividends;
(b) a known cost of capital.

So is it correct? Are share prices predictable? And if not, why not?

2.11 (a) In general terms, fundamental analysis seems to be valid. This means that if an investment analyst can foresee before anyone else that:

(i) a company's future profits and dividends are going to be different from what is currently expected; or
(ii) shareholders' cost of capital will rise or fall (for example in response to interest rate changes)

then the analyst will be able to predict a future share price movement, and so recommend clients to buy or sell the share before the price change occurs.

(b) In practice, share price movements are affected by day to day fluctuations, reflecting supply and demand in a particular period, investor confidence, market interest rate movements, and so on. Investment analysts want to be able to predict these fluctuations in prices, but fundamental analysis might be inadequate as a technique.

Some analysts, known as chartists, therefore rely on technical analysis of share price movements.

(c) In October 1987, there was a sudden and very sharp fall in share prices on all the Stock Exchanges of the world, on average by 20% to 40% but with some share prices falling by 50% or so. This crash of 1987 cannot be explained by fundamental analysis. On the other hand, a widely feared crash late in 1989 failed to materialise.

3. CHARTING OR TECHNICAL ANALYSIS

3.1 Chartists or 'technical analysts' attempt to predict share price movements by assuming that past price patterns will be repeated.

There is no real theoretical justification for this approach, but it can at times be spectacularly successful. Studies have suggested that the degree of success is greater than could be expected merely from chance. Nevertheless not even the most extreme chartist would claim that every major price movement can be predicted accurately and sufficiently early to make correct investment decisions.

3.2 Chartists do not attempt to predict every price change. They are primarily interested in trend reversals, for example when the price of a share has been rising for several months but suddenly starts to fall. There are several features of charts that are considered important. These include:
(a) resistance levels;
(b) double tops and double bottoms;
(c) 'head and shoulders' patterns.

3.3 Consider the following graph.

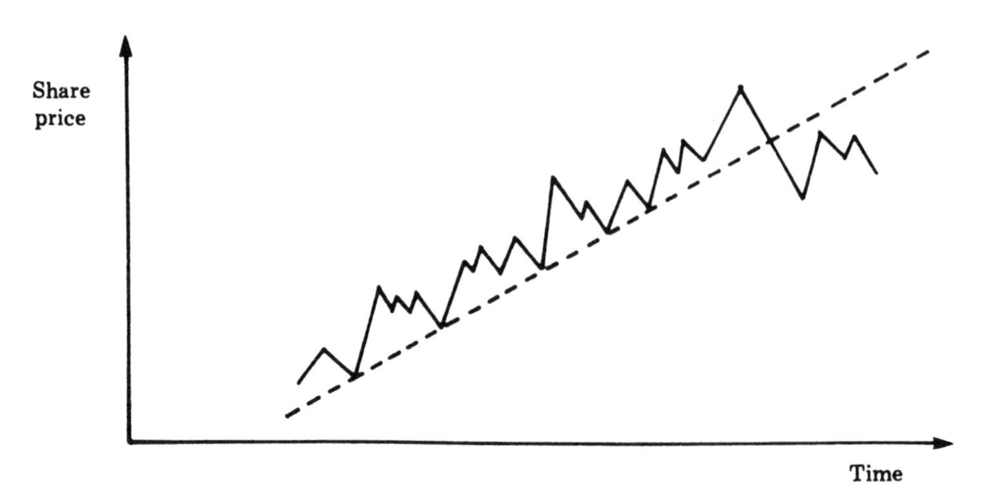

The dotted line represents the lower resistance level on a rising trend. It will be noticed that many of the troughs lie on this line, but only at the end is it breached. The chartist would claim that this breach is a good indication that the trend has been reversed.

3.4 Let us now look at a resistance level on a double top. Suppose that the price of a share has been rising steadily for some time. Recently the price fell as some investors sold to realise profits and it then rose to its maximum level for a second time before starting to fall again.

This is known as a double top and based on experience the chartist would predict that the trend has reversed. A typical double top might appear as follows.

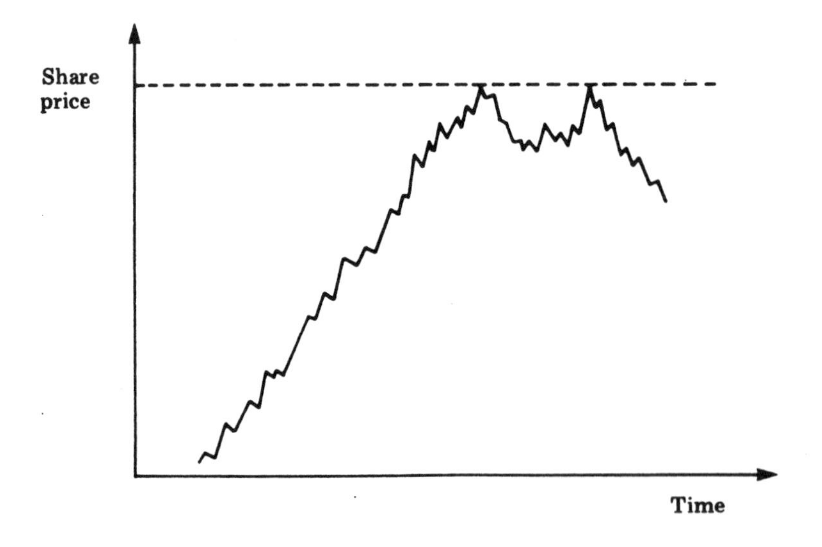

Double bottoms can be interpreted in a similar way.

3.5 Another indication of a trend reversal is the 'head and shoulders'. Consider the following graph.

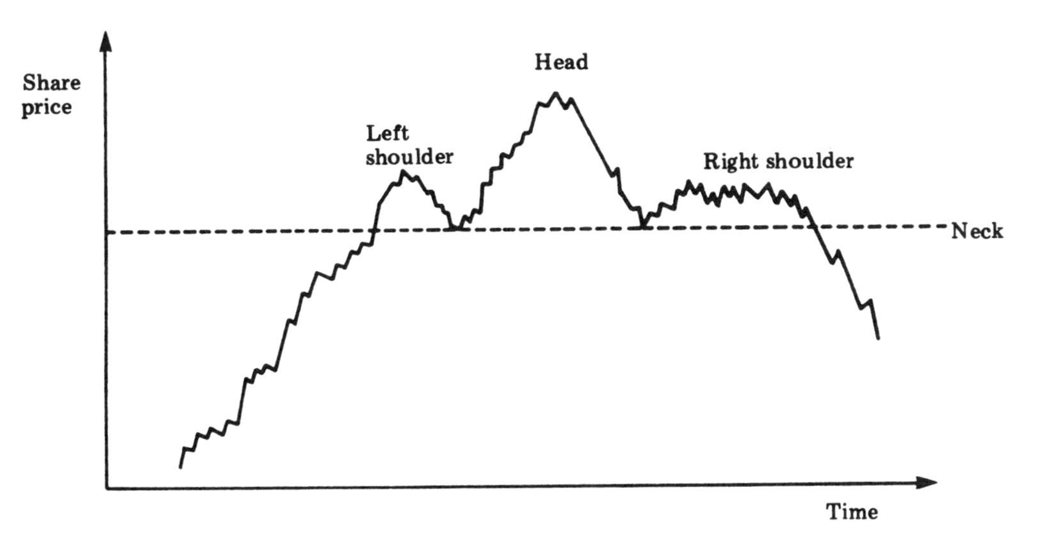

In the above graph, the price has been rising for some time before, at the left shoulder, profit taking has caused the price to drop. The price has then risen steeply again to the head before more profit taking causes the price to drop to more or less the same level as before (the neck). Although the price rises again the gains are not as great as at the head. The level of the right shoulder together with the frequent dips down towards the neck would suggest to the chartist that the upward trend previously observed is over and that a fall is imminent. The breach of the neckline is the indication to sell.

An inverse head and shoulders can be interpreted in a similar manner.

3.6 Moving averages help the chartist to examine overall trends. For example, he may calculate and plot moving averages of share prices for 20 days, 60 days and 240 days. The 20 day figures will give a reasonable representation of the actual movement in share prices after eliminating day to day fluctuations. The other two moving averages give a good idea of longer term trends.

4. RANDOM WALK THEORY

4.1 Random walk theory is consistent with the fundamental theory of share values. It accepts that a share should have an intrinsic price dependent on the fortunes of the company and the expectations of investors. One of its underlying assumptions is that all relevant information about a company is available to all potential investors who will act upon the information in a rational manner.

4.2 The key feature of random walk theory, however, is that although share prices will have an intrinsic or fundamental value, this value will be altered as new information becomes available, and that the behaviour of investors is such that the actual share price will fluctuate from day to day around the intrinsic value.

4.3 Random walk theory emerged in the late 1950s as an attempt to disprove chartist theory. H V Roberts challenged the idea that share price movements were systematic, and showed how sequences of random numbers can exhibit the same pattern as actual recorded changes of share prices on the Stock Exchange. Roberts was able to duplicate the 'head and shoulders' pattern of share price movements with random numbers, and he concluded that such 'patterns' are illusory and of no value for predicting share prices.

Random walks and an efficient stock market

4.4 Research was carried out in the late 1960s to explain why share prices in the stock market display a random walk phenomenon. This research led to the development of the efficient market hypothesis.

It can be shown that random movements in share prices will occur if the stock market operates 'efficiently' and makes information about companies, earnings, dividends and so on, freely (or cheaply) available to all customers in the market. In displaying efficiency, the stock market also lends support to the fundamental analysis theory of share prices.

5. THE EFFICIENT MARKET HYPOTHESIS

5.1 It has been argued that the UK and US stock markets are efficient capital markets, that is, markets in which:

(a) the prices of securities bought and sold reflect all the relevant information which is available to the buyers and sellers. In other words, share prices change quickly to reflect all new information about future prospects;

(b) no individual dominates the market;

(c) transaction costs of buying and selling are not so high as to discourage trading significantly.

5.2 If the stock market is efficient, share prices should vary in a rational way.

(a) If a company makes a profitable investment, shareholders will get to know about it, and the market price of its shares will rise in anticipation of future dividend increases.

(b) If a company makes a bad investment shareholders will find out and so the price of its shares will fall.

(c) If interest rates rise, shareholders will want a higher return from their investments, so market prices will fall.

The definition of efficiency

5.3 The efficiency of a stock market means the ability of a stock market to price stocks and shares fairly and quickly.

An efficient market is therefore one in which the market prices of all the securities traded on it reflect all the available information.

There is no possibility of 'speculative bubbles' in which share prices are pushed up or down, by speculative pressure, to unrealistically high or low levels.

Varying degrees of efficiency

5.4 There are three degrees or 'forms' of efficiency:

(a) weak form;
(b) semi-strong form;
(c) strong form.

5.5 Tests can be carried out on the workings of a stock market to establish whether the market operates with a particular form of efficiency.

(a) Weak form tests are made to assess whether a stock market shows at least weak form efficiency.

(b) Semi-strong form tests are made to assess whether a market shows at least semi-strong form efficiency.

(c) Strong form tests are made to assess whether a market shows strong form efficiency.

Weak form tests and weak form efficiency

5.6 The weak form hypothesis of market efficiency explains changes in share prices as the result of *new information* which becomes available to investors.

In other words, share prices only change when new information about a company and its profits have become available. Share prices do *not* change *in anticipation* of new information being announced.

5.7 Since new information arrives unexpectedly, changes in share prices should occur in a random fashion: a weak form test seeks to prove the validity of the random walk theory of share prices. In addition, since the theory states that current share prices reflect all information available from past changes in the price, if it is correct then chartist or technical analysis cannot be based on sound principles.

5.8 Research to prove that the stock market displays weak form efficiency has been based on the principle that:

(a) if share price changes are random, and
(b) if there is no connection between past price movements and new share price changes,

then it should be possible to prove statistically there is no correlation between successive changes in the price of a share, that is, that trends in prices cannot be detected.

Proofs of the absence of trends have been claimed in the work of various writers.

Semi-strong form tests and semi-strong form efficiency

5.9 Semi-strong form tests attempt to show that the stock market displays semi-strong efficiency, by which we mean that current share prices reflect both:

(a) all relevant information about past price movements and their implications; and
(b) all knowledge which is available publicly.

5.10 Tests to prove semi-strong efficiency have concentrated on the ability of the market to anticipate share price changes before new information is formally announced.

For example, if two companies plan a merger, share prices of the two companies will inevitably change once the merger plans are formally announced. The market would show semi-strong efficiency, however, if it were able to *anticipate* such an announcement, so that share prices of the companies concerned would change in advance of the merger plans being confirmed.

5.11 Research in both Britain and the USA has suggested that market prices anticipate mergers several months before they are formally announced, and the conclusion drawn is that the stock market in these countries *do* exhibit semi-strong efficiency.

5.12 It has also been argued that the market displays sufficient efficiency for investors to see through 'window dressing' of accounts by companies which use accounting conventions to overstate profits.

5.13 Suppose that a company is planning a rights issue of shares in order to invest in a new project. A semi-strong form efficient market hypothesis (unlike the weak form hypothesis) would predict that if there is public knowledge before the issue is formally announced, of the issue itself and of the expected returns from the project, then the market price (cum rights) will change to reflect the anticipated profits before the issue is announced.

Strong form tests and strong form efficiency

5.14 A strong form test of market efficiency attempts to prove that the stock market displays a strong form of efficiency, by which we mean that share prices reflect all information available:

(a) from past price changes;
(b) from public knowledge or anticipation; and
(c) from insider knowledge available to specialists or experts (such as investment managers).

It would then follow that in order to maximise the wealth of shareholders, management should concentrate simply on maximising the net present value of its investments and it need not worry, for example, about the effect on share prices of financial results in the published accounts because investors will make allowances for low profits or dividends in the current year if higher profits or dividends are expected in the future.

5.15 In theory an expert, such as an investment manager, should be able to use his privileged access to additional information about companies to earn a higher rate of return than an ordinary investor. Unit trusts should in theory therefore perform better than the average investor. Research to date has suggested, however, that this expert skill does not exist (or at least, that any higher returns earned by experts are offset by management charges).

How efficient are stock markets?

5.16 Evidence so far collected suggests that stock markets show efficiency that is at least weak form, but tending more towards a semi-strong form. In other words, current share prices reflect all or most publicly available information about companies and their securities.

However, it is very difficult to assess the market's efficiency in relation to shares which are not usually actively traded.

5.17 Fundamental analysis and technical analysis, which are carried out by analysts and investment managers, play an important role in creating an efficient stock market. This is because an efficient market depends on the widespread availability of cheap information about companies, their shares and market conditions, and this is what the firms of market makers and other financial institutions *do* provide for their clients and for the general investing public.

The implications of the efficient market hypothesis

5.18 If the strong form of the efficient market hypothesis is correct, a company's real financial position will be reflected in its share price. Its real financial position includes both its current position and its expected future profitability.

If the management of a company attempt to maximise the net present value of their investments and to make public any relevant information about those investments then current share prices will in turn be maximised.

5.19 The implication for an investor is that if the market shows strong form or semi-strong form efficiency, he can rarely spot shares at a bargain price that will soon rise sharply in value. This is because the market will already have anticipated future developments, and will have reflected these in the share price. All an investor can do, instead of looking for share bargains, is to concentrate on building up a good spread of shares (a portfolio) in order to achieve a satisfactory balance between risk and return.

Example

5.20 Company X has 3,000,000 shares in issue and company Y 8,000,000.

(a) On day 1 the market value per share is £3 for X and £6 for Y.

(b) On day 2 the management of Y decide, at a private meeting, to make a takeover bid for X at a price of £5 per share. The takeover will produce large operating savings with a present value of £8,000,000.

(c) On day 5 Y publicly announces an unconditional offer to purchase all shares of X at a price of £5 per share with settlement on day 20. Details of the large savings are not announced and are not public knowledge.

(d) On day 10 Y announces details of the savings which will be derived from the takeover.

Ignoring tax and the time value of money between day 1 and 20, and assuming the details given are the only factors having an impact on the share price of X and Y, determine the day 2, day 5 and day 10 share price of X and Y if the market is:

(a) semi-strong form efficient;
(b) strong form efficient;

in each of the following *separate* circumstances.

(i) The purchase consideration is cash as specified above.
(ii) The purchase consideration, decided upon day 2 and publicly announced on day 5, is five newly issued shares of Y for six shares of X.

Solution

5.21 (a) *Semi-strong form efficient market (i) cash offer*
With a semi-strong form of market efficiency, shareholders know all the relevant historical data and publicly available current information.

(i) Day 1 — Value of X shares: £3 each, £9,000,000 in total.
Value of Y shares: £6 each, £48,000,000 in total.

(ii) Day 2 — The decision at the *private* meeting does not reach the market, and so share prices are unchanged.

(iii) Day 5 — The takeover bid is announced, but no information is available yet about the savings.

(1) The value of X shares will rise to their takeover bid price of £5 each, £15,000,000 in total.

(2) The value of Y shares will be as follows.

	£
Previous value (8,000,000 × £6)	48,000,000
Add value of X shares to be acquired, at previous market worth (3,000,000 × £3)	9,000,000
	57,000,000
Less purchase consideration for X shares	15,000,000
New value of Y shares	42,000,000
Price per share	£5.25

The share price of Y shares will fall on the announcement of the takeover.

(iv) Day 10 The market learns of the potential savings of £8,000,000 (present value) and the price of Y shares will rise accordingly to

$$\frac{£42{,}000{,}000 + £8{,}000{,}000}{8{,}000{,}000 \text{ shares}} = £6.25 \text{ per share.}$$

The share price of X shares will remain the same as before, £5 per share.

Semi-strong form efficient market (ii) share exchange offer

(i) The share price will not change until the takeover is announced on day 5, when the value of the combined company will be perceived by the market to be (48 + 9) £57,000,000.

The number of shares in the enlarged company Y would be as follows.

Current	8,000,000
Shares issued to former X shareholders	
3,000,000 × 5/6	2,500,000
	10,500,000

The value per share in Y would change to what the market expects the value of the enlarged company to be.

$$\frac{£57{,}000{,}000}{10{,}500{,}000} = £5.43 \text{ per share}$$

The value per share in X would reflect this same price, adjusted for the share exchange terms.

$$\frac{5}{6} \text{ of } £5.43 = £4.52$$

(ii) Day 10 The value of the enlarged company would now be seen by the market to have risen by £8,000,000 to £65,000,000 and the value of Y shares would rise to

$$\frac{£65{,}000{,}000}{10{,}500{,}000} = £6.19 \text{ per share.}$$

The value per X share would be

$$\frac{5}{6} \text{ of } £6.19 = £5.16$$

(b) *Strong form efficient market (i) cash offer*

In a strong form efficient market, the market would become aware of *all* the relevant information when the private meeting takes place. The value per share would change as early as *day 2* to

(i) X: £5
(ii) Y: £6.25

The share prices would then remain unchanged until day 20.

Strong form efficient market (ii) share exchange offer

In the same way, for the same reason, the value per share would change *on day 2* to

(i) X: £5.16
(ii) Y: £6.19

and remain unchanged thereafter until day 20.

5.22 The different characteristics of a semi-strong form and a strong form efficient market thus affect the timing of share price movements, in cases where the relevant information becomes available to the market eventually. The difference between the two forms of market efficiency concerns *when* the share prices change, not by how much prices eventually change.

You should notice, however, that in neither case would the share prices remain unchanged until day 20. In a *weak form* efficient market, the price of Y's shares would not reflect the expected savings until after the savings had been achieved and reported, so that the takeover bid would result in a fall in the value of Y's shares for a considerable time to come.

The share price crash of October 1987 and the efficient market hypothesis

5.23 The crash of October 1987, in which share prices fell suddenly by 20% to 40% on the world's stock markets, has raised very serious questions about the validity of random walk theory, the fundamental theory of share values and the efficient market hypothesis.

5.24 If these theories are correct, how can shares that were valued at one level on one day suddenly be worth 40% less the next day, without any change in expectations of corporate profits and dividends?

5.25 On the other hand, a widely feared crash late in 1989 failed to happen, suggesting that stock markets may not be altogether out of touch with the underlying values of companies.

6. CONCLUSION

6.1 In Chapter 1, we set out the main financial objective of companies as the maximisation of shareholders' wealth. In this chapter, we have seen how share values may be arrived at. We may then start to see how a financial manager should behave, in order to maximise shareholders' wealth.

TEST YOUR KNOWLEDGE

The numbers in brackets refer to paragraphs of this chapter

1. What is the fundamental theory of share values? (2.1) State the formulae for the valuation of shares, assuming (a) no dividend growth (b) a constant rate of dividend growth in perpetuity. (2.2)

2. What is chartism? (3.1)

3. What is random walk theory? (4.1-4.3) How is this theory related to the efficient market hypothesis? (4.4)

4. What does efficiency mean, in the context of the efficient market hypothesis? (5.3)

5. What is weak form efficiency? (5.6)

6. What is semi-strong form efficiency? (5.9, 5.10)

7. What is strong form efficiency? (5.14)

8. How does the difference between weak form and semi-strong form efficiency matter, in terms of by how much or when share prices change? (5.22)

Now try question 3 at the end of the text

PART C

SOURCES OF FINANCE AND CAPITAL STRUCTURES

Chapter 4

SHARE CAPITAL, LOAN CAPITAL AND RETAINED EARNINGS

This chapter covers the following topics.

1. Sources of funds
2. New share issues
3. Loan stock
4. Convertibles, warrants and options
5. Dividends and retentions
6. Dividend growth and market value
7. A practical approach to dividends

1. SOURCES OF FUNDS

1.1 A company might raise new funds from the following sources.

(a) The capital markets:
   (i) new share issues, for example by companies acquiring a stock market listing for the first time;
   (ii) rights issues;
   (iii) issues of loan capital
(b) Retained earnings
(c) Bank borrowings
(d) Government sources
(e) Business expansion scheme funds
(f) Venture capital
(g) The international money and capital markets (eurocommercial paper, eurobonds and eurocurrency borrowing).

In this chapter we shall concentrate on items (a) and (b). Items (c) to (g) are covered in the next chapter.

Ordinary shares (equity)

1.2 Ordinary shares are issued to the owners of a company. They have a nominal or 'face' value, typically £1 or 50p,but shares with a nominal value of 1p, 2p or 25p are not uncommon. The market value of a quoted company's shares bears no relationship to their nominal value, except that when ordinary shares are issued for cash, the issue price must be equal to or more than the nominal value of the shares.

1.3 *Deferred ordinary shares* are a form of ordinary shares, which are entitled to a dividend only after a certain date or only if profits rise above a certain amount. Voting rights might also differ from those attached to other ordinary shares.

1.4 Ordinary shareholders put funds into their company:

(a) by paying for a new issue of shares;
(b) through retained profits.

1.5 A new issue of shares might be made in a variety of different circumstances.

(a) The company might want to raise more cash. If it issues ordinary shares for cash, should the shares be issued pro rata to existing shareholders, so that control or ownership of the company is not affected? If, for example, a company with 200,000 ordinary shares in issue decides to issue 50,000 new shares to raise cash, should it offer the new shares to existing shareholders, or should it sell them to new shareholders instead?

(i) If a company sells the new shares to existing shareholders in proportion to their existing shareholding in the company, we have a *rights issue*. In the example above, the 50,000 shares would be issued as a one for four rights issue, by offering shareholders one new share for every four shares they currently hold.

(ii) If the number of new shares being issued is small compared to the number of shares already in issue, it might be decided instead to sell them to new shareholders, since ownership of the company would only be minimally affected.

(b) The company might want to issue new shares partly to raise cash but more importantly to 'float' its shares on a stock market. When a UK company is floated, for example on the main stock market, it is a requirement of the Stock Exchange that at least a minimum proportion of its shares should be made available to the general investing public.

(c) The company might issue new shares to the shareholders of another company, in order to take it over. Takeovers are dealt with separately, in a later chapter.

2. NEW SHARE ISSUES

2.1 A company seeking to obtain additional equity funds may be:

(a) an unquoted company wishing to obtain a Stock Market or Unlisted Securities Market quotation;

(b) an unquoted company wishing to issue new shares, but without obtaining a Stock Market or USM quotation;

(c) a company which is already listed on the Stock Market or the USM wishing to issue additional new shares.

2.2 The methods by which an unquoted company can obtain a quotation on the Stock Market are:

(a) an offer for sale:
(b) a prospectus issue;
(c) a placing;
(d) an introduction.

Of these, (a) and (c) are the most common.

Offers for sale

2.3 An offer for sale is a means of selling the shares of a company to the public at large.

(a) An unquoted company may issue new shares, and sell them on the Stock Exchange, to raise cash for the company. All the shares in the company, not just the new ones, would then become marketable.

(b) Shareholders in an unquoted company may sell some of their existing shares to the general public. When this occurs, the company is not raising any new funds, but is merely providing a wider market for its existing shares (all of which would become marketable), and giving existing shareholders the chance to cash in some or all of their investment in their company.

2.4 When companies 'go public' for the first time, a *large* issue will probably take the form of an offer for sale (or occasionally an offer for sale by tender). A smaller issue is more likely to be a placing, since the amount to be raised can be obtained more cheaply if the issuing house or other sponsoring firm approaches selected institutional investors privately.

2.5 A company whose shares are already listed might issue new shares to the general public. It is likely, however, that a new issue by a quoted company will be either a placing or a rights issue, which are described later.

Issuing houses and sponsoring member firms

2.6 When an unquoted company applies for a Stock Exchange listing, it must be sponsored by a firm that is a member of the Stock Exchange. This sponsoring member firm has the responsibility of ensuring that the company meets the requirements for listing, and carries out the necessary procedures. The company will also employ the services of an issuing house, which might well be the sponsoring member firm itself. An issuing house has the job of trying to ensure a successful issue for the company's shares, by advising on an issue price for the shares, and trying to interest institutional investors in buying some of the shares.

The issue price and offers for sale

2.7 The price at which shares are offered will be critical to the success of the issue. The offer price must be advertised a short time in advance, so it is fixed without certain knowledge of the condition of the market at the time applications are invited.

In order to safeguard the success of an issue, share prices are often set lower than they might otherwise be.

It is normal practice for an issuing house to try to ensure that a share price rises to a premium above its issue price soon after trading begins. A target premium of 20% above the issue price would be fairly typical.

2.8 Companies will be keen to avoid over-pricing an issue, so that the issue is under-subscribed, leaving underwriters with the unwelcome task of having to buy up the unsold shares.

On the other hand, if the issue price is too low then the issue will be oversubscribed and the company would have been able to raise the required capital by issuing fewer shares.

2.9 The share price of an issue is usually advertised as being based on a certain P/E ratio, a ratio of the price to the company's most recent earnings per share figure in its audited accounts. The issue's P/E ratio can then be compared by investors with the P/E ratios of similar quoted companies.

Offers for sale by tender

2.10 It is often very difficult to decide upon the price at which the shares should be offered to the general public. One way of trying to ensure that the issue price reflects the value of the shares as perceived by the market is to make an offer for sale by tender.

(a) A minimum price will be fixed and subscribers will be invited to tender for shares at prices equal to or above the minimum.

(b) The shares will be allotted at the highest price at which they will all be taken up. This is known as the striking price.

2.11 Offers by tender are less common than offers for sale.

The reasons why offers for sale by tender might not be preferred are as follows.

(a) It is sometimes felt that the decision to made an offer by tender reflects badly on the issuing house's ability to determine the issue price.

(b) It is claimed that the use of tenders leaves the determination of prices to the 'uninformed public' rather than the City 'experts'. However, in practice the major influence on the striking price will be the tenders of the institutional investors.

(c) An offer for sale is more certain in the amount of finance that will be raised.

(d) Some potential investors may be deterred from applying for shares as they do not wish to have to decide on a price.

2.12 An increase in the use of offers for sale by tender might follow a general increase in share values. When share prices are generally rising, the striking price in an offer for sale by tender is likely to be higher than the issue price that would have been set if the issuing company were to select the issue price itself, since the issue price would have to be sufficiently low to be reasonably sure that the issue would be fully subscribed by investors.

Example

2.13 Byte Henderson plc is a new company that is making its first public issue of shares. It has decided to make the issue by means of an offer for sale by tender. The intention is to issue up to 4,000,000 shares (the full amount of authorised share capital). The money raised, net of issue costs of £1,000,000, would be invested in projects which would earn benefits with a present value equal to 130% of the net amount invested.

The following tenders have been received. (Each applicant has made only one offer.)

Price tendered per share	*Number of shares applied for at this price*
£	
6.00	50,000
5.50	100,000
5.00	300,000
4.50	450,000
4.00	1,100,000
3.50	1,500,000
3.00	2,500,000

(a) How many shares would be issued, and how much in total would be raised, if Byte Henderson plc chooses to:
(i) maximise the total amount raised?
(ii) issue exactly 4,000,000 shares?

(b) Harvey Goldfinger, a private investor, has applied for 12,000 shares at a price of £5.50 and has sent a cheque for £66,000 to the issuing house that is handling the issue. In both cases (a)(i) and (ii), how many shares would be issued to Mr Goldfinger, assuming that any partial acceptance of offers would mean allotting shares to each accepted applicant in proportion to the number of shares applied for? How much will Mr Goldfinger receive back out of the £66,000 he has paid?

(c) Estimate the likely market value of shares in the company after the issue, assuming that the market price fully reflects the investment information given above and that exactly 4,000,000 shares are issued.

Solution

2.14 (a) We must begin by looking at the cumulative tenders.

Price	*Cumulative number of shares applied for*	*Amount raised if price is selected, before deducting issue costs*
£		£
6.00	50,000	300,000
5.50	150,000	825,000
5.00	450,000	2,250,000
4.50	900,000	4,050,000
4.00	2,000,000	8,000,000
3.50	3,500,000	12,250,000
3.00	6,000,000	12,000,000

(i) To maximise the total amount raised, the issue price should be £3.50. The total raised before deducting issue costs would be £12,250,000.

(ii) To issue exactly 4,000,000 shares, the issue price must be £3.00. The total raised would be £12,000,000, before deducting issue costs.

(b) (i) Harvey Goldfinger would be allotted 12,000 shares at £3.50 per share. He would receive a refund of 12,000 × £2 = £24,000 out of the £66,000 he has paid.

(ii) If 4,000,000 shares are issued, applicants would receive two thirds of the shares they tendered for. Harvey Goldfinger would be allotted 8,000 shares at £3 per share and would receive a refund of £42,000 out of the £66,000 he has paid.

(c) The net amount raised would be £12,000,000 minus issue costs of £1,000,000, £11,000,000.

The present value of the benefits from investment would be 130% of £11,000,000, £14,300,000. If the market price reflects this information, the price per share would rise to $\frac{£14,300,000}{4,000,000} = £3.575$ per share.

A prospectus issue

2.15 In a prospectus issue, or public issue, a company offers its own shares to the general public. An issuing house or merchant bank may act as an agent, but not as an underwriter. This type of issue is therefore risky, and is very rare. Well known companies making a large new issue may use this method, and the company would almost certainly already have a quotation on the Stock Exchange.

A placing

2.16 A placing is an arrangement whereby the shares are not all offered to the public, but instead, the sponsoring market maker arranges for most of the issue to be bought by a small number of investors, usually institutional investors such as pension funds and insurance companies.

The choice between an offer for sale and a placing

2.17 When a company is planning a flotation on to the USM, or a full Stock Exchange listing, is it likely to prefer an offer for sale of its shares, or a placing?

Placings are much cheaper, although most of the shares will be placed with a relatively small number of (institutional) shareholders, which means that most of the shares are unlikely to be available for trading after the flotation. This is a particular problem for smaller companies.

A Stock Exchange introduction

2.18 By this method of obtaining a quotation, no shares are made available to the market, neither existing nor newly-created shares; nevertheless, the Stock Exchange grants a quotation. This will only happen where shares in a large company are already widely held, so that a market can be seen to exist. A company might want an introduction to obtain greater marketability for the shares, a known share valuation for inheritance tax purposes and easier access in the future to additional capital.

Underwriters

2.19 A company about to issue new securities in order to raise finance might decide to have the issue underwritten. Underwriters are financial institutions which agree (in exchange for a fixed fee, perhaps 2.25% of the finance to be raised) to buy at the issue price any securities which are not subscribed for by the investing public.

2.20 Underwriters remove the risk of a share issue's being under-subscribed, but at a cost to the company issuing the shares. It is not compulsory to have an issue underwritten.

(a) It is unnecessary to underwrite a placing since a purchaser for the shares is arranged in the issue process.

(b) An offer for sale by tender would only need underwriting if there is a risk that there will be under-subscription even at the minimum price.

(c) A rights issue should in theory not require underwriting, since new shares are being offered to existing shareholders. However, the underwriting of rights issues is common practice.

With underwriting, the company making the issue is sure of receiving the funds it wants to raise, net of expenses.

2.21 As an alternative to underwriting an issue, a company could choose to issue its share at a deep discount, that is, at a price well below the current market price, to ensure the success of the issue. This is less common.

A major disadvantage of issuing shares at a deep discount is that, since companies try to avoid reducing the dividends paid out per share, the total amount required for dividends in future years will be that much higher, since more shares would have to be issued at the low price to raise the amount of finance required. If the company expects only moderate growth in total earnings and dividends, the company's shareholders might even suffer a fall in earnings per share.

Pricing shares for a stock market launch

2.22 Pricing shares for a stock market launch on the main market or the USM is a task for the company's sponsor.

Factors that the sponsor will take into account are as follows.

(a) Are there similar companies already quoted, whose P/E ratios can be used for comparison? The chosen P/E ratio can be multiplied by the company's most recent EPS, as shown in the prospectus, to arrive at a draft share price. This price can be negotiated with the company's current owners.

A company which is coming to the USM will obtain a lower P/E ratio than a similar company on the main market.

(b) What are current market conditions?

(c) With what accuracy can the company's future trading prospects be forecast?

(d) It is usual to set a price which gives an immediate premium when the launch takes place. A sponsor will usually try to ensure that the market price rises to a premium of about 20% over the launch price on the day that the launch takes place.

(e) A steady growth in the share price year by year should be achievable.

Example

2.23 Launchpad plc is proposing to obtain a Stock Exchange listing, to raise £10,000,000 from a placing of new shares. Issue costs will be 8% of the gross receipts.

The company already has 4,000,000 shares in issue. The company expects to earn a post-tax profit of £4,000,000 in its next year of operations, plus a 15% post-tax return on the newly-raised funds, and to pay out 50% of its profits as dividends. Dividend growth would be 3% a year.

For the issue to be successful, Launchpad plc would have to issue shares at a 20% discount to what it considers the market value of the shares ought to be.

Shareholders will expect a net dividend yield (that is, net of the tax credit) of 12%.

Calculate a suitable issue price for the shares, and the number of shares that would have to be issued.

Solution

2.24 (a) Receipts net of issue costs from the new issue = 92% of £10,000,000
= £9,200,000

(b) Post-tax profits on the newly-raised funds in year 1 = 15% of £9,200,000
= £1,380,000

(c) Total post-tax profits in year 1 = £4,000,000 + £1,380,000
= £5,380,000

(d) Dividends in year 1 = 50% of £5,380,000
= £2,690,000

(e) Market value, based on dividend growth model, expected dividend growth of 3% a year from year 1 and a required return of 12%

$$MV = \frac{d_1}{(r - g)} = \frac{£2,690,000}{(0.12-0.03)}$$

$$= \frac{£2,690,000}{0.09}$$

$$= £29,888,888$$

(f) Let the number of shares issued be X.
Total number of shares = 4,000,000+ X
Let the share price after the issue be P.

Total market value = £29,888,888
(4,000,000 + X) P = £29,888,888

(g) Let P_d be the discount price at which the new shares must be issued, which is 20% below what the share price P ought to be.

$P_d = 0.8P$

From (f) it follows that

$$\frac{(4{,}000{,}000 + X)P_d}{0.8} = £29{,}888{,}888$$

$$4{,}000{,}000P_d + XP_d = £29{,}888{,}888 \times 0.8$$
$$= £23{,}911{,}110$$

(h) XP_d = number of new shares issued × issue price = £10,000,000

(i) Taking (g) and (h) together,

$$4{,}000{,}000P_d + 10{,}000{,}000 = £23{,}911{,}110$$
$$4{,}000{,}000\ P_d = £13{,}911{,}110$$
$$P_d = \frac{£13{,}911{,}110}{4{,}000{,}000} = £3.48$$

(j) Since

$$XP_d = £10{,}000{,}000$$
$$X = \frac{£10{,}000{,}000}{£3.48}$$
$$= 2{,}873{,}563$$

Conclusions

1. 2,873,563 shares should be issued at a price of £3.48 to raise £10,000,000.

2. The price of £3.48 is at a 20% discount to the market value after the issue. The market value will be £3.48 ÷ 0.8 = £4.35 per share.

3. After the issue, there will be 6,873,563 shares valued at £4.35 each or £29,899,999 in total. Allowing for rounding errors, this is the total valuation of £29,888,888 given in (g) above.

New issues of shares by quoted companies

2.25 When a quoted company makes an issue of new shares to raise capital, it could make an offer for sale, but it is more likely to issue the shares by means of:

(a) a rights issue; or
(b) a placing.

Rights issues

2.26 A rights issue is a method of raising new share capital by means of an offer to existing shareholders, inviting them to subscribe cash for new shares in proportion to their existing holdings.

For example, a rights issue on a one for four basis at 280p per share would mean that a company is inviting its existing shareholders to subscribe for one new share for every four shares they hold, at a price of 280p per new share. A rights issue may be made by any type of company, private or public, listed or unlisted. The analysis below, however, applies primarily to listed companies.

2.27 The major advantages of a rights issue are as follows.

(a) Rights issues are cheaper than offers for sale to the general public. This is partly because no prospectus is required, partly because the administration is simpler and partly because the cost of underwriting will be less.

(b) Rights issues are more beneficial to existing shareholders than issues to the general public. New shares are issued at a discount to the current market price, to make them attractive to investors. If the shares are issued to the general public, the benefit of the discount will be enjoyed by whoever buys the shares. A rights issue secures the discount on the market price for existing shareholders.

(c) Relative voting rights are unaffected if shareholders all take up their rights.

Deciding the issue price for a rights issue

2.28 The offer price in a rights issue will be lower than the current market price of existing shares. The size of the discount will vary, and will be larger for difficult issues. As a general guide, however, the average size of discount might be 20% to 30% (so that if the current market price of a share was, say, £2, the company would issue rights to shareholders enabling them to buy new shares at a price of perhaps £1.40 or £1.60 each).

2.29 The offer price must also be at or above the nominal value of the shares, so as not to break company law. Where the current market price of shares is below the nominal value, or only very slightly above it, a rights issue would therefore be impractical.

2.30 A company making a rights issue must set a price which is:

(a) low enough to secure the acceptance of shareholders, who are being asked to provide extra funds;
(b) not too low, so as to avoid excessive dilution of the earnings per share.

Example

2.31 Seagull plc can achieve a profit after tax of 20% on the capital employed. At present its capital structure is as follows.

	£
200,000 ordinary shares of £1 each	200,000
Retained earnings	100,000
	300,000

The directors propose to raise an additional £126,000 from a rights issue. The current market price is £1.80.

(a) Calculate the number of shares that must be issued if the rights price is: £1.60; £1.50; £1.40; £1.20.

(b) Calculate the dilution in earnings per share in each case.

Solution

2.32 The earnings at present are 20% of £300,000 = £60,000. This gives earnings per share of 30p. The earnings after the rights issue will be 20% of £426,000 = £85,200.

Rights Price	*No of new shares (£126,000 ÷ rights price)*	*EPS (£85,200 ÷ total no of shares)*	*Dilution*
£		pence	pence
1.60	78,750	30.6	+ 0.6
1.50	84,000	30.0	-
1.40	90,000	29.4	- 0.6
1.20	105,000	27.9	- 2.1

2.33 Note that at a high rights price the earnings per share are increased, not diluted. The break-even point (zero dilution) occurs when the rights price is equal to the capital employed per share: £300,000 ÷ 200,000 = £1.50.

The market price of shares after a rights issue: the theoretical ex rights price

2.34 After the *announcement* of a rights issue, there is a tendency for share prices to fall, although the extent and duration of the fall may depend on the number of shareholders and the size of their holdings. This temporary fall is due to uncertainty in the market about the consequences of the issue, with respect to future profits, earnings and dividends.

2.35 After the issue has actually been made, the market price per share will normally fall, because there are more shares in issue and the new shares were issued at a discount price.

2.36 When a rights issue is announced, all existing shareholders have the right to subscribe for new shares, and so there are rights attached to the existing shares. The shares are therefore described as being 'cum rights' (with rights attached) and are traded cum rights.

On the first day of dealings in the newly issued shares, the rights no longer exist and the old shares are now 'ex rights' (without rights attached).

2.37 In theory, the new market price will be the consequence of an adjustment to allow for the discount price of the new issue, and a *theoretical ex rights price* can be calculated.

Example

2.38 Fundraiser plc has 1,000,000 ordinary shares of £1 in issue, which have a market price on 1 September of £2.10 per share. The company decides to make a rights issue, and offers its shareholders the right to subscribe for one new share at £1.50 each for every four shares already held. After the announcement of the issue, the share price fell to £1.95, but by the time just prior to the issue being made, it had recovered to £2 per share. This market value just before the issue is known as the *cum rights price.*

What is the theoretical ex rights price?

Solution

2.39 In theory, the market price will fall after the issue, as follows.

	£
1,000,000 shares have a 'cum rights' value of (× £2)	2,000,000
250,000 shares will be issued to raise (× £1.50)	375,000
The theoretical value of 1,250,000 shares is	2,375,000

The theoretical ex rights price is $\frac{£2,375,000}{1,250,000}$ = £1.90 per share.

2.40 The same calculation is often shown as follows.

	£
Four shares have a cum rights value of (× £2)	8.00
One new share is issued for	1.50
The value of five shares is theoretically	9.50

The theoretical ex rights price is £9.50/5 = £1.90 per share.

The value of rights

2.41 The value of rights is the theoretical gain a shareholder would make by exercising his rights.

(a) Using the above example, if the price offered in the rights issue is £1.50 per share, and the market price after the issue is expected to be £1.90, the value attaching to a right is £1.90 - £1.50 = £0.40. A shareholder would therefore be expected to gain 40 pence for each new share he buys. If he does not have enough money to buy the share himself, he could sell the right to subscribe for a new share to another investor, and receive 40 pence from the sale. This other investor would then buy the new share for £1.50, so that his total outlay to acquire the share would be £0.40 + £1.50 = £1.90, the theoretical ex rights price.

(b) The value of rights attaching to existing shares is calculated in the same way. If the value of rights on a new share is 40 pence, and there is a one for four rights issue, the value of the rights attaching to each existing share is 40 ÷ 4 = 10 pence.

The theoretical gain or loss to shareholders

2.42 The possible courses of action open to shareholders are:

(a) to 'take up' or 'exercise' the rights, that is, to buy the new shares at the rights price. Shareholders who do this will maintain their percentage holdings in the company by subscribing for the new shares;

(b) to 'renounce' the rights and sell them on the market. Shareholders who do this will have lower percentage holdings of the company's equity after the issue than before the issue, and the total value of their shares will be less (on the assumption that the actual market price after the issue is close to the theoretical ex rights price);

(c) to renounce part of the rights and take up the remainder. For example, a shareholder may sell enough of his rights to enable him to buy the remaining rights shares he is entitled to with the sale proceeds, and so keep the total market value of his shareholding in the company unchanged;

(d) to do nothing at all. Shareholders may be protected from the consequences of their inaction because rights not taken up are sold on a shareholder's behalf by the company. The Stock Exchange rules state that if new securities are not taken up, they should be sold by the company to new subscribers for the benefit of the shareholders who were entitled to the rights. However, if the amount involved is small the shares can be sold for the benefit of the company. The shareholder (or the company) gets the difference between the issue price and the market price after the issue.

Unless a shareholder exercises all his rights, his proportion of the total equity of the company will decline.

Exercise

Gopher plc has issued 3,000,000 ordinary shares of £1 each, which are at present selling for £4 per share. The company plans to issue rights to purchase one new equity share at a price of £3.20 per share for every three shares held. A shareholder who owns 900 shares thinks that he will suffer a loss in his personal wealth because the new shares are being offered at a price lower than market value. On the assumption that the actual market value of shares will be equal to the theoretical ex rights price, what would be the effect on the shareholder's wealth if:

(a) he sells all the rights;
(b) he exercises half of the rights and sells the other half;
(c) he does nothing at all?

Solution

	£
Three shares 'cum rights' are worth (× £4)	12.00
One new share will raise	3.20
Four new shares will have a theoretical value of	15.20

The theoretical ex rights price is $\frac{£15.20}{4}$ = £3.80 per share

	£
Theoretical ex rights price	3.80
Price per new share	3.20
Value of rights per new share	0.60

The value of the rights attached to each existing share is $\frac{£0.60}{3}$ = £0.20.

We will assume that a shareholder is able to sell his rights for £0.20 per existing share held.

(a) If the shareholder sells all his rights:

	£
Sale value of rights (900 × £0.20)	180
Market value of his 900 shares, ex rights (× £3.80)	3,420
Total wealth	3,600

Total value of 900 shares cum rights (× £4) £3,600

The shareholder would neither gain nor lose wealth. He would not be required to provide any additional funds to the company, but his shareholding as a proportion of the total equity of the company will be lower.

(b) If the shareholder exercises half of the rights (buys 450/3 = 150 shares at £3.20) and sells the other half:

	£
Sale value of rights (450 × £0.20)	90
Market value of his 1,050 shares, ex rights (× £3.80)	3,990
	4,080
Total value of 900 shares cum rights (× £4)	3,600
Additional investment (150 × £3.20)	480
	4,080

The shareholder would neither gain nor lose wealth, although he will have increased his investment in the company by £480.

(c) If the shareholder does nothing, but all other shareholders either exercise their rights or sell them, he would lose wealth as follows.

	£
Market value of 900 shares cum rights (× £4)	3,600
Market value of 900 shares ex rights (× £3.80)	3,420
Loss in wealth	180

It follows that the shareholder, to protect his existing investment, should either exercise his rights or sell them to another investor. If he does not exercise his rights, the new securities he was entitled to subscribe for might be sold for his benefit by the company, and this would protect him from losing wealth.

The actual market price after a rights issue

2.43 The actual market price of a share after a rights issue may differ from the theoretical ex rights price.

This will occur when the expected earnings yield from the new funds raised is different from the earnings yield from existing funds in the business. The market will take a view of how profitably the new funds will be invested, and will value the shares accordingly. An example will illustrate this point.

Example

2.44 Musk plc currently has 4,000,000 ordinary shares in issue, valued at £2 each, and the company has annual earnings equal to 20% of the market value of the shares. A one for four rights issue is proposed, at an issue price of £1.50. If the market continues to value the shares on a price/earnings ratio of 5, what would be the value per share if the new funds are expected to earn, as a percentage of the money raised,

(a) 15%?
(b) 20%?
(c) 25%?

How do these values in (a), (b) and (c) compare with the theoretical ex rights price? Ignore issue costs.

Solution

2.45 The theoretical ex rights price will be calculated first.

	£
Four shares have a current value (× £2) of	8.00
One new share will be issued for	1.50
Five shares would have a theoretical value of	9.50

The theoretical ex rights price is $\frac{£9.50}{5}$ = £1.90.

2.46 The new funds will raise 1,000,000 × £1.50 = £1,500,000.

Earnings as a % of money raised	*Additional earnings*	*Current earnings*	*Total earnings after the issue*
	£	£	£
15%	225,000	1,600,000	1,825,000
20%	300,000	1,600,000	1,900,000
25%	375,000	1,600,000	1,975,000

2.47 If the market values shares on a P/E ratio of 5, the total market value of equity and the market price per share would be as follows.

Total earnings	*Market value*	*Price per share (5,000,000 shares)*
£	£	£
1,825,000	9,125,000	1.825
1,900,000	9,500,000	1.900
1,975,000	9,875,000	1.975

2.48 (a) If the additional funds raised are expected to generate earnings at the same rate as existing funds, the actual market value will probably be the same as the theoretical ex rights price.

(b) If the new funds are expected to generate earnings at a lower rate, the market value will fall below the theoretical ex rights price. If this happens, shareholders will lose.

(c) If the new funds are expected to earn at a higher rate than current funds, the market value should be above the theoretical ex rights price. If this happens, shareholders will profit by taking up their rights.

2.49 The decision by individual shareholders as to whether they take up the offer will therefore depend on:

(a) the expected rate of return on the investment (and the risk associated with it);
(b) the return obtainable from other investments (allowing for the associated risk).

Rights issues or issuing shares for cash to new investors? Pre-emptive rights

2.50 When shares are issued for cash to outside buyers, existing shareholders forfeit their *pre-emptive rights* to a rights issue.

2.51 Companies can issue shares for cash without obtaining prior approval from shareholders for each such share issue, provided that they have obtained approval from shareholders within the past 12 months to make new issues of shares for cash which are not rights issues. (This shareholder approval could be obtained at the company's AGM.)

2.52 Companies can thus issue shares for cash without having to bear the high costs of a rights issue, for example by *placing* shares for cash at a higher price than they might have been able to obtain from a rights issue.

Vendor placings

2.53 A vendor placing occurs when there is an issue of shares by one company to take over another, and these shares are then sold in a placing to raise cash for the shareholders in the target company, who are selling their shares in the takeover.

Example

2.54 AB plc wants to take over Z Ltd. AB plc wants to finance the purchase by issuing more equity shares, and the shareholders of Z Ltd want to sell their shares for cash. AB plc can arrange a vendor placing whereby:

(a) AB plc issues new shares to finance the takeover;

(b) these shares are placed by AB plc's stockbrokers (market makers) with institutional investors, to raise cash;

(c) the cash that is raised is used to pay the shareholders in Z Ltd for their shares.

Other methods of issuing shares

2.55 There are some other methods of issuing shares on the Stock Exchange. These are as follows.

(a) An *open offer* is an offer to existing shareholders to subscribe for new shares in the company but, unlike a rights issue:

(i) the offer is not necessarily pro rata to existing shareholdings;

(ii) the offer is not allotted on renounceable documents. (With rights issues the offer to subscribe for new shares must be given on a renounceable letter, so that the shareholder can sell his rights if he so wishes).

(b) A *capitalisation issue* is a 'scrip issue' of shares which does not raise any new funds. It is made to 'capitalise' reserves of the company: in effect, to change some reserves into share capital. Shareholders receive new shares pro rata to their existing shareholdings.

(c) A *vendor consideration issue* is an issue of shares whereby one company acquires the shares of another in a takeover or merger. For example, if A plc wishes to take over B plc, A might make a 'paper' offer to B's shareholders, try to buy the shares of B by offering B's shareholders newly issued shares of A. This is now a common form of share issue, because mergers and takeovers are fairly frequent events.

(d) *Employee share option schemes* are schemes for awarding shares to employees. For example, in an employee share option scheme, a company awards its employees share options, which are rights to subscribe for new shares at a later date at a predetermined price (commonly, the market price of the shares when the options are awarded). When and if the options are eventually exercised, the employees will receive the newly issued shares at a price that ought by then to be below the market price.

The timing and costs of new equity issues

2.56 New equity issues in general (offers for sale and placings as well as rights issues) will be more common when share prices are high than when share prices are low.

(a) When share price are high, investors' confidence will probably be high, and investors will be more willing to put money into companies with the potential for growth.

(b) By issuing shares at a high price, a company will reduce the number of shares it must issue to raise the amount of capital it wants. This will reduce the dilution of earnings for existing shareholders.

(c) Following on from (b), the company's total dividend commitment on the new shares, to meet shareholders' expectations, will be lower.

(d) If share prices are low, business confidence is likely to be low too. Companies may not want to raise capital for new investments until expectations begin to improve.

2.57 Typical costs of a share issue include:

(a) underwriting costs;

(b) the Stock Exchange listing fee (the initial charge) for the new securities;

(c) fees of the issuing house, solicitors' fees, auditors' fees, and fees of public relations consultants;

(d) charges for printing and distributing the prospectus;

(e) advertising, which must be done in national newspapers.

2.58 Costs vary according to whether equity or debt capital is being issued and whether the issue is a rights issue, an offer for sale or placing. With a placing, a full prospectus is not needed, advertising is cheaper and underwriting is not needed.

Some costs of flotation are variable (for example commission payable to an issuing house) but many costs are fixed (for example the costs of a prospectus, including professional fees, printing and advertising). The greater the amount of capital raised, the lower will be the costs of flotation as a percentage of the funds raised, because fixed costs are spread more thinly. High fixed costs help to explain why small companies have found it difficult and often undesirable to raise new funds through the Stock Exchange.

Rules on issues of shares

2.59 The Stock Exchange has rules affecting the choice of the method of issue. The treatment of an issue depends on the amount involved.

(a) With issues of less than £15,000,000, all shares may be placed with clients of the securities house sponsoring the issue, so long as there are at least 100 shareholders and at least one independent market maker.

(b) With issues of £15,000,000 to £30,000,000 the sponsor may place 75% of the shares on offer (up to a maximum of £15,000,000), so long as the balance is sold through an offer for sale or to brokers acting on behalf of private clients (an *intermediaries offer*). There should be at least two independent market makers.

(c) With issues of over £30,000,000, a public offer for sale is preferred to a placing, but up to 50% of the issue may be placed or firmly underwritten if there are at least three independent market makers.

In all issues, market makers other than the sponsor should be offered at least 5% of the stock issued.

Preference shares

2.60 Preference shares have a fixed percentage dividend before any dividend is paid to the ordinary shareholders. As with ordinary shares a preference dividend can only be paid if sufficient distributable profits are available, although with *cumulative* preference shares the right to an unpaid dividend is carried forward to later years. The arrears of dividend on cumulative preference shares must be paid before any dividend is paid to the ordinary shareholders.

2.61 The stated dividend (such as 7%) on preference shares is the cash dividend, not grossed up.

2.62 In recent years preference shares have formed a negligible part of new capital issues. The main reason for this is that their dividends, unlike interest on loans, are not deductible in computing profits chargeable to corporation tax.

They do have the advantages that their issue does not restrict the company's borrowing power, at least in the sense that preference share capital is not secured against assets of the business, and that the non-payment of dividend does not give the preference shareholders the right to appoint a receiver, a right which is normally given to debenture holders.

2.63 From the point of view of the investor, preference shares are less attractive than loan stock because:

(a) they cannot be secured on the company's assets;

(b) the dividend yield traditionally offered on preference dividends has been much too low to provide an attractive investment compared with the interest yields that have been available on loan stock.

3. LOAN STOCK

3.1 Loan stock is long-term debt capital raised by a company for which interest is paid, usually half yearly and at a fixed rate. Holders of loan stock are therefore long-term creditors of the company.

3.2 Loan stock has a nominal value, which is the debt owed by the company, and interest is paid at a stated 'coupon yield' on this amount. For example, if a company issues 10% loan stock, the coupon yield will be 10% of the nominal value of the stock, so that £100 of stock will receive £10 interest each year. The rate quoted is the gross rate, before tax.

3.3 *Debentures* are a form of loan stock, legally defined as the written acknowledgement of a debt incurred by a company, normally containing provisions about the payment of interest and the eventual repayment of capital.

3.4 A debenture trust deed would empower a trustee (such as an insurance company or a bank) to intervene on behalf of debenture holders if the conditions of borrowing under which the debentures were issued are not being fulfilled. This might involve:

(a) failure to pay interest on the due dates;
(b) an attempt by the company to sell off important assets contrary to the terms of the loan;
(c) a company taking out additional loans and thereby exceeding previously agreed borrowing limits established either by the Articles or by the terms of the debenture trust deed. (A trust deed might well place restrictions on the company's ability to borrow more from elsewhere until the debentures have been redeemed.)

Debentures with a floating rate of interest

3.5 These are debentures for which the coupon rate of interest can be changed by the issuer, in accordance with changes in market rates of interest. They may be attractive to both lenders and borrowers when interest rates are volatile, and preferable to fixed interest loan stock or debentures.

(a) Floating rate debentures protect borrowers from having to pay high rates of interest on their debentures when market rates of interest have fallen. On the other hand, they allow lenders to benefit from higher rates of interest on their debentures when market rates of interest go up.

(b) The *market value* of debentures depends on the coupon rate of interest, relative to market interest rates. With floating rate debentures the market value should be fairly stable (and close to par) because interest rates are varied to follow market rate changes. Stable market prices protect the value of the lenders' investment.

3.6 For example, suppose that a company issues 6% fixed rate debentures at par when the market rate of interest is 6%, and the debentures have a term to maturity of 20 years. If interest rates suddenly rise to 12%, the market value of the debentures would fall by half to £50 per cent (that is, per £100 nominal value). However, if the debentures had carried a floating rate of interest, the interest rate would have been raised to 12% and the debentures would have retained their market value at par (£100 per cent).

Deep discount bonds

3.7 Deep discount bonds are loan stock issued at a price which is at a large discount to the nominal value of the stock, and which will be redeemable at par (or above par) when they eventually mature.

For example a company might issue £1,000,000 of loan stock in 1991, at a price of £50 per £100 of stock, and redeemable at par in the year 2011.

3.8 Investors might be attracted by the large capital gain offered by the bonds, which is the difference between the issue price and the redemption value. However, deep discount bonds will carry a much lower rate of interest than other types of loan stock.

Zero coupon bonds

3.9 Zero coupon bonds are bonds that are issued *at a discount* to their redemption value, but *no interest* is paid on them. The investor gains from the difference between the issue price and the redemption value, and there is an implied interest rate in the amount of discount at which the bonds are issued (or subsequently re-sold on the market).

(a) The advantage for borrowers is that zero coupon bonds can be used to raise cash immediately, and there is no cash repayment until redemption date. The cost of redemption is known at the time of issue, and so the borrower can plan to have funds available to redeem the bonds at maturity.

(b) The advantage for lenders is restricted, unless the rate of discount on the bonds offers a high yield. The only way of obtaining cash from the bonds before maturity is to sell them, and their market value will depend on the remaining term to maturity and current market interest rates.

Security

3.10 Loan stock and debentures will often be *secured*. Security may take the form of:

(a) a *fixed charge*. Security would be related to a specific asset or group of assets, typically land and buildings. The company would be unable to dispose of the asset without providing a substitute asset for security, or without the lender's consent;

(b) a *floating charge*. With a floating charge on certain assets of the company (for example stocks and debtors), the lender's security in the event of a default of payment is whatever assets of the appropriate class the company then owns (provided that another lender does not have a prior charge on the assets). The company would be able, however, to dispose of its assets as it chose until a default took place. In the event of default, the lender would probably appoint a receiver to run the company rather than lay claim to a particular asset.

Unsecured loan stock

3.11 Not all loan stock is secured. Investors are likely to expect a higher yield with unsecured loan stock to compensate them for the extra risk. The rate of interest on unsecured loan stock may be around 1% or more higher than for secured debentures.

The redemption of loan stock

3.12 Loan stock and debentures are usually redeemable. They are issued for a term of ten years or more, and perhaps 25 to 30 years. At the end of this period, they will 'mature' and become redeemable (at par or possibly at a value above par).

3.13 Most redeemable stocks have an earliest and a latest redemption date. For example, 12% Debenture Stock 2007/09 is redeemable, at any time between the earliest specified date (in 2007) and the latest date (in 2009). The issuing company can choose the date. The decision by a company when to redeem a debt will depend on:

(a) how much cash is available to the company to repay the debt;

(b) the nominal rate of interest on the debt. If the debentures pay 12% nominal interest and current interest rates are lower, say 9%, the company may try to raise a new loan at 9% to redeem debt which costs 12%. On the other hand, if current interest rates are 14%, the company is unlikely to redeem the debt until the latest date possible, because the debentures would be a cheap source of funds.

3.14 Some loan stock does not have a redemption date, and is 'irredeemable' or 'undated'. Undated loan stock might be redeemed by a company that wishes to pay off the debt, but there is no obligation on the company to do so.

How will a company finance the redemption of long-term debt?

3.15 A company might finance the redemption of long-term debt from its own cash resources, if it has enough. Often, however, a company will repay a debt by raising cash from a new loan, thus 'renewing' its borrowing (perhaps at a different interest rate).

3.16 There is no guarantee that a company will be able to raise a new loan to pay off a maturing debt, and one item to look for in a company's balance sheet is the redemption date of current loans, to establish how much new finance is likely to be needed by the company, and when.

Mortgages

3.17 Mortgages are a specific type of secured loan. Companies place the title deeds of freehold or long leasehold property as security with an insurance company or mortgage broker and receive cash on loan, usually repayable over a specified period.

Most organisations owning property which is unencumbered by any charge should be able to obtain a mortgage up to two thirds of the value of the property.

Companies that are unable to repay debt capital

3.18 A company might get into difficulties and be unable to pay its debts. This could be:

(a) an inability to repay the debt capital when it is due for redemption;

(b) an inability, perhaps temporary, to pay interest on the debt, before the capital is due for redemption.

3.19 When this occurs, the debenture holders or loan stock holders could exercise their right to appoint a receiver and make use of whatever security they have. Occasionally, perhaps because the secured assets have fallen in value and would not realise much in a forced sale, or perhaps out of a belief that the company can improve its position soon, unpaid debenture holders *might* be persuaded to surrender their debentures in exchange for an equity interest in the company or possibly convertible debentures, paying a lower rate of interest, but carrying the option to convert the debentures into shares at a specified time in the future.

Tax relief on loan interest

3.20 As far as companies are concerned, debt capital is a potentially attractive source of finance because interest charges reduce the profits chargeable to corporation tax.

(a) A new issue of loan stock is likely to be preferable to a new issue of preference shares.

(b) Companies might wish to increase their gearing (the ratio of fixed interest capital to equity capital) in order to improve their earnings per share by benefiting from tax relief on interest payments.

Example

3.21 This example illustrates the differing effects of preference shares and loan stock on the profits attributable to the ordinary shareholders. Assuming that the basic rate of income tax is 25%, 7½% preference shares will give the same yield to an investor as 10% loan stock. Company A has in issue £1,000,000 7½% preference shares; Company B £1,000,000 of 10% loan stock. Both have profits before tax and interest of £1,500,000. It is assumed that the corporation tax rate is 33%.

	Company A	*Company B*
	£'000	£'000
Profit before tax and interest	1,500	1,500
Less interest	-	100
Profit before tax	1,500	1,400
Less tax (33%)	495	462
Profit after tax	1,005	938
Less preference dividend	75	-
Available to equity	930	938

You should note the following points.

(a) The preference dividend is the amount actually paid. In the hands of the recipient it will have a gross value for tax purposes of £100, being £75 + (25/75 × £75) and this is the same to an investor as 10% from the loan stock.

(b) The difference in the amounts available to the equity shareholders of £8,000 is due to the difference between the rate of income tax (here 25% of a £100,000 gross dividend) and the rate of corporation tax (here 33% of £100,000 interest paid).

3.22 So why do companies not borrow up to the hilt to get as much debt finance as they can? What restricts their ability or their willingness to borrow?

There are various reasons why a company might be unwilling or unable to borrow more.

(a) Interest charges have been very high in recent years, making debt capital quite expensive, even after tax relief. Interest yields are higher than *dividend* yields on equity shares.

(b) Heavy borrowing increases the financial risks for ordinary shareholders. A company must be able to pay the interest charges and eventually repay the debt from its cash resources, and at the same time maintain a healthy balance sheet which does not deter would-be creditors. There might be insufficient security for a new loan.

(c) There might be restrictions on a company's power to borrow.

3.23 The borrowing powers of a company may be restricted by several factors.

(a) The company's Articles of Association may limit borrowing. These borrowing limits cannot be altered except with the approval of the shareholders at a general meeting of the company. A typical wording of a paragraph in the Articles is as follows: 'The Directors shall restrict the borrowings ... so as to ensure that the aggregate amount of all monies borrowed by the company and/or any subsidiaries shall not at any time without the previous sanction of an ordinary resolution of the company exceed the share capital and consolidated reserves.'

(b) Trust deeds of existing loan stock may limit borrowing. These limits can only be overcome by redeeming the loan stock.

(c) Borrowing may be limited by the attitude of would-be new lenders, who expect some security for their lending, in the form of a charge on company assets, or a certain rate of interest cover, or a 'safe' debt ratio or gearing ratio for the borrowing company.

The reverse yield gap

3.24 Equities are more risky investments than loan stock. To compensate equity shareholders for the extra risk, they should expect higher returns than investors in loan stock or debentures. But this does not always happen, and when yields on loan stock are higher than yields on equities, there is a reverse yield gap.

The return on equities consists of both dividends and capital gains (or losses) in the share price.

It is often the case that interest rates on loan stock exceed dividend yields on equities. However, equity shareholders benefit from any increase in share price too and so the total return on equity then exceeds the yield on debt capital. Even so, a reverse yield gap does occur from time to time.

4. CONVERTIBLES, WARRANTS AND OPTIONS

Convertible loan stock

4.1 Convertible securities are fixed return securities (usually debentures but sometimes preference shares) that may be converted, on pre-determined dates and at the option of the holder, into ordinary shares of the company at a predetermined rate. Once converted they cannot be converted back into the original fixed return security. The conversion rate is usually stated as a conversion price or a conversion ratio.

(a) A conversion price gives the nominal value of loan stock that can be converted into one ordinary share.

(b) A conversion ratio gives the number of ordinary shares that will be obtained from the conversion of one unit of loan stock.

4.2 Conversion terms often vary over time, with the conversion price increasing in line with the expected increase in ordinary share values. For example, the conversion terms of convertible stock might be that on 1 April 1995, £2 of stock can be converted into one ordinary share, whereas on 1 April 1996, the conversion price will be £2.20 of stock for one ordinary share.

The conversion value and the conversion premium

4.3 The market value of ordinary shares into which a unit of stock may be converted is known as the *conversion value*. The conversion value will be below the value of the stock at the date of issue, but will be expected to increase as the date for conversion approaches on the assumption that a company's shares ought to increase in market value over time. The difference between the issue value of the stock and the conversion value at the date of issue, is called the *conversion premium*. The premium may be expressed as a percentage of the conversion value.

Exercise

The 10% convertible loan stock of Starchwhite plc is quoted at £142 per £100 nominal. The earliest date for conversion is in four years time, at the rate of 30 ordinary shares per £100 nominal loan stock. The share price is currently £4.15. Annual interest on the stock has just been paid.

Required

(a) What is the average annual growth rate in the share price that is required for the stockholders to achieve an overall rate of return of 12% a year compound over the next four years, including the proceeds of conversion?

(b) What is the implicit conversion premium on the stock?

Solution

(a)

Year	*Investment*	*Interest*	*Compound factor to end of year 4* 12%	*Terminal value*
	£	£		£
0	(142)		$(1.12)^4$	(223.44)
1		10	$(1.12)^3$	14.05
2		10	$(1.12)^2$	12.54
3		10	$(1.12)^1$	11.20
4		10	1.00	10.00
				(175.65)

The value of 30 shares on conversion must be at least £175.65 at the end of year 4, to provide investors with a 12% return.

The current market value of 30 shares is (× £4.15) £124.50.

The growth factor in the share price over four years needs to be

$$\frac{175.65}{124.50} = 1.4108$$

If the annual rate of growth in the share price, expressed as a proportion, is g, then

$$(1 + g)^4 = 1.4108$$
$$1 + g = 1.0899$$
$$g = 0.0899, \text{ say } 0.09$$

Conclusion. The rate of growth in the share price needs to be 9% a year (compound).

(b) The conversion premium can be expressed as an amount per share or as a percentage.

(i) As an amount per share $\frac{£142 - £(30 \times 4.15)}{30} = £0.583$ per share

(ii) As a % value $\frac{£0.583}{£4.15} \times 100\% = 14\%$

The issue price and the market price of convertible loan stock

4.4 A company will aim to issue loan stock with the greatest possible conversion premium as this will mean that, for the amount of capital raised, it will, on conversion, have to issue the lowest number of new ordinary shares. The premium that will be accepted by potential investors will depend on the company's growth potential and so on prospects for a sizeable increase in the share price.

4.5 Convertible loan stock issued at par normally has a lower coupon rate of interest than straight debentures. This lower yield is the price the investor has to pay for the conversion rights. It is, of course, also one of the reasons why the issue of convertible stock is attractive to a company.

4.6 When convertible loan stock is traded on a stock market, its *minimum market price* will be the price of straight debentures with the same coupon rate of interest. If the market value falls to this minimum, it follows that the market attaches no value to the conversion rights.

The actual market price of convertible stock will depend not only on the price of straight debt but also on the current conversion value, the length of time before conversion may take place, and the market's expectation as to future equity returns and the risk associated with these returns. If the conversion value rises above the straight debt value then the price of convertible stock will normally reflect this increase.

4.7. Most companies issuing convertible stocks expect them to be converted. They view the stock as *delayed equity*. They are often used either because the company's ordinary share price is considered to be particularly depressed at the time of issue or because the issue of equity shares would result in an immediate and significant drop in earnings per share. There is no certainty, however, that the security holders will exercise their option to convert; therefore the stock may run its full term and need to be redeemed.

Example

4.8 CD plc has issued 50,000 units of convertible debentures, each with a nominal value of £100 and a coupon rate of interest of 10% payable yearly. Each £100 of convertible debentures may be converted into 40 ordinary shares of CD plc in three years time. Any stock not converted will be redeemed at 110 (that is, at £110 per £100 nominal value of stock).

Estimate the likely current market price for £100 of the debentures, if investors in the debentures now require a pre-tax return of only 8%, and the expected value of CD plc ordinary shares on the conversion day is:

(a) £2.50 per share;
(b) £3.00 per share.

Solution

4.9 (a) *Shares are valued at £2.50 each.*
If shares are only expected to be worth £2.50 each on conversion day, the value of 40 shares will be £100, and investors in the debentures will presumably therefore redeem their debentures at 110 instead of converting them into shares.

The market value of £100 of the convertible debentures will be the discounted present value of the expected future income stream.

Year		*Cash flow*	*Discount factor* 8%	*Present value*
		£		£
1	Interest	10	0.926	9.26
2	Interest	10	0.857	8.57
3	Interest	10	0.794	7.94
3	Redemption value	110	0.794	87.34
				113.11

The estimated market value is £113.11 per £100 of debentures.

(b) *Shares are valued at £3 each*
If shares are expected to be worth £3 each, the debenture holders will convert their debentures into shares (value per £100 of stock = 40 shares × £3 = £120) rather than redeem their debentures at 110.

Year		*Cash flow/ value*	*Discount factor* 8%	*Present value*
		£		£
1	Interest	10	0.926	9.26
2	Interest	10	0.857	8.57
3	Interest	10	0.794	7.94
3	Value of 40 shares	120	0.794	95.28
				121.05

The estimated market value is £121.05 per £100 of debentures.

Exercise

Downon Howett plc is unable to pay the interest on its debt capital, which consists of £5,000,000 of 10% debenture stock. The debenture holders are entitled, under the terms of their trust deed, to appoint a receiver, but the current financial position of Downon Howett plc is so poor that the enforced liquidation of the company would not realise more than a small fraction of the amount owed to the debenture holders. The debenture holders are therefore willing to consider alternatives.

Downon Howett has suggested that either of two options might satisfy them. The debenture holders would surrender their debentures, in exchange for:

(a) 15,000,000 ordinary shares under option 1;

(b) £5,000,000 of non-interest-bearing convertible debentures under option 2. The debentures would be convertible into ordinary shares in two years time at the rate of 200 shares per £100 of stock. Alternatively, the debentures (which would not be secured) would be repayable at par after two years.

Estimates of the net realisable value of Downon Howett's assets in two years time are as follows.

Probability	*Net realisable value*
	£m
0.2	2
0.4	4
0.3	6
0.1	8

If Downon Howett does not go into liquidation, its value as a going concern after two years is estimated to be 150% of the net realisable value of its assets, and the share price will reflect this value.

Downon Howett would not be allowed to issue any additional shares, nor pay any dividend, for the next two years. There are currently 10,000,000 shares in issue.

Required

Which option would the debenture holders prefer, on the assumption that they choose the one that maximises the expected value of their wealth?

Solution

(a) If option 1 is selected, the debenture holders would own

$$\frac{15}{10 + 15} = 60\% \text{ of the shares.}$$

After two years, the EV of these shares would be as follows.

Break-up value	*Market value (going concern) 150%*	*Ex-debenture holders' share 60%*	*Probability*	*EV*
£m	£m	£m		£m
2	3	1.8	0.2	0.36
4	6	3.6	0.4	1.44
6	9	5.4	0.3	1.62
8	12	7.2	0.1	0.72
				4.14

(b) If option 2 is selected, the debenture holders could choose to demand repayment of the debentures, out of the proceeds of sale of the assets of the company, or to convert the debentures into shares.

They would own $\frac{10}{10 + 10}$ = 50% of the total number of shares.

Break-up value	*Going-concern value*	*Value of convertibles as equity*	*Value of convertibles as debt*	*Convert? *Yes or no*	*Value of debenture holders' securities*	*Probability*	*EV*
£m	£m	£m	£m		£m		£m
2	3	1.5	2.0	No	2	0.2	0.4
4	6	3	4.0	No	4	0.4	1.6
6	9	4.5	5.0	No	5	0.3	1.5
8	12	6	5.0	Yes	6	0.1	0.6
							4.1

* The answer is no if the break-up value or the total debt of £5,000,000, whichever is lower, exceeds the value of 50% of the equity of the going concern. The debenture holders will compare the value of their convertibles as debt and as shares, and opt to use them in the form that gives the greater value.

The debenture holders would prefer option 1 to option 2, but only marginally so (with a difference in expected value of only £40,000).

Warrants (or subscription rights)

4.10 A warrant is a right given by a company to an investor, allowing him to buy new shares at a future date at a fixed, pre-determined price known as the exercise price.

Warrants are usually issued as part of a package with unsecured loan stock: an investor who buys stock will also acquire a certain number of warrants.

The purpose of warrants is to make loan stock more attractive.

4.11 Once issued, warrants are detachable from the stock and can be sold and bought separately before or during the 'exercise period' (the period during which the right to use the warrants to subscribe for shares is allowed). The market value of warrants will depend on expectations of actual share prices in the future.

4.12 If for example, a warrant entitles the holder to purchase two ordinary shares at a price of £3 each, when the current market price of the shares is £3.40, the non-discounted value of a warrant would be (£3.40 - £3) × 2 = 80p.

4.13 If the current market price is below the exercise price, the value of the warrant would be zero.

A warrant may sell on the market for more or less that its value computed in the above way.

4.14 A warrant is only worth buying at its value computed as above if an investor expects the share price to rise between the date of purchase and the exercise period; otherwise, he would wait until the exercise period and buy shares at the existing market rate.

4.15 The advantages of warrants to a company are as follows.

(a) Investors are willing to accept a lower loan interest rate and less restrictive debenture provisions on loan stock or debentures issued with warrants attached.

(b) The company has an easier task in raising new loans for the reasons described in (a).

(c) The warrants also provide for additional equity funds in the future, when the rights attached to the warrants are eventually exercised.

Example

4.16 Pinafore plc has issued 1,000,000 warrants, each giving the holder the option to subscribe for one new ordinary share in the company at a price of £4 per share.

The annual return required by investors is 10%.

Estimate the value of a warrant if it is exercisable:
(i) in one year's time;
(ii) in two years time,
and the expected share price at the time of exercise will be:
(a) £3.80 per share
(b) £6.00 per share.

Solution

4.17 (a) *Expected share price £3.80.* If the expected share price is only £3.80, warrant holders will not exercise their warrants to buy a share for £4. The warrants will therefore be worthless.

(b) *Expected share price £6.* Warrant holders will exercise their option to buy new shares for £4 each, thus making a capital gain of £2 per warrant. The value of a warrant now will be the discounted present value of this future gain.

(i) In one year's time $\frac{£2}{1.10} = £1.82$

(ii) In two years's time $\frac{£2}{1.10^2} = £1.65$

Share options

4.18 Share options may be issued by a company, giving their holders the right to subscribe for new ordinary shares at a predetermined price, at a certain date in the future. When options are eventually exercised, the company will issue new shares for cash.

Share option schemes for employees

4.19 Share options might be issued by a company as a way of rewarding employees. The feature of share options is that they give the right to apply for shares at a date in the future, at a specified price that will probably be favourable to the applicant. For example, a public company whose shares are currently traded at £2 on the stock market might award share options to some of its employees, giving them the right to apply for a quantity of shares at a date in the future at a price of, say, £2. Provided that the market price of the shares rises above £2 by the time the options can be exercised, the employees would then be able to:

(a) obtain some shares, and so get an equity interest in their company; or
(b) obtain some shares and then sell them at a profit. The share options would then give, in effect, a cash bonus.

4.20 Companies which are 'floated' on the Stock Market or the Unlisted Securities Market might use the flotation as an opportunity to set up a share option scheme for employees.

Option dealings

4.21 There are also two quite different types of option that are dealt with on the Stock Exchange: negotiated options and traded options.

Negotiated options

4.22 Negotiated options are arranged individually for an investor by his stockbroker. They may, theoretically, be for any number of shares for any period of time although in practice most negotiated options are for three months. An investor may acquire a *call option* which means he is entitled to acquire the shares at the stated price within the specified period, a *put option* which means he has the right to sell the shares at the stated price within the specified period, or a two-way option or *double option*, which gives the right to buy or sell.

4.23 The advantage of an option to the investor is that he can, if his prediction of the share price movement is correct, reap a large return for a small initial cost. For example, suppose that you are interested in the shares of a quoted company called Twitchtoes plc, whose current market price is 392 - 396. (The lower price is the price at which you could sell shares, the higher price that at which you could buy shares). You believe that the share price is going to rise substantially but you cannot afford to buy a large number of shares. You decide therefore, to take a call option on 500 shares. Your broker informs you that he can get a three month option with a striking price of 398p and a cost of 20p per share. Your initial outlay will be £100 (20p × 500) plus commission which might amount to about £30. If the share price rises as you expect, you can exercise your option at any time within the three month period. For example, if the price rose to 447 - 451p after two months, you could buy 500 shares at 398p and immediately sell them for 447p, giving you a profit before costs of £245 and a net profit of £115. If the price did not rise, or even fell, you could abandon your option (you cannot be forced to take it up) and your loss would be £130.

Traded options

4.24 One of the disadvantages of negotiated options is that, because they are all different, there is no ready market for them. This problem is overcome by traded options.

4.25 Traded options (both call and put options) are for three, six or nine months and are, in almost all cases, for 1000 shares. Options are only available for a very limited list of large financially strong companies. For each company, there will be a series of options in existence at any one time. When new options are created, they are paired, one with an exercise price (similar to the striking price for negotiated options) above the current market price and one below. The former is called 'out of the money', the latter 'in the money'. For example, if the current price of X plc is 251p the exercise prices for a call option might be 240p and 260p. If the market price closes outside the range 240p -260p for at least two days, a new pair of options is created with new exercise prices; thus when market prices are moving violently there will be contracts in existence with several different exercise prices all maturing on the same date. The prices for the two types of option reflect their intrinsic value and in the money call options are always more expensive than out of the money ones.

4.26 As with negotiated options, the advantage to the investor is that the amount of initial investment required is relatively small compared with the potential gains, although the whole investment may be lost if the share price moves in the opposite direction to that expected.

5. DIVIDENDS AND RETENTIONS

5.1 Retained earnings are the single most important source of finance for UK companies. For any company, the amount of earnings retained within the business has a direct impact on the amount of dividends. Profit re-invested as retained earnings is profit that could have been paid as a dividend.

5.2 The major reasons for using retained earnings to finance new investments, rather than to pay higher dividends and then raise new equity funds for the new investments, are as follows.

(a) The management of many companies believe that retained earnings are funds which do not cost anything, although this is not true. However, it is true that the use of retained earnings as a source of funds does not lead to a payment of cash.

(b) The dividend policy of a company is in practice determined by the directors. From their standpoint, retained earnings are an attractive source of finance because investment projects can be undertaken without involving either the shareholders or any outsiders.

(c) The use of retained earnings as opposed to new shares or debentures avoids issue costs.

(d) The use of retained earnings avoids the possibility of a change in control resulting from an issue of new shares.

5.3 Another factor that may be of importance is the financial and taxation position of the company's shareholders. If, for example, because of taxation considerations, they would rather make a capital profit (which will only be taxed when the shares are sold) than receive current income, then finance through retained earnings would be preferred to other methods.

5.4 A company must restrict its self-financing through retained profits because shareholders should be paid a reasonable dividend, in line with realistic expectations, even if the directors would rather keep the funds for re-investing.

At the same time, a company that is looking for extra funds will not be expected by investors (such as banks) to pay generous dividends, nor over-generous salaries to owner-directors.

6. DIVIDEND GROWTH AND MARKET VALUE

6.1 The purpose of a dividend policy should be to maximise shareholders' wealth, which depends on both current dividends and capital gains. Capital gains can be achieved by retaining some earnings for reinvestment and dividend growth in the future.

6.2 The rate of growth in dividends is sometimes expressed, theoretically, as:

$$g = bR$$

where g is the annual growth rate in dividends
R is the proportion of profits that are retained
b is the rate of return on new investments.

Example

6.3 (a) If a company has a payout ratio of 40%, and retains the rest for investing in projects which yield 15%, the annual rate of growth in dividends could be estimated as 15% × 60% = 9%.

(b) If a company pays out 80% of its profits as dividends, and retains the rest for reinvestment at 15%, the current dividend would be twice as big as in (a), but annual dividend growth would be only 15% × 20% = 3%.

An approach to dividend and retentions policy, based on fundamental analysis of share values

6.4 A theoretical approach to dividend and retentions policy can be based on the fundamental theory of share values, which was described in Chapter 3. We will make the following assumptions.

(a) The market value of a company's shares depends on:
  (i) the size of dividends paid;
  (ii) the rate of growth in dividends;
  (iii) the shareholders' required rate of return.

(b) The rate of growth in dividends depends on how much money is reinvested in the company, and so on the rate of earnings retention.

(c) Shareholders will want their company to pursue a retentions policy that maximises the value of their shares.

6.5 The basic dividend-based formula for the market value of shares is

$$MV = \frac{d}{r}$$

where d is a constant annual dividend, and r is the shareholders' required rate of return. This formula assumes a *constant* dividend, and no dividend growth at all, so an assumption on which this formula is based is that all earnings are paid out as dividends.

6.6 Using the dividend growth model , we have

$$\text{MV ex div} = \frac{d_0(1 + g)}{(r - g)}$$

where d_0 is the current year's dividend (year 0) and g is the growth rate in earnings and dividends, so $d_0(1 + g)$ is the expected dividend in one year's time. MV ex div is the market value excluding any dividend currently payable.

Example

6.7 Tantrum plc has achieved earnings of £800,000 this year. The company intends to pursue a policy of financing all its investment opportunities out of retained earnings. There are considerable investment opportunities, which are expected to be available indefinitely. However, if Tantrum plc does not exploit any of the available opportunities, its annual earnings will remain at £800,000 in perpetuity. The following figures are available.

Proportion of earnings retained	*Growth rate in earnings*	*Required return on all investments by shareholders*
%	%	%
0	0	14
25	5	15
40	7	16

The rate of return required by shareholders would rise if earnings are retained, because of the risk associated with the new investments.

What is the optimum retentions policy for Tantrum plc? The full dividend payment for this year will be paid in the near future in any case.

Solution

6.8 Since

$$\text{MV ex div} = \frac{d(1 + g)}{(r - g)}$$

$$\text{MV cum div} = \frac{d(1 + g)}{(r - g)} + d$$

We are trying to maximise the value of shareholder wealth, which is currently represented by the *cum div* market value, since a dividend will soon be paid.

(i) If retentions are 0%

$$\text{MV cum div} = \frac{800{,}000}{0.14} + 800{,}000$$

$$= £6{,}514{,}286$$

(ii) If retentions are 25%, the current dividend will be £600,000 and

$$\text{MV cum div} = \frac{600{,}000(1.05)}{(0.15 - 0.05)} + 600{,}000$$

$$= £6{,}900{,}000$$

(iii) If retentions are 40%, the current dividend will be £480,000 and

$$\text{MV cum div} = \frac{480{,}000(1.07)}{(0.16 - 0.07)} + 480{,}000$$

$$= £6{,}186{,}667$$

The best policy (out of the three for which figures are provided) would be to retain 25% of earnings.

Dividend policy and shareholders' personal taxation

6.9 The market value of a share has been defined as the sum of all future dividends, discounted at the shareholder's marginal cost of capital. When constant dividends are expected, we have

$$MV = \frac{d}{r}$$

6.10 The cost of capital is generally taken to be a tax-free rate, ignoring the actual rates of personal taxation paid on dividends by different shareholders. To each individual shareholder, however, the dividends are subject to income tax at a rate which depends on his own tax position, and it is possible to re-define his valuation of a share as:

$$MV = \frac{d_g(1 - t)}{r_t}$$

where d_g = gross dividend (assumed to be constant each year)
t = rate of personal tax on the dividend
r_t = the shareholder's after tax marginal cost of capital.

6.11 Presumably, a company should choose between dividend payout and earnings retention so as to maximise the wealth of its shareholders; however, if not all shareholders have the same tax rates and after tax cost of capital, there might not be an optimum policy which satisfies all shareholders.

6.12 A further problem occurs when income from dividends might be taxed either more or less heavily than capital gains. Note that in the UK, individuals have an annual capital gains exemption which is not available against income, and companies are taxed on capital gains but not on dividend income.

Since the purpose of a dividend policy should be to maximise the wealth of shareholders, it is important to consider whether it would be better to pay a dividend now, subject to tax on income, or to retain earnings so as to increase the shareholders' capital gains (which will be subject to capital gains tax when the shareholders eventually sell their shares).

7. A PRACTICAL APPROACH TO DIVIDENDS

7.1 So far, we have concentrated on a theoretical approach to establishing an optimal dividend and retentions policy. A practical approach to dividends and retentions should take the following extra factors into consideration.

(a) The need to remain profitable. Dividends are paid out of profits, and an unprofitable company cannot for ever go on paying dividends out of retained profits made in the past.

(b) The law on distributable profits.

(c) Any dividend restraints which might be imposed by loan agreements.

(d) The effect of inflation, and the need to retain some profit within the business just to maintain its operating capability unchanged.

(e) The company's gearing level. If the company wants extra finance, the sources of funds used should strike a balance between equity and debt finance. Retained earnings are the most readily available source of growth in equity finance.

(f) The company's liquidity position. Dividends are a cash payment, and a company must have enough cash to pay the dividends it declares.

(g) Investors usually expect a consistent dividend policy from the company, with stable dividends each year or, even better, steady dividend growth.

(h) A large rise or fall in dividends in any year will have a marked effect on the company's share price. Stable dividends or steady dividend growth are usually needed for share price stability.

(i) The ease with which the company could raise extra finance from sources other than retained earnings. Small companies which find it hard to raise finance might have to rely more heavily on retained earnings than large companies.

(j) If a company wants extra finance to invest, retained earnings can be obtained without incurring transaction costs. Costs of raising new share capital can be high, and even bank borrowings can be quite expensive.

Exercise

Bilanben plc is a company that is still managed by the two individuals who set it up 12 years ago. In the current year, the company acquired plc status and was launched on the USM. Previously, all of the shares had been owned by its two founders and certain employees. Now, 40% of the shares are in the hands of the investing public.

The company's profit growth and dividend policy are set out below. Will a continuation of the same dividend policy as in the past be suitable now that the company is quoted on the USM?

Year	*Profits* £'000	*Dividend* £'000	*Shares in issue*
4 years ago	176	88	800,000
3 years ago	200	104	800,000
2 years ago	60	120	1,000,000
1 year ago	290	150	1,000,000
Current year	444	222 (proposed)	1,500,000

Solution

Year	*Dividend per share* p	*Dividend as % of profit*
4 years ago	11.0	50%
3 years ago	13.0	52%
2 years ago	12.0	50%
1 year ago	15.0	52%
Current year	14.8	50%

The company appears to have pursued a dividend policy of paying out half of after-tax profits in dividend.

This policy is only suitable when a company achieves a stable EPS or steady EPS growth. Investors do not like a fall in dividend from one year to the next, and the fall in dividend per share in the current year is likely to be unpopular, and to result in a fall in the share price.

The company would probably serve its shareholders better by paying a dividend of at least 15p per share, possibly more, in the current year, even though the dividend as a percentage of profit would then be higher.

---

8. CONCLUSION

8.1 This chapter has covered the main sources of long-term finance in some detail. When these sources are used, large amounts are generally involved, so the financial manager does need to consider all options carefully, looking to the possible long-term effects on the company.

Changes in dividend policy can also have an immediate impact on the share price, so such changes should not be made lightly.

TEST YOUR KNOWLEDGE

The numbers in brackets refer to paragraphs of this chapter

1. What is an offer for sale? (2.3)
2. What is a placing? (2.16)
3. What is the role of underwriters? (2.19)
4. What factors should be taken into account when setting the price of shares for launching a company on to the stock market? (2.22)
5. What courses of action are open to a shareholder when there is a rights issue of shares? (2.42)
6. What are the costs of an issue of shares on the stock market? (2.57)
7. What are zero coupon bonds? (3.9)
8. What factors will influence the market price of convertible debentures? (4.6)
9. What are warrants? (4.10)
10. What are share options? (4.18) In what ways might they be issued? (4.19, 4.20)
11. Why might retained earnings be popular with company directors as a source of finance? (5.2)
12. Give a formula for the connection between retained earnings and dividend growth. (6.2)
13. What is the dividend growth model formula for a share's market value? (6.6)
14. How does an individual shareholder's personal tax position affect the dividend policy that the shareholder would like the company to pursue? (6.10, 6.11)
15. What practical considerations should directors take into account in deciding on a dividend policy? (7.1)

Now try questions 4 and 5 at the end of the text

Chapter 5

FINANCE FROM OTHER SOURCES

This chapter covers the following topics.

1. Bank lending, leasing transactions and government assistance
2. International borrowing
3. Smaller companies

1. BANK LENDING, LEASING TRANSACTIONS AND GOVERNMENT ASSISTANCE

Bank lending

1.1 Borrowings from banks are an important source of finance to companies. Bank lending is still mainly short-term, although medium-term lending has grown considerably in recent years.

1.2 Short-term borrowing may be in the form of:

(a) an overdraft, which a company should keep within a limit set by the bank. Interest is charged (at a variable rate) on the amount by which the company is overdrawn from day to day;
(b) a short-term loan, for up to three years.

1.3 Medium-term loans are loans for a period of from three to ten years.

1.4 The rate of interest charged on medium term bank lending to large companies will be a set margin above the London Inter-Bank Offer Rate (LIBOR), with the size of the margin depending on the credit standing and riskiness of the borrower. A loan may have a fixed rate of interest or a variable interest rate, so that the rate of interest charged will be adjusted every three, six, nine or 12 months in line with recent movements in the LIBOR.

1.5 Lending to smaller companies will be at a margin above the bank's base rate and at either a variable or a fixed rate of interest. Lending on overdraft is always at a variable rate. A loan at a variable rate of interest is sometimes referred to as a *floating rate loan*.

1.6 Longer-term bank loans will sometimes be available, usually for the purchase of property, where the loan takes the form of a mortgage.

1.7 When a banker is asked by a business customer for a loan or overdraft facility, he will consider several factors. Banking students are often taught to remember the main factors by the mnemonic PARTS.

- Purpose
- Amount
- Repayment
- Term
- Security

(a) The purpose of the loan. A loan request will be refused if the purpose of the loan is not acceptable to the bank.

(b) The amount of the loan. The customer must state exactly how much he wants to borrow. The banker must verify, as far as he is able to do so, that the amount required to make the proposed investment has been estimated correctly.

(c) How will the loan be repaid? Will the customer be able to obtain sufficient income to make the necessary repayments?

(d) What would be the duration of the loan? Traditionally, banks have offered short-term loans and overdrafts, although medium-term loans are now much more common than they used to be.

(e) Does the loan require security? If so, is the proposed security adequate?

Leasing transactions

Sale and leaseback arrangements

1.8 A company which owns its premises can obtain finance by selling the property to an insurance company for immediate cash and renting it back, usually for at least 50 years, with rent reviews every few years. The property itself must be non-specialised, modern, and situated in a geographical area with good long-term prospects for increases in property value, otherwise it would offer a poor investment to the insurance company, in the event that the tenant went out of business, or stopped renting the property for some other reason.

1.9 A company would raise more cash from a sale and leaseback agreement than from a mortgage, but it should only make such an agreement if it cannot raise funds in any other way. The main disadvantages of sale and leaseback are as follows.

(a) The company loses ownership of a valuable asset which is almost certain to appreciate over time with inflation.

(b) The future borrowing capacity of the firm will be reduced, since the property could, if owned, be used to provide security for a loan.

(c) The company is contractually committed to occupying the property for many years ahead, and this can be restricting.

(d) The real cost is likely to be high, particularly as there will be frequent rent reviews.

Leasing

1.10 'Leasing' in the UK is historically associated with leasehold property, but our concern here is with leasing arrangements for machinery and equipment. A lease is an agreement between two parties, the lessor and the lessee.

(a) The lessor owns a capital asset, but allows the lessee to use it. *Finance houses* (often subsidiaries of banks) act as the lessor in such arrangements.

(b) The lessee makes payments under the terms of the lease to the lessor, for a specified period of time.

1.11 Leasing is therefore a form of rental. Leased assets have usually been plant and machinery, cars and commercial vehicles, but might also be computers, ships, aeroplanes, oil production equipment and office equipment.

There are two basic forms of lease, operating leases and finance leases.

1.12 *Operating leases* are rental agreements between a lessor and a lessee whereby:

(a) the lessor supplies the equipment to the lessee;

(b) the lessor is responsible for servicing and maintaining the leased equipment;

(c) the period of the lease is fairly short, less than the economic life of the asset, so that at the end of one lease agreement, the lessor can either:
   (i) lease the same equipment to someone else, and obtain a good rent for it; or
   (ii) sell the equipment secondhand.

1.13 Much of the growth in the UK leasing business in recent years has been in operating leases. With an operating lease, the lessor, often a finance house, purchases the equipment from the manufacturer and then leases it to the user (the lessee) for the agreed period.

1.14 *Finance leases* are lease agreements between the user of the leased asset (the lessee) and a provider of finance (the lessor) for most or all of the asset's expected useful life.

1.15 Suppose that a company decides to obtain a company car and finance the acquisition by means of a finance lease. A car dealer will supply the car. A finance house will agree to act as lessor in a finance leasing arrangement, and so will purchase the car from the dealer and lease it to the company. The company will take possession of the car from the car dealer, and make regular payments (monthly, quarterly, six monthly or annually) to the finance house under the terms of the lease.

1.16 There are other important characteristics of a finance lease.

(a) The lessee is responsible for the upkeep, servicing and maintenance of the asset. The lessor is not involved in this at all.

(b) The lease has a primary period, which covers all or most of the useful economic life of the asset. At the end of this primary period, the lessor would not be able to lease the asset to someone else, because the asset would be worn out. The lessor must therefore ensure that the lease payments during the primary period pay for the full cost of the asset as well as providing the lessor with a suitable return on his investment.

(c) It is usual at the end of the primary period to allow the lessee to continue to lease the asset for an indefinite secondary period, in return for a very low nominal rent, sometimes called a 'peppercorn rent'. Alternatively, the lessee might be allowed to sell the asset on a lessor's behalf (since the lessor is the owner) and to keep most of the sale proceeds, paying only a small percentage (perhaps 10%) to the lessor.

1.17 Under some schemes, a lessor leases equipment to the lessee for most of the equipment's life, and at the end of the lease period sells the equipment himself, with none of the sale proceeds going to the lessee.

1.18 Returning to the example of the car lease, the primary period of the lease might be three years, with an agreement by the lessee to make three annual payments of £6,000 each. The lessee will be responsible for repairs and servicing, road tax, insurance and garaging. At the end of the primary period of the lease, the lessee might be given the option either to continue leasing the car at a nominal rent (perhaps £250 a year) or to sell the car and pay the lessor 10% of the proceeds.

Why might leasing be popular?

1.19 The attractions of leases to the supplier of the equipment, the lessee and the lessor are as follows.

(a) The supplier of the equipment is paid in full at the beginning. The equipment is sold to the lessor, and apart from obligations under guarantees or warranties, the supplier has no further financial concern about the asset.

(b) The lessor invests finance by purchasing assets from suppliers and makes a return out of the lease payments from the lessee. Provided that a lessor can find lessees willing to pay the amounts he wants to make his return, the lessor can make good profits. He will also get capital allowances on his purchase of the equipment.

(c) Leasing might be attractive to the lessee:

(i) if the lessee does not have enough cash to pay for the asset, and would have difficulty obtaining a bank loan to buy it, and so has to rent it in one way or another if he is to have the use of it at all; or

(ii) if finance leasing is cheaper than a bank loan. The cost of payments under a loan *might* exceed the cost of a lease.

The lessee will be able to deduct the lease payments in computing his taxable profits.

1.20 Operating leases have these further advantages.

(a) The leased equipment does not have to be shown in the lessee's published balance sheet, and so the lessee's balance sheet shows no increase in its gearing ratio.

(b) The equipment is leased for a shorter period than its expected useful life. In the case of high-technology equipment, if the equipment becomes out of date before the end of its expected life, the lessee does not have to keep on using it, and it is the lessor who must bear the risk of having to sell obsolete equipment secondhand.

1.21 Not surprisingly perhaps, the biggest growth area in operating leasing in the UK has been in computers and office equipment (such as photocopiers and fax machines) where technology is continually improving.

Hire purchase

1.22 Hire purchase is a form of instalment credit. There are two basic forms of instalment credit, whereby an individual or business purchases goods on credit and pays for them by instalments.

(a) *Lender credit* occurs when the buyer borrows money and uses the money to purchase goods outright.

(b) *Vendor credit* occurs when the buyer obtains goods on credit and agrees to pay the vendor by instalments. Hire purchase is an example of vendor credit.

Hire purchase is similar to leasing, with the exception that ownership of the goods passes to the hire purchase customer on payment of the final credit instalment, whereas a lessee never becomes the owner of the goods.

1.23 Hire purchase agreements nowadays usually involve a finance house.

(a) The supplier sells the goods to the finance house.
(b) The supplier delivers the goods to the customer who will eventually purchase them.
(c) The hire purchase arrangement exists between the finance house and the customer.

1.24 The finance house will nearly always insist that the hirer should pay a deposit towards the purchase price, perhaps as low as 10%, or as high as 33%. The size of the deposit will depend on the finance company's policy and its assessment of the hirer. This is in contrast to a finance lease, where the lessee might not be required to make any large initial payment.

1.25 An industrial or commercial business can use hire purchase as a source of finance. With *industrial hire purchase*, a business customer obtains hire purchase finance from a finance house in order to purchase a fixed asset.

Goods bought by businesses on hire purchase include company vehicles, plant and machinery, office equipment and farming machinery. Hire purchase arrangements for fleets of motor cars are quite common, and most car manufacturers have a link with a leading finance house so as to offer hire purchase credit whenever a car is bought.

Government assistance

1.26 The government provides finance to companies in cash grants and other forms of direct assistance, as part of its policy of helping to develop the national economy, especially in high technology industries and in areas of high unemployment.

1.27 Government incentives might be offered on:

(a) a *regional basis*, giving help to firms that invest in an economically depressed area of the country;

(b) a *selective national basis*, giving help to firms that invest in an industry that the government would like to see developing more quickly, for example robotics or fibre optics.

1.28 Such assistance is, however, increasingly limited by European Community policies designed to prevent the distortion of free market competition. The UK government's powers to grant aid for modernisation and development are now severely restricted.

2. INTERNATIONAL BORROWING

2.1 Companies are able to borrow funds on the eurocurrency (money) markets and on the markets for eurobonds and eurocommercial paper.

Eurocurrency markets

2.2 A UK company might borrow money from a bank or from the investing public, in sterling. But it might also borrow in a foreign currency, especially if it trades abroad, or if it already has assets or liabilities abroad denominated in a foreign currency.

When a UK company borrows in a foreign currency from a UK bank, the loan is known as a *eurocurrency loan*.

For example, if a UK company borrows US $50,000 from its bank, the loan will be a 'eurodollar' loan. London is a centre for eurocurrency lending and companies with foreign trade interests might choose to borrow from their bank in another currency.

2.3 The eurocurrency markets involve the depositing of funds with a bank outside the country of origin of the funds and re-lending these funds for a fairly short term, typically three months. Most eurocurrency lending in fact takes place between banks of different countries, and takes the form of negotiable certificates of deposit.

International capital markets

2.4 Large companies may arrange borrowing facilities from their bank, in the form of bank loans or bank overdrafts. Instead, however, they might prefer to borrow from private investors. In other words, instead of obtaining a £10,000,000 bank loan, a company might issue 'bonds', or 'paper' in order to borrow directly from investors, with:

(a) the bank merely acting as a go-between, finding investors who will take up the bonds or paper that the borrowing company issues;

(b) interest being payable to the investors themselves, not to a bank.

2.5 In recent years, a strong market has built up which allows very large companies to borrow in this way, long-term or short-term.

Eurobonds

2.6 A eurobond is a bond issued in a European capital market, denominated in a currency which often differs from that of the country of issue and sold internationally. Eurobonds are long-term loans raised by international companies or other institutions in several countries at the same time. Such bonds can be sold by one holder to another.

The term of a eurobond issue is typically ten to 15 years.

2.7 Eurobonds may be the most suitable source of finance for a large organisation with an excellent credit rating, such as a large successful multinational company, which:

(a) requires a long-term loan to finance a big capital expansion programme (with a loan for at least five years and up to 20 years);

(b) requires borrowing which is not subject to the national exchange controls of any government (a company in country X could raise funds in the currency of country Y by means of a eurobond issue, and thereby avoid any exchange control restrictions which might exist in country X). In addition, domestic capital issues may be regulated by the government or central bank, with an orderly queue for issues. In contrast, eurobond issues can be made whenever market conditions seem favourable.

2.8 The interest rate on a bond issue may be fixed or variable.

Many variable rate issues have a minimum interest rate which the bond holders are guaranteed, even if market rates fall even lower. These bonds convert to a fixed rate of interest when market rates do fall to this level. For this reason, they are called 'drop lock' floating rate bonds.

Eurobond issues and currency risk

2.9 A borrower who is contemplating a eurobond issue must consider the exchange risk of a long-term foreign currency loan.

(a) If the money is to be used to purchase assets which will earn revenue in a currency different to that of the bond issue, the borrower will run the risk of exchange losses. These losses would be due to adverse movements in exchange rates, if the currency of the loan strengthens against the currency of the revenues out of which the bond (and interest) must be repaid. Borrowers cannot obtain long-term forward cover in the forward exchange market, and would have to accept the risks of foreign exchange exposure.

(b) If the money is to be used to purchase assets which will earn revenue in the same currency, the borrower can match these revenues with payments on the bond, and so remove or reduce the exchange risk.

Eurobonds and the investor

2.10 An investor subscribing to a bond issue will be concerned about:

(a) *security*. The borrower must be of high quality. A standard condition of a bond issue is a 'negative pledge clause' in which the borrower undertakes not to give any prior charge over its assets, during the life of the bond issue, that would rank ahead of the rights of the investors in the event of a liquidation;

(b) *marketability*. Investors will wish to have a ready market in which bonds can be bought and sold. If the borrower is of high quality the bonds or notes will be readily negotiable;

(c) *anonymity*. Investors in eurobonds tend to be attracted to this type of issue because they can preserve anonymity;

(d) *the return on the investment*.

Eurocommercial paper and sterling commercial paper

2.11 A large company can raise short-term finance by issuing commercial paper. Commercial paper (CP) is a short-term financial instrument:

(a) issued in the form of unsecured promissory notes with a fixed maturity, typically between seven days and three months. (A promissory note is a written promise to pay);

(b) issued in bearer form;

(c) issued on a discount basis (so the rate of interest on the CP is implicit in its sale value).

2.12 The term 'eurocommercial paper' refers to CP issued in any currency (usually US dollars or ecus) whereas 'sterling commercial paper' refers to CP which is denominated in sterling. Commercial paper is an example of 'securitisation', the raising of loans in the form of debt securities.

2.13 A large company which wants to raise fairly substantial sums of money by issuing commercial paper will negotiate a programme with a dealer or with several dealers, that is, with a bank or several banks. There will be a borrowing limit under the CP programme.

2.14 The flexibility of eurocommercial paper arises because the borrower is able to choose the period to maturity. For example, a company might decide that it wants to issue some new paper at the end of November, with maturity in the middle of March. However, if the interest rates that would be payable are not attractive enough at the time for this term of borrowing, the borrower can decide instead to issue paper with a maturity in (say) mid-February. Corporate borrowers are therefore able to schedule borrowing for when they expect interest rates to be most favourable to themselves.

Should borrowing be in a foreign currency or in the domestic currency?

2.15 The factors which are relevant to choosing between borrowing on the euromarkets or the domestic markets are as follows.

(a) The *currency* that the borrower wants to obtain. Multinational companies often want to borrow in a foreign currency (perhaps to reduce their foreign exchange exposure) and it might be more convenient to borrow on the euromarkets than in a foreign domestic market. Where foreign exchange exposure can be reduced by matching income in a foreign currency against interest and capital repayments on borrowing, a further advantage of euromarket borrowing is that interest rates on foreign currency borrowing might be much lower than domestic interest rates.

(b) *The cost.* There is often a small difference in interest rates between eurocurrency and domestic markets. On large borrowings, however, even a small difference in rates can result in a large difference in the total interest charged on the loan.

(c) *Timing and speed.* It may be possible to raise money on the euromarkets more quickly than on the domestic markets.

(d) *Security.* Euromarket loans are usually unsecured, whereas domestic market loans are more commonly secured. Large borrowers might wish to avoid having to give security, preferring to rely on their high credit rating.

(e) *The size of the loan.* It is often easier for a large multinational to raise very large sums on the euromarkets than in a domestic financial market.

3. SMALLER COMPANIES

3.1 The various sources of finance for companies that have been described so far are designed mainly for larger companies.

Compared to large companies, small companies have great difficulty in obtaining funds. Smaller companies are perceived as being more risky, and investors either refuse to invest or expect a higher return on their investment, which the borrowing firm must then be able to pay.

3.2 Small and unquoted companies do not have ready access to new long-term funds, except for:

(a) retained earnings;
(b) perhaps, extra finance obtained by issuing more shares to private shareholders;
(c) some bank borrowing.

So how are small companies to overcome financial restrictions and achieve a good rate of growth?

3.3 The problems of finance for small businesses have received much publicity in recent years, and some efforts have been made to provide them with access to sources of funds. Most of these sources are referred to as 'venture capital'.

Venture capital

3.4 Venture capital is money put into an enterprise which may all be lost if the enterprise fails.

A businessman starting up a new business will invest venture capital of his own, but he will probably need additional funding from a source other than his own pocket. However the term 'venture capital' is more specifically associated with putting money, *usually in return for an equity stake*, into a new business, a management buy-out or a major expansion scheme.

3.5 The institution that puts in the money recognises the gamble inherent in the funding. There is a serious risk of losing the entire investment, and it might take a long time before any profits and returns materialise. But there is also the prospect of very high profits and a substantial return on the investment. A venture capitalist will require a high expected rate of return on investments, to compensate for the high risk.

3.6 A venture capital organisation will not want to retain its investment in a business indefinitely, and when it considers putting money into a business venture, it will also consider its 'exit', that is how it will be able to pull out of the business eventually (after five to seven years, say) and realise its profits.

With the development of the Unlisted Securities Market in recent years, obtaining a quotation for the company's shares on the USM has become an attractive exit because the venture capitalists can sell their shares at the market price and so pull out of the company.

Venture capital organisations

3.7 Venture capital organisations have been operating for many years. There are now quite a large number of such organisations (a guide published in 1988 listed 150 of them) and in 1983 the British Venture Capital Association was formed, to provide a regulatory body for all the various venture capital institutions that joined it as members.

3.8 Examples of venture capital organisations are:

(a) Investors in Industry plc (the 3i group);
(b) Equity Capital for Industry;
(c) venture capital subsidiaries of the clearing banks;
(d) Business Expansion Scheme funds.

3.9 The growing interest in venture capital stems partly from the government's concern to encourage the small business private sector of the economy, and also from the 'high technology' potential that many small businessmen are currently trying to develop on a commercial basis. The high technology aspect to much venture capital funding is particularly apparent in institutions such as Prutec (founded in 1980 with funds of the Prudential Group) which specialises in new technology developments.

The 3i group

3.10 Investors in Industry plc, or the 3i group as it is more commonly known, is the biggest and oldest of the venture capital organisations. It is involved in many venture capital schemes. The 3i group has existed under various different names since 1945.

The clearing banks own 85% of the equity of 3i, and the Bank of England 15%. At the time of writing, a flotation of 3i on the stock market is under consideration.

3.11 The amount invested in a company by the 3i group can range from under £10,000 to over £5,000,000, and even larger sums can be arranged by the group, which in suitable cases will organise a syndicate of financial institutions to provide the funds.

Like other venture capitalists, the 3i group will only invest in a company if there is a reasonable chance that the company will be successful. The group's publicity material states that successful investments have three common characteristics.

(a) There is a good basic idea, a product or service which meets real customer needs.
(b) There is finance, in the right form to turn the idea into a solid business.
(c) There is the commitment and drive of an individual or group, the determination to succeed.

3.12 Investments by the 3i group are medium-term to long-term. The group's publicity material states:

'We are completely flexible in the type of finance we provide. It will take whatever form will achieve the best results subject only to the test of commercial viability. It could be either a loan, an equity subscription or a package combining the two. We will also provide hire purchase and guarantees.'

3.13 Another feature of 3i group financing is that the group will be prepared to provide additional finance at a later stage, should the company need it.

3.14 Normally, the 3i group does not try to become closely involved in the management decisions of companies it invests in. Unlike other venture capitalists, it does not usually ask for a representative of the group to be given a seat on the board of directors. However, the group has a team of staff that is available to give advice, and it also has a Ventures team which does give intensive management support to a few companies in the group's portfolio.

3.15 The types of venture that the 3i group might invest in include the following.

(a) Business start-ups. When a business has been set up by someone who has already put time and money into getting it started, the group may be willing to provide finance to enable it to get off the ground. With start-ups, the 3i group often prefers to be one of several financial institutions putting in venture capital.

(b) Business development. The group may be willing to provide development capital for a company which wants to invest in new products or new markets or to make a business acquisition, and so which needs a major capital injection.

(c) Management buyouts. These are discussed in Chapter 17 below.

(d) Helping a company where one of its owners wants to realise all or part of his investment. The 3i group may be prepared to buy some of the company's equity.

Equity Capital for Industry (ECI)

3.16 ECI was formed in 1976 with capital subscribed by institutional investors (insurance companies, investment companies, unit trusts, pension funds and the 3i group). It was intended to be a 'rescue vehicle' for ailing firms. Its aim is to provide finance, in exchange for equity or convertible preference shares, to viable companies who for certain reasons cannot raise the finance anywhere else. These reasons might be as follows.

(a) The company may lack a Stock Exchange quotation but the capital required is more than financial institutions are prepared to provide. ECI will consider investments in the range of £250,000 to about £3,000,000 or even more.

(b) A rights issue may be ruled out for technical reasons, for example because the market value of the shares is at or close to par.

(c) The company may be too highly geared, and the amount of equity capital required might be too much for a rights issue.

(d) The company may have a poor recent trading record, and without closer investigation (which ECI is prepared to give) may appear to be a poor investment.

3.17 ECI will also provide finance to a company as one of a team of venture capitalists.

Venture capital funds

3.18 Some other organisations are engaged in the creation of venture capital funds, whereby the organisation:

(a) raises venture capital funds from investors;
(b) invests in management buyouts or expanding companies.

3.19 The venture capital fund managers usually reward themselves by taking a percentage of the portfolio of the fund's investments.

The clearing banks and venture capital

3.20 In one sense, the clearing banks have been venture capitalists for many years, providing loans and overdrafts to small companies, often without security. However, an overdraft or loan is not venture capital, in the sense that the bank does not take an equity stake in the business. Even so, all businesses, old, new, small and large, rely to some extent on financial assistance from their bank.

The banks also provide venture capital in return for an equity stake through their venture capital subsidiaries.

Finding venture capital

3.21 If a small company, or an ailing company, decides that it needs financial help, and cannot get it with a bank loan or from any other normal source, its directors may decide to look for venture capital support.

3.22 When a company's directors look for help from a venture capital institution, they must recognise that:

(a) the institution will want an equity stake in the company;
(b) it will need convincing that the company can be successful (management buyouts of companies which already have a record of successful trading have been increasingly favoured by venture capitalists in recent years);
(c) it may want to have a representative appointed to the company's board, to look after its interests.

3.23 The directors of the company must then contact venture capital organisations, to try to find one or more which would be willing to offer finance. A venture capital organisation will only give funds to a company that it believes can succeed, and before it will make any definite offer, it will want from the company's management:

(a) a business plan;
(b) details of how much finance is needed and how it would be used;
(c) the most recent trading figures of the company, a balance sheet, a cash flow forecast and a profit forecast;
(d) details of the management team, with evidence of a wide range of management skills;
(e) details of major shareholders;
(f) details of the company's current banking arrangements and any other sources of finance;
(g) any sales literature or publicity material that the company has issued.

Almost 75% of requests for venture capital are rejected on an initial screening, and only about 3% of all requests survive both this screening and further investigation and result in actual investments.

Government measures to help small businesses

3.24 The government has introduced a few schemes to encourage more lending to small firms and these include:

(a) the loan guarantee scheme;

(b) the Business Expansion Scheme or BES. The BES is a tax incentive scheme to encourage investors to put up venture capital for companies;

(c) development agencies.

The loan guarantee scheme

3.25 The loan guarantee scheme was introduced by the government in 1981. It is intended to help small businesses to get a loan from the bank, when a bank would otherwise be unwilling to lend because the business cannot offer the security that the bank would want. The borrower's annual turnover must not exceed a limit which depends on the type of business. The limit for manufacturing is £2,700,000.

3.26 Under the scheme:

(a) the bank can lend up to £100,000 without security being given by the borrower;

(b) the government will guarantee 70% of the loan;

(c) the borrower must pay a 2.5% annual premium on the guaranteed part of the loan.

3.27 Most types of business can apply for such a loan through their bank. This includes sole traders and partnerships as well as limited companies. Some business activities, however, are excluded (for example agriculture, banking, education, forestry, estate agents, insurance companies, medical services, night clubs, postal and telecommunications services).

The Business Expansion Scheme (BES)

3.28 The BES is a tax incentive to investors to purchase new shares in unquoted UK companies. Individuals are entitled to tax relief on up to £40,000 a year of investments in new shares in such companies. Shares in USM companies do not qualify under the scheme. Companies are limited to raising £750,000 a year in this way.

3.29 There are two ways in which a company can obtain BES investment funds.

(a) It can approach a BES fund for equity funding. BES funds are funds which have been set up especially to pool the BES investment capital of many individuals and to invest this capital in a range of companies that qualify for BES funding. But an individual BES fund may not be willing to provide the full amount of money that a company wants.

(b) It can approach private investors directly by issuing a prospectus.

The attractions of the BES

3.30 An investor benefits in the following way. Suppose that a person with a high annual income pays income tax at the top rate (now 40%) on the top slice of his earnings, and he wishes to invest in a BES scheme to obtain tax relief. It is a condition of the BES scheme that he must invest in *new* equity shares, and hold on to his investment for a minimum of five years. We will suppose that our investor finds a suitable scheme and invests £10,000.

By investing in the BES scheme, he avoids paying tax of £4,000 and so of the £10,000, we could say that £6,000 is his own money and £4,000 is donated by the Inland Revenue.

He holds on to his shares for five years, and then sells them for £20,000. His own money of £6,000 has therefore multiplied in value over three-fold (not a bad return, but by no means impossible in practice since the original gross investment was £10,000, not £6,000). Furthermore, this gain is exempt from capital gains tax.

3.31 This favourable tax treatment for BES investors explains the popularity of the scheme. Many companies, quite sensibly, have sought the opportunity to benefit from the scheme by offering new shares to BES investors. But the companies must be able to offer:

(a) good asset backing to attract investors;

(b) good prospects of making profits and prospects of expansion and growth.

BES funds

3.32 The obvious difficulty with the BES is matching investors and companies. If an individual wants to invest £20,000 in shares that will qualify for tax relief under the BES, how does he or she find a promising company that wants to issue new shares for £20,000?

3.33 This difficulty is overcome by BES funds. BES funds are a form of venture capital fund. They are set up by a number of financial institutions (investment managers, life assurance companies, investment brokers and so on) to:

(a) collect subscriptions from investors;

(b) find companies which want to raise new capital and are prepared to issue new shares to obtain the finance. The companies must qualify under the BES;

(c) package together the subscriptions of individual investors into the fund, and buy the newly-issued shares of these companies.

Realising BES investments

3.34 Investors will expect the company to have plans for how its shareholders will be able to cash in their investment after five years, if that is what they want to do.

Planned exit routes for shareholders might be:

(a) a launch of the company on to the USM after five years;

(b) a management buy-back of the shares, the company's management arranging to purchase the shares of the BES investors from them;

(c) a takeover by a larger company.

Development agencies

3.35 The UK government has set up some development agencies (the Scottish and Welsh Development Agencies) which have been given the task of trying to encourage the development of trade and industry in their areas. The strategy of the agencies has been mainly to encourage the start-up and development of small companies, although they will also give help to larger companies too.

3.36 The assistance that a development agency might give to a firm could include:

(a) free factory accommodation, or factory accommodation at a low rent;

(b) financial assistance, in the form of:
  (i) an interest relief grant for a bank loan. A company developing its business in an area might obtain a bank loan, and the development agency will agree to compensate the bank for providing the loan at a low rate of interest;
  (ii) direct financial assistance in the form of equity finance or loans.

Franchising

3.37 Franchising is a method of expanding business on *less* capital than would otherwise be needed. For suitable businesses, it is an alternative to raising extra capital for growth.

Franchisors include Budget Rent-a-car, Dyno-rod, Express Dairy, Kall-Kwik Printing, Kentucky Fried Chicken, Prontaprint, Sketchley Cleaners and Wimpy.

3.38 Under a franchising arrangement, a franchisee pays a franchisor for the right to operate a local business, under the franchisor's trade name. The franchisor must bear certain costs (possibly for architect's work, establishment costs, legal costs, marketing costs and the costs of other support services) and will charge the franchisee an initial franchise fee to cover set-up costs, relying on the subsequent regular payments by the franchisee for an operating profit. These regular payments will usually be a percentage of the franchisee's turnover.

3.39 Although the franchisor will probably pay a large part of the initial investment cost of a franchisee's outlet, the franchisee will be expected to contribute a share of the investment himself. The franchisor may well help the franchisee to obtain loan capital to provide his share of the investment cost.

3.40 The advantages of franchises to the franchisor are as follows.

(a) The capital outlay needed to expand the business is reduced substantially.

(b) The image of the business is improved because the franchisees will be motivated to achieve good results and will have the authority to take whatever action they think fit to improve results.

3.41 The advantage of a franchise to franchisee is that he obtains ownership of a business for an agreed number of years (including stock and premises, although premises might be leased from the franchisor) together with the backing of a large organisation's marketing effort and experience. The franchisee is able to avoid some of the mistakes of many small businesses, because the franchisor has already learned from his own past mistakes and developed a scheme that works.

4. CONCLUSION

4.1 This chapter has covered a range of sources of finance outside the main UK capital markets. Note that some of the sources, such as international capital markets, are best suited to large companies, others, such as BES funds, to smaller companies, and others, such as bank borrowing, to all sizes of company. When recommending sources of finance, always bear in mind the size of the company.

TEST YOUR KNOWLEDGE

The numbers in brackets refer to paragraphs of this chapter

1. What is a floating rate loan? (1.5)
2. What factors will a banker consider when a loan is requested? (1.7)
3. What is sale and leaseback? (1.8)
4. What are the advantages of leasing equipment rather than purchasing it? (1.19, 1.20)
5. What are the eurocurrency markets? (2.2, 2.3)
6. What are eurobonds? (2.6) Who issues them? (2.7)
7. What is eurocommercial paper? (2.11, 2.12)
8. What is a venture capital fund? (3.18)
9. How might a BES investor seek to realise his investment after five years or so? (3.34)
10. What are the advantages of franchises? (3.40, 3.41)

Now try question 6 at the end of the text

Chapter 6

RAISING LONG-TERM AND SHORT-TERM FINANCE

This chapter covers the following topics.

1. The principles of capital structure
2. The appraisal of capital structures
3. Stock market ratios
3. Treasury departments

1. THE PRINCIPLES OF CAPITAL STRUCTURE

1.1 The assets of a business must be financed somehow, and when a business is growing, the additional assets must be financed by additional capital.

1.2 *Capital structure* refers to the way in which an organisation is financed, by a combination of long-term capital (ordinary shares and reserves, preference shares, debentures, bank loans, convertible loan stock and so on) and short-term liabilities such as a bank overdraft and trade creditors.

Matching assets with funds

1.3 Assets which yield profits over a long period of time should be financed by long-term funds. In this way, the returns made by the asset will be sufficient to pay either the interest cost of the loans raised to buy it, or dividends on its equity funding.

If, on the other hand, a long-term asset is financed by short-term funds, the company cannot be certain that when the loan becomes repayable, it will have enough cash (from profits) to repay it.

1.4 It is usually prudent for a company not to finance all of its short-term assets with short-term liabilities, but instead to finance short-term assets partly with short-term funding and partly with long-term funding.

Long-term capital requirements for replacement and growth

1.5 A distinction can be made between long-term capital that is needed to finance the replacement of worn-out assets, and capital that is needed to finance growth.

1.6 If a company is not growing and only needs finance to maintain its current level of operations, including the replacement of fixed assets, its main sources of funding are likely to be internally generated, provided that the rate of inflation is reasonably low.

1.7 When a company is seeking to grow, however, it will need extra finance.

Debts and financial risk

1.8 A high level of debt creates financial risk. Financial risk can be seen from the point of view of:

(a) *the company as a whole.* If a company builds up debts that it cannot pay when they fall due, it will be forced into liquidation;

(b) *creditors.* If a company cannot pay its debts, the company will go into liquidation owing creditors money that they are unlikely to recover in full;

(c) *ordinary shareholders.* A company will not make any distributable profits unless it is able to earn enough profit before interest and tax to pay all its interest charges, and then tax. The lower the profits or the higher the interest-bearing debts, the less there will be, if there is anything at all, for shareholders.

When a company has preference shares in its capital structure, ordinary shareholders will not get anything until the preference dividend has been paid.

2. THE APPRAISAL OF CAPITAL STRUCTURES

2.1 The financial risk of a company's capital structure can be measured by:

(a) a gearing ratio;
(b) interest cover;
(c) a debt ratio or debt/equity ratio

Gearing ratios

2.2 Gearing measures the relationship between shareholders' capital plus reserves, and either prior charge capital or borrowings or both.

2.3 *Prior charge capital* is capital which has:

(a) a right to payment of interest or preference dividend before there can be any earnings for ordinary shareholders;

(b) a prior claim on the company's assets in the event of a winding up.

2.4 Although there is no single definition of prior charge capital, it is usual to regard it as consisting of:

(a) any preference share capital;
(b) interest-bearing long-term debt capital;
(c) interest-bearing short-term debt capital with less than 12 months to maturity, including any bank overdraft.

However, (c) might be excluded.

2.5 Commonly used measures of gearing are based on the balance sheet values of the fixed interest and equity capital. They include:

$$\frac{\text{Prior charge capital}}{\text{Equity capital (including reserves)}}$$

$$\frac{\text{Prior charge capital}}{\text{Total capital employed*}}$$

* This can either include or exclude minority interests, deferred tax and deferred income: balance sheet items which are neither equity nor prior charge capital.

With the first definition above, a company is low geared if the gearing ratio is less than 100%, highly geared if the ratio is over 100% and neutrally geared if it is exactly 100%. With the second definition, a company is neutrally geared if the ratio is 50%, low geared below that, and highly geared above that.

Exercise

From the following balance sheet, compute the company's financial gearing ratio.

	£'000	£'000	£'000
Fixed assets			12,400
Current assets		1,000	
Creditors: amounts falling due within one year			
Loans	120		
Bank overdraft	260		
Trade creditors	430		
Bills of exchange	70		
		880	
Net current assets			120
Total assets less current liabilities			12,520
Creditors: amounts falling due after more than one year			
Debentures		4,700	
Bank loans		500	
			(5,200)
Provisions for liabilities and charges: deferred taxation			(300)
Deferred income			(250)
			6,770

	£'000
Capital and reserves	
Called up share capital	
Ordinary shares	1,500
Preference shares	500
	2,000
Share premium account	760
Revaluation reserve	1,200
Profit and loss account	2,810
	6,770

Solution

Prior charge capital	£'000
Preference shares	500
Debentures	4,700
Long term bank loans	500
Prior charge capital, ignoring short term debt	5,700
Short term loans	120
Overdraft	260
Prior charge capital, including short term interest-bearing debt	6,080

Either figure £6,080,000 or £5,700,000 could be used. If gearing is calculated with capital employed in the denominator, and capital employed is net fixed assets plus *net* current assets, it would seem more reasonable to exclude short-term interest bearing debt from prior charge capital. This is because short-term debt is set off against current assets in arriving at the figure for net current assets.

Equity = 1,500 + 760 + 1,200 + 2,810 = £6,270,000

The gearing ratio can be calculated in any of the following ways.

(a) $\frac{\text{Prior charge capital}}{\text{Equity}} \times 100\% = \frac{6,080}{6,270} \times 100\% = 97\%$

(b) $\frac{\text{Prior charge capital}}{\text{Equity plus prior charge capital}} \times 100\% = \frac{6,080}{(6,080 + 6,270)} \times 100\% = 49.2\%$

(c) $\frac{\text{Prior charge capital}}{\text{Total capital employed}} \times 100\% = \frac{5,700}{12,520} \times 100\% = 45.5\%$

2.6 A gearing ratio should not be given without stating how it has been defined. You should make your assumptions clear whenever you calculate a gearing ratio in a solution to an examination question.

Gearing ratios based on market values

2.7 An alternative method of calculating a gearing ratio is one based on market values.

$$\frac{\text{Market value of debt (including preference shares)}}{\text{Market value of equity}}$$

The advantage of this method is that potential investors in a company are able to judge the further debt capacity of the company more clearly by reference to market values than they could by looking at balance sheet values. A company with high asset values in its balance sheet might have poor profits after tax and low dividends, so that the gearing ratio based on market values might be high (with debt capital worth more than equity) whereas the gearing ratio based on balance sheet values would be lower. The company should find the task of raising new debt capital fairly difficult, because of its low profitability and consequent high gearing ratio based on market values.

2.8 The disadvantage of a gearing ratio based on market values is that it disregards the value of the company's assets, which might be used to secure further loans. A gearing ratio based on balance sheet values arguably gives a better indication of the security for lenders of fixed interest capital.

The effect of gearing on earnings

2.9 The level of gearing has a considerable effect on the earnings attributable to the ordinary shareholders. A highly geared company must earn enough profits to cover its interest charges before anything is available for equity.

Example

2.10 Suppose that two companies are identical in every respect except for their gearing. Both have assets of £20,000 and both make the same operating profits (profit before interest and tax: PBIT). The only difference between the two companies is that Nonlever Ltd is all-equity financed and Levered Ltd is partly financed by debt capital, as follows.

	Nonlever Ltd	*Levered Ltd*
	£	£
Assets	20,000	20,000
10% Loan stock	0	(10,000)
	20,000	10,000
Ordinary shares of £1	£20,000	£10,000

Because Levered Ltd has £10,000 of 10% loan stock it must make a profit before interest of at least £1,000 in order to pay the interest charges. Nonlever Ltd, on the other hand, does not have any minimum PBIT requirement because it has no debt capital. A company which is lower geared is considered less risky than a higher geared company because of the greater likelihood that its PBIT will be high enough to cover interest charges and make a profit for equity shareholders.

Operating gearing as a measure of business risk

2.11 Financial risk, as we have seen, can be measured by financial gearing.

One way of measuring *business risk* is by calculating a company's operating gearing. Business risk refers to the risk of making only low profits, or even losses, due to the nature of the business that the company is involved in.

$$\text{Operating gearing} = \frac{\text{Contribution}}{\text{Profit before interest and tax (PBIT)}}$$

Contribution is sales minus variable cost of sales, and a contribution/sales ratio represents the amount by which profits will rise or fall per £1 of sales as sales revenue rises or falls.

2.12 The significance of operating gearing is as follows.

(a) If contribution is high but PBIT is low, fixed costs will be high, and only just covered by contribution. Business risk, as measured by operating gearing, will be high.

(b) If contribution is not much bigger than PBIT, fixed costs will be low, and fairly easily covered. Business risk, as measured by operating risk, will be low.

Interest cover

2.13 Interest cover is a measure of financial risk which is designed to show the risks in terms of profit rather than in terms of capital values.

2.14 $$\text{Interest cover} = \frac{\text{Profit before interest and tax}}{\text{Interest}}$$

The reciprocal of this, the interest to profit ratio, is also sometimes used.

2.15 As a general guide, an interest cover of less than three times is considered low, indicating that profitability is too low given the gearing of the company.

The debt ratio (debt/equity ratio)

2.16 Another measure of financial risk is the debt ratio, which is the ratio of a company's total debts, long-term and short-term, to its total assets: net fixed assets plus total current assets.

Another way of expressing the debt ratio is as the ratio of debt to equity (the debt/equity ratio).

You can ignore long-term provisions and liabilities, such as deferred taxation.

2.17 There is no firm rule on the maximum safe debt ratio, but as a general guide, you might regard 50% as a safe limit to debt. In practice, many companies operate successfully with a higher debt ratio than this, but 50% is a helpful benchmark. If the debt ratio is over 50% and getting worse, the company's debt position will be worth looking at more carefully.

Limiting factors on debt financing

2.18 The gearing ratio and the debt/equity ratio indicate whether a company is likely to be successful in raising new funds by means of extra borrowing. Lenders will probably want a higher interest yield to compensate them for higher financial risk and gearing.

2.19 In addition, *ordinary shareholders* will probably want a bigger return from their shares to compensate them for a higher financial risk. The market value of shares will therefore depend on gearing, because of this premium for financial risk that shareholders will want to earn. Directors should bear in mind their responsibility to maximise the value of shares.

2.20 Business confidence and expectations of future profits are crucial factors in the determination of how much debt capital investors are prepared to lend. The level of gearing which the market will allow will therefore depend on the nature of the company wishing to borrow more funds, and the industry in which it is engaged.

(a) A company which is involved in a cyclical business, where profits are subject to periodic ups and downs, should have a relatively low gearing.

(b) A company in a business where profits are stable should be able to raise a larger amount of debt.

2.21 Gearing levels also vary between one country and another, largely as a result of differing economic and social histories. For example, in Germany and, to some extent, Japan, the capital markets are dominated by the banks. They are the main providers of both equity and loan finance and they will usually have board representation in all the companies in which they invest. It follows that they will be largely indifferent to the risk aspects of gearing when providing fresh capital to a particular company. Instead, gearing levels will be determined by other factors such as legal requirements, taxation and liquidity.

Inflation, debt capital and interest rates

2.22 The *cost* of any extra finance will reflect investors' expectations about the rate of inflation. Investors will usually want a real return on their investment, that is, a return in excess of the rate of inflation.

(a) If long-term debt finance is issued in an inflationary period the nominal interest rate needs to be high enough to convince potential investors that they will get a real return. Current market interest rates will reflect investors' expectations.

(b) However, if actual rates of inflation subsequently turn out to be lower than expected, market interest rates will probably fall. A company that issues debt capital at a high nominal interest rate would then find itself paying interest charges on its borrowings which are higher than current market rates.

2.23 Both inflation and uncertainty about future interest rate changes help to explain why:

(a) companies are unwilling to borrow long-term at high rates of interest and investors are unwilling to lend long-term when they think that interest yields might go even higher;

(b) companies therefore rely quite heavily for borrowed funds on bank borrowing and short-term borrowing (such as money market borrowing).

2.24 The advantage of short-term borrowing is that the company is not committed to paying a high interest rate for a long period.

3. STOCK MARKET RATIOS

3.1 A company will only be able to raise finance if investors think that the returns they can expect are satisfactory in view of the risks they are taking. We must therefore consider how investors appraise companies. We will concentrate on quoted companies.

3.2 Information that is relevant to market prices and returns is available from published stock market information, and in particular from certain stock market ratios. The main stock market ratios are:

(a) the dividend yield;
(b) earnings per share;
(c) the price/earnings ratio;
(d) the dividend cover;
(e) the earnings yield.

The dividend yield

3.3 The dividend yield is given by $\frac{\text{gross dividend per share}}{\text{market price per share}} \times 100\%$

3.4. The gross dividend is the dividend paid plus the appropriate tax credit. The gross dividend yield is used in preference to a net dividend yield, so that investors can make a direct comparison with (gross) interest yields from loan stock and gilts.

Example

3.5 A company pays a dividend of 15p (net) per share. The market price is 240p. What is the dividend yield if the basic rate of income tax is 25%?

$$\text{Gross dividend per share} = 15\text{p} \times \frac{100}{(100-25)} = 20\text{p}$$

$$\text{Dividend yield} = \frac{20\text{p}}{240\text{p}} \times 100\% = 8.33\%$$

Earnings per share (EPS)

3.6 EPS is widely used as a measure of a company's performance and is of particular importance in comparing results over a period of several years. A company must be able to sustain its earnings in order to pay dividends and re-invest in the business so as to achieve future growth. Investors also look for *growth* in the EPS from one year to the next.

3.7 EPS is defined as the profit in pence attributable to each ordinary share:

(a) based on the consolidated profit of the period after tax:

(i) after deducting minority interests;
(ii) after deducting preference dividends;
(iii) *but before taking into account extraordinary items*. Extraordinary items are unusual, non-repeating items that affect profit in one year. Including these items within EPS would spoil the value of the EPS as a measure of comparison with previous periods and other companies;

(b) divided by the number of ordinary shares in issue and ranking for dividend.

Exercise 1

Walter Wall Carpets plc made profits before tax in 19X8 of £9,320,000. Tax amounted to £2,800,000.

The company's share capital is as follows.

	£
Ordinary shares (10,000,000 shares of £1)	10,000,000
8% preference shares	2,000,000
	12,000,000

Calculate the EPS for 19X8.

Solution

	£
Profits before tax	9,320,000
Less tax	2,800,000
Profits after tax	6,520,000
Less preference dividend (8% of £2,000,000)	160,000
Earnings	6,360,000
Number of ordinary shares	10,000,000
EPS	63.6p

Exercise 2

Calculate the earnings per share of Orson Cart plc, given the following information.

Profits before extraordinary items and taxation	£5,050,000
Interest charges	£850,000
Tax on ordinary operations	£1,370,000
Extraordinary losses (net of tax)	£460,000
Nominal value of issued shares (25p shares)	£1,000,000

Solution

Interest charges have already been deducted in arriving at the profits before tax, and so should be ignored.

	£
Profits before tax and extraordinary items	5,050,000
Less tax on ordinary operations	1,370,000
Earnings	3,680,000
Number of shares	4,000,000
EPS	92p

3.8 EPS on its own does not tell us anything. It must be seen in the context of several other matters.

(a) EPS is used for the comparing results of a company over time. Is its EPS growing? What is the rate of growth? Is the rate of growth increasing or decreasing?

(b) Is there likely to be a significant dilution of EPS in the future, perhaps due to the exercise of share options or warrants, or the conversion of convertible loan stock into equity?

(c) EPS should not be used blindly to compare the earnings of one company with another. For example, if A plc has an EPS of 12p for its 10,000,000 10p shares and B plc has an EPS of 24p for its 50,000,000 25p shares, we must take account of the numbers of shares. When earnings are used to compare one company's shares with another, this is done using the P/E ratio or perhaps the earnings yield.

(d) If EPS is to be a reliable basis for comparing results, it must be calculated consistently. The EPS of one company must be directly comparable with the EPS of others, and the EPS of a company in one year must be directly comparable with its published EPS figures for previous years. Changes in the share capital of a company during the course of a year cause problems of comparability.

Fully diluted earnings per share

3.9 The fully diluted EPS is potentially important when analysing a company's accounts. It deals with how much the EPS might be reduced (diluted) in the future by:

(a) extra shares being issued;
(b) shares which currently do not rank for dividend becoming entitled to dividends.

3.10 The fully diluted EPS only reflects obligations that the company has already entered into, and so, shares that as at the balance sheet might foreseeably be issued in the future because:

(a) some people have a right to buy new shares, because they hold share options;

(b) the company has issued some convertible debentures or loan stock;

(c) the company has issued share warrants.

3.11 If people exercise their options, convert their convertible loan stock or use their warrants there will be more shares in issue, and so there might be dilution of the company's EPS. The fully diluted EPS is intended to indicate how much dilution of the EPS there might be, on the assumption that the maximum foreseeable number of new shares will come into existence.

3.12 The calculation of the fully diluted EPS involves adjustments to:

(a) the number of ordinary shares ranking for dividend;

(b) the earnings.

(i) If holders of convertible loan stock exercise their right to convert the stock into ordinary shares, the company would save interest payments, and so total earnings would rise by the amount of interest saved (less tax on the extra profits).

(ii) If holders of share options or share warrants exercise their right to subscribe for new shares, they will have to make some payment for the shares, albeit at a price below the market price of the company's existing shares. The funds they pay into the company would be put to use to earn more profits.

Example

3.13 Groundswell plc has 1,000,000 ordinary shares in issue. In 19X4 total earnings were £500,000. The company also has £1,800,000 of 10% convertible loan stock issue. The conversion rights are as follows.

Date	*Price per share*
	£
30.6.19X4	1.50
30.6.19X5	1.80
30.6.19X6	1.90
30.6.19X7	2.00

Calculate the fully diluted earnings per share for the year to 31 December 19X4 on the assumption that no conversion was made during 19X4.

Assume that corporation tax is at 33%.

Solution

3.14

	£	£
Earnings		500,000
Add back interest saving that would arise if the loan stock had been converted (10%)	180,000	
Less tax on these extra profits (33%)	59,400	
		120,600
		620,600

3.15 The EPS calculation is being made at the end of 19X4. By that time the greatest number of shares that would be issued on conversion would be at £1.80 per share. The price of £1.50 would yield more shares but was only available on 30 June 19X4, and that date has now gone by.

The number of shares issued would be $\frac{£1,800,000}{£1.80}$ =	1,000,000
Shares already in issue	1,000,000
Number of shares assumed to be in issue on 1.1.19X5	2,000,000

Fully diluted earnings per share = $\frac{£620,600}{2,000,000}$ = 31.03p

Example

3.16 Grumble plc has issued share options to selected employees. The dates of issue, the number of options issued, and the exercise price are as follows.

Date issued	*Number*	*Exercise price*
July 19X0	200,000	£1.20
November 19X1	300,000	£1.30

The price of 2½% Consolidated Stock on 1 January 19X2 was £20 per cent. The company has 1,000,000 shares in issue and earnings for 19X2 were £600,000. Corporation tax is at 33%.

(*Note*. SSAP 3 requires that when share options or warrants are used, the diluted EPS should be calculated on the assumptions that:

(a) the maximum number of shares are issued under the terms of the options or warrants;

(b) earnings for the period should be adjusted on the basis that the proceeds of the subscription were invested in 2½% Consolidated Stock on the first day of the period to which the EPS calculation relates, and purchased at the closing market price on the previous day.)

Calculate the fully diluted EPS.

Solution

3.17 The yield on 2½% Consols bought at £20 per cent is $2\frac{1}{2}\% \times \frac{100}{20} = 12\frac{1}{2}\%$

Subscription monies receivable = £1.20 × 200,000 + £1.30 × 300,000		£630,000
Yield on £630,000 at 12½% =		£78,750
	£	£
Earnings		600,000
Yield on £630,000 at 12½%, as above	78,750	
Less tax at 33% on these extra profits	25,988	
		52,762
		652,762
Shares at 1 January		1,000,000
Shares from options		500,000
		1,500,000

Fully diluted earnings per share = $\frac{£652,762}{1,500,000}$ = 43.52p

Fully diluted EPS and the interpretation of accounts

3.18 The bigger the potential dilution, the greater the potential question mark over the company's future performance. Dilution is of more concern for companies with a poor record of growth in profits, earnings and EPS. In contrast, if a company can point to a history of strong growth (and could argue perhaps that its share option scheme is succeeding in attracting, keeping and motivating high quality employees) an apparently poor fully diluted EPS in its accounts need not be a matter of concern.

The price earnings ratio

3.19 The P/E ratio is the most important yardstick for assessing the relative worth of a share. It is

$$\frac{\text{Market price in pence}}{\text{EPS in pence on the net basis}}$$

This is the same as

$$\frac{\text{Total market value of equity}}{\text{Total earnings on the net basis}}$$

The 'net basis' means that account is taken of the ACT effects of any dividend payments.

3.20 The value of the P/E ratio reflects the market's appraisal of the shares' future prospects. In other words, if one company has a higher P/E ratio than another it is because investors either expect its earnings to increase faster than the other's or consider that it is a less risky company or in a more secure industry.

The P/E ratio is, simply, a measure of the relationship between the market value of a company's shares and the earnings from those shares.

3.21 It is an important ratio because it relates two key considerations for investors, the market price of a share and its earnings capacity.

It is significant only as a measure of this relationship between earnings and value.

Example

3.22 A company has recently declared a dividend of 12p per share. The share price is £3.72 cum div and earnings for the most recent year were 30p per share. Calculate the P/E ratio.

Solution

3.23 $$\text{P/E ratio} = \frac{\text{MV ex div}}{\text{EPS}} = \frac{£3.60}{30\text{p}} = 12$$

Changes in EPS: the P/E ratio and the share price

3.24 In Chapter 3, the dividend valuation model or fundamental theory of share values was explained. This is the theory that share prices are related to expected future dividends on the shares.

3.25 Another approach to assessing what share prices ought to be, which is often used in practice, is a P/E ratio approach. It is a commonsense approach to share price assessment (although not as well founded in theory as the dividend valuation model), which is that:

(a) the relationship between the EPS and the share price is measured by the P/E ratio;
(b) there is no reason to suppose, in normal circumstances, that the P/E ratio will vary much over time;
(c) so if the EPS goes up or down, the share price should be expected to move up or down too, and the new share price will be the new EPS multiplied by the constant P/E ratio.

3.26 For example, if a company had an EPS last year of 30p and a share price of £3.60, its P/E ratio would have been 12. If the current year's EPS is 33p, we might expect that the P/E ratio would remain the same, 12, and so the share price ought to go up to 12 × 33p = £3.96.

Example

3.27 Annette Cord Sports Goods plc has 6,000,000 ordinary shares in issue, and the company has been making regular annual profits after tax of £3,000,000 for some years. The share price is £5.

A proposal has been made to issue 2,000,000 new shares in a rights issue, at an issue price of £4.50 per share. The funds would be used to redeem £9,000,000 of 12% debenture stock.

The rate of corporation tax is 33%.

What would be the predicted effect of the rights issue on the share price, and would you recommend that the issue should take place?

Solution

3.28 If the stock market shows semi-strong form efficiency, the share price will change on announcement of the rights issue, in anticipation of the change in EPS. The current EPS is 50p per share, and so the current P/E ratio is 10.

	£	£
Current annual earnings		3,000,000
Increase in earnings after rights issue		
Interest saved (12% × £9,000,000)	1,080,000	
Less tax on extra profits (33%)	356,400	
		723,600
Anticipated annual earnings		3,723,600
Number of shares (6,000,000 + 2,000,000)		8,000,000
EPS		£0.46545
Current P/E ratio		10
The anticipated P/E ratio is assumed to be the same		
Anticipated share price		£4.6545

The proposed share issue is a one for three rights issue, and we can estimate the theoretical ex rights price.

	£
Current value of three shares (× £5)	15.00
Rights issue price of one share	4.50
Theoretical value of four shares	19.50

Theoretical ex rights price $\frac{£19.50}{4} = £4.875.$

3.29 The anticipated share price after redeeming the debentures would be £4.6545 per share, which is less than the theoretical ex rights price. If the rights issue goes ahead and the P/E ratio remains at 10, shareholders should expect a fall in share price below the theoretical ex rights price, which indicates that there would be a capital loss on their investment. The rights issue is for this reason not recommended.

Changes in the P/E ratio over time

3.30 Changes in the P/E ratios of companies over time will depend on several factors.

(a) If interest rates go up, investors will be attracted away from shares and into debt capital. Share prices will fall, and so P/E ratios will fall.

Similarly, if interest rates go down, shares will become relatively more attractive to invest in, so share prices and P/E ratios will go up.

(b) If prospects for company profits improve, share prices will go up, and P/E ratios will rise. Share prices depend on expectations of future earnings, not historical earnings, and so a change in prospects, perhaps caused by a substantial rise in international trade, or an economic recession, will affect prices and P/E ratios.

(c) Investors' confidence might be changed by a variety of circumstances, such as:
   (i) the prospect of a change in government;
   (ii) the prospects for greater exchange rate stability between currencies.

The dividend cover

3.31 The dividend cover is the number of times the actual dividend could be paid out of current profits.

The dividend cover is equal to

$$\frac{\text{Maximum possible equity dividend that could be paid out of current profits}}{\text{Actual dividend for ordinary shareholders}}$$

The figures for the maximum dividend and the actual dividend may be either:
(a) both gross; or
(b) both net.

3.32 The dividend cover indicates:

(a) the proportion of distributable profits for the year that is being retained by the company;

(b) the level of risk that the company will not be able to maintain the same dividend payments in future years, should earnings fall.

3.33. A high dividend cover means that a high proportion of profits are being retained, which might indicate that the company is investing to achieve earnings growth in the future.

Example

3.34 The EPS of York plc is 20p. The dividend was 20% on the 25p ordinary shares. Calculate the dividend cover, assuming that there were no extraordinary items in the profit and loss account.

Solution

3.35 Dividend cover = $\frac{20\text{p}}{20\% \text{ of } 25\text{p}}$ = 4

A dividend cover of 4 means that the company is retaining 75% of its earnings for reinvestment.

The dividend cover and extraordinary profits or losses

3.36 When a company makes an extraordinary gain (or loss) during an accounting period, the gain (or loss) is excluded in the calculation of earnings and EPS, but it is included in the calculation of the maximum possible dividend for the purposes of calculating the dividend cover. The maximum possible dividend is then the total distributable profits (profits on ordinary activities plus extraordinary profits minus extraordinary losses) divided by the number of shares.

The earnings yield

3.37 The most common definition of the earnings yield currently used is

$$\frac{\text{Grossed up equivalent of EPS calculated on the net basis}}{\text{Market price per share}} \times 100\%$$

The earnings are grossed up to put the earnings yield on the same basis as the dividend yield.

Example

3.38 The EPS of Cumbria plc calculated on the net basis is 25p and the market price per ordinary share is 200p. Calculate the earnings yield assuming that the basic rate of income tax is 25%.

Solution

3.39 $$\text{Earnings yield} = \frac{25 \times 100/75}{200} \times 100\% = 16.67\%$$

The Financial Times share information service

3.40 The share information of the Financial Times is published in the following format.

19X8		*Stock*	*Price*	*+ or -*	*Div.*	*Cover*	*Yield*	*P/E ratio*
High	*Low*				*Net*		*Gross*	
243	152	Dumpy plc	221	-2	5.25	4.0	3.2	10.5
333	220	Playful plc	255 xd	...	8.25	2.5	4.3	12.1
265	138	Rotten plc	203	+ 18	2.75	5.3	1.8	13.9

(a) High/low refers to the highest and lowest prices (in pence) reached by the shares in the year.

(b) Price is the current market price, and is cum dividend unless otherwise indicated by xd (ex dividend).

(c) + or - shows the daily movement in the price.

(d) Div. net is the most recent net dividend in pence.

(e) Yield gross is the dividend yield. The basic rate of income tax is here assumed to be 25% so that for Dumpy plc the dividend yield is:

$$\frac{5.25}{221} \times \frac{100}{75} \times 100\% = 3.2\%.$$

3.41 Although the EPS is not shown, it may be calculated from the P/E ratio and the market price per share, as follows.

$$\text{EPS} = \frac{\text{Market price per share}}{\text{P/E ratio}}$$

$$\text{Dumpy plc EPS} = \frac{221\text{p}}{10.5} = 21.0\text{p}$$

4. TREASURY DEPARTMENTS

4.1 Large companies rely heavily for both long-term and short-term funds on the financial and currency markets. These markets are volatile, with interest rates and foreign exchange rates changing continually and by significant amounts. The sources of long-term capital have been covered in Chapters 4 and 5. The use of short-term money markets is covered in Chapter 23, and foreign exchange risk management is covered in Chapter 24.

4.2 Many large companies have set up separate and centralised treasury departments to manage cash and foreign currency.

The role of the treasurer

4.3 The Association of Corporate Treasurers has listed the experience it will require from its student members before they are eligible for full membership of the Association. This list of required experience gives a good indication of the roles of treasury departments.

(a) *Corporate financial objectives*

(i) financial aims and strategies;
(ii) financial and treasury policies;
(iii) financial and treasury systems.

(b) *Liquidity management: making sure the company has the liquid funds it needs, and invests any surplus funds, even for very short terms.*

(i) working capital and money transmission management;
(ii) banking relationships and arrangements;
(iii) money management.

Cash management and liquidity management are probably the most obvious responsibilities of a treasurer. In some organisations, the task is largely one of controlling stocks, debtors, creditors and bank overdrafts.

In cash-rich companies, the treasurer will invest surplus funds to earn a good yield until they are required again for another purpose.

A good relationship with one or more banks is desirable, so that the treasurer can negotiate overdraft facilities, money market loans or longer term loans at reasonable interest rates.

(c) *Funding management*

(i) funding policies and procedures;
(ii) sources of funds;
(iii) types of funds.

Funding management is concerned with all forms of borrowing, and alternative sources of funds, such as leasing and factoring.

The treasurer needs to know:

(i) where funds are obtainable;
(ii) for how long;
(iii) at what interest rate;
(iv) whether security would be required;
(v) whether interest rates would be fixed or variable.

If a company borrows, say, £10,000,000, even a difference of ¼% in the interest cost of the loan obtained would be worth £25,000 in interest charges each year.

(d) *Currency management*

(i) exposure policies and procedures;
(ii) exchange dealing, including futures and options;
(iii) international monetary economics and exchange regulations.

Currency dealings can save or cost a company considerable amounts of money, and the success or shortcomings of the corporate treasurer can have a significant impact on the profit and loss account of a company which is heavily involved in foreign trade.

(e) *Corporate finance*

(i) equity capital management;
(ii) business acquisitions and sales;
(iii) project finance and joint ventures.

Corporate finance is concerned with matters such as raising share capital, its form (ordinary or preference, or different classes of ordinary shares), obtaining a stock exchange listing, dividend policy, financial information for management, mergers, acquisitions and business sales.

(f) *Related subjects*

(i) corporate taxation (domestic and foreign tax);
(ii) risk management and insurance;
(iii) pension fund investment management.

5. CONCLUSION

5.1 In this chapter, we have seen how risk must be considered when deciding how to finance a business. If shareholders' interests are to be safeguarded, the shareholders must put up a reasonable amount of their own money as equity capital, to ensure that loan interest payments and loan capital repayments do not drive the business into insolvency.

5.2 A financial manager seeking finance from the market must be aware of how the market will view the company. A grasp of the main stock market ratios is therefore essential.

TEST YOUR KNOWLEDGE

The numbers in brackets refer to paragraphs of this chapter

1. What is a company's capital structure? (1.2)
2. How can financial risk be measured? (2.1)
3. Give three alternative formulae for gearing. (2.5, 2.7)
4. What is operating gearing? (2.11)
5. Define interest cover. (2.14)
6. How is the dividend yield calculated? (3.3)
7. How might EPS be used to judge the returns that a company is making for its equity investors? (3.8)
8. What is the P/E ratio? (3.19) Why is it significant? (3.21)
9. What makes a share's P/E ratio change over time? (3.30)
10. What is the dividend cover? (3.31) What does it indicate? (3.32, 3.33)
11. What is the earnings yield? (3.37)
12. What is the role of a treasurer? (4.3)

Now try questions 7 and 8 at the end of the text

Chapter 7

THE COST OF CAPITAL

A note on discounted cash flow

This chapter and the next chapter assume a basic understanding of the two main discounted cash flow techniques, net present value (NPV) and internal rate of return (IRR). If you are not familiar with these techniques, or if you have not used them for some time, you should first read Chapter 12, Sections 4, 5 and 6.

1. INVESTMENT DECISIONS, FINANCING DECISIONS AND THE COST OF CAPITAL

1.1 The cost of capital has two aspects to it.

(a) It is the cost of funds that a company raises and uses, and the return that investors expect to be paid for putting funds into the company.

(b) It is therefore the minimum return that a company must make on its own investments, to earn the cash flows out of which investors can be paid their return.

1.2 The cost of capital can therefore be measured by studying the returns required by investors, and then used to derive a discount rate for DCF analysis and investment appraisal.

The cost of capital as an opportunity cost of finance

1.3 The cost of capital, however it is measured, is an opportunity cost of finance, because it is the minimum return that investors require. If they do not get this return, they will transfer some or all of their investment somewhere else. Here are two examples.

(a) If a bank offers to lend money to a company, the interest rate it charges is the yield that the bank wants to receive from investing in the company, because it can get just as good a return from lending the money to someone else. In other words, the interest rate is the opportunity cost of lending for the bank.

(b) When shareholders invest in a company, the returns that they can expect must be sufficient to persuade them not to sell some or all of their shares and invest the money somewhere else. The yield on the shares is therefore the opportunity cost to the shareholders of not investing somewhere else.

The cost of capital and risk

1.4 The cost of capital has three elements.

(a) The *risk-free rate of return* is the return which would be required from an investment if it were completely free from risk. Typically, a risk-free yield would be the yield on government securities.

(b) The *premium for business risk* is an increase in the required rate of return due to the existence of uncertainty about the future and about a firm's business prospects. The actual returns from an investment may not be as high as they are expected to be. Business risk will be higher for some firms than for others, and some types of project undertaken by a firm may be more risky than other types of project that it undertakes.

(c) The *premium for financial risk* relates to the danger of high debt levels (high gearing). For ordinary shareholders, financial risk is evident in the variability of earnings after deducting payments to holders of debt capital. The higher the gearing of a company's capital structure, the greater will be the financial risk to ordinary shareholders, and this should be reflected in a higher risk premium and therefore a higher cost of capital.

1.5 Because different companies are in different types of business (varying business risk) and have different capital structures (varying financial risk) the cost of capital applied to one company may differ radically from the cost of capital of another.

2. THE COSTS OF DIFFERENT SOURCES OF FINANCE

2.1 Where a company uses a mix of equity and debt capital its overall cost of capital might be taken to be the weighted average of the cost of each type of capital, but before discussing this we must look at the cost of each source of capital: equity, preference shares, debt capital and so on.

The cost of ordinary share capital

2.2 New funds from equity shareholders are obtained:

(a) from new issues of shares;
(b) from retained earnings.

2.3 Both of these sources of funds have a cost.

(a) Shareholders will not be prepared to provide funds for a new issue of shares unless the return on their investment is sufficiently attractive.

(b) Retained earnings also have a cost. This is an opportunity cost, the dividend forgone by shareholders.

The dividend valuation model

2.4 If we begin by ignoring share issue costs, the cost of equity, both for new issues and retained earnings, could be estimated by means of a dividend valuation model, on the assumption that the market value of shares is directly related to expected future dividends on the shares.

2.5 If the future dividend per share (d) is expected to be *constant* in amount then the ex dividend share price (MV) is calculated by the formula

$$\text{MV (ex div)} = \frac{d}{(1+r)} + \frac{d}{(1+r)^2} + \frac{d}{(1+r)^3} + \ldots = \frac{d}{r}, \text{ so } r = \frac{d}{MV}$$

where r is the shareholders' cost of capital
d is the annual dividend per share, starting at year 1 and then continuing annually in perpetuity.

Assumptions in the dividend valuation model

2.6 The dividend valuation model is based on certain assumptions.

(a) The dividends from projects for which the funds are required will be of the same risk type or quality as dividends from existing operations.

(b) There would be no increase in the cost of capital, for any other reason besides (a) above, from a new issue of shares.

(c) All shareholders have perfect information about the company's future, there is no delay in obtaining this information and all shareholders interpret it in the same way.

(d) Taxation can be ignored.

(e) All shareholders have the same marginal cost of capital.

(f) There would be no issue expenses for new shares.

Share issue costs and the cost of equity

2.7 The issue of shares, whether to the general public or as a rights issue, costs money, and these costs should be considered in investment appraisal. Two approaches have been suggested.

(a) One approach is to deduct issue costs as a year 0 cash outflow of the project or projects for which the share capital is being raised. The issue costs would not affect the cost of equity capital.

(b) An alternative approach you might come across is to calculate the cost of new equity with the formula

$$r = \frac{d}{MV - X}$$

where X represents the issue costs. Thus, if the issue price of a share is £2.50, issue costs are 20p per share, and new shareholders expect constant annual dividends of 46p, the cost of new equity would be

$$\frac{46}{(250 - 20)} = 0.2 = 20\%$$

Approach (a) is recommended.

The dividend growth model

2.8 Shareholders will normally expect dividends to increase year by year and not to remain constant in perpetuity. The fundamental theory of share values states that the market price of a share is the present value of the discounted future cash flows of revenues from the share, so the market value given an expected constant annual growth in dividends would be

$$MV \text{ (ex div)} = \frac{d_0(1 + g)}{(1 + r)} + \frac{d_0(1 + g)^2}{(1 + r)^2} + \ldots$$

where MV (ex div) is the current market price
d_0 is the current net dividend
r is the shareholders' cost of capital
g is the expected annual growth in dividend payments
and both r and g are expressed as proportions.

2.9 This formula assumes a constant growth rate in dividends, but it could easily be adapted for uneven growth.

Capital growth through increases in the share price will arise from changed expectations about future dividend growth, or changes in the required return, r.

2.10 It is often convenient to assume a constant expected dividend growth rate in perpetuity. The formula in Paragraph 2.8 then simplifies to

$$MV = \frac{d_0 (1 + g)}{(r - g)}$$

2.11. Re-arranging this, we get a formula for the ordinary shareholders' cost of capital.

$$r = \frac{d_0 (1 + g)}{MV} + g$$

Some text books give an alternative formula, which comes to the same thing.

$$r = \frac{d}{MV} + g$$

where d is the dividend in year 1, so that

$$d = d_0 (1 + g)$$

The growth model is sometimes called Gordon's growth model.

Example

2.12 A share has a current market value of 96p, and the last dividend was 12p. If the expected annual growth rate of dividends is 4%, calculate the cost of equity capital.

Solution

2.13 Cost of capital

$$= \frac{12\,(1 + 0.04)}{96} + 0.04$$

$$= 0.13 + 0.04$$

$$= 0.17$$

$$= 17\%$$

Estimating the growth rate

2.14 If an examination question requires you to calculate a cost of equity using the growth model, it is likely that you will be expected to predict the future growth rate from an analysis of the growth in dividends over the past few years.

Example

2.15 The dividends and earnings of Hall Shores plc over the last give years have been as follows.

Year	*Dividends*	*Earnings*
	£	£
19X1	150,000	400,000
19X2	192,000	510,000
19X3	206,000	550,000
19X4	245,000	650,000
19X5	262,350	700,000

The company is financed entirely by equity and there are 1,000,000 shares in issue, each with a market value of £3.35 ex div.

What is the cost of equity?

What implications does dividend growth appear to have for earnings retentions?

Solution

2.16 The dividend growth model will be used.

(a) Dividends have risen from £150,000 in 19X1 to £262,350 in 19X5. The increase represents four years growth. (Check that you are aware that there are four years growth, and not five years growth, in the table.) The average growth rate, g, may be calculated as follows.

$$\text{Dividend in 19X1} \times (1 + g)^4 = \text{Dividend in 19X5}$$

$$(1 + g)^4 = \frac{\text{Dividend in 19X5}}{\text{Dividend in 19X1}}$$

$$= \frac{£262,350}{£150,000}$$

$$= 1.749$$

$$1 + g = \sqrt[4]{1.749} = 1.15$$

$$g = 0.15 = 15\%$$

(b) The growth rate over the last four years is assumed to be expected by shareholders into the indefinite future, so the cost of equity, r, is

$$\frac{d_0 (1 + g)}{MV} + g$$

$$= \frac{0.26235\ (1.15)}{3.35} + 0.15$$

$$= 0.24 = 24\%$$

(c) Retained profits will earn a certain rate of return and so growth will come from the yield on the retained funds. It might be assumed that g = bR where b is the yield on new investments and R is the proportion of profits retained for reinvestment. In our example, if we applied this assumption the future annual growth rate would be 15% if bR continued to be 15%. If the rate of return on new investments averages 24% (which is the cost of equity) and if the proportion of earnings retained is 62.5% (which it has been, approximately, in the period 19X1 - 19X5) then g = bR = 24% × 62.5% = 15%.

The cost of debt capital and the cost of preference shares

2.17 Estimating the cost of fixed interest or fixed dividend capital is much easier than estimating the cost of ordinary share capital because the interest received by the holder of the security is fixed by contract and will not fluctuate.

The cost of debt capital already issued is the rate of interest (the internal rate of return) which equates the current market price with the discounted future cash receipts from the security.

In the case of *irredeemable debt* (or preference shares) the future cash flows are the interest (or dividend) payments in perpetuity so that

$$W_0 = \frac{k}{(1+i)} + \frac{k}{(1+i)^2} + \frac{k}{(1+i)^3} \ldots$$

where W_0 is the current market price of debt capital after payment of the current interest (dividend)
k is the interest (dividend) received
i is the cost of debt (preference share) capital

$$\frac{1}{(1+i)} + \frac{1}{(1+i)^2} + \frac{1}{(1+i)^3} \ldots$$

simplifies to $\frac{1}{i}$

so

$$W_0 = \frac{k}{i} \quad \text{and} \quad i = \frac{k}{W_0}$$

2.18 If the debt is *redeemable* then in the year of redemption the interest payment will be received by the holder as well as the amount payable on redemption so

$$W_0 = \frac{k}{(1+i)} + \frac{k}{(1+i)^2} + \ldots + \frac{k + W_n}{(1+i)^n}$$

where W_n = the amount payable on redemption in year n.

2.19 The above equation cannot be simplified so 'i' will have to be calculated by trial and error, as an IRR.

The best trial and error figure to start with in calculating the cost of redeemable debt is to take the cost of debt capital as if it were irredeemable and then add the annualised capital profit that will be made from the present time to the time of redemption.

Example

2.20 Owen Allot plc has in issue 10% debentures of a nominal value of £100. The market price is £90 ex interest. Calculate the cost of this capital if the debenture is:

(a) irredeemable;
(b) redeemable at par after 10 years.

Ignore taxation.

Solution

2.21 *The cost of irredeemable debt capital is* $\frac{k}{W_0} = \frac{£10}{£90} \times 100\%$

$= 11.1\%$

2.22 *The cost of redeemable debt capital.* The cost of debt capital is 11.1% if irredeemable. The capital profit that will be made from now to the date of redemption is £10 (£100 - £90). This profit will be made over a period of ten years which gives an annualised profit of £1 which is about 1% of current market value. The best trial and error figure to try first is, therefore, 12%.

Year		*Cash flow*	*Discount factor*	*PV*	*Discount factor*	*PV*
			12%	£	11%	£
0	Market value	(90)	1.000	(90.00)	1.000	(90.00)
1-10	Interest	10	5.650	56.50	5.889	58.89
10	Capital repayment	100	0.322	32.20	0.352	35.20
				(1.30)		4.09

The approximate cost of debt capital is, therefore, $(11 + \frac{4.09}{(4.09 - -1.30)} \times 1) = 11.76\%$

2.23 The cost of debt capital estimated above represents the cost of continuing to use the finance rather than redeem the securities at their current market price. It would also represent the cost of raising additional fixed interest capital if we assume that the cost of the additional capital would be equal to the cost of that already issued. If a company has not already issued any fixed interest capital, it may estimate the cost of doing so by making a similar calculation for another company which is judged to be similar as regards risk.

Debt capital and taxation

2.24 The interest on debt capital is an allowable deduction for purposes of taxation and so the cost of debt capital and the cost of share capital are not properly comparable costs. This tax relief on interest ought to be recognised in DCF computations. One way of doing this is to include tax savings due to interest payments in the cash flows of every project. A simpler method, and one that is normally used, is to allow for the tax relief in computing the cost of debt capital, to arrive at an 'after-tax' cost of debt.

The after-tax cost of irredeemable debt capital is

$$i = \frac{k}{W_0}(1 - t)$$

where
- i is the cost of debt capital
- k is the annual interest payment
- W_0 is the current market price of the debt capital ex interest (that is, after payment of the current interest)
- t is the rate of corporation tax.

2.25 Therefore if a company pays £10,000 a year interest on irredeemable debenture stock with a nominal value of £100,000 and a market price of £80,000, and the rate of corporation tax is 33%, the cost of the debentures would be

$$\frac{10,000}{80,000}(1 - 0.33)$$

$$= 0.08375 = 8.375\%.$$

2.26 The higher the rate of corporation tax is, the greater the tax benefits in having debt finance will be compared with equity finance. In the example above, if the rate of tax had been 50%, the cost of debt would have been, after tax

$$\frac{10,000}{80,000}(1 - 0.50) = 0.0625 = 6.25\%.$$

2.27 In the case of *redeemable* debentures, the capital repayment is not allowable for tax. To calculate the cost of the debt capital to include in the weighted average cost of capital, it is necessary to calculate an internal rate of return which takes account of tax relief on the interest.

Example

2.28 (a) A company has outstanding £660,000 of 8% debenture stock on which the interest is payable annually on 31 December. The stock is due for redemption at par on 1 January 19X6. The market price of the stock at 28 December 19X2 was 103 cum interest.

Ignoring any question of personal taxation, what do you estimate to be the current market rate of interest?

(b) If a new expectation emerged that the market rate of interest would rise to 12% during 19X3 and 19X4 what effect might this have in theory on the market price at 28 December 19X2?

(c) If the effective rate of corporation tax was 33% what would be the percentage cost to the company of debenture stock in (a) above? Tax is paid each 31 December on profits earned in the year ended on the previous 31 December.

Solution

2.29 (a) The current market rate of interest is found by calculating the pre-tax internal rate of return of the cash flows shown in the table below. We must subtract the current interest (of 8% per £100 of stock) from the current market price, and use this 'ex interest' market value. A discount rate of 10% is chosen for a trial-and-error start to the calculation.

Item and date		*Year*	*Cash flow*	*Discount factor*	*Present value*
			£	10%	£
Market value (ex int)	28.12.X2	0	(95)	1.000	(95.0)
Interest	31.12.X3	1	8	0.909	7.3
Interest	31.12.X4	2	8	0.826	6.6
Interest	31.12.X5	3	8	0.751	6.0
Redemption	1.1.X6	3	100	0.751	75.1
				NPV	0

By coincidence, the market rate of interest is 10% since the NPV of the cash flows above is zero.

(b) If the market rate of interest is expected to rise in 19X3 and 19X4 it is probable that the market price in December 19X2 will fall to reflect the new rates obtainable. The probable market price would be the discounted value of all future cash flows up to 19X6, at a discount rate of 12%.

Item and date		*Year*	*Cash flow*	*Discount factor*	*Present value*
			£	12%	£
Interest	31.12.X2	0	8	1.000	8.0
Interest	31.12.X3	1	8	0.893	7.1
Interest	31.12.X4	2	8	0.797	6.4
Interest	31.12.X5	3	8	0.712	5.7
Redemption	1. 1.X6	3	100	0.712	71.2
					98.4

The estimated market price would be £98.4 per cent *cum* interest.

(c) Again we must deduct the current interest payable and use ex interest figures.

At a market value of 103

Item and date		*Year*	*Cash flow ex int*	*PV 5%*	*PV 8%*
			£	£	£
Market value		0	(95.0)	(95.0)	(95.0)
Interest	31.12.X3	1	8.0	7.6	7.4
Tax saved	31.12.X4	2	(2.6)	(2.4)	(2.2)
Interest	31.12.X4	2	8.0	7.3	6.9
Tax saved	31.12.X5	3	(2.6)	(2.2)	(2.1)
Interest	31.12.X5	3	8.0	6.9	6.4
Tax saved	31.12.X6	4	(2.6)	(2.1)	(1.9)
Redemption	1. 1.X6	3	100.0	86.4	79.4
NPV				6.5	(1.1)

The estimated cost of capital is

$$5\% + \left(\frac{6.5}{(6.5 - -1.1)} \times 3\% \right) = 7.6\%$$

The cost of floating rate debt

2.30 If a firm has floating rate debt, then the cost of an equivalent fixed interest debt should be substituted. 'Equivalent' usually means fixed interest debt with a similar term to maturity in a firm of similar standing, although if the cost of capital is to be used for project appraisal purposes, there is an argument for using debt of the same duration as the project under consideration.

The cost of convertible securities

2.31 The cost of fixed interest securities which are convertible into ordinary shares is found as follows, allowing for taxation and assuming that conversion will take place.

$$P_0 = \frac{K(1-t)}{(1+r)} + \frac{K(1-t)}{(1+r)^2} + \ldots + \frac{K(1-t)}{(1+r)^n} + \frac{V_n CR}{(1+r)^n}$$

where P_0 is the current market price of the convertible security, convertible in year n, after paying the current year's interest
K is the annual interest payment
t is the rate of corporation tax
r is the cost of capital of the convertible security holders
V_n is the market value of an ordinary share in year n
CR is the conversion ratio, that is the number of shares into which the security is convertible.

The cost of capital, r, would be calculated by finding the IRR which equates P_0 with the present value of the future cash flows.

If the cost of capital found by treating the convertibles as non-convertible debentures is higher, that higher cost should be used on the basis that the debenture holders will choose not to convert, so as to secure the higher rate of return for themselves.

Example

2.32 Some 8% convertible debentures have a current market value of £106 per cent. An interest payment was made recently.

The debentures will be convertible into equity shares in three years time, at a rate of four shares per £10 of debentures. The shares are expected to have a market value of £3.50 each at that time, and all the debenture holders are expected to convert their debentures.

What is the cost of capital to the company for the convertible debentures? Corporation tax is at 33%. Assume that tax savings occur in the same year that the interest payments arise.

Solution

2.33

			Try 12%		*Try 15%*	
Year	*Item*	*Cash flow*	*Discount factor*	*PV* £	*Discount factor*	*PV* £
0	Current MV	(106.00)	1.000	(106.00)	1.000	(106.00)
1-3	Interest less tax (K(1-t))	5.36	2.402	12.87	2.283	12.24
3	Value of shares on conversion (40 × £3.5)	140.00	0.712	99.68	0.658	92.12
				6.55		(1.64)

$$\text{Cost of capital} = 12\% + \left[\frac{6.55}{(6.55 - -1.64)} \times (15-12) \right] \%$$

$$= 12\% + 2.4\%$$

$$= 14.4\%, \text{ say } 14\%$$

The cost of short-term funds

2.34 The cost of short-term funds such as bank loans and overdrafts is the current interest being charged on such funds.

Depreciation

2.35 Depreciation, being a non-cash item of expense, is ignored in our cost of capital computations, but depreciation is a means of retaining funds within a business for new investments or replacements. For our purposes, it is sufficient to say that the cost of funds retained by depreciation *is ignored*, because it is argued that they should be taken as having a cost equal to the company's weighted average cost of capital, and so are irrelevant to the calculation of the cost of capital.

3. SPECIAL PROBLEMS

Private companies and the cost of equity

3.1 The cost of capital cannot be calculated from market values for *private companies* in the way that has been described so far, because the shares in a private company do not have a quoted market price.

Since private companies do not have a cost of equity that can be readily estimated, it follows that a big problem for private companies which want to use DCF for evaluating investment projects is how to select a cost of capital for a discount rate.

3.2 Suitable approaches might be:

(a) to estimate the cost of capital for similar public companies, but then add a further premium for additional business and financial risk;

(b) to build up a cost of capital by adding estimated premiums for business risk and financial risk to the risk-free rate of return.

Government organisations and the cost of capital

3.3 The same problem faces government organisations. Government institutions do not have a market value, and most of them do not pay interest on much or all of the finance they receive. Government activities do not involve business risk, and there is no financial risk either for the investor, which is mainly the government itself. It is therefore impossible to calculate a cost of capital for government organisations. The problem is overcome in their case by using a target 'real' rate of return set by the Treasury.

The cost of equity capital: gross dividend or net dividend yield?

3.4 We have seen that the cost of equity is calculated on the basis of net dividends (perhaps with dividend growth). This selection of net dividends rather than gross dividends for the cost of equity requires some explanation.

3.5 The net dividend is the appropriate choice because the cost of capital is used as the discount rate for the evaluation of capital projects by a company, and the company must have sufficient profits from its investments to pay shareholders the net dividends they require out of after-tax profits.

3.6 The taxation on profits is allowed for in the cash flows of each project. The discount rate is therefore applied to the cash flows of the project after tax. If a company were to make a payment of dividends out of profits, the amount available would be the net dividend, related to the after-tax profits earned.

3.7 Since the company's cost of equity is connected with the net dividends payable by the company, the company need not be concerned with the net dividends received by the shareholders after personal taxation has been deducted from the shareholders' gross dividend income. The cash return to a shareholder from his investment in the shares may well differ from the cash which the company pays out. That is, the cost of equity to the company will differ from the required net return of the shareholder.

3.8 Different shareholders may be subject to different rates of taxation, and may therefore have different preferences as to the amount of dividends they receive (and the amount of retained earnings kept within the business for capital growth). Suppose, for example, that a company pays out £75 in dividends (£100 in dividends plus tax credit) to each of two investors, A and B. If shareholder A pays tax at a marginal rate of 25% and shareholder B pays tax at a marginal rate of 40%, A will have £75 left over after tax to re-invest, and B only £60. Since the tax positions of A and B differ, although each investor would appear to agree to the same market value for their shares, it follows that they have different personal costs of capital net of tax.

4. THE WEIGHTED AVERAGE COST OF CAPITAL (WACC)

4.1 We have now looked at the costs of individual sources of capital for a company. But how does this help us to work out the cost of capital as a whole, or the discount rate to apply to DCF investment appraisals?

4.2 In many cases it will be difficult to associate a particular project with a particular form of finance. A company's funds may be viewed as a pool of resources. Money is withdrawn from this pool of funds to invest in new projects and added to the pool as new finance is raised or profits are retained. Under these circumstances it might seem appropriate to use an *average* cost of capital as the discount rate.

4.3 It is essential to note that the correct cost of capital to use in investment appraisal is the marginal cost of the funds raised (or earnings retained) to finance the investment.

The WACC might be considered the most reliable guide to the marginal cost of capital, but only on the assumption that the company continues to invest in the future, in projects of a standard level of business risk, by raising funds in the same proportions as its existing capital structure.

Example

4.4 Prudence plc is financed partly by equity and partly by debentures. The equity proportion is always kept at two thirds of the total. The cost of equity is 18% and that of debt 12%. A new project is under consideration which will cost £100,000 and will yield a return before interest of £17,500 a year in perpetuity. Should the project be accepted? Ignore taxation.

Solution

4.5 Since the company will maintain its gearing ratio unchanged, it is reasonable to assume that its marginal cost of funds equals its WACC. The weighted average cost of capital is as follows.

	Proportion	*Cost*	*Cost × Proportion*
Equity	$\frac{2}{3}$	18%	12%
Debt	$\frac{1}{3}$	12%	4%
		WACC	16%

4.6 The present value of the future returns in perpetuity can be found using the WACC as the discount rate, as follows.

$$\text{Present value of future cash flows} = \frac{\text{annual cash flow}}{\text{discount rate}} = \frac{£17,500}{0.16} = £109,375$$

4.7 The NPV of the investment is £109,375 - £100,000 = £9,375.

4.8 Another way of looking at the investment shows how using the WACC as the discount rate ensures that equity shareholders' wealth is increased by undertaking projects with a positive NPV when discounted at the WACC.

The amount of finance deemed to be provided by the debenture holders will be $\frac{1}{3}$ × £100,000 = £33,333. The interest on this will be 12% × £33,333 =£4,000, leaving £13,500 available for the equity shareholders. The return they are receiving based on their 'investment' of £66,667 will be as follows.

$$\text{Return to equity} = \frac{£13,500}{£66,667} = 0.2025 = 20.25\%$$

As this return exceeds the cost of equity capital, the project is acceptable.

Weighting

4.9 In the last example, we simplified the problem of weighting the different costs of capital by giving the proportions of capital. Two methods of weighting could be used.

(a) Weights could be based on market values (by this method, the cost of retained earnings is implied in the market value of equity).

(b) Weights could be based on book values.

Although the latter are often easier to obtain they are of doubtful economic significance. It is, therefore, more meaningful to use market values when data are available. For unquoted companies estimates of market values are likely to be extremely subjective and consequently book values may be used. When using market values it is not possible to split the equity value between share capital and reserves and only one cost of equity can be used. This removes the need to estimate a separate cost of retained earnings.

Example

4.10 The management of Custer Ackers plc are trying to decide on a cost of capital to apply to the evaluation of investment projects.

The company has an issued share capital of 500,000 ordinary £1 shares, with a current market value cum div of £1.17 per share. It has also issued £200,000 of 10% debentures, which are redeemable at par in two years time and have a current market value of £105.30 per cent, and £100,000 of 6% preference shares, currently priced at 40p per share. The preference dividend has just been paid, and the ordinary dividend and debenture interest are due to be paid in the near future.

The ordinary share dividend will be £60,000 this year, and the directors have publicised their view that earnings and dividends will increase by 5% a year into the indefinite future.

The fixed assets and working capital of the company are financed by the following.

	£
Ordinary shares of £1	500,000
6% £1 Preference shares	100,000
Debentures	200,000
Reserves	380,000
	1,180,000

Advise the management. Ignore inflation, and assume corporation tax of 33%. Assume also that tax savings occur in the same year as the interest payments to which they relate.

Solution

4.11 The cost of capital of a security is the IRR which equates the current market value of the security with its expected future cash flows. The balance sheet (accounting) values of the securities and reserves should be ignored.

(a) *Equity.* Given a 5% annual increase in dividend in perpetuity, the cost of equity capital may be estimated as

$$\frac{60{,}000\ (1 + 0.05)}{585{,}000 - 60{,}000^*} + 0.05 = 0.17 = 17\%$$

* MV ex div

(b) *Preference shares.* The cost of capital is $\frac{6p}{40p} \times 100\% = 15\%$

(c) *Debentures.* The cost of capital is the IRR of the following cash flows.

Year	*Cost*	*Interest*	*Tax relief*	*Net cash flows*
	£	£	£	£
0	(95.30)			(95.30)
1		10	(3.30)	6.70
2	100.00	10	(3.30)	106.70

Net cash flow	Try 10% Discount factor	PV	Try 8% Discount factor	PV
£		£		£
(95.30)	1.000	(95.30)	1.000	(95.30)
6.70	0.909	6.09	0.926	6.20
106.70	0.826	88.13	0.857	91.44
		(1.08)		2.34

The IRR is approx 8% $+ \dfrac{2.34}{(2.34 - -1.08)} \times (10-8)\%$

$= 9.37\%$, say 9%

(d) *Weighted average cost of capital*

Item	*Market value*	*Cost of capital*	*Product*
	£		£
Ordinary shares*	525,000	17%	89,250
Preference shares	40,000	15%	6,000
Debentures*	190,600	9%	17,154
	755,600		112,404

* ex div and ex interest

WACC $= \dfrac{112,404}{755,600} = 0.149 = 14.9\%$, say 15%

(e) The management of Custer Ackers plc may choose to add a premium for risk on top of this 15% and apply a discount rate of, say, 18% to 20% in evaluating projects.

Argument for and against using the WACC

Arguments for using the WACC

4.12 The weighted average cost of capital is recommended for use in investment appraisal on the assumptions that:

(a) new investments must be financed by new sources of funds: retained earnings, new share issues, new loans and so on;

(b) the cost of capital to be applied to project evaluation must reflect the marginal cost of new capital; and

(c) the weighted average cost of capital reflects the company's long-term future capital structure, and capital costs. If this were not so, the current weighted average cost would become irrelevant because eventually it would not relate to any actual cost of capital.

4.13 It has been argued that the current weighted average cost of capital should be used to evaluate projects, because a company's capital structure changes only very slowly over time; therefore the marginal cost of new capital should be roughly equal to the weighted average cost of current capital.

If this view is correct, then by undertaking investments which offer a return in excess of the WACC, a company will increase the market value of its ordinary shares in the long run. This is because the excess returns would provide surplus profits and dividends for the shareholders.

Arguments against using the WACC

4.14 The arguments against using the WACC as the cost of capital for investment appraisal are based on criticisms of the assumptions that are used to justify use of the WACC.

4.15 The main arguments against the WACC are as follows.

(a) New investments undertaken by a company might have different *business risk* characteristics from the company's existing operations. As a consequence, the return required by investors might go up (or down) if the investments are undertaken, because their business risk is perceived to be higher (or lower).

(b) The finance that is raised to fund a new investment might substantially change the capital structure and the perceived *financial risk* of investing in the company. Depending on whether the project is financed by equity or by debt capital, the perceived financial risk of the entire company might change. This must be taken into account when appraising investments.

(c) Many companies raise *floating rate* debt capital as well as fixed interest debt capital. With floating rate debt capital, the interest rate is variable, and is altered every three or six months or so in line with changes in current market interest rates. The cost of debt capital will therefore fluctuate as market conditions vary. Floating rate debt is difficult to incorporate into a WACC computation, and the best that can be done is to substitute an 'equivalent' fixed interest debt capital cost in place of the floating rate debt cost.

5. THE COST OF CAPITAL, THE NPV OF NEW PROJECTS AND THE VALUE OF SHARES

5.1 Using the dividend valuation model, it can be argued that the total value of a company's shares will increase by the NPV of any project that is undertaken, provided that there is no change in the company's WACC.

We shall begin by considering this argument for companies financed entirely by equity, so that the WACC and the cost of equity are the same.

5.2 Suppose that a company relying on equity as its only source of finance wishes to invest in a new project. If the money is raised by issuing new share capital to the existing shareholders and the inflows generated by the new project are used to increase dividends, then the project will have to show a positive NPV at the shareholders' marginal cost of capital, because otherwise the shareholders would not agree to provide the new capital.

5.3 The gain to the shareholders after acceptance of the new project will be the difference between the market value of the company before acceptance of the new project and the market value of the company after acceptance of the new project *less* the amount of funds raised from the shareholders to finance the project.

The market value of the shares will increase by

$$\frac{A_1}{(1+r)} + \frac{A_2}{(1+r)^2} + \frac{A_3}{(1+r)^3} + \ldots - \text{(Cost of project)}$$

where $A_1, A_2 \ldots$ are the additional dividends at years 1, 2 and so on
r is the shareholders' marginal cost of capital.

This is the NPV of the project.

Investments financed by retained profits

5.4 If for some reason there is a limit to the number of new shares that a company can issue to its shareholders and a company could undertake many projects with positive net present values, then reducing its dividend payment would increase the supply of capital available. Even though in the short term dividends will be reduced, this will be more than compensated for in the long term by the fact that extra cash inflows generated by the investments will increase dividends in the future. Indeed, it can be argued that no dividends should be paid until all projects with positive net present values have been financed.

Example

5.5 Hubble plc, which has just paid its current dividend, expects to pay dividends of £6,000 at year 1, £6,000 at year 2 and £8,000 a year from then onwards.

A new project has just been discovered which will require an outlay of £3,000 at year 1 and will yield cash inflows of £2,000 each year for two years. If the project is accepted dividends will be adjusted accordingly. The shareholders' marginal cost of capital is estimated at 15%.

If the shareholders were told at year 0 that the project was going to be accepted and they were given full information about the project, what should be the theoretical increase in the market value of the company's shares?

Solution

5.6 (a) The market value of company at the end of year 0 before acceptance of the new project is

$$\frac{£6{,}000}{1.15} + \frac{£6{,}000}{1.15^2} + \frac{£8{,}000}{1.15^3} + \frac{£8{,}000}{1.15^4} + \ldots \text{ (£8,000 pa in perpetuity)}$$

The value at year 2 of £8,000 receivable each year from year 3 onwards is

$\frac{£8{,}000}{0.15}$ = £53,333 which means that the above computation can be simplified to

$$\frac{£6{,}000}{1.15} + \frac{£6{,}000}{1.15^2} + \frac{£53{,}333}{1.15^2} = £50{,}080$$

(b) The market value of the company at year 0 after acceptance of the new project is

$$\frac{£3{,}000}{1.15} + \frac{£8{,}000}{1.15^2} + \frac{£10{,}000}{1.15^3} + \frac{£8{,}000}{1.15^4} + ... \text{ (£8,000 pa in perpetuity)}$$

The year 1 dividend will be £3,000 lower than before and the years 2 and 3 dividends will be £2,000 higher than before.

$$\frac{£3{,}000}{1.15} + \frac{£8{,}000}{1.15^2} + \frac{£10{,}000}{1.15^3} + \frac{£53{,}333}{1.15^3} = £50{,}300$$

(c) The market value of the company at year 0 would increase by £220 (£50,300 - £50,080) after acceptance of the project. The £220 can be proved as follows.

(i) NPV of the project at year 1 $= \frac{£2{,}000}{1.15^2} + \frac{£2{,}000}{1.15} - £3{,}000$

$= £(1{,}512 + 1{,}739 - 3{,}000) = £251$

(ii) NPV at year 0 of £251 receivable at the end of year 1

$= \frac{£251}{1.15} = £218$

This NPV of £218 is the same as the increase in the market value of £220, allowing for a rounding error of £2.

5.7 In the example above the shareholders would in theory benefit from a sudden rise in the price equal to the net present value of the new project as soon as the project was accepted. In practice, however, this is unlikely to happen for the following reasons.

(a) It would only happen if there is a strong form efficient market, or if dividend forecasts are published and are believed.

(b) Shareholders do not necessarily make rational decisions, so market values may not in practice respond to changes in future dividend expectations.

Conclusions for ungeared companies

5.8 If an all equity company undertakes a project, and it is financed in such a way that its cost of capital remains unchanged, the total market value of ordinary shares will increase by the amount of the NPV of the project.

If the market has strong form efficiency the shares will increase in value as soon as details of the intended project become available in advance of extra profits actually being earned and extra dividends actually being received from the project.

Geared companies

5.9 The situation is the same if a company has debt capital in its capital structure.

Example

5.10 Trubshaw plc is financed 50% by equity and 50% by debt capital. The cost of equity is 20% and the cost of debt is 14%. Ignoring tax, this means that Trubshaw's WACC is 17%.

The company currently pays out all its profits as dividends, and expected dividends are £800,000 a year into the indefinite future.

A project is under consideration which would cost £1,200,000, to be financed half by a new issue of equity and half by a new loan. It would increase annual profits before interest by £340,000. The costs of equity and debt capital would be unchanged.

(a) What is the NPV of the project?
(b) By how much would the value of equity increase if the project is undertaken?

Solution

5.11 The NPV of the project is as follows.

Year	*Cash flow*	*Discount factor*	*Present value*
	£	17%	£
0	(1,200,000)	1.0	(1,200,000)
1 - ∞	340,000	1/0.17	2,000,000
		NPV	800,000

The market value of the company as a whole will increase by £2,000,000, which is the project's NPV plus the cost of the investment. Of this, £1,000,000 will be debt capital and £1,000,000 will be equity.

5.12 To maintain the 50:50 debt:equity ratio, the cost of the investment will be financed by £1,000,000 debt capital and £200,000 equity. It would not be financed by £600,000 of each. This is because the NPV of £800,000 will add to the value of equity *only*, not to the value of the debt capital. If new equity of £200,000 is issued, the NPV of £800,000 will increase the market value of equity by £1,000,000 in total, which matches the new loan capital of £1,000,000.

5.13 The increased value of equity can be proved as follows.

	£
Annual profit from project, before interest	340,000
Less interest cost (£1,000,000 × 14%)	140,000
Increase in annual profits and dividends	200,000
Cost of equity	÷ 20%
Increase in the market value of equity	£1,000,000

5.14 This example therefore illustrates that given an unchanged WACC, the value of equity will be increased by the NPV of any project which is undertaken, with the NPV calculated using a discount rate equal to the WACC.

6. CONCLUSION

6.1 As you will see from this chapter, every source of finance has a cost. In deciding how to finance a company, the costs of all sources must be considered.

6.2 Financial managers need a cost of capital to use in making decisions. A weighted average might seem a reasonable cost to use, but you should appreciate the arguments against, as well as those for, using it.

TEST YOUR KNOWLEDGE

The numbers in brackets refer to paragraphs of this chapter

1. A cost of capital can be said to consist of three elements. What are they? (1.4)

2. What is the dividend valuation model formula for the cost of equity:

   (a) with no dividend growth? (2.5)
   (b) with dividend growth? (2.8 - 2.11)

3. How is the after-tax cost of debt capital calculated? (2.24 - 2.27)

4. How is the cost of convertible securities calculated? (2.31)

5. Why should a weighted average cost of capital be used as the discount rate, instead of the cost of the funds that are specifically used to finance each new investment? (4.2)

6. On what assumption is it appropriate to use the weighted average cost of capital as the discount rate for investment evaluation? (4.3)

7. Should weightings be based on the market values or the book values of the sources of capital? (4.9)

8. What are the arguments against using the WACC as the discount rate? (4.15)

Now try questions 9 and 10 at the end of the text

Chapter 8

MODIGLIANI AND MILLER: THE EFFECT OF CAPITAL STRUCTURE

This chapter covers the following topics.

1. Gearing, financial risk and the cost of capital
2. Traditional and net operating income views of WACC
3. Modigliani-Miller (MM) theory without taxation
4. Modigliani-Miller theory adjusted for taxation
5. The adjusted present value (APV) method of project evaluation
6. Modigliani-Miller theory on the irrelevance of dividend policy

1. GEARING, FINANCIAL RISK AND THE COST OF CAPITAL

1.1 A high level of debt creates financial risk. The financial risk of a company's capital structure can be measured by a gearing ratio.

The method of calculating a gearing ratio which is appropriate for investment evaluation is one based on market values. Gearing is measured as

$$\frac{\text{Market value of debt (including preference shares)}}{\text{Market value of equity}}$$

1.2 Because of the financial risk associated with gearing, higher gearing will increase the rate of return required by ordinary shareholders, and may also affect the yield required by long-term creditors. It follows that a company's gearing level could have a bearing on its weighted average cost of capital.

Example

1.3 Whitebait plc is a company financed by £1 ordinary share capital and irredeemable debentures. The debentures carry a nominal rate of 12% and have a current market value at par. The company has paid an annual dividend of 40p per share in the past and is expected to continue to do so in the future. The market value per share is £2 ex div. The total market value of equity is £6,000,000, and of debentures, £2,000,000.

1.4 Whitebait plc is now considering a major new project which will cost £2,000,000, and return annual net cash flows in perpetuity of £378,000 (before interest). The company proposes to finance the project with a new issue of 12% debentures at par.

The rights of the existing debenture holders will be protected, so it is expected that the cost of existing debt will be unchanged, and its market value will remain the same.

The returns from the new project carry the same degree of risk as the returns from existing projects, therefore the *business* risk of the company as a whole is unaffected, and there should be no increase in the company's cost of capital to allow for additional business risk.

However, the higher gearing will increase the *financial* risk for shareholders. If the project is accepted and financed in the manner proposed, there will be an increase of 4% in the cost of equity.

Ignore taxation, and assume that all earnings before interest will be paid out as interest and dividends in the year they are received.

Decide whether Whitebait plc should undertake the project, and calculate by how much the choice of the method of financing influences the decision.

Solution

1.5 The project is a major one, and therefore its method of financing will affect the company's capital structure substantially. It is important that the full effect of the marginal cost of finance should be taken into consideration.

1.6 The marginal cost of finance is not just 12%, the cost of the new debentures, because the new funds will also cause an increase in the cost of existing equity. This effect on the overall cost of capital should be allowed for in evaluating the project.

1.7 The project will be evaluated on the assumptions that:

(a) the market value of equity is determined by the level of dividends and the equity cost of capital;

(b) a project should not be undertaken unless it increases the wealth of shareholders, that is, the market value of equity.

1.8 *Workings*

(a) The current cost of equity is $\frac{40p}{£2} = 0.2 = 20\%$

(b) The cost of equity after acceptance of the project would be 20% + 4% = 24%, because of the increase in financial risk.

(c) The current weighted average cost of capital is as follows.

Item	*Market value*	*Cost*	*Product*
	£		£
Equity	6,000,000	20%	1,200,000
Existing debentures	2,000,000	12%	240,000
	8,000,000		1,440,000

The current weighted average cost of capital is $\frac{1,440}{8,000} = 18\%$

(d) The new weighted average cost of capital cannot be calculated until the market value of equity after acceptance of the project is known.

1.9 The effect of the project on equity market values can be estimated with the dividend valuation model. The effect on ordinary dividends of accepting the project and financing it in the manner proposed is as follows.

		£
Present annual earnings before interest		1,440,000
Add annual earnings before interest from new project		378,000
		1,818,000
Deduct interest	£	
Existing debentures	240,000	
New debentures	240,000	
		480,000
Annual earnings and dividends for equity if the project is accepted, in perpetuity		1,338,000
New cost of equity = 24%		
New market value of equity (£1,338,000 ÷ 24%)		£5,575,000

1.10

	£
Existing market value of equity	6,000,000
Market value of equity if the project is accepted	5,575,000
Loss in shareholder wealth from acceptance of the project	425,000

The project should not be undertaken because shareholders' wealth would be reduced.

1.11 The reasons for not accepting the project can be analysed into two separate considerations.

(a) Would the project have been acceptable if the company had raised funds which maintained the existing weighted average cost of capital?

(b) Has the change in the weighted average cost of capital, resulting from financing the project in a particular way, influenced the decision whether or not to accept the project?

1.12 We will look at each of these factors in turn.

(a) *What would have happened if the WACC had been kept unchanged?*
If the company had maintained its weighted average cost of capital, the project's NPV would have been calculated at a discount rate of 18%.

Year	*Cash flow*		*PV at 18%*
	£		£
0	(2,000,000)		(2,000,000)
1 onwards	378,000	(÷0.18)	2,100,000
		NPV +	100,000

The total annual earnings before interest of £1,818,000 would have been valued at

$$\frac{£1,818,000}{0.18} = £10,100,000$$

Subtracting the total market value of debt (£4,000,000) the market value of equity would be £6,100,000 which represents an increase in shareholders' wealth of £100,000 above the existing market value. That is, share values would rise by an amount equal to the NPV of the project, as predicted by the fundamental theory of share values.

(b) *How has the change in capital structure affected the project's viability?*
The method of financing must therefore be the reason for deciding to reject the project.

The new weighted average cost of capital is as follows.

Item	*Market value*	*Cost*	*Product*
	£		£
Equity	5,575,000	24%	1,338,000
Existing debentures	2,000,000	12%	240,000
New debentures	2,000,000	12%	240,000
	9,575,000		1,818,000

The new weighted average cost of capital is $\frac{£1,818}{£9,575} = 0.19 = 19\%$

If the company had maintained a weighted average cost of capital of 18%, the value of annual cash flows of £1,818,000 would have been £10,100,000 (see (a) above).

	£
Value of annual cash flows at 18%	10,100,000
Value of annual cash flows at 19%	9,575,000
Loss in value due to increase in WACC	525,000

The method of financing the project accounts for a loss in shareholder wealth of £525,000.

(c) The two causes can now be brought together.

	£
NPV of the project at the current WACC	100,000
Effect of financing on share values	(525,000)
Loss in shareholder wealth	(425,000)

This is the total figure calculated previously.

Gearing, project appraisal and the source of funds to finance a new project

1.13 The previous example attempts to suggest that a project which has a positive NPV when its cash flows are discounted at the WACC might be financially harmful to shareholders if it is financed in the wrong way. This conclusion can be taken one step further.

If a project is viable (has a positive NPV) when it is discounted at the current WACC, then it would be worthwhile provided that the new funds which are raised to finance it leave the company's WACC unchanged.

Exercise

Mazarin plc has a constant annual cash inflow of £700,000 and has the following capital structure.

	Market value	*Dividends/interest*
	£'000	£'000
Equity: 2,000,000 £1 shares	3,000	540
£2,000,000 of 8% perpetual debentures	2,000	160
	5,000	700

It has a new project costing £1,600,000 which will return £280,000 a year in perpetuity.If the project is financed by an issue of 14% perpetual debentures at par it is thought that shareholders will want an increase in their return of 3% to compensate them for the extra financial risk. The cash inflow from the new project will, after interest has been paid on the additional finance, be passed on to shareholders in dividends.

Required

(a) Calculate the gain or loss to shareholders if the project is financed in the manner proposed.

(b) Analyse the cause of the gain or loss.

(c) How should the finance be raised if Mazarin plc considers its existing capital structure to be optimal? (You may assume that the cost of the individual elements within the capital structure will remain the same.)

Ignore taxation.

Solution

(a) The marginal cost of finance is not 14% because the cost of equity will be affected by the project being undertaken.

The current cost of equity is $\frac{540}{3,000} = 0.18 = 18\%$.

The new cost of equity would be (18 + 3%) = 21%.

The current weighted average cost of capital is as follows.

Item	*Market value*	*Cost*	*Product*
	£'000		
Equity	3,000	0.18	540
8% Debentures	2,000	0.08	160
	5,000		700

$$\text{WACC} = \frac{700}{5,000} = 0.14 \text{ or } 14\%$$

The effect on ordinary dividend after accepting the project and financing it in the manner proposed is as follows.

	£'000	£'000
Present annual earnings before interest		700
Add annual cash flows from project		280
		980
Deduct interest:		
on existing 8% debentures	160	
on £1,600,000 14% debentures	224	
		384
		596

New cost of equity	21%
New market value of equity (£596,000 ÷ 21%)	£2,838,095

	£'000
New value of equity	2,838
Less existing value of equity	3,000
Loss in shareholder wealth from acceptance of the project	(162)

(b) If the company were to maintain its WACC of 14% the NPV of the project would be as follows.

	£'000
PV of future cash flows in perpetuity (£280,000 ÷ 14%)	2,000
Less PV of capital outlays	1,600
NPV of project	400

The new WACC after financing the project in the manner proposed would be as follows.

Item	*Market value*	*Cost*	*Product*
	£'000		£'000
New value of equity	2,838	0.21	596
8% debentures	2,000	0.08	160
14% debentures	1,600	0.14	224
	6,438		980

$$\text{WACC} = \frac{980}{6,438} = 0.15222$$

The annual cash flows of £980,000 would give the following values for the company.

	£'000
At a WACC of 14%	7,000
At a WACC of 15.222%	6,438
Loss in value due to change in WACC	(562)

Summary

	£'000
NPV at current WACC	400
Loss in value due to the choice of financing method	(562)
Net loss from the project	(162)

(c) Since the project has a positive NPV of £400,000 at the current WACC of 14%, it should finance the project in such a way that the WACC remains unchanged.

This means maintaining a capital structure in which the ratio of the market value of equity to the market value of debt is 60% : 40% (£3m : £2m).

The revised total value of the company after the project is undertaken should be £980,000/0.14 = £7,000,000. Of this, £4,200,000 (60%) should be equity and £2,800,000 (40%) should be debt capital. This means that:

(i) the debt capital should increase in market value by £2,800,000 - £2,000,000 = £800,000;

(ii) equity should increase in market value by £4,200,000 - £3,000,000 = £1,200,000, including the gain in market value arising from the project's positive NPV of £400,000. This means that new equity of £1,200,000 - £400,000 = £800,000 should be raised, either by a new issue of shares or by withholding dividends.

Gearing and shareholders' investment decisions

1.14 It should be apparent from the foregoing that the value of equity is related, not only to the size of dividends and the cost of equity, but also to the weighted average cost of capital. This connection will now be investigated in greater detail.

We will assume that a shareholder would be prepared to accept a change in the gearing of a company, and therefore a change in the required rate of return for equity, provided that the effect of this change in gearing would be to increase the value of his shares, or at the very least to leave them unchanged.

2. TRADITIONAL AND NET OPERATING INCOME VIEWS OF WACC

2.1 There are two main theories about the effect of changes in gearing on the weighted average cost of capital and share values. These are:

(a) the 'traditional' view;
(b) the net operating income approach, for which a behavioural justification has been provided by Modigliani and Miller.

2.2. The assumptions on which these theories are based are as follows.

(a) The company pays out all its earnings as dividends.

(b) The gearing of the company can be changed immediately by issuing debt to repurchase shares, or by issuing shares to repurchase debt. There are no transaction costs for issues.

(c) The earnings of the company are expected to remain constant in perpetuity and all investors share the same expectations about these future earnings.

(d) Business risk is also constant, regardless of how the company invests its funds.

(e) Taxation, for the time being, is ignored.

The traditional view of WACC

2.3 The traditional view is as follows.

(a) As the level of gearing increases the cost of debt remains unchanged up to a certain level of gearing. Beyond this level, the cost of debt will increase.

(b) The cost of equity rises as the level of gearing increases.

(c) The weighted average cost of capital does not remain constant, but rather falls initially as the proportion of debt capital increases, and then begins to increase as the rising cost of equity (and possibly of debt) becomes more significant.

(d) The optimum level of gearing is where the company's weighted average cost of capital is minimised.

2.4 The traditional view about the cost of capital is shown in the following graph. It shows that the weighted average cost of capital will be minimised at a particular level of gearing P.

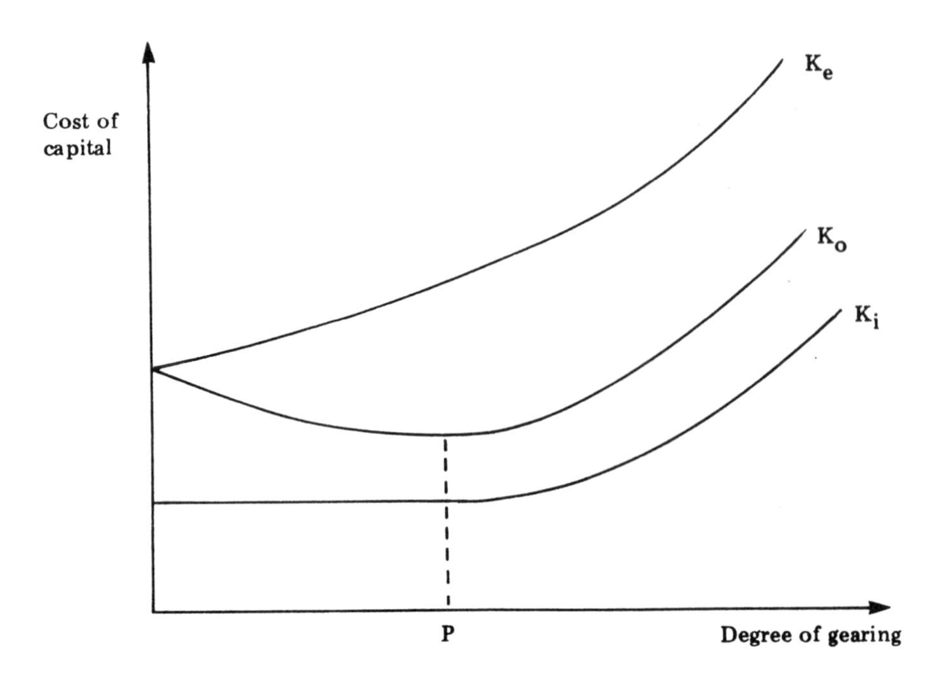

K_e is the cost of equity
K_i is the cost of debt
K_o is the weighted average cost of capital

2.5 The traditional view is that the weighted average cost of capital, when plotted against the level of gearing, is saucer shaped.

The optimum capital structure is where the weighted average cost of capital is lowest, at point P.

The net operating income view of WACC

2.6 The net operating income approach takes a different view of the effect of gearing on WACC. It assumes that the weighted average cost of capital is unchanged, regardless of the level of gearing, because of the following two factors.

(a) The cost of debt remains unchanged as the level of gearing increases.

(b) The cost of equity rises in such a way as to keep the weighted average cost of capital constant.

This would be represented on a graph as follows.

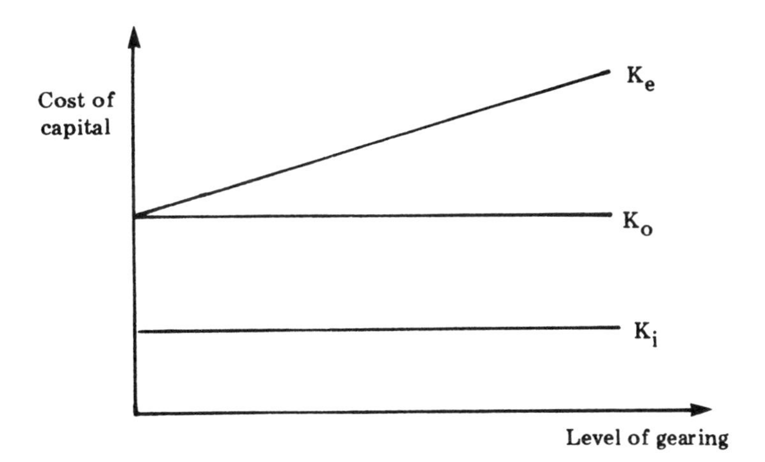

Example

2.7 A company has £5,000 of debt at 10% interest, and earns £5,000 a year before interest is paid. There are 2,250 issued shares, and the weighted average cost of capital of the company is 20%.

The market value of the company should be as follows.

Earnings	£5,000
Weighted average cost of capital	0.2
	£
Market value of the company (£5,000 ÷ 0.2)	25,000
Less market value of debt	5,000
Market value of equity	20,000

The cost of equity is therefore $\frac{5,000 - 500}{20,000} = \frac{4,500}{20,000} = 22.5\%$

and the market value per share is $\frac{4,500}{2,250} \times \frac{1}{0.225} = £8.89$

2.8 Suppose that the level of gearing is increased by issuing £5,000 more of debt at 10% interest to repurchase 562 shares (at a market value of £8.89 per share) leaving 1,688 shares in issue.

The weighted average cost of capital will, according to the net operating income approach, remain unchanged at 20%. The market value of the company should still therefore be £25,000.

	£
Earnings	5,000
Weighted average cost of capital	0.2
	£
Market value of the company	25,000
Less market value of debt	10,000
Market value of equity	15,000

Annual dividends will now be £5,000 - £1,000 interest = £4,000.

The cost of equity has risen to $\frac{4,000}{15,000} = 26.667\%$ and the market value per share is still

$\frac{4,000}{1,688} \times \frac{1}{0.2667} = £8.89$

2.9 The conclusion of the net operating income approach is that the level of gearing is a matter of indifference to an investor, because it does not affect the market value of the company, nor of an individual share. This is because as the level of gearing rises, so does the cost of equity in such a way as to keep both the weighted average cost of capital and the market value of the shares constant.

Although, in our example, the dividend per share rises from £2 to £2.37 the increase in the cost of equity is such that the market value per share remains at £8.89.

3. MODIGLIANI-MILLER (MM) THEORY WITHOUT TAXATION

3.1 Modigliani and Miller (1958) developed a defence of the net operating income approach to the effect of gearing on the cost of capital. Their view is that investors would use *arbitrage* to keep the weighted average cost of capital constant when changes in a company's gearing occur.

Arbitrage

3.2 Arbitrage is trading in shares and debt to profit by different prices in different companies. An example will be used to explain how it works.

Example

3.3 Consider two companies, Ordinary plc and Levered plc, in the same risk class, which are identical in all respects except that Ordinary plc is financed entirely by equity whereas the capital structure of Levered plc includes £40,000 of debt at 8% interest.

We will assume that the annual earnings of both companies (before interest) are the same, £20,000, and we will begin by considering the traditional view of the cost of capital, and suppose that the cost of equity in the unlevered company is 13½%, and in the levered company, it is higher at 14%.

The market valuation of each company, according to the traditional view, would be as follows.

	Ordinary plc	*Levered plc*
	£	£
Annual earnings	20,000	20,000
Less interest	-	3,200
Available for equity (earnings = dividends)	20,000	16,800
Cost of equity	0.135	0.14
	£	£
Market value of equity	148,148	120,000
Market value of debt	-	40,000
Market value of company	148,148	160,000
Weighted average cost of capital (PBIT ÷ market value)	13.5%	12.5%
Gearing ratio	0%	33.3%

3.4 The two companies, identical in every respect except their gearing, are therefore assumed by the traditional view to have different market values. MM argue that this situation could not last for long because investors in Levered plc would soon see that they could get the same return for a smaller investment by investing in Ordinary plc. Exercising arbitrage, they would sell their shares in Levered plc and buy shares in Ordinary plc.

This sale would:

(a) drive up the price of Ordinary plc shares (thereby lowering the cost of its equity capital); and

(b) force down the price of Levered plc shares (thereby raising the cost of its equity capital);

until the total market value of each company is the same. Arbitrage would then cease.

3.5 Arbitrage would occur as follows. Suppose Mr Onepercent owns 1% of the equity in Levered plc. These would have a market value of (1% × £120,000)= £1,200. He would notice that Ordinary plc makes the same annual earnings as Levered plc (£20,000) but with a smaller investment (£148,148 compared to £160,000). He would therefore take the following steps.

(a) He would sell his shares in Levered plc for £1,200.

(b) He would borrow £400 at 8% interest. This amount is equivalent to 1% of the debt of Levered plc (£40,000 at 8%). In this way, Mr Onepercent would have substituted personal gearing for the corporate gearing of Levered plc. His assets would be as follows.

£	
1,200	from the sale of his shares
400	borrowed at 8%
1,600	which is 1% of the value of Levered plc.

His personal gearing ratio (400/1,200 = 33.3%) is the same as the gearing ratio of Levered plc, and so MM would argue that his financial risk is in no way changed by this process of arbitrage.

(c) He would then buy 1% of the equity of Ordinary plc for £148,148 × 1% = £1,481.48. To do this, he would use the borrowed £400 plus £1081.48 of his own money.

(d) His annual earnings from Ordinary plc would be as follows.

	£
1% of £20,000	200
Less the interest he must repay on his personal loan (8% of £400)	32
Net earnings	168

This is exactly the same as he would earn from keeping 1% of the equity of Levered plc (1% of £16,800) but he can earn this from a smaller net investment of £1,081.48 rather than £1,200.

(e) Alternatively, if he spends the entire £1,600 in purchasing shares of Ordinary plc, his annual earnings would be a dividend of

$\frac{1{,}600}{148{,}148} \times$ £20,000 = £216 less loan repayments of £32, leaving him with £184, which is £16 more than he currently earns from his Levered plc investment.

3.6 Rational investors will continue to substitute personal gearing for corporate gearing, and buy shares in Ordinary plc, until the price of these shares has risen, the price of Levered Limited shares has fallen, and the market values of the two companies are the same. At this point:

(a) the cost of equity in the company with the higher gearing (Levered plc) will be higher than the cost of equity in the other company;

(b) because both the market values and the annual earnings of the companies are the same, the weighted average costs of capital must be the same, despite the difference in gearing.

The Modigliani-Miller propositions, ignoring taxes

3.7 We can now set out the propositions of Modigliani and Miller, ignoring tax relief on the interest charged on debt capital.

3.8 The following symbols will be used.

V_u = the market value of an ungeared (all equity) company

V_g = the total market value of a geared company, which is similar in every respect to the ungeared company (same profits before interest and same business risk) except for its capital structure

D = the market value of the debt capital in a geared company. (The debt capital is assumed, for simplicity, to be irredeemable)

V_{eg} = the market value of the equity in a geared company, and so $V_g = V_{eg} + D$

K_u = the cost of equity in an ungeared company

K_g = the cost of equity in the geared company

K_d = the cost of debt capital.

Proposition 1 (ignoring taxation): the total market value of a company and the WACC

3.9 MM suggested that the total market value of any company is independent of its capital structure, and is given by discounting its expected return at the appropriate rate. The value of a geared company is therefore as follows.

$$V_g = V_u$$

$$V_g = \frac{\text{Profit before interest}}{\text{WACC}}$$

$$V_u = V_g = \frac{\text{Earnings in an ungeared company}}{K_u}$$

Proposition 2 (ignoring taxation): the cost of equity in a geared company

3.10 MM went on to argue that the expected return on a share in a geared company equals the expected cost of equity in a similar but ungeared company, plus a premium related to financial risk.

3.11 The premium for financial risk can be calculated as the debt/equity ratio multiplied by the difference between the cost of equity for an ungeared company and the *risk-free* cost of debt capital.

$$K_g = K_u + [(K_u - K_d) \times \frac{D}{V_{eg}}]$$

The part of the formula to the right of the plus sign is the value of the premium for financial risk.

Example

3.12 The cost of equity in an all equity company is 15%. The WACC is therefore also 15%.

Another company is identical in every respect to the first, except that it is geared, with a debt:equity ratio of 1:4. The cost of debt capital is 5% and this is a risk-free cost of debt. What is this second company's WACC?

Solution

3.13 $K_g = 15\% + ((15 - 5)\% \times \frac{1}{4}) = 17.5\%$.

	Weighting	*Cost*		*Product*
Equity	80%	17.5%		14%
Debt	20%	5.0%		1%
			WACC =	15%

The WACC in the geared company is the same as in the ungeared company.

Example

3.14 Loesch plc is an all equity company and its cost of equity is 12%.

Berelco plc is similar in all respects to Loesch plc, except that it is a geared company, financed by £1,000,000 of 3% debentures (current market price £50 per cent) and 1,000,000 ordinary shares (current market price £1.50 ex div).

What is Berelco's cost of equity and weighted average cost of capital?

Solution

3.15 $K_d = 3\% \times \frac{100}{50} = 6\%$

$K_g = 12\% + [(12\% - 6\%) \times \frac{500}{1,500}] = 14\%$

	Market value		*Cost*		
	£'000				
Equity	1,500	×	0.14	=	210
Debt	500	×	0.06	=	30
	2,000				240

$\text{WACC} = \frac{240}{2,000} = 0.12 = 12\%$

This is the same as Loesch plc's WACC. As gearing is introduced, the cost of equity rises, but in such a way that the WACC does not change.

Weaknesses in MM theory

3.16 MM theory has been criticised on four main grounds.

(a) The risks for the investor may differ between personal gearing and corporate gearing. In the example in Paragraph 3.5 Mr Onepercent stands, financially, to lose no more than £1,200, which is in his stake in a company (Levered plc) with limited liability. If he practises arbitrage, he would stand to lose his personal investment in Ordinary plc (£1,481.48 - £400 = £1,081.48) plus his debt repayment (£400), a total of £1,481.48. The financial risk is consequently greater.

(b) The cost of borrowing for an individual is likely to be higher than the cost of borrowing for a company. MM assume that the cost is the same for personal and corporate borrowers.

(c) Transaction costs will restrict the arbitrage process.

(d) MM theory initially ignored taxation.

3.17 Further weaknesses in the MM theory are as follows.

(a) In practice, it may be impossible to identify firms with identical business risk and operating characteristics.

(b) Some earnings may be retained and so the simplifying assumption of paying out all earnings as dividends would not apply.

(c) Investors are assumed to act rationally which may not be the case in practice.

These weaknesses are not critical, however, and would not on their own invalidate MM theory.

3.18. MM also acknowledge that when the level of gearing gets high, the cost of debt will rise. They argue, however, that this does not affect the weighted average cost of capital because the cost of equity falls at the same time as risk seeking investors are attracted to buying shares in the company.

3.19 When a company's gearing reaches very high levels, it may be perceived as being in danger of insolvency, and its market value will be very low (instead of being very high, as MM would predict). MM ignored the possibility of bankruptcy, and so their theory may not be valid at very high levels of gearing.

4. MODIGLIANI-MILLER THEORY ADJUSTED FOR TAXATION

4.1 Allowing for taxation reduces the cost of debt capital by multiplying it by a factor (1 - t) where t is the rate of corporation tax (assuming the debt to be irredeemable). So far, our analysis of MM theory has ignored the tax relief on debt interest, which makes debt capital cheaper to a company, and therefore reduces the weighted average cost of capital where a company has debt in its capital structure.

4.2 MM modified their theory to admit that tax relief on interest payments does lower the weighted average cost of capital. They claimed that the weighted average cost of capital will continue to fall, up to gearing of 100%.

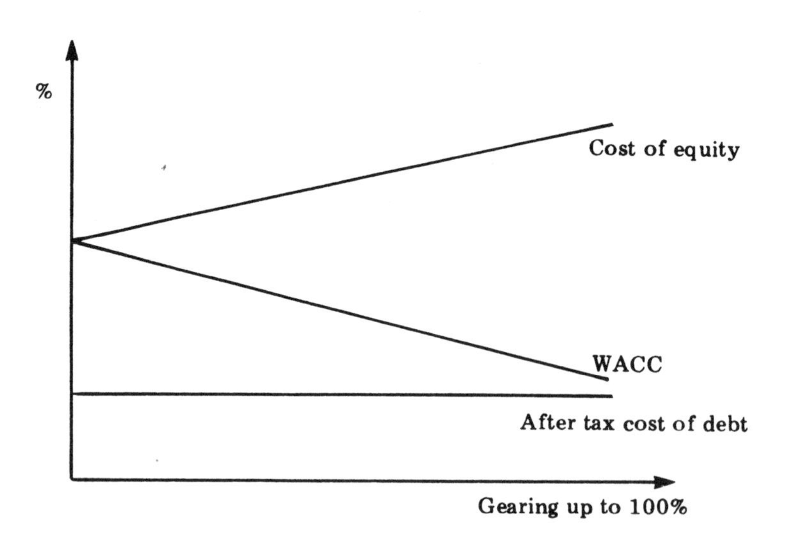

The adjustment to the MM cost of equity formula to allow for taxes

4.3 The formula for the cost of equity in a geared company becomes

$$K_g = K_u + (1 - t) \left[(K_u - K_d) \times \frac{D}{V_{eg}} \right]$$

where t is the corporation tax rate and K_d is the pre-tax (gross) cost of debt capital.

The financial risk premium is adjusted by a factor of (1-t).

4.4 Thus assuming a corporation tax rate of 33%, the geared company's cost of equity in the example in Paragraphs 3.12 and 3.13 would be

$$15\% + \left[\frac{(1 - 0.33)\,1}{4} \times (15\% - 5\%) \right] = 16.675\%$$

and its WACC would be

$$(0.8 \times 16.675\%) + (0.2 \times 5\% \times 0.67) = 13.34\% + 0.67\% = 14.01\%$$

4.5 This is below the ungeared company's WACC which is 15%. So higher gearing reduces the WACC.

4.6 Similarly, in the example in Paragraph 3.14, and assuming a corporation tax rate of 33%, Berelco plc's cost of equity would be

$$12\% + \left[(1 - 0.33) \times (12 - 6)\% \times \frac{500}{1,500} \right]$$

$$= 13.34\%$$

and its WACC would be

$$(\tfrac{3}{4} \times 13.34\%) + (\tfrac{1}{4} \times 6\% \times 67\%) = 11.01\%.$$

This is below Loesch plc's WACC of 12%.

4.7 From the formula in Paragraph 4.3 we can derive

$$WACC_g = K_u \left[\frac{V_{eg} + (1-t) D}{V_g}\right] = K_u \left[1 - \frac{tD}{D + V_{eg}}\right]$$

where $WACC_g$ is the weighted average cost of capital of a geared company, and K_u is the cost of equity and the WACC of a similar ungeared company.

4.8 Using the figures previously given in Paragraphs 3.14, 3.15 and 4.6, the WACC of Berelco plc would be

$$\begin{aligned} WACC &= 12\% \left[\frac{1{,}500 + (0.67)(500)}{1{,}500 + 500}\right] \\ &= 12\%\ (0.9175) \\ &= 11.01\% \end{aligned}$$

Is there an optimum level of gearing?

4.9 We have now seen that MM modified their theory to say that when taxation is taken into account, the WACC will continue to fall as the level of gearing increases. The arbitrage process still operates, although the actions of investors will be influenced by their personal rates of taxation.

4.10 MM argued that since WACC falls as gearing rises, and the value of a company should rise as its WACC falls, the value of a geared company will always be greater than its ungeared counterpart, but only by the amount of the debt-associated tax saving of the geared company.

$$V_g = V_u + Dt$$

Example

4.11 Notnil plc and Newbegin plc are companies in the same industry. They have the same business risk and operating characteristics, but Notnil is a geared company whereas Newbegin is all equity financed. Notnil plc earns three times as much profit before interest as Newbegin plc. Both companies pursue a policy of paying out all their earnings each year as dividends.

The market value of each company is currently as follows.

		Notnil plc		*Newbegin plc*
		£m		£m
Equity	(10m shares)	36	(20m shares)	15
Debt	(£12m of 12% loan stock)	14		
		50		15

The annual profit before interest of Notnil is £3,000,000 and that of Newbegin is £1,000,000. The rate of corporation tax is 33%.

It is thought that the current market value per ordinary share in Newbegin plc is at the equilibrium level, and that the market value of Notnil's debt capital is also at its equilibrium level. There is some doubt, however, about whether the value of Notnil's shares is at its equilibrium level.

Apply the MM formula to establish the equilibrium price of Notnil's shares.

Solution

4.12 $V_g = V_u + Dt$

V_u = the market value of an ungeared company. Since Notnil earnings (before interest) are three times the size of Newbegin's, V_u is three times the value of Newbegin's equity: 3 × £15,000,000 = £45,000,000.

Dt = £14,000,000 × 33% = £4,620,000

V_g = £45,000,000 + £4,620,000 = £49,620,000.

Since the market value of debt in Notnil plc is £14,000,000, it follows that the market value of Notnil's equity should be £49,620,000 - £14,000,000 = £35,620,000.

$$\text{Value per share} = \frac{£35,620,000}{10,000,000} = £3.562 \text{ per share}$$

Since the current share price is £3.60 per share, MM would argue that the shares in Notnil are currently over-valued by the market, but only by £380,000 in total or 3.8p per share.

4.13 Now let us relate the MM company valuation formula to the process of arbitrage.

Example

4.14 Lenox plc and Groves plc are two companies operating in the same industry. They have the same business risk, and are identical in most other respects. The annual earnings before interest and tax are £40,000 for each company. The only differences between the companies are in their financial structures and their market values. Details of these are given below.

Lenox plc

	£
Ordinary shares of £1	30,000
Share premium account	10,000
Profit and loss account	110,000
Shareholders' funds	150,000
12% loan stock (newly issued)	100,000
	250,000

Lenox's ordinary shares have a market value of 600 pence, and the 12% loan stock is trading at £100.

Groves plc

	£
Ordinary shares of £1	50,000
Share premium account	6,000
Profit and loss account	100,000
Shareholders' funds	156,000

Groves' shares have a market value of 400 pence.

Corporation tax is at 33%.

Suppose that you are the owner of 1% of the equity of Lenox plc. If you agreed with the propositions of Modigliani and Miller, would you retain your shares in Lenox or could you improve your financial position? Ignore personal taxes.

Solution

4.15 A difficulty with this problem is the need to allow for tax relief on corporate debt, when working out how an investor should gear himself up so as to achieve personal gearing which is the same as the geared company. Check the solution carefully on this point.

According to MM theory, where there are corporate taxes, the value of a geared company will always be greater than the value of its ungeared counterpart, but only by the amount of the debt-associated tax saving of the geared company. This is expressed by the formula

$$V_g = V_u + Dt$$

If actual market values do not conform to this formula, it would follow that one company is incorrectly valued by the market relative to the other.

4.16 Let us assume that the shares of Groves, the ungeared company, are correctly valued by the market at 400 pence. We would then predict that the total market value of Lenox, the geared company, should be (V_u + Dt).

	£
Market value of Groves shares (50,000 × £4)	200,000
Market value of Lenox debt multiplied by tax rate (100,000 × 33%)	33,000
Correct market value of Lenox plc	233,000

Actual market value of Lenox

	£
Market value of Lenox shares (30,000 × £6)	180,000
Market value of Lenox debt capital	100,000
	280,000

4.17 We can conclude that Lenox plc is over-valued by the market and so an investor in Lenox shares can improve his or her financial position by:

(a) selling all his or her shares in Lenox;
(b) gearing himself or herself, by personal borrowing, so as to achieve the same personal gearing as Lenox;
(c) buying shares in Groves.

This action will increase the investor's income without any change in the investor's business or financial risk. This process of arbitrage should continue until the equilibrium of $V_g = V_u + Dt$ is restored.

4.18 1% of the equity of Lenox has a current market value of 1% × £180,000 = £1,800.

	£
Sell 1% holding of shares in Lenox to receive	1,800
Borrow, through personal borrowing*, an amount equal to 1% of the market value of Lenox's debt capital, adjusted to allow for the tax relief that Lenox gets on the debt interest (1% × £100,000 × 0.67)	670
	2,470

(* The rate of interest on personal borrowing is assumed to be the same as the market rate of interest on corporate debt, which is 12%).

The investor should now invest £2,470 in the equity of Groves plc, and can buy £2,470 ÷ £200,000 = 1.235% of Groves' shares.

4.19 The investor's income will now be higher than before, but because personal gearing has been substituted for corporate gearing, there is no change in the investor's financial risk. The increase in income can be illustrated as follows.

	Holding 1% shares in Lenox plc	*Holding 1.235% of shares in Groves plc with personal gearing*
	£	£
Earnings before interest and tax	40,000	40,000
Less interest charge for the company	12,000	0
	28,000	40,000
Less tax (33%)	9,240	13,200
Earnings, assumed equal to dividends	18,760	26,800
	£	£
Investor's share		
1% of Lenox	187.60	
1.235% of Groves		330.98
Less interest on personal debt (12% × £670)	0	80.40
Investor's net income	187.60	250.58

The investor can increase his or her annual income by £(250.58 - 187.60) = £62.98 through this arbitrage process.

Empirical testing and conclusion

4.20 It might be imagined that empirical testing should have been carried out by now either to prove or to disprove MM theory. Given, however, that MM accept that the weighted average cost of capital declines after allowing for tax, and that traditional theorists argue in favour of a flattish bottom to the weighted average cost of capital curve, it is very difficult to prove that one theory is preferable to the other.

5. THE ADJUSTED PRESENT VALUE (APV) METHOD OF PROJECT EVALUATION

5.1 We have seen that a company's gearing level has implications for both the value of its equity shares and its WACC. The viability of an investment project will depend partly on how the investment is financed, and how the method of finance affects gearing.

5.2 The net present value method of investment appraisal is to discount the cash flows of a project at a cost of capital. This cost of capital might be the WACC, but it could also be another cost of capital, perhaps one which allows for the risk characteristics of the individual project.

5.3 An alternative method of carrying out project appraisal is to use the adjusted present value or APV method.

The APV method involves two stages.

(a) Evaluate the project first of all as if it were all equity financed, and so as if the company were an all equity company.

(b) Make adjustments to allow for the effects of the method of financing that has been used.

Example

5.4 A company is considering a project that would cost £100,000 to be financed 50% by equity (cost 21.6%) and 50% by debt (pre-tax cost 12%). The financing method would maintain the company's WACC unchanged.

The cash flows from the project would be £36,000 a year in perpetuity, before interest charges.

Corporation tax is at 33%.

Appraise the project using firstly the NPV method and secondly the APV method.

Solution

5.5 *The NPV method*
We can use the NPV method because the company's WACC will be unchanged.

	Cost	*Weighting*	*Product*
	%		%
Equity	21.60	0.5	10.80
Debt (67% of 12%)	8.04	0.5	4.02
		WACC	14.82

Annual cash flows in perpetuity from the project are as follows.

	£
Before tax	36,000
Less tax (33%)	11,880
After tax	24,120

NPV of project = - £100,000 + (£24,120 ÷ 0.1482)
= - £100,000 + £162,753
= + £62,753

5.6 Since £100,000 of new investment is being created, the value of the company will increase by £100,000 + £62,753 = £162,753, of which 50% must be debt capital.

The company must raise 50% × £162,753 = £81,376 of 12% debt capital, and (the balance) £18,624 of equity. The NPV of the project will raise the value of this equity from £18,624 to £81,377 thus leaving the gearing ratio at 50:50.

5.7 *The APV method*
The APV method is as follows.

(a) First, we need to know the cost of equity in an ungeared company. The MM formula we can use to establish this is

$$K_g = K_u + (1 - t)\,[\,(K_u - K_d)\,\frac{D}{V_{eg}}\,]$$

$$21.6\% = K_u + (0.67)\,[\,(K_u - 12\%)\,\frac{50}{50}\,]$$

$$21.6\% = K_u + 0.67\,K_u - 8.04\%$$

$$1.67K_u = 29.64\%$$

$$K_u = 17.748503\%$$

(b) Next, we calculate the NPV of the project as if it were all equity financed. The cost of equity would be 17.748503%

$$NPV = \frac{£24{,}120}{0.17748503} - £100{,}000$$

$$= +\,£35{,}899$$

(c) Next, we can use the MM formula for the relationship between the value of geared and ungeared companies, to establish the effect of gearing on the value of the project. £81,376 will be financed by debt.

$$V_g = V_u + Dt$$

$$= +\,£35{,}899 + (£81{,}376 \times 0.33)$$

$$= £62{,}753$$

5.8 The value Dt represents the present value of the tax shield on debt interest, that is the present value of the savings arising from tax relief on debt interest.

Annual interest charge = 12% of £81,376 = £9,765.12.

Tax saving (33% × £9,765.12)	=	£3,222.49
Cost of debt (pre-tax)		12%
PV of tax savings in perpetuity		$\frac{£3{,}222.49}{0.12}$
	=	£26,854

Dt = £81,376 × 0.33 = £26,854 is a quicker way of deriving the same value.

5.9 The APV and NPV approaches produce the same conclusion. However, the APV method can also be adapted to allow for financing which changes the gearing structure and the WACC. In this respect, it is superior to the NPV method.

5.10 Suppose, for example, that in the previous example, the entire project were to be financed by debt. The APV of the project would be calculated as follows.

(a) The NPV of project if all equity financed is

$$\frac{£24,120}{0.17748503} - £100,000$$

$$= +£35,899 \text{ (as before)}$$

(b) The adjustment to allow for the method of financing is the present value of the tax relief on debt interest in perpetuity.

$$Dt = £100,000 \times 0.33$$
$$= £33,000$$

(c) $$APV = £35,899 + £33,000$$
$$= +£68,899$$

The project would increase the value of equity by £68,899.

Example

5.11. A company is considering a project with a four year life, costing £1,600,000. The project will be financed half by a 14% loan and half by a rights issue of shares.

Corporation tax is at 33%.

The costs of raising the loan will be £10,000 and the rights issue costs will be £40,000.

The project will earn cash flows after tax as follows.

Year	£
1	400,000
2	800,000
3	600,000
4	600,000

Tax is payable in the same year that the profits arise.

If the project were all equity financed, an appropriate cost of capital would be 18%.

What is the APV of the project?

Solution

5.12 (a) If the project were all equity financed, its NPV would be as follows.

Year	*Cash flow*	*Discount factor*	*PV*
	£	18%	£
0	(1,600,000)	1.000	(1,600,000)
1	400,000	0.847	338,800
2	800,000	0.718	574,400
3	600,000	0.609	365,400
4	600,000	0.516	309,600
			(11,800)

The NPV is negative.

(b) Next, make adjustments for the method of financing used.

(i) The annual interest payment on a loan of £800,000 at 14% is £112,000. The consequent annual reduction in tax is £112,000 × 33% = £36,960.

(ii) The present value of the tax shield, discounted at the pre-tax cost of debt (14%) is as follows.

Years	*Cash flow*	*Discount factor*	*PV*
	£	14%	£
1 - 4	36,960	2.914	107,701

Summary

	£	£
NPV, if all equity financed		(11,800)
PV of tax shield (years 1-4)		107,701
Issue costs		
Loan	(10,000)	
Rights issue	(40,000)	
		(50,000)
Adjusted present value		+ 45,901

Because of the method of financing chosen, the project is a worthwhile undertaking, with an APV of + £45,901.

The advantages and disadvantages of the APV method

5.13 The main advantage of the APV method is that it can be used to evaluate all the effects of the method of financing a project.

5.14 The NPV technique can allow for the financing side-effects implicitly, by adjusting the discount rate used. In contrast, the APV technique allows for the financing side-effects explicitly.

5.15 The main difficulties with the APV technique are:

(a) establishing a suitable cost of equity, for the initial DCF computation as if the project were all-equity financed;

(b) identifying all the costs associated with the method of financing.

6. MODIGLIANI-MILLER THEORY ON THE IRRELEVANCE OF DIVIDEND POLICY

6.1 In the final section of this chapter, we shall consider whether dividend policy is a means of influencing shareholders' wealth.

The irrelevance argument: Modigliani and Miller

6.2 There are two opposing schools of thought: one side accepts the argument that dividend policy is irrelevant to the market value of shares, and the other side claims that an active dividend policy should be pursued as a means of maximising shareholders' wealth.

6.3 The most well-known support for the irrelevance argument comes from Modigliani and Miller. They argued that in a tax-free world, shareholders are indifferent between dividends and capital gains, and the value of a company is determined solely by the earning power of its assets and investments.

6.4 MM argue that if a company with investment opportunities decides to pay a dividend, so that retained earnings are insufficient to finance all its investments, the shortfall in funds will be made up by obtaining additional funds from outside sources. The consequent loss of value in the existing shares, as a result of obtaining outside finance instead of using retained earnings, is exactly equal to the amount of the dividend paid. A company should therefore be indifferent between paying a dividend (and obtaining new outside funds) and retaining earnings.

6.5 In answer to criticisms that certain shareholders will show a preference for either high dividends or capital gains, MM argued that if a company pursues a consistent dividend policy, it will attract a 'clientele' consisting of those preferring its particular pay-out ratio. One clientele is as good as another in terms of the valuation it implies for the company.

The case in favour of the relevance of dividend policy (and against MM's views)

6.6 There are strong arguments against MM's view that dividend policy is irrelevant as a means of affecting shareholder's wealth. We have already seen that:

(a) differing rates of taxation or tax allowances for dividends and capital gains can create a preference for a high dividend or high earnings retention;

(b) dividend retention should be preferred by companies in a period of capital rationing;

(c) due to imperfect markets and the possible difficulties of selling shares easily at a fair price, shareholders might need high dividends in order to have funds to invest in opportunities outside the company.

6.7 Further arguments against the Modigliani-Miller position include the following.

(a) Markets are not perfect. Because of transaction costs on the sale of shares, investors who want some cash from their investments should prefer to receive dividends rather than to sell some of their shares to get the cash they want.

(b) Information available to shareholders is imperfect, and they are not aware of the future investment plans and expected profits of their company. Even if management were to provide them with profits forecasts, these forecasts would not necessarily be accurate or believable. As a consequence of imperfect information:

(i) companies are normally expected at least to maintain the level of dividends from one year to the next. Failure to maintain the dividend level would undermine the investors' confidence in the future;

(ii) in practice, undertaking a new investment project with a positive NPV will not immediately increase the market value of shares by the amount of the NPV because markets do not show strong form efficiency. It is only gradually, as the profits from the investment begin to affect profits and dividends, that the market value of the shares will rise.

(c) Perhaps the strongest argument against the MM view is that shareholders will tend to prefer a current dividend to future capital gains (or deferred dividends) because the future is less certain.

7. CONCLUSION

7.1 The theories discussed in this chapter may seem to be far removed from the realities of day-to-day decision making. However, the directors of a company have a duty to act in the company's interests, and if there is an optimum level of gearing they should do their best to estimate and achieve it.

TEST YOUR KNOWLEDGE

1. AB plc has a WACC of 16%. It is financed partly by equity (cost 18%) and partly by debt capital (cost 10%). The company is considering a new project which would cost £5,000,000 and would yield annual profits of £850,000 before interest charges. It would be financed by a loan at 10%. As a consequence of the higher gearing, the cost of equity would rise to 20%. The company pays out all profits as dividends, which are currently £2,250,000 a year.

   (a) What would be the effect on the value of equity of undertaking the project?
   (b) To what extent can you analyse the increase or decrease in equity value into two causes, the NPV of the project at the current WACC and the effect of the method of financing?

   Ignore taxation. The traditional view of WACC and gearing is assumed in this question. (See below)

2. The cost of equity in an ungeared company is 18%. The cost of risk free debt capital is 8%.

   (a) What is the cost of equity in a similar geared company, according to MM, which is 75% equity financed and 25% debt financed, assuming corporation tax at a rate of 33%?

   (b) What is the WACC of the geared company, allowing for taxation? (See below)

3. CD plc and YZ plc are identical in every respect except for their gearing. The market value of each company is as follows.

CD plc		*YZ plc*	
	£m		£m
Equity (5m shares)	?	(8m shares)	24
Debt (£20m of 5% loan stock)	10		
	?		24

   According to MM theory, what is the value of CD plc shares, given a corporation tax rate of 33%. (See below)

4. A project costing £100,000 is to be financed by £60,000 of irredeemable 12% debentures and £40,000 of new equity. The project will yield an annual cash flow of £21,000 in perpetuity. If it were all equity financed, an appropriate cost of capital would be 15%. The corporation tax rate is 33%. What is the project's APV? (See below)

Now try question 11 at the end of the text

Solutions

1. (a)

	£
Current profits and dividends	2,250,000
Increase in profits and dividends (£850,000 less extra interest 10% × £5,000,000)	350,000
New dividends, if project is undertaken	2,600,000
New cost of equity	÷ 20%
	£
New MV of equity	13,000,000
Current MV of equity (£2,250,000 ÷ 0.18)	12,500,000
Increase in shareholder wealth from project	500,000

(b) (i) NPV of project if financed at current WACC

$$= \frac{£850,000}{0.16} - £5,000,000 = +£312,500$$

(ii) The effect of financing on share values must be to increase the MV of equity by the remaining £187,500, which indicates that the effect of financing the project in the manner proposed will be to increase the company's gearing, but to reduce its WACC.

2. (a) $K_g = 18\% + (1 - 0.33)\ [(18 - 8)\% \times \frac{25}{75}] = 20.233\%$

(b) $WACC_g = 18\%\ [1 - \frac{0.33\ (25)}{(25 + 75)}]$

$= 18\% \times 0.9175 = 16.515\%$

3. Value of CD plc in total = $V_g = V_u + Dt$ where V_u is the value of YZ plc.

$V_g = £24,000,000 + £10,000,000 \times 33\% = £27,300,000$.

CD plc's equity is valued at £27,300,000 - debt of £10,000,000 = £17,300,000, or £3.46 per share.

4.

	£
NPV if all equity financed: £21,000/0.15 - £100,000	40,000
PV of the tax shield: £60,000 × 12% × 33%/0.12	19,800
APV	59,800

Chapter 9

PORTFOLIO THEORY

This chapter covers the following topics.

1. Portfolios and portfolio theory
2. Investors' preferences

1. PORTFOLIOS AND PORTFOLIO THEORY

1.1 A portfolio is the collection of different investments that make up an investor's total holding.

A portfolio might be:

(a) the investments in stocks and shares of an investor;
(b) the investments in capital projects of a company.

1.2 Portfolio theory is concerned with establishing guidelines for building up a portfolio of stocks and shares, or a portfolio of projects. The same theory applies to both stock market investors and to companies with capital projects to invest in.

Factors in the choice of investments

1.3 There are five major factors to be considered when an investor chooses investments, no matter whether the investor is an institutional investor, a company making an investment or a private individual investor.

(a) *Security.* Investments should at least maintain their capital value.

(b) *Liquidity.* Where the investments are made with short-term funds, they should be convertible back into cash at short notice.

(c) *Return.* The funds are invested to made money. The highest return compatible with safety should be sought.

(d) *Spreading risks.* The investor who puts all his funds into one type of security risks everything on the fortunes of that security. If it performs badly, his entire investment will make a loss. A better (and more secure) policy is to spread investments over several types of security, so that losses on some may be offset by gains on others.

(e) *Growth prospects.* The most profitable investments are likely to be in businesses with good growth prospects.

Portfolios: expected return and risk

1.4 When an investor has a portfolio of securities, he will *expect* the portfolio to provide a certain return on his investment.

1.5 The *expected return* from the portfolio will be a weighted average of the expected returns of the investments in the portfolio, weighted by the proportion of total funds invested in each. Thus if 70% of the portfolio relates to a security which is expected to yield 10% and 30% to a security expected to yield 12%, the portfolio's expected return is (70% × 10%) + (30% × 12%) = 10.6%.

1.6 The *risk* in an investment, or in a portfolio of investments, is that the actual return will not be the same as the expected return. The actual return may be higher, but it may be lower. A prudent investor will want to avoid too much risk, and will hope that the actual returns from his portfolio are much the same as what he expected them to be.

1.7 The risk of a security, and the risk of a portfolio, can be measured as the standard deviation of expected returns, given estimated probabilities of actual returns.

Example

1.8 Suppose that the return from an investment has the following probability distribution.

Return x %	*Probability* p	*Expected value* px
8	0.2	1.6
10	0.2	2.0
12	0.5	6.0
14	0.1	1.4
		11.0

The expected return is 11%, and the standard deviation of the expected return is as follows. The symbol $\bar{x}$ refers to the expected value of the return, 11%.

Return x %	$x - \bar{x}$ %	p		$p(x - \bar{x})^2$
8	-3	0.2		1.8
10	-1	0.2		0.2
12	1	0.5		0.5
14	3	0.1		0.9
			Variance	3.4

Standard deviation $= \sqrt{3.4} = 1.84\%$

Thus, the expected return is 11% with a standard deviation of 1.84%.

1.9 The risk of an investment might be high or low, depending on the nature of the investment.

(a) Low risk investments usually give low returns.
(b) High risk investments might give high returns, but with more risk of disappointing results.

So how does holding a *portfolio* of investments affect expected returns and investment risk?

Diversification as a means of reducing risk

1.10 Portfolio theory states that individual investments cannot be viewed simply in terms of their risk and return. The relationship between the return from one investment and the return from other investments is just as important.

1.11 The relationship between investments can be one of three main types.

(a) *Positive correlation.* When there is positive correlation between investments, if one investment does well (or badly) it is likely that the other will perform likewise. Thus if you buy shares in one company making umbrellas and in another which sells raincoats you would expect both companies to do badly in dry weather.

(b) *Negative correlation.* If one investment does well the other will do badly, and vice versa. Thus if you hold shares in one company making umbrellas and in another which sells ice cream, the weather will affect the companies differently.

(c) *No correlation.* The performance of one investment will be independent of how the other performs. If you hold shares in a mining company and in a leisure company, it is likely that there would be no relationship between the profits and returns from each.

1.12 This relationship between the returns from different investments is measured by the correlation coefficient. A figure close to +1 indicates high positive correlation, and a figure close to -1 indicates high negative correlation. A figure of 0 indicates no correlation.

1.13 If investments show high negative correlation, then by combining them in a portfolio overall risk would be reduced. Risk will also be reduced by combining in a portfolio investments which have no significant correlation.

Example

1.14 Security A and Security B have the following expected returns.

Probability	*Security A Return*	*Security B Return*
0.1	15%	10%
0.8	25%	30%
0.1	35%	50%

1.15 The expected return from each security is as follows.

Probability	*Security A* Return %	EV %	*Security B* Return %	EV %
0.1	15	1.5	10	1
0.8	25	20.0	30	24
0.1	35	3.5	50	5
	Expected return =	25.0	Expected return =	30

1.16 The variance of the expected return for each security is $\Sigma p(x - \bar{x})^2$

Probability	*Security A*			*Security B*		
	Return			*Return*		
p	x	$x - \bar{x}$	$p(x - \bar{x})^2$	y	$y - \bar{y}$	$p(y - \bar{y})^2$
0.1	15	(10)	10	10	(20)	40
0.8	25	0	0	30	0	0
0.1	35	10	10	50	20	40
	$\bar{x}$ = 25	Variance =	20	$\bar{y}$ = 30	Variance =	80

1.17 The standard deviation is the square root of the variance.

Security A: $\sqrt{20}$ = 4.472%

Security B: $\sqrt{80}$ = 8.944%

Security B therefore offers a higher return than security A, but at a greater risk.

1.18 Let us now assume that an investor acquires a portfolio consisting of 50% A and 50% B. The *expected return* from the portfolio will be 0.5 × 25% + 0.5 × 30% = 27.5%. This is less than the expected return from security B alone, but more than that from security A. The combined portfolio should be less risky than security B alone (although in this example of just a two-security portfolio, it will be more risky than security A alone except when returns are negatively correlated).

1.19 We can work out the standard deviation of the expected return:

(a) if there is perfect positive correlation between the returns from each security, so that if A gives a return of 15%, then B will give a return of 10% and so on;

(b) if there is perfect negative correlation between the returns from each security, so that if A gives a return of 15%, B will yield 50%, if A gives a return of 35%, B will yield 10%, and if A gives a return of 25%, B will yield 30%;

(c) if there is no correlation between returns, and so the probability distribution of returns is as follows.

A	*B*		*p*
%	%		
15	10	(0.1 × 0.1)	0.01
15	30	(0.1 × 0.8)	0.08
15	50	(0.1 × 0.1)	0.01
25	10	(0.8 × 0.1)	0.08
25	30	(0.8 × 0.8)	0.64
25	50	(0.8 × 0.1)	0.08
35	10	(0.1 × 0.1)	0.01
35	30	(0.1 × 0.8)	0.08
35	50	(0.1 × 0.1)	0.01
			1.00

Perfect positive correlation

1.20 The standard deviation of the portfolio may be calculated as follows, given an expected return of 27.5%.

Probability	*Return from 50% A*	*Return from 50% B*	*Combined portfolio return*		
p			x	$(x - \bar{x})$	$p(x - \bar{x})^2$
	%	%	%		
0.1	7.5	5	12.5	(15)	22.5
0.8	12.5	15	27.5	0	0
0.1	17.5	25	42.5	15	22.5
				Variance =	45.0

The standard deviation is $\sqrt{45} = 6.71\%$

Perfect negative correlation

1.21 The standard deviation of the portfolio, given an expected return of 27.5%, is as follows.

Probability	*Return from 50% A*	*Return from 50% B*	*Combined portfolio return*		
p			x	$(x - \bar{x})$	$p(x - \bar{x})^2$
	%	%	%		
0.1	7.5	25	32.5	5	2.5
0.8	12.5	15	27.5	0	0
0.1	17.5	5	22.5	(5)	2.5
				Variance =	5.0

The standard deviation is $\sqrt{5} = 2.24\%$

1.22 *No correlation*

The standard deviation of the portfolio, given an expected return of 27.5%, is as follows.

Probability	*Return from 50% A*	*Return from 50% B*	*Combined portfolio return*		
p			x	$(x - \bar{x})$	$p(x - \bar{x})^2$
	%	%	%		
0.01	7.5	5	12.5	(15)	2.25
0.08	7.5	15	22.5	(5)	2.00
0.01	7.5	25	32.5	5	0.25
0.08	12.5	5	17.5	(10)	8.00
0.64	12.5	15	27.5	0	0.00
0.08	12.5	25	37.5	10	8.00
0.01	17.5	5	22.5	(5)	0.25
0.08	17.5	15	32.5	5	2.00
0.01	17.5	25	42.5	15	2.25
				Variance =	25.00

The standard deviation is $\sqrt{25} = 5\%$

Conclusion

1.23 You should notice that for the same expected return of 27.5%, the standard deviation (the risk)

(a) is highest when there is perfect positive correlation between the returns of the individual securities in the portfolio;

(b) is lower when there is no correlation;

(c) is lowest when there is perfect negative correlation. The risk is then less than for either individual security taken on its own.

Another way of calculating the standard deviation of a portfolio

1.24 A quick way of calculating the standard deviation of the returns from a portfolio of *two* investments is to use the formula

$$\sigma_p = \sqrt{(W_a)^2\sigma_a^2 + (W_b)^2\sigma_b^2 + 2(W_a)(W_b)(r)(\sigma_a)(\sigma_b)}$$

where:

σ_p is the standard deviation of a portfolio of two investments, A and B
σ_a is the standard deviation of the returns from investment A
σ_b is the standard deviation of the returns from investment B
σ_a^2, σ_b^2 are the variances of returns from investment A and B (the squares of the standard deviations)
W_a is the weighting or proportion of investment A in the portfolio
W_b is the weighting or proportion of investment B in the portfolio
r is the correlation coefficient of returns from investment A and B

$$= \frac{\text{Covariance of investments A and B}}{\sigma_a \times \sigma_b}$$

Example

1.25 We will use the previous example of the portfolio of 50% security A and 50% security B.

(a) When there is perfect positive correlation between the returns from A and B, r = 1.

$$\begin{aligned}\sigma_p^2 &= (0.5)^2\,20 + (0.5)^2\,80 + 2\,(0.5)\,(0.5)\,(1)\,(\sqrt{20})(\sqrt{80})\\ &= 5 + 20 + 0.5\,(4.472)\,(8.944)\\ &= 45\end{aligned}$$

The standard deviation of the portfolio is $\sqrt{45} = 6.71\%$

(b) When there is perfect negative correlation between returns from A and B, r = -1.

$$\begin{aligned}\sigma_p^2 &= (0.5)^2 20 + (0.5)^2 80 + 2\,(0.5)\,(0.5)\,(-1)\,(\sqrt{20})(\sqrt{80})\\ &= 5 + 20 - 0.5(4.472)(8.944)\\ &= 5\end{aligned}$$

The standard deviation of the portfolio is $\sqrt{5} = 2.24\%$

(c) When there is no correlation between returns from A and B, r = 0.

$$\begin{aligned}\sigma_p^2 &= (0.5)^2 20 + (0.5)^2 80 + 2\,(0.5)\,(0.5)\,(0)\,(\sqrt{20})(\sqrt{80})\\ &= 5 + 20 + 0\\ &= 25\end{aligned}$$

The standard deviation of the portfolio is $\sqrt{25} = 5\%$

1.26 These are exactly the same figures for standard deviations that were calculated earlier.

2. INVESTORS' PREFERENCES

2.1 Investors must choose a portfolio which gives them a satisfactory balance between:

(a) the expected returns from the portfolio;

(b) the risk that actual returns from the portfolio will be higher or lower than expected. Some portfolios will be more risky than others.

2.2 Traditional investment theory suggests that rational investors wish to maximise return and minimise risk. Thus if two portfolios have the same element of risk, the investor will choose the one yielding the higher return. Similarly, if two portfolios offer the same return the investor will select the portfolio with the lesser risk.

This can be illustrated by the following diagram.

Figure 1: an investor's indifference curve

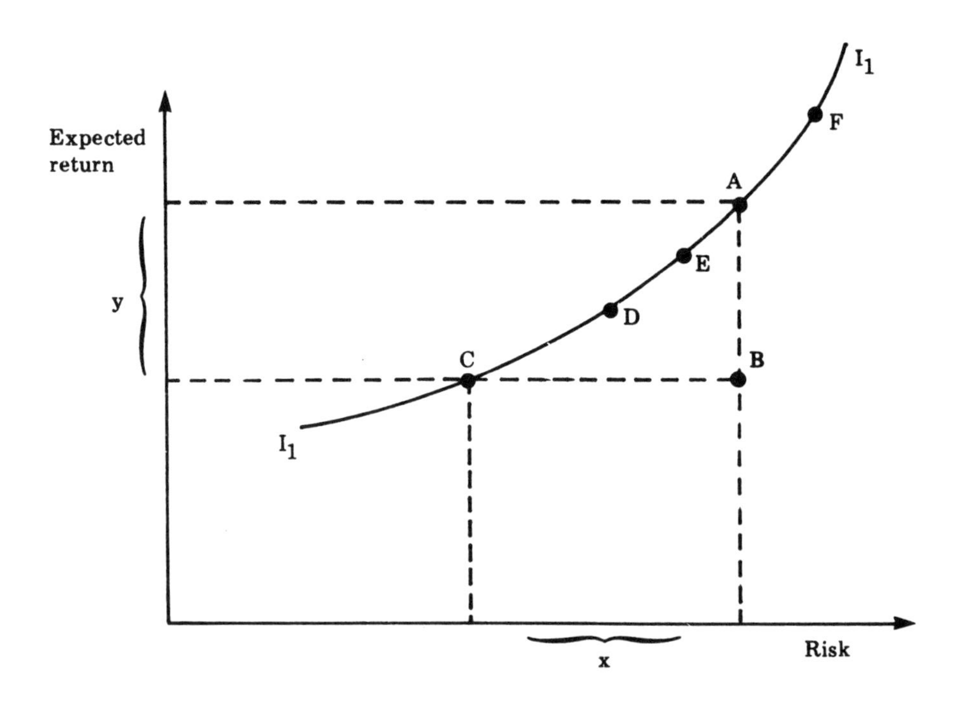

2.3 Portfolio A will be preferred to portfolio B because it offers a higher expected return for the same level of risk. Similarly, portfolio C will be preferred to portfolio B because it offers the same expected return for lower risk. (A and C are said to *dominate* portfolio B). But whether an investor chooses portfolio A or portfolio C will depend on the individual's attitude to risk, whether he wishes to accept a greater risk for a greater expected return.

2.4 The curve I_1 is an investor's *indifference curve.*

The investor will have no preference between any portfolios which give a mix of risk and expected return which lies on the curve. Thus, to the investor the portfolios A, C, D, E and F are all just as good as each other, and all of them are better than portfolio B.

2.5 An investor would prefer combinations of return and risk on indifference curve A to those on curve B (figure 2) because curve A offers higher returns for the same degree of risk (and less risk for the same expected returns). For example, for the same amount of risk x, the expected return on curve A is y_1, whereas on curve B it is only y_2.

Figure 2: indifference curves compared

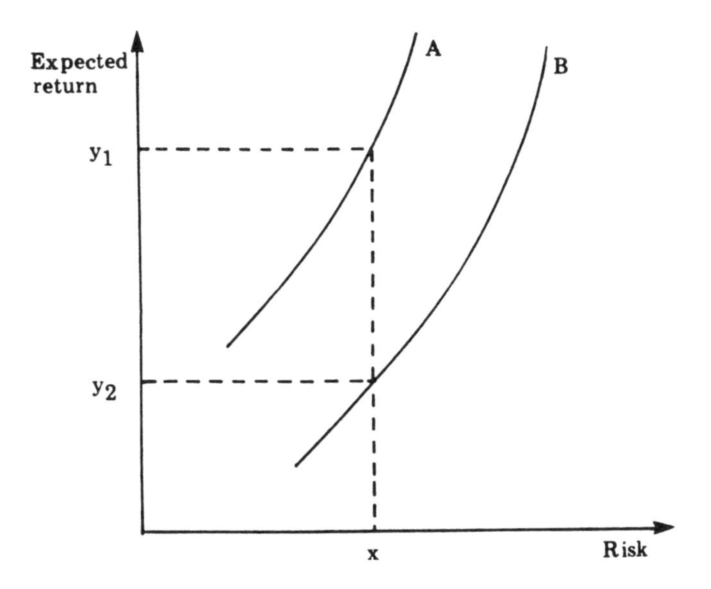

Efficient portfolios

2.6 If we drew a graph (figure 3) to show the expected return and the risk of the many possible portfolios of investments, we could (according to portfolio theory) plot an egg-shaped cluster of dots on a scattergraph as follows.

Figure 3: the efficient frontier of available investment portfolios

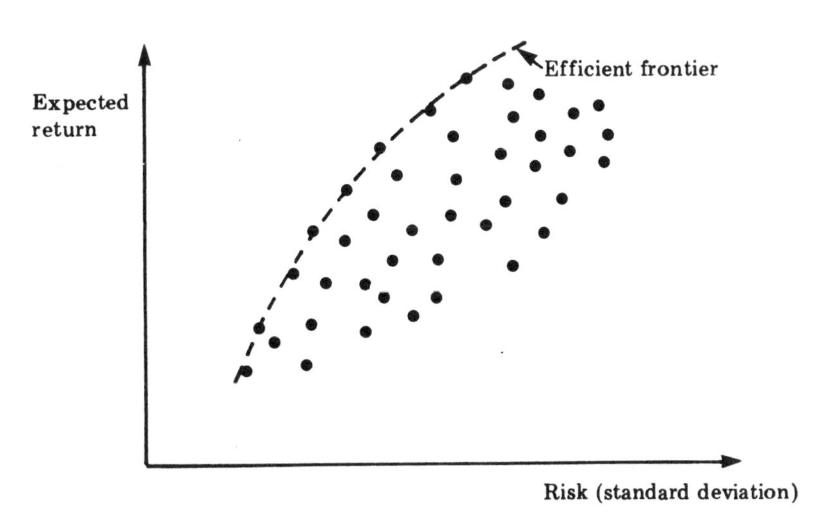

In this graph, there are some portfolios which would not be as good as others. However, there are other portfolios which are neither better nor worse than each other, because they have either a higher expected return but a higher risk, or a lower expected return but a lower risk. These portfolios lie along the so-called 'efficient frontier' of portfolios which is shown as a dotted line in the above graph. Portfolios on this efficient frontier are called 'efficient' portfolios.

2.7 We can now place an investor's indifference curves on the same graph as the possible portfolios of investments (the egg-shaped scatter graph), as in figure 4.

Figure 4: the optimum portfolio (ignoring risk-free securities)

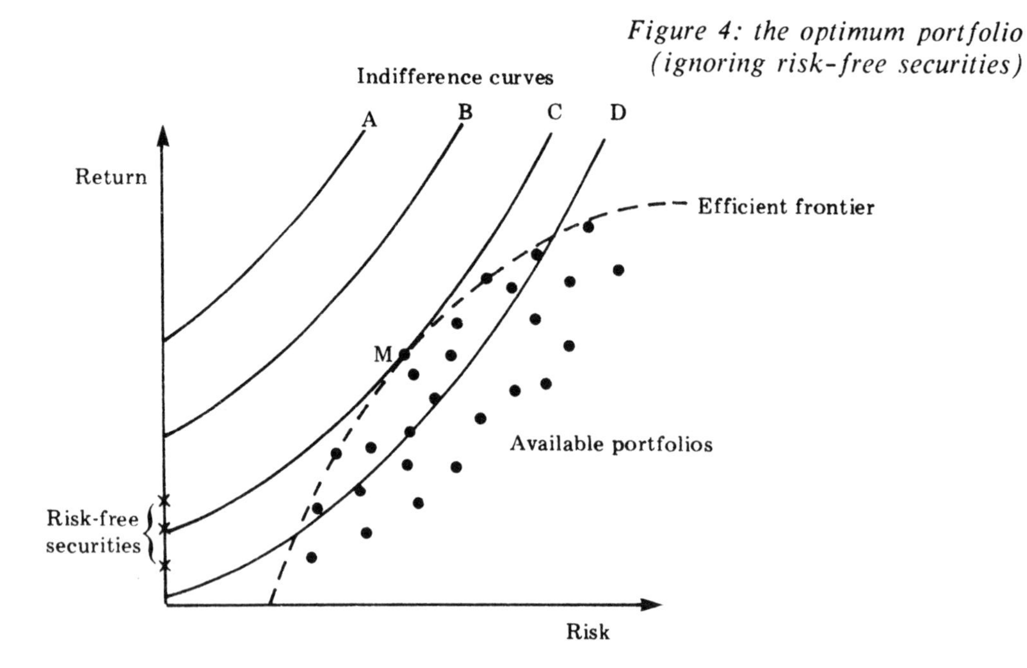

An investor would prefer a portfolio of investments on indifference curve A to a portfolio on curve B, which in turn is preferable to a portfolio on curve C which in turn is preferable to curve D. No portfolio exists, however, which is on curve A or curve B.

2.8 The optimum portfolio (or portfolios) to select is one where an indifference curve touches the efficient frontier of portfolios at a tangent. In figure 4, this is the portfolio marked M, where indifference curve C touches the efficient frontier at a tangent. Any portfolio on an indifference curve to the right of curve C, such as one on curve D, would be worse than M.

Risk-free investments

2.9 The efficient frontier is a curved line, not a straight line. This is because the additional return for accepting a greater level of risk will not be constant. The curve eventually levels off because a point will be reached where no more return can be offered to an investor for accepting more risk.

2.10 All the portfolios under consideration carry some degree of risk. But some investments are risk-free. It is extremely unlikely that the British Government would default on any payment of interest and capital on its stocks. Thus government stocks can be taken to be risk-free investments.

2.11 If we introduce a risk-free investment into the analysis we can see that the old efficient frontier is superseded (figure 5).

Figure 5: the capital market line

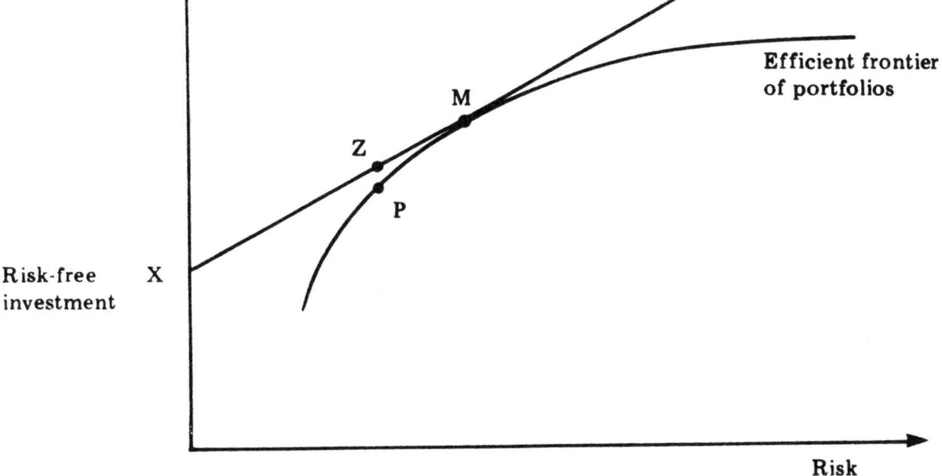

2.12 The straight line XZME is drawn at a tangent to the efficient frontier and cuts the y axis at the point of the risk-free investment's return. The line (known as the 'capital market line' (CML)) becomes the new efficient frontier.

2.13 Portfolio M is the same as in figure 4. It is the efficient portfolio which will appeal to the investor most, ignoring risk-free investments. Portfolio Z is a mixture of the investments in portfolio M and risk-free investments. Investors will prefer portfolio Z (a mixture of risky portfolio M and the risk-free investment) to portfolio P because a higher return is obtained for the same level of risk.

2.14 The only portfolio consisting entirely of *risky* investments a rational investor should want to hold is portfolio M. All other risky portfolios are inefficient (because they are below the CML).

2.15 As with the curvilinear frontier, one portfolio on the capital market line is as attractive as another to a rational investor. One investor may wish to hold portfolio Z, which lies 2/3 of the way along the CML between risk-free investment X and portfolio M (that is, a holding comprising 2/3 portfolio M and 1/3 risk-free securities).

Another investor may wish to hold portfolio E, which entails putting all his funds in portfolio M and borrowing money at the risk-free rate to acquire more of portfolio M.

2.16 We have said that investors will only want to hold one portfolio of risky investments: portfolio M. This may be held in conjunction with a holding of the risk-free investment (as with portfolio Z). Alternatively, an investor may borrow funds to augment his holding of M (as with portfolio E).

Therefore:
(a) since all investors wish to hold portfolio M; and
(b) all shares quoted on the Stock Exchange must be held by investors; it follows that
(c) all shares quoted on the Stock Exchange must be in portfolio M.

2.17 Thus portfolio M is the 'market portfolio' and each investor's portfolio will contain a proportion of it. (Although in the real world, investors do not hold every quoted security in their portfolio, in practice a well-diversified portfolio will 'mirror' the whole market in terms of weightings given to particular sectors, high income and high capital growth securities, and so on.)

2.18 However, in practice, investors *might* be able to build up a small portfolio that 'beats the market' or might have a portfolio which performs worse than the market average. The following exercise illustrates this.

Exercise

The following data relate to four different portfolios of securities.

Portfolio	*Expected rate of return*	*Standard deviation of return on the portfolio*
	%	%
K	11	6.7
L	14	7.5
M	10	3.3
N	15	10.8

The expected rate of return on the market portfolio is 8.5% with a standard deviation of 3%. The risk-free rate is 5%.

Identify which of these portfolios could be regarded as 'efficient'.

Solution

To answer this question, we can start by drawing the CML (see below).

(a) When risk = 0, return = 5.
(b) When risk = 3, return = 8.5.

These points can be plotted on a graph and joined up, and the line can be extended to produce the CML.

The individual portfolios K, L, M and N can be plotted on the same graph.

(a) Any portfolio which is above the CML is efficient.
(b) Any portfolio which is below the CML is inefficient.

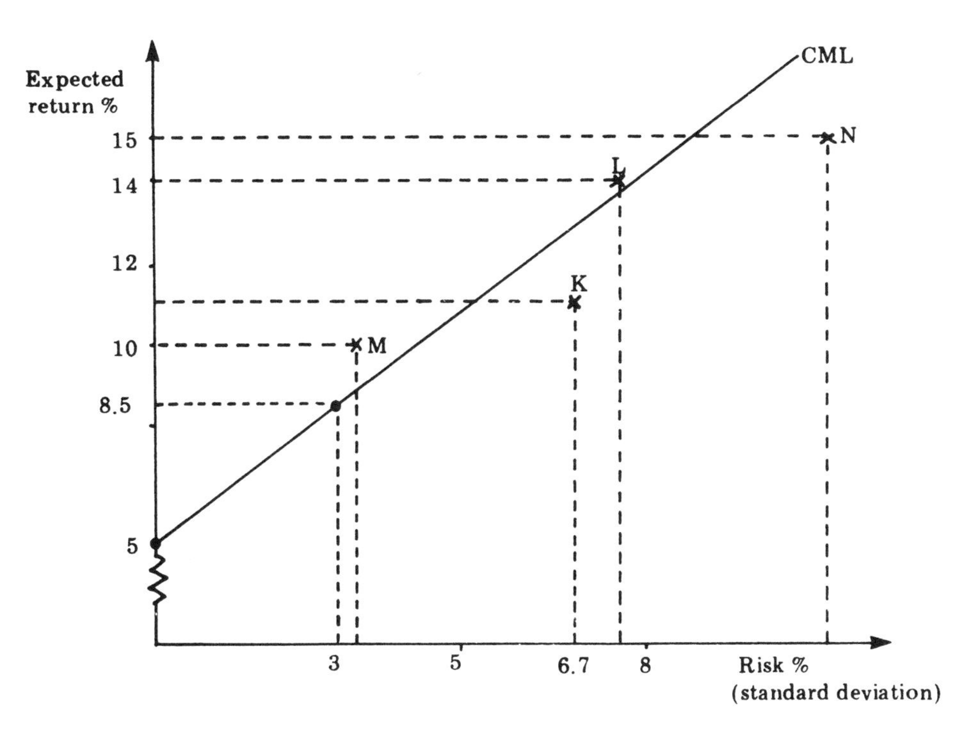

(a) Portfolio M is very efficient.
(b) Portfolio L is also efficient.
(c) Portfolios K and N are inefficient.

If you prefer numbers to graphs, we can tackle the problem in a slightly different way, by calculating the formula for the CML.

Let the standard deviation of a portfolio be x.
Let the return from a portfolio be y.

The CML formula is $y = r_f + bx$.

where r_f is the risk-free rate of return. Here, this is 5.

To calculate b, we can use the high-low method.

When $x = 3$, $y = 8.5$

When $x = 0$, $y = 5$

Therefore $b = \frac{(8.5-5)}{(3-0)} = \frac{3.5}{3} = 1.6667$

The CML is y = 5 + 1.16667x

Portfolio	*Standard deviation x*	*CML return*		*Actual return*	*Efficient or inefficient portfolio*
			%	%	
K	6.7	(5 + 1.16667 × 6.7)	12.8	11	Inefficient
L	7.5	(5 + 1.16667 × 7.5)	13.8	14	Efficient
M	3.3	(5 + 1.16667 × 3.3)	8.9	10	Very efficient
N	10.8	(5 + 1.16667 × 10.8)	17.6	15	Inefficient

If the actual return exceeds the CML return for the given amount of risk, the portfolio is efficient.

Here, L is efficient and M is even more efficient, but K and N are inefficient.

The return on the market portfolio M

2.19 The expected returns from portfolio M will be higher than the return from risk-free investments because the investors expect a greater return for accepting a degree of investment risk.

The size of the risk premium will increase as the risk of the market portfolio increases. We can show this with an analysis of the capital market line (figure 6).

Figure 6: the risk premium in required returns from a portfolio

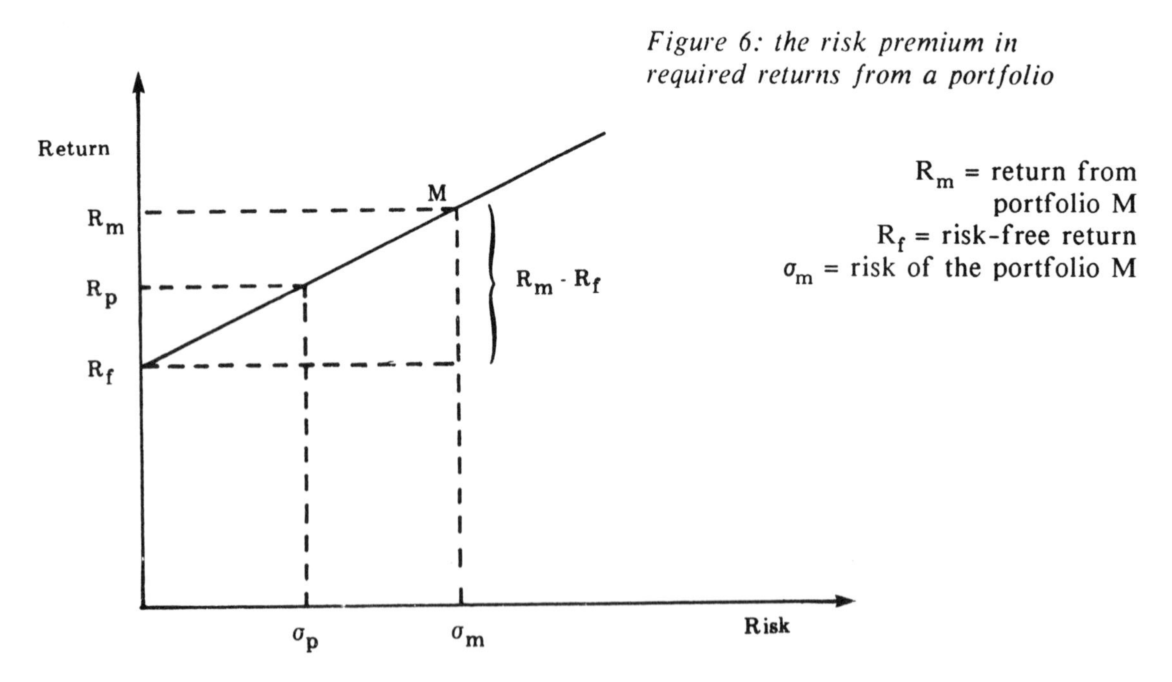

2.20 The formula for the CML was expressed as y = a + bx in the previous exercise, where a is the risk-free rate of return and bx represents the increase in the return as the risk goes up.

2.21 Let Rf = the risk-free rate of return
Rm = the return on market portfolio M
Rp = the return on portfolio P, which is a mixture of investments in portfolio M and risk-free investments
Y_m = the risk (standard deviation) of returns in portfolio M
Y_p = the risk (standard deviation) of returns in portfolio P

The gradient of the CML can be expressed as $\frac{Rm - Rf}{\sigma_m}$

This represents the extent to which the required returns from a portfolio should exceed the risk-free rate of return, to compensate investors for risk.

The beta factor

2.22 The equation of the CML can be expressed as: $Rp = Rf + \left(\frac{Rm - Rf}{\sigma_m} \right) \sigma_p$

where $\left(\frac{Rm - Rf}{\sigma_m} \right) \sigma_p$ is the risk premium that the investor should require as compensation for accepting portfolio risk σ_p.

2.23 The risk premium can be re-arranged into:

$$\frac{\sigma p}{\sigma m} \quad (Rm - Rf)$$

The expression $\frac{\sigma p}{\sigma m}$ is referred to as a *beta factor*, so that an investor's required return from a portfolio can be stated as

$$Rp = Rf + \beta \ (Rm - Rf)$$

2.24 The beta factor (β) can therefore be used to measure the extent to which a portfolio's return (or indeed an individual investment's return) should exceed the risk-free rate of return. The beta factor is multiplied by the difference between the average return on market securities (Rm) and the risk-free return (Rf) to derive the portfolio's or investment's risk premium. This risk premium will include both a business risk and a financial risk element in it.

2.25 This equation forms the basis of the Capital Asset Pricing Model (CAPM), which we shall look at in the next chapter.

3. CONCLUSION

3.1 Portfolio theory takes account of the fact that many investors have a range of investments which are unlikely all to change values in step. The investor should be concerned with his or her overall position, not with the performance of individual investments.

TEST YOUR KNOWLEDGE

The numbers in brackets refer to paragraphs of this chapter

1. What are the factors in choosing a portfolio of investments? (1.3)

2. How is the expected return from a portfolio measured? (1.5)

3. Returns from investments might be positively correlated, negatively correlated, or uncorrelated. How does correlation of returns from individual investments affect the risk of a portfolio? (1.23)

4. What is the formula for calculating the standard deviation of returns from a two-investment portfolio? (1.24)

5. How are the expected returns and risks of portfolios on the efficient frontier related to each other? (2.6)

6. Give an example of a risk-free investment. (2.10)

7. What is the equation of the Capital Market Line? (2.22). Use this to derive an expression for the beta factor. (2.23)

8. How is the beta factor used? (2.23, 2.24)

Now try question 12 at the end of the text

Chapter 10

THE CAPITAL ASSET PRICING MODEL

This chapter covers the following topics.

1. Risk and the CAPM
2. Calculating a beta factor
3. CAPM and portfolio management
4. Gearing and the β values of companies' equity
5. Practical implications of CAPM

1. RISK AND THE CAPM

1.1 The Capital Asset Pricing Model (CAPM) brings together aspects of portfolio theory, share valuations, the cost of capital and gearing.

1.2 The uses of the CAPM include:

(a) trying to establish what the 'correct' equilibrium market value of a company's shares;

(b) trying to establish the cost of a company's equity (and the company's average cost of capital), taking account of the risk characteristics of a company's investments, both business and financial risk.

It therefore provides an approach to establishing a cost of equity capital which is an alternative to the dividend valuation model.

Systematic risk and unsystematic risk

1.3 Whenever an investor invests in some shares, or a company invests in a new project, there will be some risk involved. The actual return on the investment might be better or worse than that hoped for.

To some extent, risk is unavoidable (unless the investor settles for risk-free securities such as gilts). Investors must take the rough with the smooth and for reasons outside their control, returns might be higher or lower than expected. Provided that the investor diversifies his investments in a suitably wide portfolio, the investments which perform well and those which perform badly should tend to cancel each other out, and much risk can be diversified away. In the same way, a company which invests in a number of projects will find that some do well and some do badly, but taking the whole portfolio of investments, average returns should turn out much as expected.

1.4 Risks that can be diversified away are referred to as *unsystematic risk.*

1.5 But there is another sort of risk too. Some investments are by their very nature more risky than others. This has nothing to do with chance variations up or down in actual returns compared with what an investor should expect. This inherent risk cannot be diversified away, and it is referred to as *systematic risk* (or market risk).

1.6 Systematic risk must therefore be accepted by any investor, unless he invests entirely in risk-free investments. In return for accepting systematic risk, an investor will expect to earn a return which is higher than the return on a risk-free investment.

1.7 The amount of systematic risk in an investment varies between different types of investment.

(a) Some industries by their nature are more risky than others. For example, it might be that the systematic risk in the operating cash flows of a company in a high technology industry is greater than the systematic risk for a company which operates a chain of supermarkets.

(b) In the same way, some individual projects will be more risky than others and so the systematic risk involved in an investment to develop a new product would be greater than the systematic risk of investing in a replacement asset.

Systematic risk and unsystematic risk: implications for investments

1.8 The implications of systematic risk and unsystematic risk are as follows.

(a) If an investor wants to avoid risk altogether, he must invest entirely in risk-free securities.

(b) If an investor holds shares in just a few companies, there will be some unsystematic risk as well as systematic risk in his portfolio, because he will not have spread his risk enough to diversify away the unsystematic risk. To eliminate unsystematic risk, he must build up a well-diversified portfolio of investments.

(c) If an investor holds a balanced portfolio of all the stocks and shares on the stock market, he will incur systematic risk which is exactly equal to the average systematic risk in the stock market as a whole.

(d) Shares in individual companies will have systematic risk characteristics which are different to this market average. Some shares will be less risky and some will be more risky than the stock market average. Similarly, some investments will be more risky and some will be less risky than a company's 'average' investments.

Systematic risk and the CAPM

1.9 The Capital Asset Pricing Model is mainly concerned with:

(a) how systematic risk is measured;
(b) how systematic risk affects required returns and share prices.

Systematic risk is measured using beta factors.

1.10 CAPM theory includes the following propositions.

(a) Investors in shares require a return in excess of the risk-free rate, to compensate them for systematic risk.

(b) Investors should not require a premium for unsystematic risk, because this can be diversified away by holding a wide portfolio of investments.

(c) Because systematic risk varies between companies, investors will require a higher return from shares in those companies where the systematic risk is bigger.

1.11 The same propositions can be applied to capital investments by companies.

(a) Companies will want a return on a project to exceed the risk-free rate, to compensate them for systematic risk.

(b) Unsystematic risk can be diversified away, and so a premium for unsystematic risk should not be required.

(c) Companies should want a bigger return on projects where systematic risk is greater.

Market risk and returns

1.12 The CAPM was first formulated for investments in stocks and shares on the market, rather than for companies' investments in capital projects. It is based on a comparison of the systematic risk of individual investments (shares in a particular company) and the risk of all shares in the market as a whole. Market risk is the average risk of the market as a whole. Taking all the shares on a stock market together, the total expected returns from the market will vary because of systematic risk. The market as a whole might do well or it might do badly.

Risk and returns from an individual security

1.13 In the same way, an individual security may offer prospects of a return of x%, but with some risk (business risk and financial risk) attached. The return (the x%) that investors will require from the individual security will be higher or lower than the market return, depending on whether the security's systematic risk is greater or less than the market average.

1.14 A major assumption in CAPM is that there is a linear relationship between the return obtained from an individual security and the average return from all securities in the market.

Example

1.15 The following information is available about the performance of an individual company's shares and the stock market as a whole.

	Individual company	*Stock market as a whole*
Price at start of period	105.0	480.0
Price at end of period	110.0	490.0
Dividend during period	7.6	39.2

1.16 The return on the company's shares (R_s) and the return on the 'market portfolio' of shares (R_m) may be calculated as

$$\frac{\text{Capital gain (or loss) + dividend}}{\text{Price at start of period}}$$

$$R_s = \frac{(110 - 105) + 7.6}{105} = 0.12 \qquad R_m = \frac{(490 - 480) + 39.2}{480} = 0.1025$$

1.17 A statistical analysis of 'historic' returns from a security and from the 'average' market may suggest that a linear relationship can be assumed to exist between them. A series of comparative figures could be prepared (month by month) of the return from a company's shares and the average return of the market as a whole. The results could be drawn on a scattergraph and a 'line of best fit' drawn (using linear regression techniques) as follows.

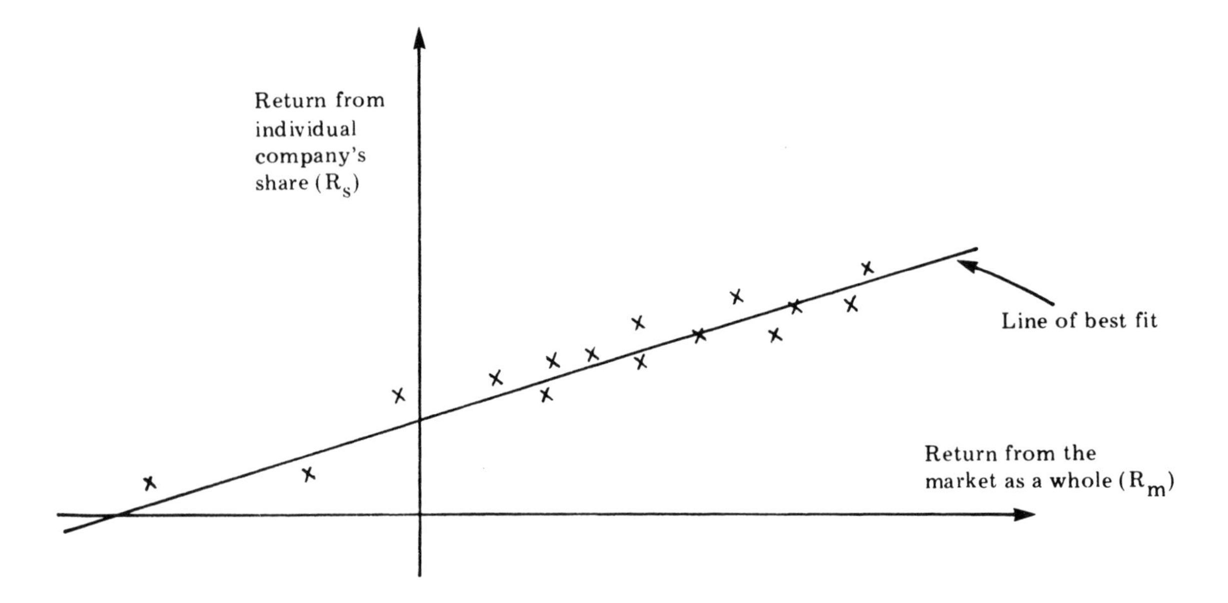

1.18 This analysis would show three things.

(a) The return from the security (Rs) and the return from the market as a whole will tend to rise or fall together.

(b) The return from the security may be higher or lower than the market return. This is because the systematic risk of the individual security differs from that of the market as a whole. The graph above corresponds to a security which is riskier than the market (higher returns).

(c) The scattergraph may not give a good line of best fit, unless a large number of data items are plotted, because actual returns are affected by unsystematic risk as well as by systematic risk.

Note that returns can be negative. A share price fall represents a capital loss, which is a negative return.

1.19 The conclusion from this analysis is that individual securities will be either more or less risky than the market average in a fairly predictable way. The measure of this relationship between market returns and an individual security's returns, reflecting differences in systematic risk characteristics, can be developed into a *beta factor* for the individual security.

The beta factor and the market risk premium

1.20 A share's *beta factor* is the measure of its volatility in terms of market risk.

1.21 The beta factor of the market as a whole is 1.0. Market risk makes market returns volatile and the beta factor is simply a basis or yardstick against which the risk of other investments can be measured.

1.22 For example, suppose that returns on shares in XYZ plc tend to vary twice as much as returns from the market as a whole, so that if market returns went up 3%, say, returns on XYZ plc shares would be expected to go up by 6% and if market returns fell by 3%, returns on XYZ plc shares would be expected to fall by 6%. The beta factor of XYZ plc shares would be 2.0.

1.23 Thus if the average market return rises by, say, 2%, the return from a share with a beta factor of 0.8 should rise by 1.6% in response to *the same conditions* which have caused the market return to change. The *actual* return from the share might rise by, say, 2.5%, or even fall by, say, 1%, but the difference between the actual change and a change of 1.6% due to general market factors would be attributed to unsystematic risk factors unique to the company or its industry.

1.24 It is an essential principle of CAPM theory that unsystematic risk can be cancelled out by diversification. In a well-balanced portfolio, an investor's gains and losses from the unsystematic risk of individual shares will tend to cancel each other out. In other words, if shares in X plc do worse than market returns and the beta factor of X's shares would predict, shares in Y plc will do better than predicted, and the net effect will be self-cancelling elimination of the specific (unsystematic) risk from the portfolio, leaving the average portfolio return dependent only on:

(a) changes in the average market return; and

(b) the beta factors of shares in the portfolio.

Excess returns over returns on risk-free investments

1.25 The Capital Asset Pricing Model also makes use of the principle that returns on shares in the market as a whole are expected to be higher than the returns on risk-free investments. The difference between market returns and risk-free returns is called an *excess* return.

For example, if the return on British Government stocks is 9% and market returns are 13%, the excess return on the market's shares as a whole is 4%.

1.26 The difference between the risk-free return and the expected return on an individual security can be measured as the excess return for the market as a whole multiplied by the security's beta factor. Thus, if shares in DEF plc have a beta of 1.5 when the risk-free return is 9% and the expected market return is 13%, then the expected return on DEF plc shares would exceed the risk- free return by 1.5(13 - 9)% = 6% and the total expected return on DEF shares would be (9 + 6)% = 15%.

1.27 If the market returns fall by 3% to 10%, say, the expected return on DEF plc shares would fall by 1.5 × 3% = 4.5% to 10.5%, being 9% + 1.5(10 - 9)% = 10.5%.

The Capital Asset Pricing Model formula

1.28 The CAPM is a statement of the principles explained above. It can be stated as follows.

$$(R_s - R_f) = \beta (R_m - R_f)$$

where
- R_s is the expected return from an individual security
- R_f is the risk-free rate of return
- R_m is the return from the market as a whole
- β is the beta factor of the individual security

1.29 The CAPM formula can be rearranged into:

$$R_s = R_f + \beta (R_m - R_f)$$

Alpha values

1.30 A share's alpha value is a measure of its abnormal return, which is the amount by which the share's returns are currently above or below what would be expected, given its systematic risk.

Example

1.31 ABC plc's shares have a beta value of 1.2 and an alpha value of +2%. The market return is 10% and the risk-free rate of return is 6%.

Expected return 6% + 1.2 (10-6)% = 10.8%

Current return	=	Expected return ± alpha value
	=	10.8% + 2% = 12.8%

1.32 Alpha values:

(a) are only temporary, abnormal returns;
(b) can be positive or negative;
(c) over time, will tend towards zero for any individual share, and for a well-diversified portfolio taken as a whole will be 0;
(d) if positive, might attract investors into buying the share to benefit from the abnormal return, so that the share price will temporarily go up.

The CAPM and share prices

1.33 The CAPM can be used not only to estimate expected returns from securities with differing risk characteristics, but also to predict the value of shares.

Example

1.34. Company X and company Y both pay an annual cash return to shareholders of 34.048 pence per share and this is expected to continue in perpetuity. The risk-free rate of return is 8% and the current average market rate of return is 12%. Company X's β coefficient is 1.8 and company Y's is 0.8.

What is the expected return from companies X and Y respectively, and what would be the predicted market value of each company's shares?

Solution

1.35 (a) The expected return for X is 8% + 1.8(12% - 8%) = 15.2%
(b) The expected return for Y is 8% + 0.8(12% - 8%) = 11.2%

The dividend valuation model can now be used to derive expected share prices.

(c) The predicted value of a share in X is $\frac{34.048p}{0.152} = 224$ pence

(d) The predicted value of a share in Y is $\frac{34.048p}{0.112} = 304$ pence

The actual share price of X and Y might be higher or lower than 224p and 304p. If so, CAPM analysis would conclude that the share is currently either overpriced or underpriced.

2. CALCULATING A BETA FACTOR

2.1 The beta factor for a particular security can be calculated by plotting its return against the market return and drawing the line of best fit. The equation of this line can be derived by regression analysis.

The β factor is the gradient of the line. It can be calculated by using the following formula.

$$\beta = \frac{n\Sigma xy - \Sigma x \Sigma y}{n\Sigma x^2 - (\Sigma x)^2}$$

where β = the beta coefficient
x = the return from the market
y = the return from the security
n = the number of pairs of data for x and y.

2.2 Another formula for calculating the beta value of a company's shares is

$$\beta = \frac{(\text{cov } x,y)}{\text{var } (x)}$$

where (cov x,y) is the covariance of returns on an individual company's shares (y) with returns for the market as a whole (x) and var (x) is the variance of returns for the market as a whole.

Example

2.3 The risk-free rate of return is 6% and the market rate of return is 11%. The standard deviation of returns for the market as a whole is 40%. The covariance of returns for the market with returns for the shares of Peapod plc is 19.2%.

Since the variance is the square of a standard deviation, the beta value for Peapod plc is

$$\frac{0.192}{0.4^2} = \frac{0.192}{0.16} = 1.20$$

The cost of equity capital for Peapod plc would therefore be 6% + 1.2(11 - 6)% = 12%.

2.4 Yet another formula for calculating a share's beta factor is

$$\beta = \frac{\sigma_s \ \rho_{sm}}{\sigma_m}$$

where σ_s is the standard deviation of returns on the shares of a company
σ_m is the standard deviation of returns on equity for the market as a whole
ρ_{sm} is the correlation coefficient between total returns on equity for the stock market as a whole and total returns on the shares of the individual company.

Example

2.5 We are given the following information.

The average stock market return on equity	= 15%
The risk-free rate of return (pre-tax)	= 8%
Company X: dividend yield	= 4%
Company X: share price rise (capital gain)	= 12%
Standard deviation of total stock market return on equity	= 9%
Standard deviation of total return on equity of Company X	= 10.8%
Correlation coefficient between Company X return on equity and average stock market return on equity	= 0.75

What is the beta factor for Company X shares, and what does this information imply for the actual returns and actual market value of Company X shares?

Solution

2.6 (a)

$$\beta = \frac{\sigma_s \ \rho_{sm}}{\sigma_m}$$

$$= \frac{10.8\% \times 0.75}{9\%}$$

$$= 0.9$$

(b) The cost of Company X equity should therefore be

$$R_s = 8\% + 0.9(15 - 8)\%$$
$$= 14.3\%$$

2.7 The actual returns on Company X equity are 4% + 12% = 16%. This implies that:

(a) the actual returns include extra returns due to unsystematic risk factors; or

(b) if there are no unsystematic risk factors, the price of Company X shares is currently lower than it should be.

3. CAPM AND PORTFOLIO MANAGEMENT

3.1 Just as an individual security has a beta factor, so too does a portfolio of securities.

(a) A portfolio consisting of all the securities on the stock market (in the same proportions as the market as a whole), excluding risk free securities, will have an expected return equal to the expected return for the market as a whole, and so will have a beta factor of 1.

(b) A portfolio consisting entirely of risk-free securities will have a beta factor of 0.

(c) The beta factor of an investor's portfolio is the weighted average of the beta factors of the securities in the portfolio.

Example

3.2 A portfolio consisting of five securities could have its beta factor computed as follows.

Security	*Percentage of portfolio*	*Beta factor of security*	*Weighted beta factor*
A plc	20%	0.90	0.180
B plc	10%	1.25	0.125
C plc	15%	1.10	0.165
D plc	20%	1.15	0.230
E plc	35%	0.70	0.245
	100%	Portfolio beta =	0.945

3.3 If the risk-free rate of return is 12% and the average market return is 20%, the expected return from the portfolio would be 12% + 0.945(20 - 12)% = 19.56%

3.4 The calculation could have been made as follows.

Security	*Beta factor*	*Expected return* $(R_f + \beta(R_m - R_f))$	*Weighting*	*Weighted return*
		%		%
A plc	0.90	19.2	20%	3.84
B plc	1.25	22.0	10%	2.20
C plc	1.10	20.8	15%	3.12
D plc	1.15	21.2	20%	4.24
E plc	0.70	17.6	35%	6.16
			100%	19.56

4. GEARING AND THE β VALUES OF COMPANIES' EQUITY

4.1 The gearing of a company will affect the risk of its equity. If a company is geared and its financial risk is therefore higher than the risk of an all-equity company, then the β value of the geared company's equity will be higher than the β value of a similar ungeared company's equity.

4.2 The CAPM is consistent with the propositions of Modigliani and Miller.

MM argue that as gearing rises, the cost of equity rises to compensate shareholders for the extra financial risk of investing in a geared company. This financial risk is an aspect of systematic risk, and ought to be reflected in a company's beta factor.

Example

4.3 The cost of equity in an all-equity company is 15%. A similar company, identical in every respect except gearing, has an equity:debt ratio of 4:1. The cost of debt, which is virtually risk free, is 5%. Corporation tax is at the rate of 33%.

The return from the market portfolio is 10%. The risk-free rate of return, as indicated already, is 5%.

4.4 The beta factor of the ungeared company can be calculated using the CAPM.

$$15\% = 5\% + \beta\,(10\% - 5\%)$$
$$\beta = 2$$

4.5 Using the MM formula for the cost of equity in a geared company, the cost of equity of the geared company in this example would be

$$K_g = K_u + (1-t)\,[(K_u - K_d)\,\frac{D}{V_{eg}}\,]$$

$$= 15\% + (1 - 0.33)\ [(15-5) \times \frac{1}{4}\ ]\%$$

$$= 16.675\%$$

4.6 The beta factor of the geared company is found as follows.

$$16.675\% = 5\% + \beta\,(10\% - 5\%)$$
$$\beta = 2.335$$

As we would expect, the extra financial risk in the geared company means that its beta factor is higher than in the similar ungeared company.

Another formula for the cost of equity in a geared company

4.7 One of MM's propositions is that the cost of equity in a geared company (K_g) is equal to the cost of equity in a similar ungeared company (with the same business risk characteristics) plus a premium for financial risk, and

$$K_g = K_u + (1-t)(K_u - K_d)\frac{D}{V_{eg}} \qquad (1)$$

K_d, the cost of debt, was assumed by MM to be a *risk-free* cost (R_f). Thus since the CAPM is

$$K_u = R_f + \beta_u\,(R_m - R_f) \qquad (2)$$

where β_u is the beta factor of the ungeared company, it is possible to substitute (2) in (1) to get

$$K_g = R_f + \beta_u\,(R_m - R_f)\left[1 + \frac{(1-t)D}{V_{eg}}\right]$$

4.8 This equation states that the cost of equity in a geared company is the same as the cost of equity in an ungeared company *except* that the size of the premium over the risk free rate of return, $\beta_u\,(R_m - R_f)$, is adjusted by a factor $\left(1 + \frac{(1-t)D}{V_{eg}}\right)$

Example

4.9 Suppose that a company is financed partly by debt capital (market value £5,000,000) and partly by equity capital (market value £20,000,000).

It is similar in its business risk to another company which is entirely equity financed and is known to have a β value of 1.1. The average market return is 12% and the risk-free rate of return is 8%.

4.10 The cost of equity in the geared company (which we should expect to be higher than the cost of equity in the ungeared company, because of the higher financial risk) can be calculated as follows, assuming a tax rate of 33%.

Since $K_u = 8\% + 1.1\,(12\% - 8\%) = 12.4\%$

$$K_g = 8\% + 1.1(12\% - 8\%)\left[1 + \frac{0.67 \times 5}{20}\right]$$

$$= 13.137\%$$

Beta values and the effect of gearing: geared betas and ungeared betas

4.11 The connection between MM theory and the CAPM means that it is also possible to establish a mathematical relationship between the β value of an ungeared company and the β value of a similar, but geared, company.

4.12 The β value of a geared company will be higher than the β value of a company identical in every respect except that it is all-equity financed. This is because of the extra financial risk.

The mathematical relationship between the 'ungeared' and 'geared' betas is as follows.

$$\beta_u = \frac{\beta_g}{[1 + \frac{D(1-t)}{V_{eg}}]}$$

where
- β_u is the beta factor of an ungeared company: the ungeared beta
- β_g is the beta factor of a similar, but geared company: the geared beta
- D is the market value of the debt capital in the geared company
- V_{eg} is the market value of the equity capital in the geared company
- t is the rate of corporation tax.

4.13 Re-arranging this, we have

$$\beta_g = \beta_u [1 + \frac{D(1-t)}{V_{eg}}]$$

$$\beta_g = \beta_u + \beta_u [\frac{D(1-t)}{V_{eg}}]$$

4.14 Note that the geared beta is equal to the ungeared beta plus a premium for financial risk which equals

$$\beta_u [\frac{D(1-t)}{V_{eg}}]$$

Example

4.15 Two companies are identical in every respect except for their capital structure. Their market values are in equilibrium, as follows.

	Geared plc	*Ungeared plc*
	£'000	£'000
Annual profit before interest and tax	1,000	1,000
Less interest (4,000 × 8%)	320	0
	680	1,000
Less tax at 33%	224	330
Profit after tax = dividends	456	670
	£'000	£'000
Market value of equity	3,900	6,700
Market value of debt	4,180	0
Total market value of company	8,080	6,700

The total value of Geared plc is higher than the total value of Ungeared plc, which is consistent with MM's proposition that $V_g = V_u + Dt$.

All profits after tax are paid out as dividends, and so there is no dividend growth.

The beta value of Ungeared plc has been calculated as 1.0.

The debt capital of Geared plc can be regarded as risk-free.

Calculate:
(a) the cost of equity in Geared plc;
(b) the market return $R_{m;}$
(c) the beta value of Geared plc.

Solution

4.16 (a) Since its market value is in equilibrium, the cost of equity in Geared plc can be calculated as

$$\frac{d}{MV} = \frac{456}{3,900} = 11.69\%$$

(b) The beta value of Ungeared plc is 1.0, which means that the expected returns from Ungeared plc are exactly the same as the market returns, and so $R_m = 10\%$.

(c)
$$\beta_g = \beta_u \left[1 + \frac{(1 - t)D}{V_{eg}}\right]$$

$$= 1.0\left[1 + \frac{0.67(4,180)}{3,900}\right]$$

$$= 1.72$$

The beta of Geared plc, as we should expect, is higher than the beta of Ungeared plc.

Using the geared and ungeared beta formula to estimate a beta factor for a company

4.17 Another way of estimating a beta factor for a company's equity is to use data about the returns of other quoted companies which have similar operating characteristics: that is, to use the beta values of other companies' equity to estimate a beta value for the company under consideration.

4.18 The beta values estimated for the firm under consideration must be adjusted to allow for differences in gearing from the firms whose equity beta values are known. The formula for geared and ungeared beta values can be applied.

Example

4.19 The management of Crispy plc wish to estimate their company's equity beta value. The company, which is an all-equity company, has only recently gone public and insufficient data is available at the moment about its own equity's performance to calculate the company's equity beta. Instead, it is thought possible to estimate Crispy's equity beta from the beta values of quoted companies operating in the same industry and with the same operating characteristics as Crispy.

Details of three similar companies are as follows.

(a) Snapp plc has an observed equity beta of 1.15. Its capital structure at market values is 70% equity and 30% debt. Snapp plc is very similar to Crispy plc except for its gearing.

(b) Crackle plc is an all-equity company. Its observed equity beta is 1.25. It has been estimated that 40% of the current market value of Crackle is caused by investment in projects which offer high growth, but which are more risky than normal operations and which therefore have a higher beta value. These investments have an estimated beta of 1.8, and are reflected in the company's overall beta value. Crackle's normal operations are identical to those of Crispy.

(c) Popper plc has an observed equity beta of 1.35. Its capital structure at market values is 60% equity and 40% debt. Popper has two divisions, X and Y. The operating characteristics of X are identical to those of Crispy but those of Y are thought to be 50% more risky than those of X. It is estimated that X accounts for 75% of the total value of Popper, and Y for 25%.

The tax rate is 33%.

(a) Assuming that all debt is virtually risk-free, calculate three estimates of the equity beta of Crispy, from the data available about Snapp, Crackle and Popper respectively.

(b) Now assume that Crispy plc is not an all-equity company, but instead is a geared company with a debt:equity ratio of 2:3 (based on market values). Estimate the equity beta of Crispy from the data available about Snapp.

Solution

4.20 (a) *Snapp plc - based estimate*

$$\beta_g = \beta_u(1 + (1 - t)\frac{D}{E})$$

$$1.15 = \beta_u(1 + (1 - 0.33)\frac{30}{70})$$

$$1.15 = 1.28714\beta_u$$

$$\beta_u = 0.89$$

(b) *Crackle plc - based estimate*

If the beta value of normal operations of Crackle is β_n, and we know that the high-risk operations have a beta value of 1.8 and account for 40% of Crackle's value, we can estimate a value for β_n.

Overall beta = 0.4(high risk beta) + 0.6(normal operations beta)

$1.25 = 0.4(1.8) + 0.6\ \beta_n$

$\beta_n = 0.88$

Since Crackle is an all-equity company, this provides the estimate of Crispy's equity beta.

(c) *Popper plc - based estimate*

It is easiest to arrive at an estimate of Crispy's equity beta by calculating the equity beta which Popper would have had if it had been an all-equity company instead of a geared company.

$$\beta_g = \beta_u(1 + (1 - t)\frac{D}{E})$$

$$1.35 = \beta_u(1 + (1 - 0.33)\frac{0.4}{0.6})$$

$$\beta_u = \frac{1.35}{1.44667} = 0.93318$$

This equity beta estimate for Popper plc is a weighted average of the beta values of divisions X and Y, so that

$$0.93318 = 0.75\beta_x + 0.25\beta_y$$

where β_x and β_y are the beta values for divisions X and Y respectively. We also know that Y is 50% more risky than X, so that $\beta_y = 1.5\beta_x$.

$$0.93318 = 0.75\beta_x + 0.25(1.5\beta_x)$$
$$\beta_x = 0.83$$

Since Crispy plc is similar in characteristics to division X, the estimate of Crispy's equity beta is 0.83.

4.21 If Crispy plc is a geared company with a market-value based gearing ratio of 2:3, we can use the geared and ungeared beta formula again. The ungeared beta value, based on data about Snapp, was 0.89. The geared beta of Crispy would be estimated as

$$\beta_g = 0.89\,(1 + \frac{(1 - 0.33)2}{3})$$
$$= 1.29$$

Weaknesses in the formula

4.22 The problems with using the geared and ungeared beta formula for calculating a firm's equity beta from data about other firms are as follows.

(a) It is difficult to identify other firms with identical operating characteristics.

(b) Estimates of beta values from share price information are not wholly accurate. They are based on statistical analysis of historical data, and as the previous example shows, estimates using one firm's data will differ from estimates using another firm's data. The beta values for Crispy estimated from Snapp, Crackle and Popper are all different.

(c) There may be differences in beta values between firms caused by:

(i) different cost structures (for example the ratio of fixed costs to variable costs);
(ii) size differences between firms;
(iii) debt capital not being risk-free;

(d) If the firm for which an equity beta is being estimated has opportunities for growth that are recognised by investors, and which will affect its equity beta, estimates of the equity beta based on other firms' data will be inaccurate, because the opportunities for growth will not be allowed for.

4.23 Perhaps the most significant simplifying assumption is that to link MM theory to the CAPM, it must be assumed that the cost of debt (K_d) is a risk-free rate of return. This is obviously unrealistic. Companies may default on interest payments or capital repayments on their loans. It has been estimated that corporate debt has a beta value of 0.2 or 0.3.

4.24 The consequence of making the assumption that debt is risk free is that the formulae tend to understate K_u, and so to:

(a) overstate the financial risk in a geared company;
(b) understate the business risk in geared and ungeared companies by a compensating amount.

In other words β_u will be a bit higher and β_g will be a bit lower than the formulae suggest.

5. PRACTICAL IMPLICATIONS OF CAPM

5.1 The implications of CAPM theory for an investor are as follows.

(a) He should decide what beta factor he would like to have for his portfolio. He might prefer a portfolio beta factor of greater than 1, in order to expect above-average returns when market returns exceed the risk-free rate, but he would then expect to lose heavily if market returns fall. On the other hand, he might prefer a portfolio beta factor of 1 or even less.

(b) He should seek to invest in shares with low beta factors in a bear market, when average market returns are falling. He should then also sell shares with high beta factors.

(c) He should seek to invest in shares with high beta factors in a bull market, when average market returns are rising.

An investor can measure the beta factor of his portfolio by obtaining information about the beta factors of individual securities. These are obtainable from a variety of investment analysts such as the London Business School's Financial Services.

Limitations of the Capital Asset Pricing Model for the selection of a portfolio of securities

5.2 Under the Capital Asset Pricing Model, the return required from a security is related to its systematic risk rather than its total risk. If we relax some of the assumptions upon which the model is based, then the total risk may be important. In particular, the following points should be considered.

(a) The model assumes that the costs of insolvency are zero, or in other words, that all assets can be sold at going concern prices and that there are no selling, legal or other costs. In practice, the costs of insolvency cannot be ignored. Furthermore, the risk of insolvency is related to a firm's total risk rather than just its systematic risk.

(b) The model assumes that the investment market is efficient. If it is not, this will limit the extent to which investors are able to eliminate unsystematic risk from their portfolios.

(c) The model also assumes that portfolios are well diversified and so need only be concerned with systematic risk. However, this is not necessarily the case, and undiversified or partly-diversified shareholders should also be concerned with unsystematic risk and will seek a total return appropriate to the total risk that they face.

5.3 The major sources of difficulty in applying the CAPM in practice are:

(a) the need to determine the excess return (R_m - R_f). Expected, rather than historical, returns should be used, although historical returns are used in practice;

(b) the need to determine the risk-free rate. A risk-free investment might be a government security. However, interest rates vary with the term of the lending;

(c) errors in the statistical analysis used to calculate β values.

The CAPM and project appraisal

5.4 The CAPM can be used instead of the dividend valuation model to establish an equity cost of capital to use in project appraisal.

The cost of equity is $K_e = R_f + \beta_e [R_m - R_f]$ where β_e is the beta value for the company's equity capital.

Example

5.5 A company is financed by a mixture of equity and debt capital, whose market values are in the ratio 3:1. The debt capital, which is considered risk-free, yields 10% before tax. The average stock market return on equity capital is 18%. The beta value of the company's equity capital is estimated as 0.9. The tax rate is 33%.

What would be an appropriate cost of capital to be used for investment appraisal of new projects with the same systematic risk characteristics as the company's current investment portfolio?

Solution

5.6 An appropriate cost of capital to use, assuming no change in the company's financial gearing, is its WACC. However, the CAPM can be used to estimate the cost of the company's equity.

$$K_e = 10\% + 0.95(16-10)\%$$
$$= 15.7\%$$

5.7 The after tax cost of debt is $0.67 \times 10\% = 6.7\%$.

The WACC is therefore

$$(\tfrac{3}{4} \times 15.7\%) + (\tfrac{1}{4} \times 6.7\%) = 13.45\%.$$

The cost of capital to use in project appraisal is 13.45%.

How is the WACC different using the CAPM?

5.8 You might be wondering how the WACC is different when we use the CAPM compared to the method of calculating the WACC which was described in the earlier chapter on the cost of capital. The only difference, in fact, is the method used to calculate the cost of the firm's equity: the dividend valuation model or the CAPM.

5.9 Using the different techniques for measuring the cost of equity will produce two different values for these reasons.

(a) The dividend valuation model uses expectations of actual dividends and current share values. Dividends may include extra or lower returns caused by unsystematic risk variations, as well as systematic risk. Share prices might not be in equilibrium.

(b) The CAPM considers systematic risk only, and assumes equilibrium in the stock market.

5.10 If dividends reflect systematic risk only, and if stock market prices are in equilibrium, the dividend valuation model and the CAPM should produce roughly the same estimates for the cost of a firm's equity and for its WACC.

Using the CAPM to establish a discount rate for the appraisal of major diversification projects

5.11 If a company plans to invest in a project which involves diversification into a new business, the investment will involve a different level of systematic risk from that applying to the company's existing business. A discount rate should be calculated which is specific to the project, and which takes account of both the project's systematic risk and the company's gearing level.

5.12 A discount rate can be found using the CAPM, although the discount rate that is calculated is not exactly correct. A method that can be used is as follows.

(a) *Step 1.* Get an estimate of the systematic risk characteristics of the project's operating cash flows by obtaining published beta values for companies in the industry into which the company is planning to diversify.

(b) *Step 2.* Adjust these beta values to allow for the company's capital gearing level. This adjustment is done in two stages.

   (i) *Stage 2A.* Convert the beta values of other companies in the industry to ungeared betas, using the formula

$$\beta u = \frac{\beta g}{[(1 + \frac{D(1-t)}{V_{eg}}]}$$

   (ii) *Stage 2B.* Having obtained an ungeared beta value, convert it back to a geared beta, which reflects the company's own gearing ratio, using the formula

$$\beta_g = \beta_u \; (1 + \frac{D(1-t)}{V_{eg}})$$

(c) *Step 3.* Having estimated a project-specific geared beta, use the CAPM to estimate:

   (i) a project-specific cost of equity; and
   (ii) a project-specific cost of capital, based on a weighting of this cost of equity and the cost of the company's debt capital.

Example

5.13 A company's debt:equity ratio, by market values, is 2:5. The corporate debt, which is assumed to be risk-free, yields 11% before tax. The beta value of the company's equity is currently 1.1. The average returns on stock market equity are 16%.

The company is now proposing to invest in a project which would involve diversification into a new industry, and the following information is available about this industry.

(a) Average beta coefficient of equity capital = 1.59
(b) Average debt:equity ratio in the industry = 1:2 (by market value).

The rate of corporation tax is 33%.

What would be a suitable cost of capital to apply to the project?

Solution

5.14 Convert the geared beta value for the industry to an ungeared beta for the industry.

$$\beta_u = \frac{1.59}{1 + \frac{1(1 - 0.33)}{2}}$$

$$= 1.19$$

Convert this ungeared industry beta back into a geared beta, which reflects the company's own gearing level of 2:5.

$$\beta_g = 1.19\left[1 + \frac{2(1 - 0.33)}{5}\right]$$

$$= 1.51$$

5.15 This is a project-specific beta for the firm's equity capital, and so using the CAPM, we can estimate the project-specific cost of equity as

$$K_e = 11\% + 1.51(16\% - 11\%)$$

$$= 18.55\%$$

5.16 The project will presumably be financed in a gearing ratio of 2:5 debt to equity, and so the project-specific cost of capital ought to be

$$\left[\frac{5}{7} \times 18.55\%\right] + \left[\frac{2}{7} \times 67\% \times 11\%\right]$$

$$= 15.4\%$$

Exercise

Irwell plc is a quoted company which is financed by 10,000,000 ordinary shares and £5,000,000 of irredeemable 8% debentures. The market value of the shares is £2 each ex div, and an annual dividend of 40p per share is expected to be paid in perpetuity. The debentures are considered to be risk-free and are valued at par.

The company is wondering whether to invest in a project which would cost £2,000,000 and yield £380,000 a year before tax in perpetuity. The project has an estimated beta value of 1.25.

The return from a well-diversified market portfolio is 16%.

Required

(a) Calculate the weighted average cost of capital of the company.
(b) Calculate the beta of the company.
(c) Calculate the beta of an equivalent ungeared company.
(d) Advise the company whether or not the project should be accepted.

Ignore taxation.

Solution

(a) Cost of equity $= \frac{40p}{£2} \times 100\% = 20\%$

Cost of debt = 8%

WACC	*Market value*		*Cost*		
	£m				
Equity	20	×	0.20	=	4.0
Debt	5	×	0.08	=	0.4
	25				4.4

$$\text{WACC} = \frac{4.4}{25} = 0.176$$

(b)

$$\begin{aligned} \text{Cost of equity} &= R_f + \beta (R_m - R_f) \\ 0.20 &= 0.08 + \beta (0.16 - 0.08) \\ 0.08\beta &= 0.12 \\ \beta &= 1.5 \end{aligned}$$

(c) The value of the ungeared beta, ignoring tax, is

$$\beta_u = \frac{\beta g}{[1 + \frac{D}{V_{eg}}]} = \frac{1.5}{(1 + \frac{5}{20})}$$

$$= 1.2$$

(d) The required return from a project with a β of 1.25 is 0.08 + 1.25(0.16 - 0.08) = 0.18

The actual return from the project would be

$$\frac{380{,}000}{2{,}000{,}000} = 0.19$$

This exceeds the required yield of 18% and so the project should be undertaken.

The usefulness and the limitations of the CAPM for capital investment decisions

5.17 The CAPM produces a required return based on the expected return of the market, expected project returns, the risk-free interest rate and the variability of project returns relative to the market returns.

Its main advantage when used for investment appraisal is that it produces a discount rate which is based on the systematic risk of the individual investment. It can be used to compare projects of all different risk classes and is therefore superior to an NPV approach which uses only one discount rate for all projects, regardless of their risk.

5.18 The model was developed with respect to securities; by applying it to an investment within the firm, the company is assuming that the shareholder wishes investments to be evaluated as if they were securities in the capital market and thus assumes that all shareholders will hold diversified portfolios and will not look to the company to achieve diversification for them.

5.19 The greatest practical problems with the use of the CAPM in capital investment decisions are as follows.

(a) It is hard to estimate returns on projects under different economic environments, market returns under different economic environments and the probabilities of the various environments.

(b) The CAPM is really just a single period model. Few investment projects last for one year only and to extend the use of the return estimated from the model to more than one time period would require both project performance relative to the market and the economic environment to be reasonably stable.

In theory, it should be possible to apply the CAPM for each time period, thus arriving at successive discount rates, one for each year of the project's life. In practice, this would exacerbate the estimation problems mentioned above and also make the discounting process much more cumbersome.

(c) It may be hard to determine the risk-free rate of return. Government securities are usually taken to be risk-free, but the return on these securities varies according to their term to maturity.

6. CONCLUSION

6.1 The capital asset pricing model has many applications, as we have seen in this chapter. However, you should not think of it as the only approach to the cost of equity, or to project appraisal. You should learn the formulae, not only to be able to use them but also to be able to criticise the CAPM.

TEST YOUR KNOWLEDGE

The numbers in brackets refer to paragraphs of this chapter

1. Distinguish between systematic risk and unsystematic risk. (1.4, 1.5)

2. How would we expect the returns from an individual security (shares in an individual company) to be related to the average returns from all shares in market? (1.18)

3. The risk-free rate of return is 7%. The average market return is 11%.
   (a) What will be the return expected from a share whose β factor is 0.9?
   (b) What would be the share's expected value if it is expected to earn an annual dividend of 5.3p, with no capital growth? (See below)

4. The standard deviation of market returns is 50%, and the expected market return (R_m) is 12%. The risk-free rate of return is 9%. The covariance of returns for the market with returns on shares in Anxious plc has been 20%. Calculate a beta value and a cost of capital for Anxious plc equity. (See below)

5. Two companies are identical in every respect except for their capital structure. XY plc has a debt: equity ratio of 1:3, and its equity has a β value of 1.20. PQ plc has a debt:equity ratio of 2:3. Corporation tax is at 33%. Estimate a β value for PQ plc's equity. (See below)

6. What is the consequence of making the assumption in CAPM analysis that corporate debt is risk free, when in reality it has a (low) beta value? (4.23, 4.24)

7. What is the difference between using the CAPM and using the dividend valuation model for calculating a cost of equity and a WACC? (5.8 - 5.10)

Now try questions 13 and 14 at the end of the text

Solutions

3. (a) $7\% + 0.9\ (11\% - 7\%) = 10.6\%$

   (b) $\dfrac{5.3p}{10.6\%} = 50$ pence

4. (a) The variance of market returns is $0.50^2 = 0.25$

   $\beta = \dfrac{0.20}{0.25} = 0.8$

   (b) Cost of Anxious equity $= 9\% + 0.8\ (12 - 9)\%$
   $= 11.4\%$

5. Estimate an ungeared beta from XY plc data.

   $$\beta_u = \frac{1.20}{1 + \frac{1(0.67)}{3}} = 0.98093$$

   Estimate a geared beta for PQ plc using this ungeared beta.

   $$\beta_g = 0.98093\ [1 + \frac{2(0.67)}{3}\ ] = 1.42.$$

PART D

THE FIRM'S INVESTMENT DECISION

Chapter 11

LONG-TERM FINANCIAL PLANNING AND CORPORATE MODELS

This chapter covers the following topics.

1. Financial management decisions
2. Financial planning as part of long-term strategic planning

1. FINANCIAL MANAGEMENT DECISIONS

1.1 Maximising the wealth of shareholders generally implies maximising profits consistent with long-term stability. It is often found that short-term gains must be sacrificed in the interests of the company's long-term prospects. In the context of this overall objective, there are three main types of decisions facing financial managers.

(a) Investment decisions
(b) Financing decisions
(c) Dividend decisions.

In practice, these three areas are interconnected and should not be viewed in isolation.

Investment decisions

1.2 Investment decisions involve committing funds to:

(a) *internal investment* projects (and withdrawing from such projects should they turn out to be unprofitable);

(b) *external investment* decisions, involving the takeover of another company or a merger;

(c) *disinvestment* decisions, involving selling a part of the business, such as an unwanted subsidiary company.

Financing decisions

1.3 The assets of a company must be financed by share capital and reserves, long-term liabilities or short-term liabilities. When a company is growing, it will need additional finance from one or more of these sources.

1.4 The financial manager must know:

(a) where additional funds can be obtained and at what cost;
(b) the effect on a company's profitability and value of using any particular source of funds;
(c) the effect on financial risk of using any particular source of funds.

1.5 A company ought to be profitable, but it must be 'liquid' too, so that it always has access to enough cash to pay creditors and employees.

Financing decisions therefore include cash management.

The opportunity cost of finance

1.6 Financial management is concerned with obtaining funds for investment, and investing those funds profitably so as to maximise the value of the firm. It is not enough to invest at a profit; it is necessary to invest so that the profits are sufficient to pay lenders a satisfactory amount of interest. If a company cannot pay interest at the market rate demanded by lenders, the lenders will prefer to invest elsewhere on the capital market, where they can get this rate. There is a market 'opportunity cost' of funds which a company must expect to pay for new finance.

1.7 Similarly, if a company cannot make big enough profits, shareholders will be dissatisfied. The company will not be able to raise funds from new issues of shares, because investors will not be attracted. Existing shareholders who wish to sell their shares will find that buyers, who can invest in whatever securities they choose, will offer a comparatively low price, and the market price of the shares will be depressed. Since investors have a wide range of shares available to them, there is a market opportunity cost of equity.

Dividend decisions

1.8 Ordinary shareholders expect to earn dividends, and the value of a company's shares will be related to the amount of dividends that a company has been paying, and also to prospects of future dividends.

1.9 Dividend decisions are also directly related to financing decisions, since retained profits are the most important source of new funds for companies. What a company pays as dividends out of profits cannot be retained in the business to finance future growth, and profits retained represent a withholding of dividends.

2. FINANCIAL PLANNING AS PART OF LONG-TERM STRATEGIC PLANNING

2.1 Financial objectives will not be achieved, except by luck, unless management know what they are trying to achieve, and plan how to achieve the objectives.

2.2 Quantified targets for the achievement of financial objectives should therefore be set out in a financial plan. The financial plan should cover a number of years, perhaps three to five years, or ten years, or even longer. The financial plan should be a part of the overall strategic plan of the organisation.

The steps in the financial planning process include:

(a) producing financial forecasts on the basis of assumptions relating to demand, inflation and external factors such as the general state of the economy and the activities of the organisation's competitors;

(b) drawing up contingency plans to cover the possibility that financial targets will not be met, and taking precautionary measures against adverse changes (for example, in interest rates or exchange rates);

(c) establishing the financial requirements of the plan and arranging to secure the necessary funding from the most appropriate sources;

(d) monitoring and review of the plan against actual events.

The problems of uncertainty

2.3 The main problem with planning and forecasting, especially in the longer term, is uncertainty. Forecasts about economic events and changes in a market or an industry will be very difficult to make, and planners must accept that even the best forecasts will not be wholly accurate.

(a) A sales forecast might be for an annual growth of 10% in sales for the next five years. But how reliable are the assumptions made?

(b) Similarly, a company might forecast that on the assumption that the exchange rate of sterling against the US dollar falls by 5% next year, export sales will rise by 8%. How can exchange rate movements be forecast accurately, and so how reliable is this forecast?

2.4 (a) Managers should make forecasts based on realistic assumptions. Many large companies use the services of economic consultants to predict demand in the economy, the rate of inflation, interest rates and foreign exchange rates.

(b) Managers should be clear about what assumptions have been used in their forecasts and plans.

(c) Forecasts ought to be reviewed continually in the light of changing circumstances, and plans should be re-assessed when changes are significant.

2.5 Planners should also try to assess the consequences of forecasts being inaccurate. Three methods of assessing uncertainty are as follows.

(a) *Ask 'what if' questions.* A forecast is prepared, based on certain assumptions. The forecaster or planner can then carry out sensitivity analysis by finding the answers to questions such as:
   (i) what if sales growth is only 5% a year, not 10%?
   (ii) what if costs rise by 5% more than anticipated?
   (iii) what if the introduction of a new project is held up by 12 months?
   (iv) what if interest rates are 10% rather than 8%?
   (v) what if the rate of corporation tax is put up to 40%, or what if the VAT rate is increased to 20%?

(b) *Prepare a probability distribution of possible outcomes.* An alternative technique for assessing uncertainty is to prepare a probability distribution for the range of different possible outcomes; for example:

Annual sales growth

%	*Probability*
0	0.05
1	0.15
2	0.25
3	0.25
4	0.30

A probability distribution could be prepared for any key variable in the business plan, such as wage levels, raw material costs, productivity levels, interest rates, foreign exchange rates, sales and so on.

From the probability distributions, forecasts can be prepared of:
(i) the expected value (EV) of (for example) sales or profits;
(ii) the probability distribution of (for example) sales or profits.

(c) *Prepare pessimistic, optimistic and most likely forecasts.* A forecast can be prepared for each of three possible outcomes:
(i) the worst that might happen;
(ii) the best that might happen;
(iii) the most likely outcome.

2.6 Companies might also wish to:

(a) make *contingency plans*, for what should be done in the event that something occurs in the future that has not been allowed for in the main plan. For example, a company that exports many of its goods to an overseas country might have been warned of the possibility of import controls or exchange controls being imposed by the government of that country. The company might therefore draw up a contingency plan for what it should do if this occurs;

(b) protect itself whenever possible against adverse change, by means of *risk management*. Companies can, at a cost, protect themselves against adverse movements in interest rates or foreign exchange rates. We shall look in some detail at risk management in later chapters.

Financial planning models

2.7 A computer model can be constructed (or a computer modelling package purchased) incorporating certain variables. These variables might include:

(a) fixed assets;
(b) current assets;
(c) liabilities;
(d) revenues from the sale of different products;
(e) payments for various items of operating cost;
(f) taxation;
(g) sources of funds (equity, loans, preference shares);
(h) dividends and interest rates.

2.8 The inter-relationships between the variables will be specified in the model. For example, an increase in sales will affect the cost of sales, debtors, creditors, cash, fixed assets, profits, taxation and dividends in a way specified by the model, according to assumptions about the contribution/sales ratio, price inflation for various cost items, asset turnover ratios, taxation rates and capital allowances and dividend cover.

2.9 The model can be used to plan ahead, and the future profitability of the company can be estimated. If the company needs extra funds, the amount required can be assessed, and steps taken at an early stage to ensure that they will be available. If the model forecasts unsatisfactory profits and dividends, management will be aware that they need to devise long-term strategies now to improve results in future years.

Different types of model

2.10 A model can be:

(a) *deterministic:* each variable is given a specific value, for example sales growth will be 10% in year 1, 8% in year 2 and 6% in year 3;

(b) *stochastic or probabilistic:* some variables are given a probability distribution of different values, for example:

Sales growth in year 1		*Sales growth in year 2*		*Sales growth in year 3*	
%	*Probability*	%	*Probability*	%	*Probability*
8	0.1	7	0.1	4	0.2
9	0.2	8	0.4	5	0.3
10	0.6	9	0.3	6	0.4
11	0.1	10	0.2	7	0.1

2.11 Another type of financial planning model is an *optimising* model. This is described below.

2.12 *Uncertainty analysis* can be carried out.

(a) With deterministic models, this can be done by asking 'what if' questions. For example, in a deterministic model, the initial forecast might assume cost inflation of 3% a year for two years and 5% a year for the next three years. The future could then also be predicted on the varied assumption that costs will rise by 6% a year for five years.

(b) With stochastic models, this can be done by analysing the probability of different outcomes. For example, taking the figures in paragraph 2.10(b), it can be calculated that the expected value of sales growth is 9.7% in year 1, 8.6% in year 2 and 5.4% in year 3, but that there is an $0.1 \times 0.1 \times 0.2 = 0.002$ probability of sales growth being just 8% in year 1, 7% in year 2 and 4% in year 3.

Optimising models

2.13 It might also be possible to use a financial model to decide what plan will optimise the achievement of the organisation's financial objectives.

2.14 One type of optimising model is a linear programming model, which you should recall is a model for maximising or minimising an objective function, subject to certain constraints. In the case of financial modelling, a linear programming model might be formulated:

(a) to maximise shareholders' wealth (expressed, perhaps, as the share value);

(b) subject to certain constraints, which might be
  (i) financial (such as shortage of funds) or
  (ii) non-financial such as
    (1) resource productivity, such as maximum output per employee per year;
    (2) environmental, such as maximum consumption of raw materials;
    (3) social, such as employee welfare, for example maximum or minimum retirement age.

On-line information retrieval systems (OLIRS) or external databases

2.15 Planning and decision-making rely on accurate and complete information. Financial managers often rely on externally provided information systems as the source of much current information about other companies (which might be targets for takeover bids), certain markets (such as commodity and foreign exchange markets), share prices, or business and economic matters.

2.16 Some companies specialise in providing an external 'electronic reference library' or on-line information retrieval system to make this information available to subscribers. This is an externally supplied database. Subscribers can gain access to the supplier's information from a terminal in their office and pay a fee for access to the data.

A number of firms provide on-line information systems on commercial and tax matters, such as Datastream, Data-Star, Extel and Butterworths.

2.17 The value of an OLIRS or external database to companies arises from the need for:

(a) comprehensive data, which the company's own information systems might not be able to provide. For example information on company accounts is available through Extel's database system;

(b) rapid access to data;

(c) up-to-date data. Some information changes so quickly (for example commodity market prices, share prices, money market interest rates and foreign exchange rates) that companies are unable to keep fully up-to-date information systems themselves, and so rely on a specialised OLIRS to do this for them.

3. CONCLUSION

3.1 In this chapter, we have set out the types of decision a financial manager has to make, in seeking to attain the company's financial objectives. We have also considered the main problem facing business decision makers, uncertainty, and possible responses to it.

TEST YOUR KNOWLEDGE

The numbers in brackets refer to paragraphs of this chapter

1. Investment decisions can be grouped into three categories. What are they? (1.2)
2. What does 'the opportunity cost of finance' mean? (1.6, 1.7)
3. What is corporate modelling? (2.7 - 2.9)
4. Give examples of external databases that a financial manager might use. (2.16)

Now try question 15 at the end of the text

Chapter 12

CAPITAL EXPENDITURE DECISIONS

This chapter covers the following topics.

1. Methods of investment appraisal
2. The accounting rate of return (ARR) method
3. The payback method
4. Discounted cash flow (DCF) methods
5. The net present value (NPV) method
6. The internal rate of return (IRR) method
7. The NPV and the IRR methods compared

1. METHODS OF INVESTMENT APPRAISAL

1.1 Having obtained capital from investors, how should management set about the task of investing the capital in its operations so as to:

(a) provide an adequate return for investors;

(b) achieve the company's financial objective of maximising the wealth of its shareholders?

1.2 Proposed investments should be properly appraised, and found to be worthwhile, before a decision is taken to go ahead.

1.3 The principal methods of evaluating capital projects are:

(a) the return on investment method, or accounting rate of return method;
(b) the payback method;
(c) discounted cash flow (DCF):
  (i) the net present value method (NPV);
  (ii) the internal rate of return method (IRR).

Of these, DCF is by far the most important, although (a) and (b) are often used by small and medium-sized firms.

1.4 When stating the cash flows associated with a project, you should refer to now as 'year 0', the time one year in the future as 'year 1' and so on.

2. THE ACCOUNTING RATE OF RETURN (ARR) METHOD

2.1 A capital investment project may be assessed by calculating the return on investment (ROI) or accounting rate of return (ARR) and comparing it with a pre-determined target level. Unfortunately, there are several different definitions of the ARR. One of the most popular is:

$$\text{ARR} = \frac{\text{Estimated average profits}}{\text{Estimated average investment}} \times 100\%$$

Others are:

$$\text{ARR} = \frac{\text{Estimated total profits}}{\text{Estimated initial investment}} \times 100\%$$

$$\text{ARR} = \frac{\text{Estimated average profits}}{\text{Estimated initial investment}} \times 100\%$$

2.2 There are various arguments in favour of each of definitions above. The important thing is that the method selected should be used consistently. For examination purposes we recommend the first definition unless the question clearly indicates that some other one is to be used.

2.3 The accounting rate of return method of appraising a capital project is to estimate the accounting rate of return that the project will yield. If it exceeds a target rate of return, the project should be undertaken.

Example

2.4 A company has a target accounting rate of return of 20% (using the first definition in Paragraph 2.1), and is now considering the following project.

Capital cost of asset	£80,000
Estimated life	4 years

Estimated profit before depreciation

	£
Year 1	20,000
Year 2	25,000
Year 3	35,000
Year 4	25,000

The capital asset would be depreciated by 25% of its cost each year, and would have no residual value.

Should the project be undertaken?

Solution

2.5 The annual profits after depreciation, and the mid-year net book value of the asset, would be as follows.

Year	*Profit after depreciation* £	*Mid-year net book value* £	*ARR in the year*
1	0	70,000	0
2	5,000	50,000	10%
3	15,000	30,000	50%
4	5,000	10,000	50%

2.6 As the table shows, the ARR is low in the early stages of the project, partly because of low profits in Year 1 but mainly because the net book value of the asset is much higher early on in its life.

2.7 The project does not achieve the target ARR of 20% in its first two years, but exceeds it in years 3 and 4. So should it be undertaken?

2.8 When the accounting rate of return from a project varies from year to year, it makes sense to take an overall view of the project's return. In this case, we should look at the return as a whole over the four year period.

		£
Total profit before depreciation over four years		105,000
Total profit after depreciation over four years		25,000
Average annual profit after depreciation		6,250
Original cost of investment		80,000
Average net book value over the four year period	$\frac{80,000 + 0}{2}$	40,000

2.9 $$\text{ARR} = \frac{\text{Average annual profit}}{\text{Average net book value}} = \frac{£\ 6,250}{£40,000} = 15.63\%$$

So the project should not be undertaken because it would fail to yield the target return of 20%.

The comparison of mutually exclusive projects

2.10 The ARR method of capital investment appraisal can also be used to compare two or more projects which are mutually exclusive, that is, only one of them can be undertaken. The project with the highest ARR should be selected (provided that its expected ARR is higher than the company's target ARR).

The drawbacks of the ARR method

2.11 The ARR method of capital investment appraisal has the serious drawback that it does not take account of the *timing* of the profits from an investment.

2.12 Whenever capital is invested in a project, money is tied up until the project begins to earn profits which pay back the investment. Money tied up in one project cannot be invested anywhere else until the profits are realised. Management should be aware of the benefits of early repayments from an investment, which will provide money for other investments.

3. THE PAYBACK METHOD

3.1 The payback method evaluates projects by considering how long a project would take to pay back the initial investment made in it. This is the *payback period*.

3.2 Study the returns shown below for two mutually exclusive projects, A and B.

	Project A	*Project B*
	£	£
Cost	50,000	50,000
Residual value after five years	nil	nil
Profits before depreciation		
Year 1	10,000	40,000
Year 2	15,000	30,000
Year 3	20,000	10,000
Year 4	25,000	5,000
Year 5	30,000	5,000

3.3 The ARR of each project, measured as average annual profit after depreciation as a percentage of the average investment, would be as follows.

(a) Project A $\frac{10,000}{25,000} = 40\%$

(b) Project B $\frac{8,000}{25,000} = 32\%$

3.4 Using ARR to select the preferred investment, project A would be selected.

But the profits from project A, ignoring depreciation, would not repay the initial investment of £50,000 until year 4. By the end of the third year, it would have paid back £45,000 and so it would be about a fifth of the way through the fourth year that the investment would be paid back. This is the payback period.

In contrast, project B pays back the original investment about a third of the way through the second year.

3.5 So although project A has the higher ARR, project B pays back more quickly. If the company:

(a) has a cash shortage, and/or
(b) has other investments which it would undertake if it had the money,

then the company's management might decide to choose project B instead of project A, because of its quicker payback.

3.6 You should note that when payback is calculated, we take profit *before* depreciation, because we wish to estimate the cash returns from a project, and depreciation is not a cash outflow.

Setting a target payback period

3.7 Payback is often used as a first screening method. A company might have a target payback period, and it would reject a capital project unless its payback period is less than a certain number of years, perhaps five years.

Why is payback alone an inadequate investment appraisal technique?

3.8 Payback should not be used on its own to evaluate capital investments because projects with short payback periods might make much smaller profits overall than other projects which have longer payback periods but which make high profits at the end of their lives.

4. DISCOUNTED CASH FLOW (DCF) METHODS

4.1 The ARR method of project evaluation ignores the timing of cash flows and the opportunity cost of capital tied up. Payback considers the time it takes to recover the original investment cost, but ignores total profits over a project's life.

Discounted cash flow, or DCF for short, is an investment appraisal technique which takes into account both the time value of money and also total profitability over a project's life. DCF is therefore superior to both ARR and payback as a method of investment appraisal.

4.2 Two important points about DCF are as follows.

(a) DCF looks at the *cash flows* of a project, not the accounting profits. Cash flows are considered because they show the costs and benefits of a project when they occur. For example, the capital cost of a project will be the original cash outlay, and not the depreciation charge which is used to spread the capital cost over the asset's life in the financial accounts.

(b) The timing of cash flows is taken into account by discounting them. The effect of discounting is to give a bigger weighting to cash flows that occur earlier: £1 earned after one year will be worth more than £1 earned after two years, which in turn will be worth more than £1 earned after five years. This is the concept of the *time value of money*.

4.3 Various reasons could be suggested as to why £1 now is worth more than £1 in the future.

(a) *Uncertainty*. The business world is full of risk. It can never be certain that money will be received until it arrives.

This is an important argument, and uncertainty must always be considered in investment appraisal. But this argument does *not* explain why the discounted cash flow technique should be used to reflect the time value of money. Other techniques can be used to allow for uncertainty and these are discussed in Chapter 13.

(b) *Inflation.* Inflation clearly means that £1 now is worth more than £1 in the future. However, even if there were no inflation at all, discounted cash flow techniques would still be used for investment appraisal. It is of course necessary to allow for inflation, and this is considered in Chapter 14.

(c) An individual attaches more weight to current pleasures than to future ones, and would rather have £1 to spend now than £1 in a year's time. One reason suggested to justify the use of the discounted cash flow technique is this 'subjective time preference' of individuals who have the choice of consuming or investing their wealth. The return from investments must be sufficient to persuade individuals to invest now. Discounting is a measure of this time preference.

Discounting

4.4 Discounting is compounding in reverse.

Suppose that a company has £10,000 to invest. If it could be invested at 10% compound, the value of the investment with interest would build up as follows.

(a) After one year	£10,000 × 1.10	=	£11,000
(b) After two years	£10,000 × 1.10^2	=	£12,100
(c) After three years	£10,000 × 1.10^3	=	£13,310

and so on.

4.5 This is compounding. The formula for the future value of an investment plus accumulated interest after n time periods is

$$FV = PV\ (1 + r)^n$$

where FV is the future value of the investment with interest
PV is the present value of the investment
r is the compound rate of return per time period, expressed as a proportion (so 10% = 0.10, 5% = 0.05 and so on)
n is the number of time periods.

4.6 *Discounting* starts with the future value, and converts a future value to a present value. For example, if a company expects to earn a compound rate of return of 10% on its investments, how much would it need to invest now to have an investment of:

(a) £11,000 after 1 year?
(b) £12,100 after 2 years?
(c) £13,310 after 3 years?

4.7 The answer is £10,000 in each case, and we can calculate it by discounting, as follows.

(a) $£11,000 \times \frac{1}{1.10} = £10,000$

(b) $£12,100 \times \frac{1}{1.10^2} = £10,000$

(c) $£13,310 \times \frac{1}{1.10^3} = £10,000$

4.8 The discounting formula to calculate the present value of a future sum of money at the end of n time periods is

$$PV = FV \frac{1}{(1 + r)^n}$$

where the symbols have the same meanings as in Paragraph 4.5.

4.9 Discounting can be applied to both money receivable and money payable. By discounting all payments and receipts from a capital investment to their present values, we can compare them on a common basis at values which take account of when the various cash flows will take place.

Example

4.10 Spender Ltd expects the cash inflow from an investment to be £40,000 after two years and another £30,000 after three years. Its target rate of return is 12%.

(a) What is the present value of these future returns?

(b) What does this present value signify?

Solution

4.11

Year	*Cash flow*	*Discount factor at 12%*	*Present value*
	£		£
2	40,000	$\frac{1}{1.12^2} = 0.797$	31,880
3	30,000	$\frac{1}{1.12^3} = 0.712$	21,360
		Total PV	53,240

The present value of the future returns, discounted at 12%, is £53,240. This means that if Spender Ltd can invest now to earn a return of 12% on its investments, it would have to invest £53,240 now to earn £40,000 after two years plus £30,000 after three years.

Relevant cash flows

4.12 The cash flows to consider when making decisions are only those that are directly relevant to the decision under consideration.

4.13 A relevant cost is a future cash flow arising as a consequence of a decision. It follows that:

(a) any costs incurred in the past; and

(b) any committed costs which will be incurred regardless of whether or not an investment is undertaken;

are not relevant cash flows because they have occurred, or will occur whatever investment decision is taken.

4.14 Here is a reminder of some examples of relevant costs.

(a) Materials, if they have already been purchased, have a relevant cost which is the higher of

(i) their net scrap value or disposal value;
(ii) the cash profits they would earn in their next most profitable use.

Their actual cost is irrelevant, because the cost has been incurred in the past, and only future cash flows are relevant.

(b) Overhead costs should be dealt with carefully.

(i) Only cash expenditures are relevant, and so overhead items such as depreciation and notional rent should be ignored.

(ii) In a system of absorption costing, the fixed overhead absorption rate is always irrelevant, because it has nothing to do with cash flows. (The variable overhead absorption rate is likely to be relevant, in contrast, but only because the absorption rate is designed to match the rate of expenditure on variable overhead items as output increases.)

Example

4.15 Mown Down plc is wondering whether to invest £700,000 in manufacturing operations abroad, which are assumed at the moment to have a four year life.

Annual sales and costs would be as follows.

	£'000	£'000
Sales		950
Materials	250	
Labour	150	
Overheads	250	
Head office charge	50	
Depreciation	150	
		850
Annual profit		100

The residual value of the investment at the end of four years would be £100,000.

(a) Labour and overheads represent incremental cash cost items, payable in the year to which they relate.

(b) The head office charge is an apportionment of Mown Down plc's head office administrative costs.

If the investment goes ahead, Mown Down plc would lose some of its overseas sales to the country in which the subsidiary will operate. The estimated annual loss of sales is 1,000 units, and the price and cost per unit are as follows.

	£	£
Price		100
Variable costs	60	
Overhead absorbed	20	
		80
Profit		20

Included in variable costs is £20 for Material A, which is currently in short supply. The quantity not used by Mown Down plc to make 1,000 units of the exported product could be used to make 1,000 units of another product that earns a contribution of £10 per unit. This material is expected to be in short supply for years 1 and 2 only.

Identify the relevant cash flows to be used in appraising the project.

Solution

4.16 The following costs are not relevant.

(a) The head office charge.

(b) Depreciation.

(c) Absorbed overheads of the product made in the UK by Mown Down plc.

The relevant costs of the lost export sales are as follows.

	Years 1 and 2	*Years 3 and 4*
	£	£
Lost contribution: £(100-60) = £40 per unit	40,000	40,000
Less contribution that could be earned by using the materials elsewhere* (£10 per unit)	10,000	0
Annual loss of contribution	30,000	40,000

* Only relevant in years 1 and 2, when the material is in short supply.

4.17 The cash flows relevant to an appraisal of the project are as follows.

Year	*Capital* £	*Cash flows from profits abroad*** £	*Loss of contribution from exports* £	*Net cash flow* £
0	(700,000)			(700,000)
1		300,000	(30,000)	270,000
2		300,000	(30,000)	270,000
3		300,000	(40,000)	260,000
4	100,000	300,000	(40,000)	360,000

**(In £'000) 950 - 250 - 150 - 250 = 300.

The two methods of using DCF

4.18 The two methods of using DCF to evaluate capital investments are:
(a) the net present value (NPV) method;
(b) the internal rate of return (IRR) method.

5. THE NET PRESENT VALUE (NPV) METHOD

5.1 The net present value (NPV) of a project is the value obtained by discounting all cash outflows and inflows at a chosen target rate of return or 'cost of capital', and taking the net total (inflows minus outflows).

5.2 (a) *If the NPV is positive*, then the cash inflows from the investment will yield a return in excess of the cost of capital, and so the project should be undertaken.

(b) *If the NPV is negative*, then the cash inflows from the investment will yield a return below the cost of capital, and so the project should not be undertaken.

(c) *If the NPV is exactly zero*, then the cash inflows from the investment will yield a return which is exactly the same as the cost of capital, so the company should be indifferent between undertaking and not undertaking the project.

Example

5.3 Slogger Ltd is considering a capital investment, where the estimated cash flows are as follows.

Year	*Cash flow* £
0	(100,000)
1	60,000
2	80,000
3	40,000
4	30,000

The company's cost of capital is 15%.
What is the NPV of the project, and should it be undertaken?

Solution

5.4

Year	*Cash flow*	*Discount factor*	*Present value*
	£	15%	£
0	(100,000)	1.000	(100,000)
1	60,000	$\frac{1}{(1.15)} = 0.870$	52,200
2	80,000	$\frac{1}{(1.15)^2} = 0.756$	60,480
3	40,000	$\frac{1}{(1.15)^3} = 0.658$	26,320
4	30,000	$\frac{1}{(1.15)^4} = 0.572$	17,160
		NPV =	56,160

Note that the discount factor for any cash flow now, that is, at year 0, is always 1.0, regardless of what the cost of capital is.

The PV of cash inflows exceeds the PV of cash outflows by £56,160, which means that the project has a yield in excess of 15%. It should therefore be undertaken.

Discount tables for the present value of £1

5.5 The discount factor that we use in discounting is $\frac{1}{(1+r)^n} = (1+r)^{-n}$

Instead of having to calculate this factor every time we can use tables.

Discount tables for the present value of £1, for different values of r and n, are shown at the start of this text. Discount tables to three decimal places will be available to you in your examination.

Exercise

LCH Ltd manufactures product X which it sells for £5 a unit. Variable costs of production are currently £3 a unit, and fixed costs 50p a unit. A new machine is available which would cost £90,000 but which could be used to make product X for a variable cost of only £2.50 a unit. Fixed costs, however, would increase by £7,500 a year as a direct result of purchasing the machine. The machine would have an expected life of four years and a resale value after that time of £10,000. Sales of product X are 75,000 units a year. If LCH Ltd expects to earn at least 12% from its investments, should the machine be purchased?

Assume that all cash flows spread over a year take place at the end of the year. Ignore taxation.

Solution

Savings are 75,000 × (£3 - £2.50) = £37,500 a year.
Additional costs are £7,500 a year.
Net cash savings are therefore £30,000 a year.

All future cash flows arising as a direct consequence of the decision should be taken into account. It is assumed that the machine will be sold for £10,000 at year 4.

Year	*Cash flow*	*PV factor*	*PV of cash flow*
	£	12%	£
0	(90,000)	1.000	(90,000)
1	30,000	0.893	26,790
2	30,000	0.797	23,910
3	30,000	0.712	21,360
4	40,000	0.636	25,440
		Net present value	+ 7,500

The NPV is positive and so the project is acceptable.

The timing of cash flows

5.6 To use discounting, we must attach precise times to cash flows. The following guidelines may be applied.

(a) A cash outlay to be incurred at the beginning of an investment project occurs in year 0. The present value of £1 now, in year 0 is

$$\frac{1}{(1 + r)^0} = £1$$

regardless of the value of r (the cost of capital).

(b) A cash outlay, saving or inflow which occurs during the course of a year is assumed to occur all at once at the end of the year. Therefore receipts of £10,000 spread over the first year are taking to occur 'at year 1', the time one year from now.

(c) A cash outlay, saving or inflow which occurs at the beginning of a year is taken to occur at the end of the previous year. Therefore a cash outlay of £5,000 at the beginning of the second year is taken to occur at the end of the first year, that is, 'at year 1'.

Annuity tables

5.7 In the last exercise, the calculations could have been simplified for years 1 to 3 as follows.

$$\begin{aligned} & 300 \times 0.893 \\ + & 300 \times 0.797 \\ + & 300 \times 0.712 \\ = & 300 \times 2.402 \end{aligned}$$

5.8 Where there is a constant cash flow for several years (in this case £30,000 a year for years 1 to 3) we can calculate the present value by adding together the discount factors for the individual years. These total factors are 'cumulative present value' factors or 'annuity' factors. They are shown in the table of cumulative present value factors at the start of this text. You will be given a table like this in your examination. (2.402, for example, is in the column for 12% and the year 3 row).

The formula which yields the cumulative present value factors is

$$\frac{1}{r}\left[1 - \frac{1}{(1+r)^n}\right]$$

where r is the discount rate as a proportion
n is the number of years.

Exercise

(a) What is the present value of £1,000 earned each year from years 1 to 10, when the required return on investment is 11%?

(b) What is the present value of £100 earned each year from years 3 to 6 when the cost of capital is 5%?

Solution

(a) The PV of £1,000 earned each year from year 1 to year 10 at 11% is £1,000 × 5.889 = £5,889.

(b) The PV of £100 earned each year from year 3 to year 6 at 5% is as follows.

PV of £1 a year for years 1 to 6	=	5.076
Less PV of £1 a year for years 1 to 2	=	1.859
PV of £1 a year for years 3 to 6	=	3.217

£100 × 3.217 = £321.7, say £322

Exercise

The Woodstock Skyscraper Company takes on a three year lease of a building for which it pays £20,000 as a lump sum payment. It then sub-lets the building to Linus for the three years at a fixed annual rent. If the Woodstock Skyscraper Company expects to earn at least 16% a year from its investments, what should the annual rent be?

Solution

As the rent is fixed for three years, there will be a constant cash flow from year to year.

Let the annual rent be £R.

£R × (PV of £1 a year for three years at 16%) = PV of rental income

The present value of rental income over the three year period must be at least £20,000.

The annuity factor for £1 at 16% for years 1 to 3 is 2.246.

$$R \times 2.246 = 20{,}000$$

$$R = \frac{20{,}000}{2.246} = £8{,}905$$

The annual rent should be £8,905 for the company to earn 16% on its investment of £20,000.

5.9 Here is another example which includes both the identification of relevant costs and the use of annuity tables.

Example

5.10 Elsie Ltd is considering the manufacture of a new product which would involve the use of both a new machine (costing £150,000) and an existing machine, which cost £80,000 two years ago and has a current net book value of £60,000. There is sufficient capacity on this machine, which has so far been under-used.

Annual sales of the product would be 5,000 units at a selling price of £32 a unit. Unit costs would be as follows.

	£
Direct labour (4 hours at £2 an hour)	8
Direct materials	7
Fixed costs including depreciation	9
	24

The project would have a five year life, after which the new machine would have a net residual value of £10,000. Because direct labour is in short supply, labour resources would have to be diverted from other work which currently earns a contribution of £1.50 per direct labour hour. The fixed overhead absorption rate would be £2.25 an hour (£9 a unit) but actual expenditure on fixed overheads would not alter.

Working capital requirements would be £10,000 in the first year, rising to £15,000 in the second year and remaining at this level until the end of the project, when all working capital would be recovered.

The company's cost of capital is 20%. Ignore taxation.

Is the project worthwhile?

Solution

5.11 The relevant cash flows are as follows.

(a)	Year 0	Purchase of new machine	£150,000
			£
(b)	Years 1 to 5	Contribution from new product 5,000 units × £(32 - 15)	85,000
		Less contribution forgone 5,000 × (4 × £1.50)	30,000
			55,000

(c) The project requires £10,000 of working capital at the start of the first year and a further £5,000 at the start of the second year.

Increases in working capital reduce the net cash flow for the period to which they relate. When the working capital tied up in the project is recovered at the end of the project, it will provide an extra cash inflow.

(d) All other costs, which are past costs, notional accounting costs, or costs which would be incurred anyway, are irrelevant to the investment decision.

The NPV is calculated as follows

Year	*Equipment* £	*Working capital* £	*Contribution* £	*Net cash flow* £	*Discount factor* 20%	*PV of net cash flow* £
0	(150,000)	(10,000)		(160,000)	1.000	(160,000)
1		(5,000)		(5,000)	0.833	(4,165)
1-5			55,000	55,000	2.991	164,505
5	10,000	15,000		25,000	0.402	10,050
					NPV =	10,390

The NPV is positive and the project is worthwhile, although there is not much margin for error. Some risk analysis of the project is recommended.

Annual cash flows in perpetuity

5.12 You need to know how to calculate the cumulative present value of £1 a year for ever.

When the cost of capital is r, the cumulative PV of £1 a year in perpetuity (starting one year from now) is £1/r.

Example

5.13 A company with a cost of capital of 14% is considering an investment in a project costing £500,000 that would yield cash inflows of £100,000 a year in perpetuity. Should the project be undertaken?

Solution

5.14

Year	Cash flow	Discount factor	Present value
	£	14%	£
0	(500,000)	1.0	(500,000)
1 - ∞	100,000	1/0.14 = 7.14	714,000
		Net present value	214,000

The NPV is positive and so the project should be undertaken.

6. THE INTERNAL RATE OF RETURN (IRR) METHOD

6.1 By the NPV method of discounted cash flow, present values are calculated by discounting at a target rate of return, or cost of capital, and the difference between the present value of costs and the present value of benefits is the NPV.

In contrast, the internal rate of return method is to calculate the rate of return which the project is expected to achieve, that is, the rate at which the NPV is zero.

If the expected rate of return exceeds the target rate of return, the project should be undertaken.

6.2 The internal rate of return (IRR) is found approximately using interpolation. The result is usually fairly accurate, and the method is much quicker than finding the IRR exactly.

6.3 The interpolation method requires you to calculate two net present values, using rates for the cost of capital which are likely to give NPV's close to zero. As a rough guide, try starting at a return figure which is two thirds of the accounting rate of return (using the first formula in Paragraph 2.1).

Example

6.4 A company is trying to decide whether to buy a machine for £80,000 which will save costs of £20,000 a year for five years and which will have a resale value of £10,000 at the end of that period. What is the IRR of the project?

Solution

6.5 The ARR would be $\frac{20{,}000 - \text{depreciation of } 14{,}000}{\frac{1}{2} \text{ of } (80{,}000 + 10{,}000)} = \frac{6{,}000}{45{,}000} = 13.3\%$

Two thirds of this is 8.9% and so we can start by trying 9%.

Year	Cash flow	PV factor	PV of cash flow
	£	9%	£
0	(80,000)	1.000	(80,000)
1-5	20,000	3.890	77,800
5	10,000	0.650	6,500
			4,300

6.6 The NPV is positive, which means that the IRR is more than 9%. We will try 12%.

Year	*Cash flow*	*PV factor*	*PV of cash flow*
	£	12%	£
0	(80,000)	1.000	(80,000)
1-5	20,000	3.605	72,100
5	10,000	0.567	5,670
			(2,230)

This is negative. The IRR is therefore greater than 9% (NPV = +4,300) but less than 12% (NPV = -2,230).

6.7 The interpolation method uses the formula

$$IRR \simeq A + \left[\frac{a}{a-b} \times (B-A)\right]$$

where A is one discount rate
B is the other discount rate
a is the NPV at rate A
b is the NPV at rate B

This formula works even if a and b are a long way from zero, or if both are positive or both are negative, but it gives the best approximations when one is positive and one negative, and both are close to zero.

6.8 We therefore have the following estimate for the IRR.

$$IRR = 9\% + \left[\frac{4,300}{4,300 - -2,230} \times (12 - 9)\right]\% = 10.98\%, \text{ say } 11\%$$

This is only an approximation. The NPV at 10.98% is in fact -£105. The true IRR is 10.93%.

7. THE NPV AND THE IRR METHODS COMPARED

7.1 Because the NPV and IRR methods are both discounted cash flow techniques there is a relationship between them. This relationship can be shown on a graph where the y axis represents the NPV and the x axis shows the discount rate. The graph shows how the NPV varies with the discount rate.

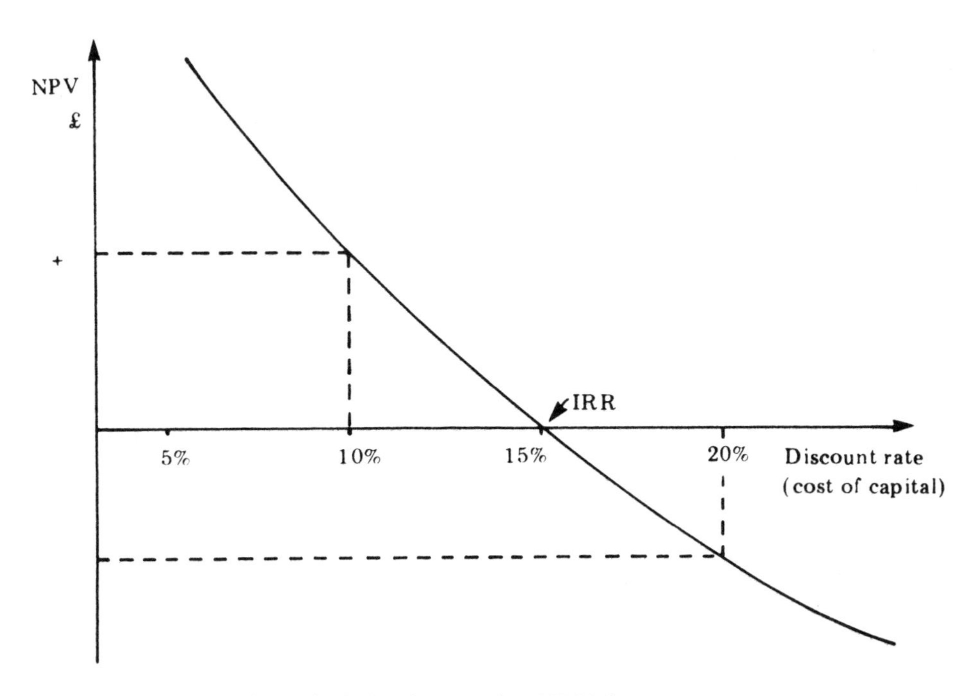

The higher the cost of capital the lower the NPV becomes.

(a) Using a discount rate of 10%, the NPV is positive.
(b) Using a discount rate of 20%, the NPV is negative.
(c) Using a discount rate of 15%, the NPV is zero, so 15% is the internal rate of return.

7.2 If the investment decision were based on whether the project earns at least 10%, it would be:

(a) accepted, using the NPV method, because the NPV at 10% is positive;
(b) accepted, using the IRR method, because the IRR exceeds 10%.

The two methods will give the same decisions for individual projects: if a project is acceptable using the NPV criterion, it will also be acceptable using the IRR criterion.

7.3 However, this does not mean that there is nothing to choose between the two methods.

7.4 The main advantage of the IRR method is that the information it provides is more easily understood by managers, especially non-financial managers.

For example, it is fairly easy to understand the meaning of the following.

> 'The project is expected to earn a yield of 25%, and have an initial capital outlay of £100,000. The yield is in excess of the target yield of 15% for investments.'

It is not so easy to understand the meaning of the following.

> 'The project will cost £100,000 and will have an NPV of £30,000 when discounted at the minimum required rate of 15%.'

This may explain why the IRR method is very widely used by venture capitalists to appraise investments.

7.5 In other respects, however, the IRR method has serious disadvantages.

(a) It might be tempting to confuse IRR and accounting return. The ARR and the IRR are two completely different measures. If managers were given information about both ARR and IRR, it might be easy to confuse the two.

(b) The IRR method ignores the relative sizes of investments.

Both the following projects have an IRR of 18%.

	Project A	*Project B*
	£	£
Cost, year 0	350,000	35,000
Annual savings, years 1 to 6	100,000	10,000

Project A is bigger and so more profitable but if the only information on which the projects were judged were to be their IRR of 18%, project B would seem just as beneficial as project A, which is not the case.

(c) The IRR method should not be used to select between mutually exclusive projects.

This follows on from point (b) and it is the most significant criticism of the IRR method.

Mutually exclusive projects

7.6 When there are two or more projects and only one project can be chosen from amongst them, the project with the highest NPV should be chosen. The reason for this will be explained with an example.

Example

7.7 A company is considering two mutually exclusive options, option A and option B. The cash flows for each would be as follows.

Year		*Option A*	*Option B*
		£	£
0	Capital outlay	(10,200)	(35,250)
1	Net cash inflow	6,000	18,000
2	Net cash inflow	5,000	15,000
3	Net cash inflow	3,000	15,000

The company's cost of capital is 16%.

7.8 The NPV of each project is calculated as follows.

		Option A		*Option B*	
Year	*Discount factor*	*Cash flow*	*Present value*	*Cash flow*	*Present value*
	16%	£	£	£	£
0	1.000	(10,200)	(10,200)	(35,250)	(35,250)
1	0.862	6,000	5,172	18,000	15,516
2	0.743	5,000	3,715	15,000	11,145
3	0.641	3,000	1,923	15,000	9,615
		NPV =	+610	NPV =	+1,026

However, the IRR of option A is 20%, and the IRR of option B is only 18%.

7.9 Using NPVs, option B would be preferred, but using IRRs, option A would be preferred.

7.10 Option B is better. This is because the differences in the cash flows between the two options, when discounted at the cost of capital of 16%, show that the present value of the incremental benefits from option B compared with option A exceed the present value of the incremental costs.

This can be re-stated in either of the following ways.

(a) The NPV of the differential cash flows is positive, and so it is worth spending the extra capital to get the extra benefits.

(b) The IRR of the differential cash flows exceeds the cost of capital of 16%, and so it is worth spending the extra capital to get the extra benefits.

7.11

Year	*Option A cash flow*	*Option B cash flow*	*Difference*	*Discount factor 16%*	*Present value of difference*
	£	£	£		£
0	(10,200)	(35,250)	(25,050)	1.000	(25,050)
1	6,000	18,000	12,000	0.862	10,344
2	5,000	15,000	10,000	0.743	7,430
3	3,000	15,000	12,000	0.641	7,692
				NPV of difference	416

The NPV of the difference, of course is the difference between the NPV of option A (£610) and the NPV of option B (£1,026).

The IRR of the differential cash flows is a little over 18%.

Mutually exclusive projects with unequal lives

7.12 The same conflict between the IRR and NPV methods can arise when a comparison has to be made between mutually exclusive projects with unequal lives. The preference for the NPV method is unchanged, for the same reasons as before.

8. CONCLUSION

8.1 This chapter has covered the mathematics of investment appraisal in detail. While it is of course important to practise calculations, do not neglect the pros and cons of the different methods, and the concept of the time value of money.

8.2 The objective of a company should be to maximise the wealth of its shareholders. The fundamental theory of share values is based on DCF principles. This theory states that the value of a company is the present value of all its expected future dividend payments to shareholders, and since dividend payments come from cash profits, the value of a company is the present value of all its future expected cash profits. A new investment with an expected NPV that is positive should add to the company's value by the amount of the NPV.

TEST YOUR KNOWLEDGE

The numbers in brackets refer to paragraphs of this chapter

1. Give a formula for the accounting rate of return. (2.1)
2. What is a project's payback period? (3.1)
3. Why is £1 now worth more than £1 at a later time? (4.3)
4. A cost of £20,000 is expected to occur near the beginning of the third year. To what year should the £20,000 be allocated in DCF analysis? (5.6)
5. The annuity factor at 9% for years 1 to 5 is 3.890. For years 1 to 6 is 4.486 and for years 1 to 8 it is 5.535. What is the PV of £10,000 a year for years 6 to 8? (See below)
6. A seven year project will need working capital of £50,000 from the start of the first year. What should the cash flows be in a DCF analysis, to allow for the effects of increases or decreases in working capital on cash flows? (See below)
7. What is the PV of £9,000 a year in perpetuity, discounted at a cost of capital of 12%? (See below)
8. What are the disadvantages of the IRR method as compared to the NPV method? (7.5)

Now try question 16 at the end of the text

Solutions

5. Years 6 to 8 = years 1 to 8 minus years 1 to 5. (5.535 - 3.890) × £10,000 = £16,450.

6. Year 0 -£50,000. Year 7 + £50,000

7. $\dfrac{£9,000}{0.12} = £75,000$

Chapter 13

THE TREATMENT OF RISK

> **This chapter covers the following topics.**
>
> 1. Business risk
> 2. Methods of treating risk

1. BUSINESS RISK

1.1 Risk as described here is the *business risk* of an investment. This is in contrast to financial risk which is the risk that a geared company may not make enough profit, after paying the interest on its borrowings, to finance a satisfactory dividend.

Business risk can be defined as the potential volatility of profits caused by the nature and type of business operations involved.

1.2 There are three elements in business risk.

(a) *The inherent risk of the industry or market itself.* For example, the fashion industry is a higher risk industry than the food processing industry; and to a UK firm, export markets in the Third World are likely to be higher risk markets than the UK market.

(b) *The stage in the product's life cycle.* Every product has a life cycle, and the 'classical' product life cycle consists of four stages.
(i) Introduction
(ii) Growth
(iii) Maturity
(iv) Decline.

When an investment is made in a product which is in its introductory phase, there is a high risk that it will fail to win market acceptance, and will have a very short market life. When an investment is made in a declining product, the risk of a rapid decline in sales is high.

(c) *The proportion of fixed costs in total costs.* When an investment involves a high proportion of fixed costs, it will need to achieve a high sales volume just to break even, and so the business risk will be high.

1.3 In this chapter, we will consider how to allow for business risk when appraising projects. Another topic, the reduction of overall risk by building up a diverse portfolio of investments, was covered in Chapter 9 above.

2. METHODS OF TREATING RISK

2.1 The methods of treating risk when appraising capital expenditure projects include the following.

(a) Adjusting the discount rate to allow a premium on the cost of capital for risk.
(b) Expecting projects to pay back, or achieve a positive net present value within a certain time limit.
(c) Sensitivity analysis.
(d) Using probability estimates of cash flows.
(e) Simulation modelling.

Adjusting the discount rate

2.2 In this method of allowing for risk, a premium is added to the discount rate as a safety margin. Marginally profitable projects are then less likely to have a positive NPV.

For example, if a company's true cost of capital is 10%, all capital projects might be evaluated using a discount rate of 15%. Projects which would have a positive NPV at a discount rate of 10% but a negative NPV at 15% would then be considered too risky to undertake.

2.3 This method recognises that risky investments ought to earn a higher return as reward for the risks that are taken. However, if the same increased discount rate is applied to all the proposed capital projects, no distinction would be made between more risky and less risky investments. And how is the size of the risk premium decided anyway?

Applying a time limit to the payback period

2.4 Estimates of future cash flows are difficult to make at the best of times, and estimates of cash flows several years ahead are quite likely to be inaccurate. It is also difficult to control capital projects over a long period, to ensure that the expected benefits are fully realised.

2.5 A method of limiting the risk on a capital project is to apply a payback time limit, so that a project should not be undertaken unless it pays back within, say, four years.

2.6 There are two ways of applying a payback time limit.

(a) A project might be expected to pay back within a certain time limit, and in addition show a positive NPV from its net cash flows.

(b) Alternatively, a project might be expected to pay back *in discounted cash flow terms* within a certain time period. For example, a project might be required to have a positive NPV on its cumulative cash flows by year 4.

Example

2.7 A company plans to spend £700,000 now on a project that is expected to last for 15 years. The annual cash benefits are expected to be £150,000. The target DCF rate of return is 12%. In addition, the company requires all capital projects to have achieved payback in DCF terms by the year 5. Should the project be undertaken?

Solution

2.8 The NPV of the project over a 15 year period is positive.

Year	*Cash flow*	*Discount factor* 12%	*Present* value
	£		£
0	(700,000)	1.00	(700,000)
1-15	150,000	6.81	1,021,650
			321,650

2.9 However, the project does not pay back in DCF terms by year 5.

Year	*Cash flow*	*Discount factor*	*Present value*	*Cumulative NPV*
	£	12%	£	£
0	(700,000)	1.000	(700,000)	(700,000)
1	150,000	0.893	133,950	(566,050)
2	150,000	0.797	119,550	(446,500)
3	150,000	0.712	106,800	(339,700)
4	150,000	0.636	95,400	(244,300)
5	150,000	0.567	85,050	(159,250)

Since it fails to pay back in discounted cash flow terms by year 5, the project would be rejected.

2.10 In this example, the project NPV would become positive between year 7 and year 8. This can be confirmed by looking at the cumulative discount tables to see where the discount factor at 12% exceeds

$$\frac{£700,000}{£150,000} = 4.67.$$

The reason for rejecting the project would be that since it fails to pay back in DCF terms within five years, it relies too heavily on the estimates of cash flows in the later years of the project's life to be considered a safe enough investment.

Sensitivity analysis

2.11 Sensitivity analysis is applied by varying the expected cash flows of a project, to measure what would happen if the investment were to work out somewhat worse than expected. We could, for example, re-calculate the NPV if:

(a) the initial cost of the investment were 5% higher than expected;
(b) running costs were 10% higher or savings were 10% lower than expected;
(c) costs were 5% higher *and* savings 5% lower than expected.

2.12 If the NPV is negative when costs are increased a little, or benefits are reduced a little, the project would be rejected on the grounds that it is too sensitive to variations in one or more key cost or revenue items.

Measuring the margin of error

2.13 By this method of sensitivity analysis, we calculate:

(a) the percentage increases in costs above what is expected; or
(b) the percentage shortfall in benefits below what is expected;

which would have to occur before a project would only just break even.

Example

2.14 Nevers Ure Ltd is considering a project with the following cash flows.

Year	*Purchase of plant*	*Running costs*	*Savings*
	£	£	£
0	(7,000)		
1		2,000	6,000
2		2,500	7,000

The cost of capital is 8%. Measure the sensitivity of the project to changes in the levels of expected costs and savings.

Solution

2.15 The PVs of the cash flows are as follows.

Year	*Discount factor*	*PV of plant cost*	*PV of running costs*	*PV of savings*	*PV of net cash flow*
	8%	£	£	£	£
0	1.000	(7,000)			(7,000)
1	0.926		(1,852)	5,556	3,704
2	0.857		(2,143)	5,999	3,856
		(7,000)	(3,995)	11,555	560

The project has a positive NPV and would appear to be worthwhile. The changes in cash flows which would need to occur for the project to break even (NPV = 0) are as follows.

(a) Plant costs would need to increase by a PV of £560, that is by $\frac{560}{7,000}$ = 8%

(b) Running costs would need to increase by a PV of £560, that is by $\frac{560}{3,995}$ = 14%

(c) Savings would need to fall by a PV of £560, that is by $\frac{560}{11,555}$ = 4.8%

(d) The effect of changes to any combination of the cash flows could be calculated. For example, the project would only just break even if running costs were 7% higher and savings (at the same time) 2.4% lower than expected.

The weaknesses of sensitivity analysis

2.16 (a) In spite of the possibility of checking the sensitivity of a project's NPV to changes in the cash flows from two or more items in conjunction, as suggested in paragraph 2.19 (d) above, it is more usual for sensitivity analysis to be applied to each cost or revenue item individually. This is often unrealistic, because items are often interdependent.

(b) Sensitivity analysis does not examine the *probability* that any particular variation in costs or revenues might occur. Just how likely is it that running costs will be 5% higher than expected?

The certainty equivalent approach

2.17 In this method, the expected cash flows of the project are converted to riskless equivalent amounts. The greater the risk of an expected cash flow, the smaller the 'certainty-equivalent' value (for receipts) or the larger the certainty equivalent value (for payments).

Example

2.18 Dark Ages Ltd, whose cost of capital is 10%, is considering a project with the following expected cash flows.

Year	*Cash flow*	*Discount factor*		*Present value*
	£	10%		£
0	(9,000)	1.000		(9,000)
1	7,000	0.909		6,363
2	5,000	0.826		4,130
3	5,000	0.751		3,755
			NPV	+5,248

The project would seem to be clearly worthwhile. However, because of the uncertainty about the future cash receipts, the management decides to reduce them to 'certainty-equivalents' by taking only 70%, 60% and 50% of the years 1, 2 and 3 cash flows respectively. (Note that this method of risk adjustment allows for different risk factors in each year of the project.) On this basis, is the project worthwhile?

Solution

2.19 The risk-adjusted NPV of the project is as follows.

Year	*Cash flow*	*PV factor*		*PV*
	£			£
0	(9,000)	1.000		(9,000)
1	4,900	0.909		4,454
2	3,000	0.826		2,478
3	2,500	0.751		1,878
			NPV =	- 190

The project is too risky and should be rejected.

2.20 The disadvantage of the 'certainty-equivalent' approach is that the amount of the adjustment to each cash flow is decided subjectively by management.

Probability estimates of cash flows

2.21 A probability distribution of expected cash flows can often be estimated, and this may be used:

(a) to calculate an expected value of the NPV;
(b) to measure risk, for example by

(i) calculating the worst possible outcome and its probability;
(ii) calculating the probability that the project will fail to achieve a positive NPV;
(iii) calculating the standard deviation of the NPV.

Example

2.22 A company is considering a project involving the outlay of £300,000 which it estimates will generate cash flows over its two year life at the probabilities shown in the following table.

Cash flows for project
Year 1

Cash flow £	*Probability*
100,000	0.25
200,000	0.50
300,000	0.25
	1.00

Year 2

If cash flow in Year 1 is: £	*there is a probability of:*	*that the cash flow in Year 2 will be:* £
100,000	0.25	Nil
	0.50	100,000
	0.25	200,000
	1.00	
200,000	0.25	100,000
	0.50	200,000
	0.25	300,000
	1.00	
300,000	0.25	200,000
	0.50	300,000
	0.25	350,000
	1.00	

The company's investment criterion for this type of project is 10% DCF.

What is the expected value (EV) of the project's NPV, and what is the probability that the NPV will be negative?

Solution

2.23 The present values of the cash flows are as follows.

Year	*Cash flow* £'000	*Discount factor* 10%	*Present value* £'000
1	100	0.909	90.9
1	200	0.909	181.8
1	300	0.909	272.7
2	100	0.826	82.6
2	200	0.826	165.2
2	300	0.826	247.8
2	350	0.826	289.1

2.24 The possible cash flows and their probabilities are as follows.

Year 1 PV of cash flow £'000	*Probability*	*Year 2 PV of cash flow* £'000	*Probability*	*Joint prob*	*Total PV of cash inflows* £'000	*EV of PV of cash inflows* £'000
(1)	(a)	(2)	(b)	(a)×(b)	(1)+(2)	
90.9	0.25	0	0.25	0.0625	90.9	5.6813
90.9	0.25	82.6	0.50	0.1250	173.5	21.6875
90.9	0.25	165.2	0.25	0.0625	256.1	16.0063
181.8	0.50	82.6	0.25	0.1250	264.4	33.0500
181.8	0.50	165.2	0.50	0.2500	347.0	86.7500
181.8	0.50	247.8	0.25	0.1250	429.6	53.7000
272.7	0.25	165.2	0.25	0.0625	437.9	27.3688
272.7	0.25	247.8	0.50	0.1250	520.5	65.0625
272.7	0.25	289.1	0.25	0.0625	561.8	35.1125
						344.4189

	£
EV of PV of cash inflows	344,419
Less project cost	300,000
EV of NPV	44,419

2.25 Since the EV of the NPV is positive, the project should go ahead unless the risk is unacceptably high.

The probability that the project will have a negative NPV is the probability that the total PV of cash inflows is less than £300,000. From the table of figures, we can establish that this probability is 0.0625 + 0.125 + 0.0625 + 0.125 = 0.375 or 37.5%. This might be considered an unacceptably high risk.

The standard deviation of the NPV

2.26 One way of measuring risk, given probabilities and an expected value, is to calculate the standard deviation of the NPV.

Example

2.27 Frame plc is considering which of two mutually exclusive projects, A or B, to undertake. There is some uncertainty about the running costs with each project, and a probability distribution of the NPV for each project has been estimated, as follows.

Project A		*Project B*	
NPV	*Probability*	*NPV*	*Probability*
£'000		£'000	
- 20	0.15	+ 5	0.2
+ 10	0.20	+ 15	0.3
+ 20	0.35	+ 20	0.4
+ 40	0.30	+ 25	0.1

Which project should the company choose, if either?

Solution

2.28 We can begin by calculating the EV of the NPV for each project.

Project A			*Project B*		
NPV	*Prob*	*EV*	*NPV*	*Prob*	*EV*
£'000		£'000	£'000		£'000
- 20	0.15	(3.0)	5	0.2	1.0
10	0.20	2.0	15	0.3	4.5
20	0.35	7.0	20	0.4	8.0
40	0.30	12.0	25	0.1	2.5
		18.0			16.0

Project A has a higher EV of NPV, but what about the risk of variation in the NPV above or below the EV? This can be measured by the standard deviation of the NPV.

2.29 The standard deviation of a project's NPV, s, can be calculated as

$$s = \sqrt{\Sigma p (x - \bar{x})^2}$$

where $\bar{x}$ is the EV of the NPV.

Project A, $\bar{x} = 18$				*Project B*, $\bar{x} = 16$			
x	p	$x - \bar{x}$	$p(x-\bar{x})^2$	x	p	$x - \bar{x}$	$p(x-\bar{x})^2$
£'000		£'000		£'000		£'000	
- 20	0.15	- 38	216.6	5	0.2	- 11	24.2
10	0.20	- 8	12.8	15	0.3	- 1	0.3
20	0.35	+ 2	1.4	20	0.4	+ 4	6.4
40	0.30	+ 22	145.2	25	0.1	+ 9	8.1
			376.0				39.0

Project A:

$s = \sqrt{376}$

$= 19.391$

$= £19,391$

Project B:

$s = \sqrt{39.0}$

$= 6.245$

$= £6,245$

Although Project A has a higher EV of NPV, it also has a higher standard deviation of NPV, and so has greater business risk associated with it.

2.30 Which project should be selected? Clearly, it depends on the attitude of the company's management to business risk.

(a) If management are prepared to take the risk of a low NPV in the hope of a high NPV, they will opt for project A.

(b) If management are risk-averse, they will opt for the less risky project B.

Simulation models

2.31 When project cash flows are given in terms of probability distributions, it might be appropriate to use simulation to establish a probability distribution of the project's expected NPV, instead of simply calculating an expected value.

Example

2.32 The following probability estimates have been prepared for a proposed project.

	Year	*Probability*	£
Cost of equipment	0	1.00	(40,000)
Revenue each year	1-5	0.15	40,000
		0.40	50,000
		0.30	55,000
		0.15	60,000
Running costs each year	1-5	0.10	25,000
		0.25	30,000
		0.35	35,000
		0.30	40,000

The cost of capital is 12%. How might a simulation model be used to assess the project's NPV?

Solution

2.33 A simulation model could be constructed by assigning a range of random number digits to each possible value for each of the uncertain variables, as follows.

Revenue			*Running costs*		
£	*Prob*	*Random numbers*	£	*Prob*	*Random numbers*
40,000	0.15	00 - 14	25,000	0.10	00 - 09
50,000	0.40	15 - 54	30,000	0.25	10 - 34
55,000	0.30	55 - 84	35,000	0.35	35 - 69
60,000	0.15	85 - 99	40,000	0.30	70 - 99

Random numbers would be generated, probably by a computer program, and these would be used to assign values to each of the uncertain variables.

2.34 For example, if random numbers 378420015689 were generated, the values assigned to the variables would be as follows.

	Revenue		*Costs*	
Calculation	*Random No*	*Value*	*Random No*	*Value*
		£		£
1	37	50,000	84	40,000
2	20	50,000	01	25,000
3	56	55,000	89	40,000

2.35 The NPV would be calculated many times over using the values established in this way with more random numbers, and the results would be analysed to provide:

(a) an expected NPV for the project;
(b) a statistical distribution pattern for the possible variation in the NPV above or below this average.

2.36 The decision whether to go ahead with the project would then be made on the basis of expected return and risk.

Which method of analysing risk is best?

2.37 (a) The problem with *adjusting the discount rate* to make it higher for more risky projects is that it is hard to decide what the size of the adjustment ought to be. Unless there is a rational basis for the size of the adjustment, this method of risk analysis will be unreliable.

(b) Setting a *time limit to the (discounted or undiscounted) payback period* has the merit of compelling projects to earn a satisfactory return before the end of their operational life, and so of building in a safety margin in case things go wrong. However:

(i) it should not be used on its own. The total expected NPV from a project over its entire life should be taken into consideration, not just its payback period;

(ii) it will discourage companies from investing in projects with very good long-term prospects, just because they will offer only small returns in the short term. In some industries, long-term investments might be desirable.

(c) *Sensitivity analysis* is an important technique, and helps managers to assess the effect on a project's NPV of higher costs or lower benefits than anticipated, or delayed benefits.

The main drawback to sensitivity analysis is that it ignores the probabilities of the different outcomes.

(d) *Analysing probabilities* is a useful technique, with a project's NPV being calculated as an expected value and with risk being measured and quantifiable.

The main drawback to probability analysis, however, is the difficulty of estimating the probabilities of the different outcomes.

(e) *Simulation modelling* provides a more complex analysis of probabilities. For projects where a complex analysis of probabilities and risk will be helpful, because of the large number of uncertainties, simulation modelling may be needed to provide a useful analysis of risk. But simulation modelling should not be used for project evaluation where a simpler method of risk analysis would be just as good.

3. CONCLUSION

3.1 This chapter has covered a wide range of techniques for incorporating an appraisal of business risk into decision making. While it is important to be able to use these techniques, it is equally important to be able to select an appropriate technique. For example, simulation models would be of little use in the absence of information about the probabilities of various outcomes.

TEST YOUR KNOWLEDGE

1. A project would cost £500,000 now, and would yield net cash profits of £125,000 a year for ten years. The company's cost of capital is 15%. When would the project pay back in discounted cash flow terms? (See below)

2. The cash flows of a project are set out below, together with PV calculations.

Year	*Discount factor*	*Capital cost*	*Savings*		*Running costs*		*Present value*
	15%	£	£	£	£	£	£
0	1.000	(140,000)					(140,000)
1	0.870		200,000	174,000	(150,000)	(130,500)	43,500
2	0.756		300,000	226,800	(180,000)	(136,080)	90,720
3	0.658		200,000	131,600	(160,000)	(105,280)	26,320
		(140,000)		532,400		(371,860)	20,540

How sensitive is the project to variations in costs or savings? Would you recommend that the project be undertaken? (See below)

3. The expected NPV from a project is £7,000,000 as follows.

NPV	*Probability*	*EV of NPV*
£m		£m
- 20	0.2	- 4
+ 10	0.5	+ 5
+ 20	0.3	+ 6
		+ 7

What is the standard deviation of the project's NPV? Would the project be undertaken if it is company policy *not* to undertake projects whose standard deviation of EV of NPV is greater than 100% of the EV of NPV? (See below)

Now try questions 17 and 18 at the end of the text

Solutions

1. £500,000/£125,000 = 4.000. From annuity tables for a 15% interest rate, 4.000 occurs about mid-way between year 6 and year 7. The project pays back in DCF terms during the seventh year.

2. Capital cost $\frac{20,540}{140,000}$ = 14.7%

   Savings $\frac{20,540}{532,400}$ = 3.8%

   Running costs $\frac{20,540}{371,860}$ = 5.5%

   The project would have a negative NPV if its capital cost is more than 14.7% above estimate, or if savings are more than 3.8% below estimate, or if running costs are more than 5.5% above estimate.

   The decision whether or not to undertake the project would depend on management's confidence in the accuracy of the estimated cash flows. Without further information, it might be guessed that the risk in the project is quite high.

3. $\bar{x} = 7$ (£m)

NPV x £m	p	$x - \bar{x}$	$p(x - \bar{x})^2$
- 20	0.2	- 27	145.8
+ 10	0.5	3	4.5
+ 20	0.3	13	50.7
			201.0

   $s = \sqrt{201} = 14.2$

   The standard deviation (14.2) is over 200% of the EV of NPV (7) and so the company would not undertake the project.

Chapter 14

INFLATION. TAXATION

This chapter covers the following topics.

1. Inflation
2. Taxation

1. INFLATION

1.1 So far we have not considered the effect of inflation on the appraisal of capital investment proposals.

As the inflation rate increases so will the minimum return required by an investor. For example, you might be happy with a return of 5% in an inflation-free world, but if inflation was running at 15% you would expect a considerably greater yield.

Example

1.2 A company is considering investing in a project with the following cash flows.

Time	*Actual cash flows*
	£
0	(15,000)
1	9,000
2	8,000
3	7,000

The company requires a minimum return of 20% under the present and anticipated conditions. Inflation is currently running at 10% a year, and this rate of inflation is expected to continue indefinitely. Should the company go ahead with the project?

1.3 Let us first look at the company's required rate of return. Suppose that it invested £1,000 for one year on 1 January, then on 31 December it would require a minimum return of £200. With the initial investment of £1,000, the total value of the investment by 31 December must therefore increase to £1,200. During the course of the year the purchasing value of the pound would fall due to inflation. We can restate the amount received on 31 December in terms of the purchasing power of the pound at 1 January as follows.

Amount received on 31 December in terms of the value of the pound at 1 January $= \dfrac{£1,200}{(1.10)^1} = £1,091$

1.4 In terms of the value of the pound at 1 January, the company would make a profit of £91 which represents a rate of return of 9.1% in 'today's money' terms. This is known as the real rate of return. The required rate of 20% is a money rate of return (sometimes called a nominal rate of return). The money rate measures the return in terms of the pound which is, of course, falling in value. The real rate measures the return in constant price level terms.

The two rates of return and the inflation rate are linked by the equation

$$(1 + \text{money rate}) = (1 + \text{real rate}) \times (1 + \text{inflation rate})$$

where all the rates are expressed as proportions.

In our example,

$$(1 + 0.20) = (1 + 0.091) \times (1 + 0.10) = 1.20$$

Which rate is used in discounting?

1.5 We must decide which rate to use for discounting, the real rate or the money rate. The rule is as follows.

(a) If the cash flows are expressed in terms of the actual number of pounds that will be received or paid on the various future dates, we *must* use the money rate for discounting.

(b) If the cash flows are expressed in terms of the value of the pound at time 0 (that is, in constant price level terms), we *must* use the real rate.

1.6 The cash flows given in Paragraph 1.2 are expressed in terms of the actual number of pounds that will be received or paid at the relevant dates. We should, therefore, discount them using the money rate of return.

Time	*Cash flow*	*Discount factor*	*PV*
	£	20%	£
0	(15,000)	1.000	(15,000)
1	9,000	0.833	7,497
2	8,000	0.694	5,552
3	7,000	0.579	4,053
			2,102

The project has a positive net present value of £2,102.

1.7 The future cash flows can be re-expressed in terms of the value of the pound at time 0 as follows, given inflation at 10% a year.

Time	*Actual cash flow*	*Cash flow at time 0 price level*
	£	£
0	(15,000)	(15,000)
1	9,000	$9{,}000 \times \frac{1}{1.10} = 8{,}182$
2	8,000	$8{,}000 \times \frac{1}{(1.10)^2} = 6{,}612$
3	7,000	$7{,}000 \times \frac{1}{(1.10)^3} = 5{,}259$

1.8 The cash flows expressed in terms of the value of the pound at time 0 can now be discounted using the real rate of 9.1%.

Time	*Cash flow*	*Discount factor*	*PV*
	£	9.1%	£
0	(15,000)	1.00	(15,000)
1	8,182	$\frac{1}{1.091}$	7,500
2	6,612	$\frac{1}{(1.091)^2}$	5,555
3	5,259	$\frac{1}{(1.091)^3}$	4,050
		NPV	2,105

1.9 The NPV is the same as before (and the present value of the cash flow in each year is the same as before) apart from rounding errors with a net total of £3.

Costs and benefits which inflate at different rates

1.10 Not all costs and benefits will rise in line with the general level of inflation. In such cases, we can apply the money rate to inflated values to determine a project's NPV.

Example

1.11 Rice Ltd is considering a project which would cost £5,000 now. The annual benefits, for four years, would be a fixed income of £2,500 a year, plus other savings of £500 a year in year 1, rising by 5% each year because of inflation. Running costs will be £1,000 in the first year, but would increase at 10% each year because of inflating labour costs. The general rate of inflation is expected to be 7½% and the company's required money rate of return is 16%. Is the project worthwhile?

Ignore taxation.

Solution

1.12 The cash flows at inflated values are as follows.

Year	*Fixed income*	*Other savings*	*Running costs*	*Net cash flow*
	£	£	£	£
1	2,500	500	1,000	2,000
2	2,500	525	1,100	1,925
3	2,500	551	1,210	1,841
4	2,500	579	1,331	1,748

The NPV of the project is as follows.

Year	*Cash flow*	*Discount factor*	*PV*
	£	16%	£
0	(5,000)	1.000	(5,000)
1	2,000	0.862	1,724
2	1,925	0.743	1,430
3	1,841	0.641	1,180
4	1,748	0.552	965
			+ 299

The NPV is positive and the project would seem to be worthwhile.

Example

1.13 Antsnest plc is considering whether to establish a new subsidiary operation in Scotland. The cost of the fixed asset investment would be £1,000,000 in total, with £750,000 payable at once and the remainder payable after one year. A further investment of £300,000 in working capital would be required.

The management of Antsnest expect all their investments to justify themselves financially within a four year planning horizon. The net disposal value of the fixed assets after four years is expected to be zero.

The operation would incur fixed costs of £520,000 a year in the first year, including depreciation of £200,000. These costs, excluding depreciation, are expected to increase by 5% each year because of inflation. The operation would involve the manufacture and sale of a standard unit, with a unit selling price and unit variable cost of £12 and £6 respectively in the first year and expected annual increases because of inflation of 4% and 7% respectively. Annual sales are expected to be 125,000 units.

The company's money cost of capital is 14%.

Is the project viable? Ignore taxation.

Solution

1.14 *Workings*

1. *Fixed costs*

		£
Year 1	(520,000 - 200,000)	320,000
Year 2		336,000
Year 3		352,800
Year 4		370,440

2. *Contribution*

Year	*Unit selling price*	*Unit variable cost*	*Unit contribution*	*Units*	*Total contribution*
	£	£	£		£
1	12.00	6.00	6.00	125,000	750,000
2	12.48	6.42	6.06	125,000	757,500
3	12.98	6.87	6.11	125,000	763,750
4	13.50	7.35	6.15	125,000	768,750

1.15 *NPV calculation*

Year	*Fixed assets*	*Working capital*	*Contribution less fixed costs*	*Net cash flow*	*Discount factor 14%*	*Present value*
	£	£	£	£		£
0	(750,000)	(300,000)		(1,050,000)	1.000	(1,050,000)
1	(250,000)		430,000	180,000	0.877	157,860
2			421,500	421,500	0.769	324,134
3			410,950	410,950	0.675	277,391
4		300,000	398,310	698,310	0.592	413,400
						122,785

The NPV is positive, and so ignoring considerations of risk, the project is viable.

Variations in the expected rate of inflation

1.16 If the rate of inflation is expected to change, the calculation of the money cost of capital is slightly more complicated.

Example

1.17 Mr Gable has just received a dividend of £1,000 on his shareholding in Gonwithy Windmills plc. The market value of the shares is £8,000 ex div.

What is the (money) cost of the equity capital, if dividends are expected to rise because of inflation by 10% in years 1, 2 and 3, before levelling off at this year 3 amount?

Solution

1.18 The money cost of capital is the internal rate of return of the following cash flows.

Year	*Cash flow*	*PV at 15%*	*PV at 20%*
	£	£	£
0	(8,000)	(8,000)	(8,000)
1	1,100	957	916
2	1,210	915	840
3 - ∞	1,331 pa	6,709	4,622
		581	(1,622)

The IRR is approximately $15\% + \left[\frac{581}{581 - -1{,}622} \times (20-15) \right] \% = 16.3\%$, say 16%

Expectations of inflation and the effects of inflation

1.19 When managers evaluate a particular project, or when shareholders evaluate their investments, they can only guess at what the rate of inflation is going to be. Their expectations will probably be wrong, at least to some extent, because it is extremely difficult to forecast the rate of inflation accurately. The only way in which uncertainty about inflation can be allowed for in project evaluation is by risk and uncertainty analysis.

1.20 Inflation has the following effects.

(a) Since fixed assets and stocks will increase in money value, the same quantities of assets must be financed by increasing amounts of capital.

(i) If the future rate of inflation can be predicted, management can work out how much extra finance the company will need, and take steps to obtain it (for example by increasing retentions of earnings, or borrowing).

(ii) If the future rate of inflation cannot be predicted with accuracy, management should guess at what it will be and plan to obtain extra finance accordingly. However, plans should also be made to obtain 'contingency funds' if the rate of inflation exceeds expectations. For example, a higher bank overdraft facility might be negotiated, or a provisional arrangement made with a bank for a loan.

(b) Inflation means higher costs and higher selling prices. The effect of higher prices on demand is not necessarily easy to predict. A company that raises its prices by 10% because the general rate of inflation is running at 10% might suffer a serious fall in demand.

(c) Inflation, because it affects financing needs, is also likely to affect gearing, and so the cost of capital.

2. TAXATION

2.1 So far, in looking at project appraisal, we have ignored taxation. However, payments of tax, or reductions of tax payments, are cash flows and ought to be considered in DCF analysis.

2.2 In the study guide to the syllabus, it is stated that in questions involving the impact of taxation, any assumptions to be used will be specified.

Typical assumptions are as follows.

(a) Corporation tax is payable in the year following the one in which the taxable profits are made. Thus, if a project increases taxable profits by £10,000 in year 2, there will be a tax payment, assuming tax at 33%, of £3,300 in year 3.

This is not always the case in examination questions. Look out for questions which state that tax is payable in the same year as that in which the profits arise.

(b) Net cash flows from a project should be considered as the taxable profits arising from the project (unless an indication is given to the contrary).

Capital allowances

2.3 Capital allowances are used to reduce taxable profits, and the consequent reduction in a tax payment should be treated as a cash saving arising from the acceptance of a project.

2.4 Writing down allowances are allowed on the cost of *plant and machinery* at the rate of 25% on a *reducing balance* basis. Thus if a company purchases plant costing £80,000, the subsequent writing down allowances would be as follows.

Year	*Capital allowance*	*Reducing balances (RB)*
	£	£
1 (25% of cost)	20,000	60,000
2 (25% of RB)	15,000	45,000
3 (25% of RB)	11,250	33,750
4 (25% of RB)	8,437	25,313

When the plant is eventually sold, the difference between the sale price and the reducing balance amount at the time of sale will be treated as

(i) a taxable profit if the sale price exceeds the reducing balance; and
(ii) a tax-allowable loss if the reducing balance exceeds the sale price. Examination questions often assume that this loss will be available immediately, though in practice the balance less the sale price continues to be written off at 25% a year as part of a pool balance unless the asset has been de-pooled.

The cash saving on the capital allowances (or the cash payment for the charge) is calculated by multiplying the allowance (or charge) by the corporation tax rate.

2.5 Assumptions about capital allowances could be simplified in an exam question. For example, you might be told that capital allowances can be claimed at the rate of 25% of cost on a straight line basis (that is, over four years), or a question might refer to 'tax allowable depreciation', so that the capital allowances equal the depreciation charge.

2.6 There are two possible assumptions about the time when capital allowances start to be claimed.

(a) It can be assumed that the first claim for capital allowances occurs at the start of the project (at year 0) and so the first tax saving occurs one year later (at year 1).

(b) Alternatively it can be assumed that the first claim for capital allowances occurs later in the first year, so the first tax saving occurs one year later, that is, year 2.

2.7 You should state clearly which assumption you have made. Assumption (b) is more prudent, because it defers the tax benefit by one year, but assumption (a) is also perfectly feasible. It is very likely, however that an examination question will indicate which of the two assumptions is required.

Example

2.8 A company is considering whether or not to purchase an item of machinery costing £40,000 in 19X5. It would have a life of four years, after which it would be sold for £5,000. The machinery would create annual cost savings of £14,000.

The machinery would attract writing down allowances of 25% on the reducing balance basis which could be claimed against taxable profits of the current year, which is soon to end. A balancing allowance or charge would arise on disposal.

The rate of corporation tax is 33%. Tax is payable one year in arrears.

The after-tax cost of capital is 8%.

Assume that tax payments occur in the year following the transactions.

Should the machinery be purchased?

Solution

2.9 The first capital allowance is claimed against year 0 profits.

Cost: £40,000

Year	*Allowance*	*Reducing balance (RB)*	
	£	£	
(0) 19X5 (25% of cost)	10,000	30,000	(40,000 - 10,000)
(1) 19X6 (25% of RB)	7,500	22,500	(30,000 - 7,500)
(2) 19X7 (25% of RB)	5,625	16,875	(22,500 - 5,625)
(3) 19X8 (25% of RB)	4,219	12,656	(16,875 - 4,219)
(4) 19X9 (25% of RB)	3,164	9,492	(12,656 - 3,164)

	£
Sale proceeds, end of fourth year	5,000
Less reducing balance, end of fourth year	9,492
Balancing allowance	4,492

2.10 Having calculated the allowances each year, the tax savings can be computed. The year of the cash flow is one year after the year for which the allowance is claimed.

Year of claim	*Allowance*	*Tax saved*	*Year of tax payment/saving*
	£	£	
0	10,000	3,300	1
1	7,500	2,475	2
2	5,625	1,856	3
3	4,219	1,392	4
4	7,656	2,526	5
	35,000 *		

* Net cost £(40,000 - 5,000) = £35,000

These tax savings relate to capital allowances. We must also calculate the extra tax payments on annual savings of £14,000.

2.11 The net cash flows and the NPV are now calculated as follows.

Year	*Equipment*	*Savings*	*Tax on saving*	*Tax saved on capital allowances*	*Net cash flow*	*Discount factor 8%*	*Present value of cash flow*
	£	£	£	£	£		£
0	(40,000)				(40,000)	1.000	(40,000)
1		14,000		3,300	17,300	0.926	16,020
2		14,000	(4,620)	2,475	11,855	0.857	10,160
3		14,000	(4,620)	1,856	11,236	0.794	8,921
4	5,000	14,000	(4,620)	1,392	15,772	0.735	11,592
5			(4,620)	2,526	(2,094)	0.681	(1,426)
							5,267

The NPV is positive and so the purchase appears to be worthwhile.

An alternative and quicker method of calculating tax payments or savings

2.12 In the above example, the tax computations could have been combined, as follows.

Year	*0*	*1*	*2*	*3*	*4*
	£	£	£	£	£
Cost savings	0	14,000	14,000	14,000	14,000
Capital allowance	10,000	7,500	5,625	4,219	7,656
Taxable profits	(10,000)	6,500	8,375	9,781	6,344
Tax at 33%	3,300	(2,145)	(2,764)	(3,228)	(2,094)

2.13 The net cash flows would then be as follows.

Year	*Equipment*	*Savings*	*Tax*	*Net cash flow*
	£	£	£	£
0	(40,000)			(40,000)
1		14,000	3,300	17,300
2		14,000	(2,145)	11,855
3		14,000	(2,764)	11,236
4	5,000	14,000	(3,228)	15,772
5			(2,094)	(2,094)

The net cash flows are exactly the same as calculated previously in Paragraph 2.11.

Example

2.14 Flagwaver plc is considering whether to establish a subsidiary in the USA, at a cost of $2,400,000. This would be represented by fixed assets of $2,000,000 and working capital of $400,000. The subsidiary would produce a product which would achieve annual sales of $1,600,000 and incur cash expenditures of $1,000,000 a year.

The company has a planning horizon of four years, at the end of which it expects the realisable value of the subsidiary's fixed assets to be $800,000.

It is the company's policy to remit the maximum funds possible to the parent company at the end of each year.

Tax is payable at the rate of 35% in the USA and is payable one year in arrears. A double taxation treaty exists between the UK and the USA and so no UK taxation is expected to arise.

Tax allowable depreciation is at a rate of 25% on a straight line basis on all fixed assets.

Because of the fluctuations in the exchange rate between the US dollar and sterling, the company would protect itself against the risk by raising a eurodollar loan to finance the investment.

The company's cost of capital for the project is 16%.

Calculate the NPV of the project.

Solution

2.15 The simplified tax rule here is that writing down allowances are 25% straight line over four years. The annual allowance is 25% of US$2,000,000 = $500,000, from which the annual tax saving would be (at 35%) $175,000.

Year	*Investment*	*Contribution*	*Tax on contribution and realisable value*	*Tax saved (writing down allowance) & tax on realisable value*	*Net cash flow*	*Discount factor 16%*	*Present value*
	$m	$m	$m	$m	$m		$m
0	(2.4)				(2.400)	1.000	(2.400)
1		0.6		0.175	0.775	0.862	0.668
2		0.6	(0.21)	0.175	0.565	0.743	0.420
3		0.6	(0.21)	0.175	0.565	0.641	0.362
4	1.2 *	0.6	(0.21)	0.175	1.765	0.552	0.974
5			(0.21)	(0.28) **	(0.490)	0.476	(0.233)
							(0.209)

* Fixed assets realisable value $800,000 plus working capital $400,000

** It is assumed that tax would be payable on the realisable value of the fixed assets, since the tax written down value of the assets would be zero. 35% of $800,000 is $280,000.

2.16 The NPV is negative and so the project would not be viable at a discount rate of 16%.

Taxation and DCF

2.17 The effect of taxation on capital budgeting is theoretically quite simple. Organisations must pay tax, and the effect of undertaking a project will be to increase or decrease tax payments each year. These incremental tax cash flows should be included in the cash flows of the project for discounting to arrive at the project's NPV.

2.18 When taxation is ignored in the DCF calculations, the discount rate will reflect the pre-tax rate of return required on capital investments. When taxation included in the cash flows, a post-tax required rate of return should be used.

The taxation aspects of leasing and hire purchase

2.19 Leasing was described in Chapter 7 as a source of medium-term or long-term funding. Our interest here is in *finance leases*, not operating leases.

2.20 When a company makes an investment decision to acquire an item of equipment, it might also have to decide whether to purchase the equipment, or whether to acquire it under a finance lease arrangement. Another alternative would be a hire purchase arrangement. Tax considerations may influence the decision.

2.21 (a) If a company purchases an item of equipment outright it can claim whatever capital allowances are available on the cost of the asset.

(b) If a company leases an item, it can claim the annual lease payments against tax, but it cannot claim any capital allowances. These are claimed by the lessor instead.

2.22 When a company acquires a capital asset under a *hire purchase agreement*, it will eventually obtain full legal title to the asset. The HP payments consist partly of 'capital' payments towards the purchase of the asset, and partly of interest charges.

2.23 For example, if a company buys a car costing £10,000 under an HP agreement, the car supplier might provide HP finance over a three year period at an interest cost of 10%, and the HP payments might be, say, as follows.

	Capital element	*Interest element*	*Total HP payment*
	£	£	£
Year 0: down payment	2,540	0	2,540
Year 1	2,254	746	3,000
Year 2	2,479	521	3,000
Year 3	2,727	273	3,000
Total	10,000	1,540	11,540

2.24 The tax position on hire purchase arrangements is as follows.

(a) The buyer obtains whatever capital allowances are available, based on the capital element of the cost. Capital allowances on the full capital element of the cost can be used from the time the asset is acquired.

(b) In addition, interest payments within the HP payments are an allowable expense against tax, spread over the term of the HP agreement.

(c) Capital payments within the HP payments, however, are not allowable against tax.

3. CONCLUSION

3.1 Inflation is a feature of all economies, and it must be accommodated in financial planning. The mathematics of relating real and money rates of return are fairly straightforward. Do not, however, forget the very great practical difficulty of predicting the rate of inflation.

3.2 Taxation is also a major practical consideration for businesses. It is vital to take it into account in making decisions.

TEST YOUR KNOWLEDGE

1. The money cost of capital is 11%. The expected annual rate of inflation is 5%. What is the real cost of capital? (See below)

2. A company wants a minimum real return of 3% a year on its investments. Inflation is expected to be 8% a year. What is the company's minimum money cost of capital? (See below)

3. Here are a project's cash flows, at today's prices.

Year	*Purchase cost*	*Running costs*	*Revenue*
	£	£	£
0	(70,000)		
1		(25,000)	60,000
2		(30,000)	70,000
3		(20,000)	50,000

Selling prices are expected to rise by 5% each year *after* the first year and running costs by 8% a year *after* the first year. The company's money cost of capital is 12%.

What is the project's NPV? (See below)

4. A company is considering the purchase of an item of equipment, which would earn profits before tax of £25,000 a year. Depreciation charges would be £20,000 a year for six years. Capital allowances would be £30,000 a year for the first four years. Corporation tax is at 33%.

What would be the annual net cash inflows of the project:

(a) for the first four years;
(b) for the fifth and sixth years,

assuming that tax payments occur in the same year as the profits giving rise to them, and there is no balancing charge or allowance when the machine is scrapped at the end of the sixth year? (See below)

5. A company is considering the purchase of a machine for £150,000. It would be sold after four years for an estimated realisable value of £50,000. By this time capital allowances of £120,000 would have been claimed. The rate of corporation tax is 33%.

What are the tax implications of the sale of the machine at the end of four years? (See below)

Now try question 19 at the end of the text

Solutions

1. $\frac{1.11}{1.05}$ = 1.057. The real cost of capital is 5.7%.

2. (1.03)(1.08) = 1.1124. The money cost of capital is 11.24%.

3.

Year	*Running costs*	*Revenue*	*Net cash flow*	*Discount factor 12%*	*Present value*
	£	£	£	£	£
0			(70,000)	1.000	(70,000)
1	(25,000)	60,000	35,000	0.893	31,255
2	(32,400)	73,500	41,100	0.797	32,757
3	(23,328)	55,125	31,797	0.712	22,639
				NPV =	+16,651

4. (a) *Years 1-4*

	Years 1-4	*Years 5-6*
	£	£
Profit before tax	25,000	25,000
Add back depreciation	20,000	20,000
Net cash inflow before tax	45,000	45,000
Less capital allowance	30,000	0
	15,000	45,000
Tax at 33%	4,950	14,850

Years 1 - 4 Net cash inflow after tax £45,000 - £4,950 = £40,050

Years 5 - 6 Net cash inflow after tax = £45,000 - £14,850 = £30,150

5. There will be a balancing charge on the sale of the machine, of £(50,000 - (150,000 - 120,000)) = £20,000. This will give rise to a tax payment of 33% × £20,000 = £6,600.

Chapter 15

CAPITAL RATIONING

This chapter covers the following topics.

1. Single period capital rationing
2. Multi-period capital rationing
3. Dividends and capital rationing

1. SINGLE PERIOD CAPITAL RATIONING

1.1 Capital rationing arises when finance available for new investment is limited to an amount that prevents acceptance of all projects with positive net present values.

This situation might arise for the following reasons.

(a) Raising money through the stock market may not be possible if share prices are depressed.

(b) There may be restrictions on bank lending due to government controls.

(c) The costs associated with making small issues of capital may be too great.

(d) Lending institutions may consider a company too risky to be given any more loans.

1.2 We shall begin our analysis by assuming that capital rationing occurs in a single period, and that capital is freely available at all other times.

1.3 The following further assumptions will be made.

(a) If a project is not accepted and undertaken during the period of capital rationing, the opportunity to undertake it is lost. It cannot be postponed until a subsequent period when no capital rationing exists.

(b) There is complete certainty about the outcome of each project, so that the choice between projects is not affected by considerations of risk.

(c) Projects are divisible, so that it is possible to undertake, say, half of Project X in order to earn half of the NPV of the whole project.

Example

1.4 Hard Times Ltd is considering four projects, W, X, Y and Z, which have the following estimated cash flows and NPVs (at a cost of capital of 10%).

Project	*Year 0*	*Year 1*	*Year 2*	*NPV*
	£	£	£	£
W	(10,000)	6,000	7,000	+ 1,240
X	(20,000)	14,000	10,000	+ 991
Y	(30,000)	10,000	28,000	+ 2,230
Z	(40,000)	30,000	20,000	+ 3,801

1.5 Without capital rationing, all four projects would be viable investments.

However, if only £60,000 is available in year 0, the company will optimise its return by maximising the NPV generated per pound spent in year 0. Putting projects in order in this way is called *project ranking*.

Project	*NPV*	*Outlay in year of rationing (year 0)*	*NPV per £1 spent in year 0*	*Priority of project*
	£	£	£	
W	1,240	10,000	0.124	1st
X	991	20,000	0.050	4th
Y	2,230	30,000	0.074	3rd
Z	3,801	40,000	0.095	2nd

1.6 The £60,000 available would be spent as follows.

Project	*Priority*	*Outlay*	*NPV*
		£	£
W	1st	10,000	1,240
Z	2nd	40,000	3,801
Y (balance)*	3rd	10,000	743 ($\frac{1}{3}$ of 2,230)
		60,000	5,784

* Projects are divisible. By spending the balancing £10,000 on project Y, one third of the full investment would be made to earn one third of the NPV.

The opportunity cost of capital

1.7 The internal rates of return (IRRs) for the four projects in the above example are as follows.

Project	*IRR (approx)*	*Ranking*
W	19%	1st
X	14%	4th
Y	15%	3rd
Z	16%	2nd

1.8 It is no coincidence that the ranking of projects by IRR gives the same result as the ratio of NPV to outlay in year 0. This will happen when there is single period rationing and no projects involve capital expenditure in any other year.

1.9 In the example, the projects selected were W, Z and a part of Y. It follows that:

(a) any project which does not have an IRR at least as great as that of project Y (about 15%) should be rejected;

(b) if any project suddenly appeared which offered a return in excess of the IRR of project Y, it should be accepted at the expense of some (or all) of project Y, and then even possibly at the expense of project Z or W.

1.10 The IRR of the marginal project, project Y, is the opportunity cost of capital.

Where there is a single period of capital rationing, and projects have outlays in that year only, it is possible to apply the opportunity cost of capital as a discount rate in evaluating projects.

1.11 A major theoretical drawback to discounting by the opportunity cost of capital is that until the optimum selection of projects has been found, it is impossible to decide what the opportunity cost of capital is. This means that once it has been calculated, it is too late to be of any use in deciding what projects to accept.

1.12 Thus, in our example, if a new project P is discovered, which costs £20,000 in year 0, has an NPV of £2,000 and an IRR of 17%, its ratio of NPV to capital outlay in the year of rationing would be

$$\frac{£2,000}{£20,000} = 0.1$$

thus ranking it second to project W, above both projects Z and Y. Given £60,000 of capital in year 0, the new investment programme would be as follows.

Project	*Ranking*		*Outlay*	*NPV*	
			£	£	
W	1st		10,000	1,240	
P (new project)	2nd		20,000	2,000	
Z	3rd	(balance)	30,000	2,851	($\frac{3}{4}$ of £3,801)
			60,000	6,091	

1.13 The opportunity cost of capital has now risen, due to the introduction of project P, to the IRR of project Z, which is 16%. This can only be established after the optimal investment programme has been revised.

1.14 Another drawback to the use of the opportunity cost of capital is that if there is single period capital rationing, but projects will involve capital expenditure in more than one period, the IRRs can give the wrong ranking of projects. The correct basis on which to establish priorities is the ratio NPV:outlay in the year of rationing.

Exercise

Bleak House Ltd is experiencing capital rationing in year 0, when only £60,000 of investment finance will be available. No capital rationing is expected in future periods, but none of the three projects under consideration by the company can be postponed. The expected cash flows of the three projects are as follows.

Project	*Year 0*	*Year 1*	*Year 2*	*Year 3*	*Year 4*
	£	£	£	£	£
A	(50,000)	(20,000)	20,000	40,000	40,000
B	(28,000)	(50,000)	40,000	40,000	20,000
C	(30,000)	(30,000)	30,000	40,000	10,000

The cost of capital is 10%. Decide which projects should be undertaken in year 0, in view of the capital rationing, given that projects are divisible.

Solution

The ratio of NPV at 10% to outlay in year 0 (the year of capital rationing) is as follows.

Project	*NPV*	*Outlay in Year 0*	*Ratio*	*Ranking*
	£	£		
A	5,700	50,000	0.114	3rd
B	3,290	28,000	0.118	2nd
C	4,380	30,000	0.146	1st

The optimal investment policy is as follows.

Ranking	*Project*	*Year 0 outlay*		*NPV*
		£		£
1st	C	30,000		4,380
2nd	B	28,000		3,290
3rd	A (balance)	2,000	(4% of 5,700)	228
NPV from total investment				7,898

Postponing projects

1.15 We have so far assumed that projects cannot be postponed until year 1. If this assumption is removed, the choice of projects in year 0 would be made by reference to the loss of NPV from postponement.

Example

1.16 The figures in the previous exercise will be used to illustrate the method. If any project, A, B or C, were delayed by one year, the "NPV" would now relate to year 1 values, so that in year 0 terms, the NPVs would be as follows.

		NPV in Year 1		NPV in Year 0 Value	Loss in NPV
		£		£	£
(a)	Project A	5,700 × $\frac{1}{1.10}$	=	5,182	518
(b)	Project B	3,290 × $\frac{1}{1.10}$	=	2,991	299
(c)	Project C	4,380 × $\frac{1}{1.10}$	=	3,982	398

1.17 An index of postponability would be calculated as follows.

Project	*Loss in NPV from one-year postponement*	*Outlay deferred from year 0*	*Postponability index (loss/outlay)*
	£	£	
A	518	50,000	0.0104
B	299	28,000	0.0107
C	398	30,000	0.0133

1.18 The loss in NPV by deferring investment would be greatest for Project C, and least for Project A. It is therefore more profitable to postpone A, rather than B or C, as follows.

Investment in year 0

Project	*Outlay*		*NPV*
	£		£
C	30,000		4,380
B	28,000		3,290
A (balance)	2,000	(4% of 5,700)	228
	60,000		7,898

Investment in year 1 (balance)

Project A	£48,000	(96% of 5,182)	4,975
Total NPV (as at year 0) of investments in years 0 and 1			12,873

2. MULTI-PERIOD CAPITAL RATIONING

2.1 When capital is expected to be in short supply for more than one period, the selection of an optimal investment programme cannot be made by ranking projects according to a simple NPV:capital outlay ratio. Other techniques, notably linear programming, should be used.

Example

2.2 Scrooge Ltd is settling its capital budget for 19X3 and 19X4. It is estimated that the cash available for investment will be £80,000 in 19X3 and £70,000 in 19X4. The company's cost of capital is 10%, and the projects which are available in these years and which offer a positive NPV are as follows.

Project	*19X3*	*19X4*	*19X5*	*19X6*	*19X7*	*NPV at 10% at year 0 (19X3)*
	£'000	£'000	£'000	£'000	£'000	£
A	(50)	(20)	40	30	20	+ 1,073
B	(30)	(40)	30	30	30	+ 1,016
C	(20)	(30)	30	10	23	+ 741
D	(31)	(15)	20	20	20	+ 577
E	0	(10)	4	5	2.32	+ 443 *

* This NPV is expressed as at 19X3, not 19X4.

2.3 The two constraints preventing the acceptance of all five worthwhile projects are:

(a) the funds available in 19X3;
(b) the funds available in 19X4.

We have multi-period capital rationing, and linear programming techniques can be used to select an investment programme which will give the maximum NPV within the capital rationing limitations.

2.4 A linear programming problem would be formulated as follows.

(a) Let a be the proportion of Project A accepted
b be the proportion of Project B accepted
c be the proportion of Project C accepted
d be the proportion of Project D accepted
e be the proportion of Project E accepted.

(b) The objective is to maximise the NPV from the total investment in 19X3 and 19X4:

maximise $1{,}073a + 1{,}016b + 741c + 577d + 443e$

subject to the following constraints.

$50a + 30b + 20c + 31d$	≤ 80	(Year 0 investment)
$20a + 40b + 30c + 15d + 10e$	≤ 70	(Year 1 investments)
a, b, c, d, e	≤ 1	
a, b, c, d, e	≥ 0	

The optimal solution

2.5 The simplex method would probably be used to derive a solution, and although you will not be expected to produce a solution by this method in your examination, some understanding of the optimal solution may be helpful.

2.6 The optimal solution is as follows.

Project	*Proportion accepted*	*Outlay Year 0* £'000	*Outlay Year 1* £'000	*NPV* £'000
A	100.00%	50.000	20.0	1,073
C	100.00%	20.000	30.0	741
E	100.00%	-	10.0	443
B	20.25%	6.075	8.1	206
D	12.66%	3.925	1.9	73
		80.000	70.0	2,536

2.7 All available funds in 19X3 and 19X4 are used. Since these funds are effective constraints in our solution, they must have dual prices. These may also be calculated by the simplex method as follows.

Dual price of funds in 19X3 : an NPV of about £10 per £1,000 of outlay
Dual price of funds in 19X4 : an NPV of about £18 per £1,000 of outlay

In other words, if another £1,000 of funds could be made available in either 19X3 or 19X4, the revised investment programme would yield an additional NPV of £10 (19X3) or £18 (19X4).

3. DIVIDENDS AND CAPITAL RATIONING

3.1 In theory, if a company's management wishes to maximise the wealth of their shareholders, there should be no dividend payments during a period of capital rationing.

However, a company may wish to pay a dividend to maintain a consistent dividend policy for its shareholders. The greater the dividend, the less will be the NPV from retained earnings.

Example

3.2 Continuing the example of Scrooge Ltd in Paragraphs 2.2 - 2.6, suppose that the company's management decide that there must be a dividend payment of at least £15,000 at the end of 19X3. How would the formulation of the linear programming problem be affected? (Assume that cash inflows from projects during 19X3 should be ignored, so that they do not add to the available capital at the end of 19X3.)

Solution

3.3 Let x be the amount of dividend paid at the end of 19X3.

The objective function is to maximise shareholder wealth.

The objective is to maximise 1,073a + 1,016b + 741c + 577d + 443e + 0.909x

subject to the following constraints.

$$\begin{aligned}
50a + 30b + 20c + 31d &\leq 80 \\
20a + 40b + 30c + 15d + 10e + x &\leq 70 \\
a, b, c, d, e &\leq 1 \\
x &\geq 15 \\
a, b, c, d, e &\geq 0
\end{aligned}$$

3.4 The optimal solution will give the value of dividend as the minimum allowable, so that in this example, x = 15 (£15,000). All other funds will be retained in order to increase the NPV from investments.

4. CONCLUSION

4.1 There are various limitations to the use of the techniques described in this chapter. The most significant of these are as follows.

(a) It has been assumed that fractions of projects may be accepted, whereas in practice, this might not be so.

(b) No account has been taken of the risk associated with the various projects, and the attitudes towards risk of a company's management and shareholders.

(c) Interdependencies between projects have not been allowed for. For example, if Project A is undertaken without Project B, the costs of Project A might be higher (or revenues lower) than if Project B were undertaken at the same time.

(d) Linear relationships are assumed, so that if a fraction of Project X were undertaken, the costs and benefits would accrue in the same proportion, to give a proportionate NPV. In practice, there might be economies or diseconomies of scale, so that if, say, half of Project X were undertaken, the NPV might be only, say, a quarter of the NPV of the entire project.

TEST YOUR KNOWLEDGE

The numbers in brackets refer to paragraphs of this chapter

1. When might capital rationing occur? (1.1)

2. How should projects be ranked for acceptance if there is capital rationing in year 0 only, and:
   (a) projects are divisible;
   (b) projects not undertaken now will be lost forever? (1.5)

3. How should projects be ranked for acceptance if there is multi-period capital rationing? (2.1)

4. What are the limitations of capital rationing techniques? (4.1)

5. Coasters Ltd is considering its capital investment programme for 19X0 and 19X1. The company's cost of capital is 15%. The directors of Coasters Ltd have reduced their initial list of projects to five, the expected cash flows of which are as follows.

		Cash flows at 1 January			
Project	*19X0*	*19X1*	*19X2*	*19X3*	*NPV at 15%*
	£	£	£	£	£
A	- 60,000	+ 30,000	+ 25,000	+ 25,000	+ 1,600
B	- 30,000	- 20,000	+ 25,000	+ 45,000	+ 1,300
C	- 40,000	- 50,000	+ 60,000	+ 70,000	+ 8,300
D	0	- 80,000	+ 45,000	+ 55,000	+ 900
E	- 50,000	+ 10,000	+ 30,000	+ 40,000	+ 7,900

None of the above projects can be delayed. All the projects are divisible; outlays may be reduced by any proportion and inflows will then be reduced by the same proportion. No project can be undertaken more than once. Coasters Ltd is able to invest surplus funds in a bank deposit account yielding an annual return of 10%.

Show which projects should be undertaken if capital available for investment is limited to £100,000 at 1 January 19X0, but is not limited thereafter. (See below)

Now try question 20 at the end of the text

Solution

5. The company should undertake those projects with the highest NPV per unit of outlay at year 0.

Project	*NPV / Year 0 outlay*	*NPV per £1 of outlay* £	*Ranking*
A	$\frac{1.6}{60}$	0.027	4
B	$\frac{1.3}{30}$	0.043	3
C	$\frac{8.3}{40}$	0.207	1
E	$\frac{7.9}{50}$	0.158	2

The projects to be undertaken are as follows.

Project	*Year 0 outlay required* £'000	*% of project undertaken*	*Actual year 0 outlay* £'000
C	40	100	40
E	50	100	50
B	30	$33\frac{1}{3}$	10
			100

In addition, the whole of project D would be undertaken, since this requires no year 0 outlay.

Chapter 16

ASSET REPLACEMENT DECISIONS. LEASE OR BUY DECISIONS

This chapter covers the following topics.

1. Replacement decisions
2. Replacement cycles
3. Non-identical replacement
4. Replacement decisions and inflation
5. Lease or buy decisions

1. REPLACEMENT DECISIONS

1.1 A company may buy a new fixed asset to replace an existing, ageing asset or else to expand its business.

Some replacement assets have greater production capacity than the assets they replace, so that both expansion and replacement occurs with the same purchase. In this chapter, however, we shall focus on replacement decisions.

1.2 The following factors are involved in replacement decisions.

(a) *Operating and maintenance costs.* As an asset gets older, it may become more expensive to operate and maintain. The longer replacement is deferred, the more expensive these running costs become.

(b) *Capital costs.* Replacement assets involve an outlay of capital expenditure which would be deferred by postponing the replacement. Occasionally (for example with computer equipment) delaying replacement may be:

(i) an advantage, because new, improved technology might be available in a year or two, so that postponing the replacement would mean that the new technology could be purchased as soon as it is available;

(ii) on the other hand, a disadvantage, because by delaying replacement, the company might not be taking advantage of new technology which is already available.

(c) *Realisable values*. The realisable value of an asset will decline as the asset gets older. Early replacement means that a higher resale value should be obtained for existing equipment.

(d) *Taxation and investment incentives*. A company's replacement decisions will be influenced by taxation (particularly capital allowances) and by the availability of government investment incentives.

In our discussion of asset replacement decisions taxation will be assumed to be included within the net cash flows given in the examples.

(e) *Opportunity costs*. A new asset is probably capable of greater productivity than an ageing asset, so any delay in replacement may involve the loss of output which would have been obtainable from a new asset.

1.3 Two types of replacement decision will be considered.

(a) The replacement of an existing asset with a new, but identical, asset. The problem is therefore simply one of deciding how frequently the asset should be replaced, that is of finding the optimum replacement cycle.

(b) The replacement of an existing asset with a different asset.

2. REPLACEMENT CYCLES

2.1 The following example will be used to show methods of deciding how frequently an asset should be replaced where the new asset will be identical to the old.

2.2 Noel Hayter Ltd operates a machine which has the following costs and resale values over its four year life.

Purchase cost £25,000.

	Year 1	*Year 2*	*Year 3*	*Year 4*
	£	£	£	£
Running costs (cash expenses)	7,500	10,000	12,500	15,000
Resale value (end of year)	15,000	10,000	7,500	2,500

How frequently should the asset be replaced? The company's cost of capital is 10%.

2.3 There are three methods of deciding the optimum replacement cycle.
(a) The lowest common multiple method
(b) The finite horizon method
(c) The equivalent annual cost method.

2.4 All three methods recognise that a replacement asset will eventually be replaced itself by an asset which will also in its turn be replaced. That is, replacements are assumed to occur into the indefinite future. The options in our example are to replace the machine:

(a) every year
(b) every two years;
(c) every three years;
(d) every four years.

To compare these options, we must assess the cost of each one over a comparable period of time.

The lowest common multiple method

2.5 The lowest common multiple method is as follows.

(a) Estimate cash flows over a period of time which is the lowest common multiple of all the replacement cycles under consideration. Thus for replacement cycles of one, two, three or four years, the lowest common multiple is 12 years. In 12 years there would be:

(i) 12 complete replacement cycles of one year; or
(ii) six complete replacement cycles of two years; or
(iii) four complete replacement cycles of three years; or
(iv) three complete replacement cycles of four years.

(b) Discount these cash flows over the lowest common multiple time period. The option with the lowest present value of cost will be the optimum replacement cycle.

2.6 In our example, we can calculate the annual cash flows as follows.

(a) *Replacement every year*

Year		£	£
0	Purchase		(25,000)
1	Running cost	(7,500)	
	Resale value	15,000	
	New purchase	(25,000)	
			(17,500)
2-11	Same as year 1		
12	Running cost	(7,500)	
	Resale value	15,000	
			7,500

The new purchase at the end of year 12 is ignored, because this starts a new 12-year cycle for all four replacement options.

(b) *Replacement every two years*

Year		£	£
0	Purchase		(25,000)
1	Running cost		(7,500)
2	Running cost	(10,000)	
	Resale value	10,000	
	New purchase	(25,000)	
			(25,000)
3,5,7,9,11	Same as year 1		
4,6,8,10	Same as year 2		
12	Running cost	(10,000)	
	Resale value	10,000	
			0

(c) *Replacement every three years*

Year		£	£
0	Purchase		(25,000)
1	Running cost		(7,500)
2	Running cost		(10,000)
3	Running cost	(12,500)	
	Resale value	7,500	
	New purchase	(25,000)	
			(30,000)
4,7,10	Same as year 1		
5,8,11	Same as year 2		
6,9	Same as year 3		
12	Running cost	(12,500)	
	Resale value	7,500	
			(5,000)

(d) *Replacement every four years*

Year		£	£
0	Purchase		(25,000)
1	Running cost		(7,500)
2	Running cost		(10,000)
3	Running cost		(12,500)
4	Running cost	(15,000)	
	Resale value	2,500	
	New purchase	(25,000)	
			(37,500)
5,9	Same as year 1		
6,10	Same as year 2		
7,11	Same as year 3		
8	Same as year 4		
12	Running cost	(15,000)	
	Resale value	2,500	
			(2,500)

2.7 We can now go on to calculate the present value for each replacement policy.

	Replacement every year		*Replacement every 2 years*		*Replacement every 3 years*		*Replacement every 4 years*	
Year	*Cash flow*	*PV at 10%*	*Cash flow*	*PV at 10%*	*Cash flow*	*PV at 10%*	*Cash flow*	*PV at 10%*
	£	£	£	£	£	£	£	£
0	(25,000)	(25,000)	(25,000)	(25,000)	(25,000)	(25,000)	(25,000)	(25,000)
1	(17,500)		(7,500)	(6,818)	(7,500)	(6,818)	(7,500)	(6,818)
2	(17,500)		(25,000)	(20,650)	(10,000)	(8,260)	(10,000)	(8,260)
3	(17,500)		(7,500)	(5,632)	(30,000)	(22,530)	(12,500)	(9,388)
4	(17,500)		(25,000)	(17,075)	(7,500)	(5,123)	(37,500)	(25,613)
5	(17,500)		(7,500)	(4,658)	(10,000)	(6,210)	(7,500)	(4,658)
6	(17,500)	(113,663)	(25,000)	(14,100)	(30,000)	(16,920)	(10,000)	(5,640)
7	(17,500)		(7,500)	(3,848)	(7,500)	(3,848)	(12,500)	(6,413)
8	(17,500)		(25,000)	(11,675)	(10,000)	(4,670)	(37,500)	(17,513)
9	(17,500)		(7,500)	(3,180)	(30,000)	(12,720)	(7,500)	(3,180)
10	(17,500)		(25,000)	(9,650)	(7,500)	(2,895)	(10,000)	(3,860)
11	(17,500)		(7,500)	(2,625)	(10,000)	(3,500)	(12,500)	(4,375)
12	7,500	2,393	0	0	(5,000)	(1,595)	(12,500)	(3,988)
PV of costs		(136,270)		(124,911)		(120,089)		(124,706)

2.8 The cheapest policy would be to replace the machine every three years, because this has the lowest total present value of costs.

The finite horizon method

2.9 The lowest common multiple method can be tedious when the maximum life of the asset is more than about three years. If the maximum life were, say, seven years, the replacement options would be every 1, 2, 3, 4, 5, 6 or 7 years, and the lowest common multiple would be 420 years.

2.10 The finite horizon method is to calculate the present value of costs for each option over a fairly long period (perhaps 15 or 20 years), because the present values of cash flows beyond this period are unlikely to affect the ranking of the replacement options.

The equivalent annual cost method

2.11 When there is no inflation, the equivalent annual cost method is the quickest method of deciding the optimum replacement cycle. It is necessary to calculate the present value of costs for each replacement cycle, but over one cycle only.

	Replace every year		*Replace every 2 years*		*Replace every 3 years*		*Replace every 4 years*	
Year	*Cash flow*	*PV at 10%*	*Cash flow*	*PV at 10%*	*Cash flow*	*PV at 10%*	*Cash flow*	*PV at 10%*
	£	£	£	£	£	£	£	£
0	(25,000)	(25,000)	(25,000)	(25,000)	(25,000)	(25,000)	(25,000)	(25,000)
1	7,500	6,818	(7,500)	(6,818)	(7,500)	(6,818)	(7,500)	(6,818)
2			0	0	(10,000)	(8,260)	(10,000)	(8,260)
3					(5,000)	(3,755)	(12,500)	(9,388)
4							(12,500)	(8,538)
		(18,182)		(31,818)		(43,833)		(58,004)

2.12 These costs are not comparable, because they refer to different time periods.

The equivalent annual cost method of comparing these cash flows is to calculate, for each length of replacement cycle, an equivalent annual cost. It is calculated as

$$\frac{\text{The PV cost over one replacement cycle}}{\text{The cumulative present value factor for the number of years in the cycle}}$$

2.13 In our example, given a discount rate of 10%, we have the following figures.

		Equivalent Annual Cost
		£
(a)	Replacement every year	
	$\frac{£(18,182)}{0.909}$	(20,002)
(b)	Replacement every two years	
	$\frac{£(31,818)}{1.736}$	(18,328)
(c)	Replacement every three years	
	$\frac{£(43,833)}{2.487}$	(17,625)
(d)	Replacement every four years	
	$\frac{£(58,004)}{3.170}$	(18,298)

The optimum replacement policy is the one with the lowest equivalent annual cost, in this case to replace every three years. This is the same conclusion reached by the lowest common multiple method.

2.14 The equivalent annual cost method is recommended as being quicker and less cumbersome than either of the other methods described.

3. NON-IDENTICAL REPLACEMENT

3.1 When a machine will be replaced by a machine of a different type, there is a different replacement problem. The decision is now 'when should the existing asset be replaced?' rather than 'how frequently?'

Example

3.2 Suppose that the machine of Noel Hayter Ltd, in our previous example in Paragraph 2.2, is a new machine, which will be introduced to replace a non-identical existing machine, which is nearing the end of its life and has a maximum remaining life of only three years. The company wishes to decide when is the best time to replace the old machine, and estimates of relevant costs have been drawn up as follows.

Year	*Resale value of current machine*	*Extra expenditure and opportunity costs of keeping the existing machine in operation during the year*
	£	£
0	8,500	0
1	5,000	9,000
2	2,500	12,000
3	0	15,000

3.3 When is the best time to replace the existing machine? The costs of the new machine will be those given in Paragraph 2.2, so that the optimum replacement cycle for the new machine will be three years as already calculated, with an equivalent annual cost of £17,625 (paragraph 2.13(c)).

Solution

3.4 The best time to replace the existing machine will be the option which gives the lowest NPV of cost in perpetuity, for both the existing machine and the machine which eventually replaces it.

The present value of costs in perpetuity of the *new* machine is

$$\frac{£17,625}{0.1} = £176,250$$

3.5. This present value of £176,250 relates to the beginning of the year when the first annual cash flow occurs, so that if replacement occurs now, the first annuity payment is at year 1, and the PV is a year 0 value. If replacement occurs at the end of the first year, the first annuity payment is at year 2, and the PV is a year 1 value, and so on.

3.6 The total cash flows of the replacement decision may now be presented as follows. These cash flows show the PV of cost in perpetuity of the new machine and its replacements, the running costs of the existing machine, and the resale value of the existing machine, at year 0, 1, 2 or 3 as appropriate.

Year	*Replace now*	*Replace in 1 year*	*Replace in 2 years*	*Replace in 3 years*
	£	£	£	£
0	(176,250)	-	-	-
	8,500			
1	-	(176,250)		
		(9,000)	(9,000)	(9,000)
		5,000		
2	-	-	(176,250)	
			(12,000)	(12,000)
			2,500	
3	-	-	-	(176,250)
				(15,000)

3.7 The PVs of the replacement options are as follows.

	Year	*Cash flow*	*Discount factor*	*Present value*
		£	10%	£
Replace now	0	(176,250)		
		8,500		
		(167,750)	1.000	(167,750)
Replace in one year	1	(176,250)		
		(9,000)		
		5,000		
		(180,250)	0.909	(163,847)
Replace in two years	1	(9,000)	0.909	(8,181)
	2	(185,750)	0.826	(153,430)
				(161,611)
Replace in three years	1	(9,000)	0.909	(8,181)
	2	(12,000)	0.826	(9,912)
	3	(191,250)	0.751	(143,629)
				(161,722)

3.8 The optimum policy is to replace the existing machine in two years time, because this has the lowest total PV of costs.

4. REPLACEMENT DECISIONS AND INFLATION

4.1 The short-cut annuity techniques described above can only be used when inflation is ignored. If inflation affects costs and residual values over time, it is not possible to calculate an equivalent annual cost and the only satisfactory methods of making replacement decisions are:

(a) for replacement of identical assets, the lowest common multiple method or the finite horizon method (inflated costs would have to be estimated as accurately as possible over the relevant period of time);

(b) for non-identical replacements, the finite horizon method.

The replacement option with the lowest present value of (inflated) costs discounted to present values should be selected.

5. LEASE OR BUY DECISIONS

5.1 There are several ways of evaluating a decision whether to lease an asset, or to purchase it by another means of finance.

5.2 The *traditional method* is to take the view that a decision to lease is a financing decision, which can only be made after a decision to acquire the asset has already been taken. It is therefore necessary to make a two-stage decision, as follows.

(a) An acquisition decision is made on whether the asset is worth having. The PVs of operational costs and benefits from using the asset are found to derive an NPV.

(b) A financing decision is then made if the acquisition is justified by a positive NPV. This is the decision on whether to lease or buy.

5.3 The traditional method is complicated by the need to choose a discount rate for each stage of the decision.

(a) The cost of capital that should be applied to the cash flows for the acquisition decision is the cost of capital that the firm would normally apply to its project evaluations, typically its weighted average cost of capital.

(b) The cost of capital that should be applied to the (differential) cash flows for the financing decision is the cost of borrowing.

(i) We assume that if the firm decided to purchase the equipment, it would finance the purchase by borrowing funds (rather than out of retained profits).

(ii) We therefore compare the cost of borrowing with the cost of leasing (or hire purchase) by applying this cost of borrowing to the financing cash flows.

5.4 Taxation should be allowed for in the cash flows, so that the traditional method would recommend:

(a) discounting the cash flows of the acquisition decision at the firm's after-tax cost of capital;

(b) discounting the cash flows of the financing decision at the after-tax cost of borrowing.

Example

5.5 Mallen and Mullins Ltd has decided to install a new milling machine. The machine costs £20,000 and it would have a useful life of five years with a trade-in value of £4,000 at the end of the fifth year. Additional cash profits from the machine would be £8,000 a year for five years. A decision has now to be taken on the method of financing the project. Two methods of finance are being considered.

(a) The company could purchase the machine for cash, using bank loan facilities on which the current rate of interest is 14% before tax.

(b) The company could lease the machine under an agreement which would entail payment of £4,800 at the end of each year for the next five years.

The company's weighted average cost of capital is 12% after tax. The rate of corporation tax is 33%. If the machine is purchased, the company will be able to claim an annual writing down allowance of 25% of the reducing balance.

Advise the management on:

(a) whether to acquire the machine;

(b) the most economical method of finance;

(c) any other matter which should be considered before finally deciding which method of finance should be adopted.

Solution

5.6 The traditional method begins with the acquisition decision. The cash flows of the project should be discounted at 12%. The first writing down allowance is assumed to be claimed in the first year resulting in a saving of tax at year 2.

Capital allowances

Year	*Allowance*	£
1	25% of £20,000	5,000
2	75% of £5,000	3,750
3	75% of £3,750	2,813
4	75% of £2,813	2,110
		13,673
5	£(20,000 - 13,673 - 4,000)	2,327

Taxable profits and tax liability

Year	*Cash profits*	*Capital allowance*	*Taxable profits*	*Tax at 33%*
	£	£	£	£
1	8,000	5,000	3,000	990
2	8,000	3,750	4,250	1,403
3	8,000	2,813	5,187	1,712
4	8,000	2,110	5,890	1,944
5	8,000	2,327	5,673	1,872

NPV calculation for the acquisition decision

Year	*Equipment*	*Cash profits*	*Tax*	*Net cash flow*	*Discount factor*	*Present value*
	£	£	£	£	12%	£
0	(20,000)			(20,000)	1.000	(20,000)
1		8,000		8,000	0.893	7,144
2		8,000	(990)	7,010	0.797	5,587
3		8,000	(1,403)	6,597	0.712	4,697
4		8,000	(1,712)	6,288	0.636	3,999
5	4,000	8,000	(1,944)	10,056	0.567	5,702
6			(1,872)	(1,872)	0.507	(949)
					NPV	6,180

5.7 The NPV is positive, and so we conclude that the machine should be acquired, regardless of the method used to finance the acquisition.

5.8 The second stage is the financing decision, and cash flows are discounted at the after-tax cost of borrowing, which is at 14% × 67% = 9.38%, say 9%.

5.9 The only cash flows that we need to consider are those which will be affected by the choice of the method of financing. The operating savings of £8,000 a year, and the tax on these savings, can be ignored.

(a) *Differential cash flows*

Year	*Item*	*Cash flow*	*Discount factor*	*PV*
		£	9%	£
0	Equipment cost	(20,000)	1.000	(20,000)
5	Trade-in value	4,000	0.650	2,600
	Tax savings, from allowances			
2	33% × £5,000	1,650	0.842	1,389
3	33% × £3,750	1,238	0.772	956
4	33% × £2,813	928	0.708	657
5	33% × £2,110	696	0.650	452
6	33% × £2,327	768	0.596	458
				(13,488)

(b) *The PV of leasing costs*

Year	*Lease payment*	*Savings in tax (33%)*	*Discount factor*	*PV*
	£	£	9%	£
1-5	(4,800) pa		3.890	(18,672)
2-6		1,584 pa	3.569	5,653
			Net PV of leasing	(13,019)

5.10 The cheaper option would be to lease the machine. However, other matters to be considered include the following.

(a) *Running expenses.* The calculations assume that the running costs are the same under each alternative. This may not be so. Expenses like maintenance, consumable stores, insurance and so on may differ between the alternatives.

(b) *The effect on cash flow.* Purchasing requires an immediate outflow of £20,000 compared to nothing for leasing. This effect should be considered in relation to the company's liquidity position, which in turn will affect its ability to discharge its debts and to pay dividends.

(c) *Alternative uses of funds.* The proposed outlay of £20,000 for purchase should be considered in relation to alternative investments.

(d) *The trade-in value.* The net present value of purchase is materially affected by the trade-in value of £4,000 in the fifth year. This figure could be very inaccurate.

5.11 A disadvantage of the traditional approach to making a lease or buy decision is that if there is a negative NPV when the operational cash flows of the project are discounted at the firm's cost of capital, the investment will be rejected out of hand, with no thought given to how the investment might be financed. It is conceivable, however, that the costs of leasing might be so low that the project would be worthwhile provided that the leasing option were selected. If this is so, an investment opportunity should not be rejected without first giving some thought to its financing costs.

5.12 Other methods of making lease or buy decisions are as follows.

(a) Compare the cost of leasing with the cost of purchase, and select the cheaper method of financing; then calculate the NPV of the project on the assumption that the cheaper method of financing is used. In other words, make the financing decision first and the acquisition decision afterwards.

(b) Calculate an NPV for the project under each of two assumptions about financing.

(i) The machine is purchased.
(ii) The machine is leased.

Select the method of financing which gives the higher NPV, provided that the project is viable (that is, has a positive NPV). In other words, combine the acquisition and financing decisions together into a single-stage decision. This method is illustrated in the following example.

Example

5.13 In the case of Mallen and Mullins Ltd the NPV with purchase would be + £6,180. This was calculated in Paragraph 5.6 The NPV with leasing would be as follows. A discount rate of 12% is used here.

Year	*Profit less leasing cost*	*Tax at 33%*	*Net cash flow*	*Discount factor*		*PV*
	£	£	£	12%		£
1	3,200		3,200	0.893		2,858
2	3,200	(1,056)	2,144	0.797		1,709
3	3,200	(1,056)	2,144	0.712		1,527
4	3,200	(1,056)	2,144	0.636		1,364
5	3,200	(1,056)	2,144	0.567		1,216
6		(1,056)	(1,056)	0.507		(535)
				NPV	+	8,139

In this case, leasing is preferable, because the NPV is £1,959 higher.

Operating leases

5.14 Since operating leases are a form of renting, the only cash flows to consider for this type of leasing are:

(a) the lease payments;
(b) tax saved: operating lease payments are allowable expenses for tax purposes.

6. CONCLUSION

6.1 The techniques covered in Sections 1 to 4 of this chapter enable us to work out when assets should be replaced. However, we should bear in mind the limitations of these techniques. In particular, in a period of technical progress it is very unlikely that new assets will be *identical* to old ones.

6.2 The decision whether to lease or buy assets can be an important one for many businesses. Computations such as those set out here are needed to avoid expensive mistakes.

TEST YOUR KNOWLEDGE

The numbers in brackets refer to paragraphs of this chapter

1. A machine costs £50,000. Its maximum life is three years. Resale values and running costs for the machine each year over its life are as follows.

	Year		
	1	*2*	*3*
	£	£	£
Running costs	8,000	12,000	16,000
Resale value	40,000	30,000	20,000

   The company's cost of capital is 12%.

   How frequently should the asset be replaced? Use the equivalent annual cost method. (See below)

2. What is the traditional method for lease or buy decisions? (5.2)

3. How is taxation dealt with in the traditional method? (5.4)

4. What factors other than net present values should be considered when making lease or buy decisions? (5.10)

5. Give two alternatives to the traditional method of making lease or buy decisions. (5.12)

Now try questions 21 and 22 at the end of the text

Solution

1.

	Year	*Cash flow*	*Discount factor* 12%	*Present value*	*Equivalent annual cost*
		£	£	£	£
Replace every year	0	(50,000)	1.000	(50,000)	
	1	32,000	0.893	28,576	
				(21,424)	÷ 0.893
					= £(23,991)
Replace every two years	0	(50,000)	1.000	(50,000)	
	1	(8,000)	0.893	(7,144)	
	2	18,000	0.797	14,346	
				(42,798)	÷ 1.690
					= £(25,324)
Replace every three years	0	(50,000)	1.000	(50,000)	
	1	(8,000)	0.893	(7,144)	
	2	(12,000)	0.797	(9,564)	
	3	4,000	0.712	2,848	
				(63,860)	÷ 2.402
					= £(26,586)

Replacement every year is the cheapest option.

Chapter 17

AMALGAMATIONS, MERGERS AND TAKEOVERS. MANAGEMENT BUYOUTS

This chapter covers the following topics.

1. Amalgamations and takeovers
2. The conduct and financing of a takeover
3. The position of shareholders
4. Other matters in takeovers
5. Demergers
6. Management buyouts
7. Buy-ins

1. AMALGAMATIONS AND TAKEOVERS

1.1 A takeover is the purchase of a controlling interest in one company by another company. Takeovers are also called acquisitions, and are a form of 'external' investment.

An amalgamation is a *merger* between two separate companies to form a single company.

1.2 In practice, the distinction between amalgamations and takeovers is not always clear, for example when a large company 'merges' with another smaller company. The methods used for mergers are often the same as the methods used to make takeovers.

The reasons for an amalgamation or a takeover

1.3 When two or more companies join together, there should be a 'synergistic' effect.

Synergy can be described as the 2 + 2 = 5 effect, whereby a group after a takeover achieves combined results that reflect a better rate of return than was being achieved by the same resources used in two separate operations before the takeover. If company A, which makes annual profits of £200,000 merges with company B, which also makes annual profits of £200,000, the combined annual profits of the merged companies should be more than £400,000.

1.4 The main reasons why one company may wish to acquire the shares or the business of another are as follows.

(a) *Operating economies.* There are many ways in which operating economies can be realised through a combination of companies. Duplicate (and competing) facilities can be eliminated.

(b) *Management acquisition.* It is sometimes recognised that a company neither has, nor is likely to obtain in the immediate future, a management team of sufficient quality to ensure continued growth. In these circumstances it may be best to seek an amalgamation with another company which has aggressive and competent management.

(c) *Diversification.* The management of many companies may feel that the long term interest of the shareholders will be best served by spreading risk through diversification.

(d) *Asset backing.* A company in a risky industry with a high level of earnings relative to the net assets may attempt to reduce its overall risk by acquiring a company with substantial assets.

(e) *The quality of earnings.* A company may reduce its risk by acquiring another with less risky earnings.

(f) *Finance and liquidity.* A company may be able to improve its liquidity and its ability to raise new finance through the acquisition of another more financially stable company.

(g) *Growth.* A company may achieve growth through acquisition more cheaply than through internal expansion.

1.5 The aim of a merger or acquisition should be to make profits in the long term as well as in the short term.

(a) Acquisitions may provide:

(i) a means of entering a market at a lower cost than would be incurred if the company tried to develop its own resources;

(ii) a means of acquiring the business of a competitor. Acquisitions or mergers which might reduce or eliminate competition in a market may be prohibited by the Monopolies and Mergers Commission.

(b) Mergers, especially in Britain, have tended to be more common in industries with a history of little growth and low returns. Highly profitable companies tend to seek acquisitions rather than mergers.

Factors in a takeover decision

1.6 Several factors will influence a decision to try to take over a target business. These include the following.

Price factors

(a) What would the cost of acquisition be?

(b) Would the acquisition be worth the price?

(c) Alternatively, factors (a) and (b) above could be expressed in terms of:
What is the highest price that it would be worth paying to acquire the business?

The value of a business could be assessed in terms of:

(i) its earnings;
(ii) its assets;
(iii) its prospects for sales and earnings growth;
(iv) how it would contribute to the short-term and long-term strategy of the 'predator' company.

Other factors

(a) Would the takeover be regarded as desirable by the predator company's shareholders and (in the case of quoted companies) the stock market in general?

(b) Are the owners of the target company amenable to a takeover bid? Or would they be likely to adopt defensive tactics to resist a bid?

(c) What form would the purchase consideration take? An acquisition is accomplished by buying the shares of a target company. The purchase consideration might be cash, but the purchasing company might issue new shares (or loan stock) and exchange them for shares in the company taken over. If purchase is by means of a share exchange, the former shareholders in the company taken over will acquire an interest in the new, enlarged company.

(d) How would the takeover be reflected in the published accounts of the predator company?

(e) Would there be any other potential problems arising from the proposed takeover, such as:

(i) future dividend policy;
(ii) service contracts for key personnel?

1.7 The share price in takeovers will be discussed in some detail in the next chapter on the valuation of businesses. In this chapter, we will consider the other factors listed above.

2. THE CONDUCT AND FINANCING OF A TAKEOVER

Will the bidding company's shareholders approve of a takeover?

2.1 When a company is planning a takeover bid for another company, its board of directors should give some thought to how its own shareholders might react to the bid.

2.2 A company does not have to ask its shareholders for their approval of every takeover, but:

(a) when a large takeover is planned by a listed company involving the issue of a substantial number of new shares by the predator company (to pay for the takeover), Stock Exchange rules may require the company to obtain the formal approval of its shareholders to the takeover bid at a general meeting (probably an extraordinary general meeting, called specifically to approve the takeover bid);

(b) if shareholders, and the stock market in general, think the takeover is not a good one the market value of the company's shares is likely to fall. The company's directors have a responsibility to protect their shareholders' interests, and are accountable to them at the annual general meeting of the company.

2.3 A takeover bid might seem unattractive to shareholders of the bidding company because:

(a) it might reduce the EPS of their company;
(b) the target company is in a risky industry, or is in danger of going into liquidation;
(c) it might reduce the net asset backing per share of the company, because the target company will probably be bought at a price which is well in excess of its net asset value.

Will a takeover bid be resisted by the target company?

2.4 Quite often, a takeover bid will be resisted. Resistance comes from:

(a) the target company's board of directors, who adopt defensive tactics;
(b) eventually, the target company's shareholders, who can refuse to sell their shares to the bidding company.

2.5 Resistance can be overcome by offering a higher price. In cases where an *unquoted* company is the target company, if resistance to a takeover cannot be overcome, the takeover will not take place, and negotiations would simply break down.

2.6 In cases where the target company is a *quoted* company, the situation is different. The target company will have many shareholders, some of whom will want to accept the offer for their shares, and some of whom will not. In addition, the target company's board of directors might resist a takeover, even though their shareholders might want to accept the offer.

2.7 Because there are likely to be major differences of opinion about whether to accept a takeover bid or not, the Stock Exchange has issued formal rules for the conduct of takeover bids, in the City code on takeovers and mergers.

Contesting an offer: defensive tactics

2.8 The directors of a target company must act in the interests of their shareholders, employees and creditors. They may decide to contest an offer on several grounds.

(a) The offer may be unacceptable because the terms are poor. Rejection of the offer may lead to an improved bid.

(b) The merger or takeover may have no obvious advantage.

(c) Employees may be strongly opposed to the bid.

(d) The founder members of the business may oppose the bid, and appeal to the loyalty of other shareholders.

2.9 When a company receives a takeover bid which the board of directors considers unwelcome, the directors must act quickly to fight off the bid.

The steps that might be taken to thwart a bid or make it seem less attractive include:

(a) issuing a forecast of attractive future profits and dividends to persuade shareholders that to sell their shares would be unwise, that the offer price is too low, and that it would be better for them to retain their shares to benefit from future profits, dividends and capital growth. Such profit and dividend forecasts can be included in 'defence documents' circulated to shareholders, and in press releases;

(b) lobbying the Office of Fair Trading and/or the Department of Trade and Industry to have the offer referred to the Monopolies and Mergers Commission;

(c) launching an advertising campaign against the takeover bid. One technique is to attack the accounts of the predator company;

(d) finding a 'white knight', a company which will make a welcome takeover bid;

(e) making a counter-bid for the predator company. This can only be done if the companies are of reasonably similar size;

(f) arranging a management buyout.

2.10 The tactics that can be used in fighting off a takeover bid are restricted by the City code, which is described later.

2.11 Takeover bids, when contested, can be very expensive, involving:

(a) costs of professional services, such as a merchant bank and a public relations agency;
(b) advertising costs;
(c) underwriting costs;
(d) interest costs;
(e) possibly also a capital loss on the sale and then re-purchase of some of the target company's shares, although a capital gain is equally likely.

Gaining the consent of the target company shareholders

2.12 A takeover bid will only succeed if the predator company can persuade enough shareholders in the target company to sell their shares. Shareholders will only do this if:

(a) they are dissatisfied with the performance of their company and its shares; or
(b) they are attracted by a high offer and the chance to make a good capital gain.

The Monopolies and Mergers Commission

2.13 A company might have to consider whether its proposed takeover would be drawn to the attention of the Monopolies and Mergers Commission. Under the terms of the Monopolies and Mergers Act, the Office of Fair Trading (the OFT) is entitled to scrutinize all mergers and takeovers above a certain size. If the OFT thinks that a merger or a takeover might be against the public interest, it will refer it to the Monopolies and Mergers Commission.

Proposed mergers can be notified to the OFT in advance. If no referral is made to the Monopolies and Mergers Commission within (normally) 20 days, the merger can proceed without fear of a referral.

2.14 The function of the Commission is to advise the government. If the Commission finds that a merger or takeover is against the public interest it can make recommendations to the Department of Trade and Industry (or to any other body, including the companies involved in the bid).

2.15 The result of an investigation by the Commission might be:

(a) a withdrawal of the proposal for the merger or takeover, in anticipation of its rejection by the Commission;

(b) acceptance or rejection of the proposal by the Commission;

(c) acceptance of the proposal by the Commission subject to the new company agreeing to certain conditions laid down by the Commission, for example on prices, employment or arrangements for the sale of the group's products.

The European Commission

2.16 The European Commission, rather than the Monopolies and Mergers Commission, must approve mergers where the worldwide turnovers of all the companies concerned total more than 5,000,000,000 ecus (about £3,500,000,000) or at least two companies involved each have European Community-wide turnovers of at least 250,000,000 ecus (about £175,000,000). However, the European Commission does not regulate mergers where each company derives at least two thirds of its European Community-wide turnover from one and the same member state: such mergers remain within the remit of the Monopolies and Mergers Commission (or similar bodies in other states).

The ecu turnover limits set out here are likely to be sharply reduced by 1993.

The purchase consideration

2.17 The terms of a takeover will involve a purchase of the shares of the target company for cash or for 'paper' (shares, or possibly loan stock). A purchase of a target company's shares with shares of the predator company is referred to as a *share exchange*.

Cash purchases

2.18 If the purchase consideration is in cash, the shareholders of the target company will simply be bought out. For example, suppose that there are two companies.

	Big Ltd	*Small Ltd*
Net assets (book value)	£1,500,000	£200,000
Number of shares	100,000	10,000
Earnings	£2,000,000	£40,000

Big Ltd negotiates a takeover of Small Ltd for £400,000 in cash.

2.19 As a result, Big Ltd will end up with:

(a) Net assets (book value) of
£1,500,000 + £200,000 - £400,000 cash = £1,300,000;

(b) 100,000 shares (no change);

(c) expected earnings of £2,040,000, minus the loss of interest (net of tax) which would have been obtained from the investment of the £400,000 in cash which was given up to acquire Small Ltd.

Purchases with paper

2.20 One company can acquire another company by issuing shares to pay for the acquisition. The new shares might be issued:

(a) in exchange for shares in the target company. Thus, if A plc acquires B Ltd, A plc might issue shares which it gives to B Ltd's shareholders in exchange for their shares. The B Ltd shareholders therefore become new shareholders of A plc. This is a takeover for a 'paper' consideration. Paper offers will often be accompanied by a cash alternative;

(b) to raise cash on the stock market, which will then be used to buy the target company's shares. To the target company shareholders, this is a cash bid.

2.21 Sometimes, a company might acquire another in a share exchange, but the shares are then sold immediately on a stock market to raise cash for the seller. For example, A plc might acquire B Ltd by issuing shares which it gives to B's shareholders; however A plc's stockbrokers arrange to 'place' these shares with other buyers, and so sell the newly-issued shares for cash on behalf of the ex-shareholders of B Ltd. This sort of arrangement, which is a mixture of (a) and (b), is called a 'vendor placing.'

2.22 Whatever the detailed arrangements of a takeover with paper, the end result will be an increase in the issued share capital of the company making the takeover.

The choice between a cash offer and a paper offer

2.23 The choice between cash and paper offers (or a combination of both) will depend on how the different methods are viewed by the company and its existing shareholders, and on the attitudes of the shareholders of the target company.

The factors that the directors of the bidding company must consider include the following.

(a) *The company and its existing shareholders*

(i) *Dilution of earnings per share.* A fall in the EPS attributable to the existing shareholders is undesirable, but it might occur when the purchase consideration is in equity shares.

(ii) *The cost to the company.* The use of loan stock (or of cash borrowed elsewhere) will be cheaper to the acquiring company than equity as the interest will be allowable for tax purposes. A direct consequence of this is that dilution of earnings may be avoided. If convertible loan stock is used, the coupon rate could probably be slightly lower than with ordinary loan stock.

(iii) *Gearing.* A highly geared company may find that the issue of additional loan stock either as consideration or to raise cash for the consideration may be unacceptable to some or all of the parties involved.

(iv) *Control.* In takeovers involving a relatively large new issue of ordinary shares the effective control of the company can change considerably. This could be unpopular with the existing shareholders.

(v) *An increase in authorised share capital.* If the consideration is in the form of shares, it may be necessary to increase the company's authorised capital. This would involve calling a general meeting to pass the necessary resolution.

(vi) *Increases in borrowing limits.* A similar problem arises if a proposed issue of loan stock will required a change in the company's borrowing limit as specified in the Articles.

(b) *The shareholders in the target company*

(i) *Taxation.* If the consideration is in cash many investors may find that they face an immediate liability to tax on a realised capital gain, whereas the liability would be postponed if the consideration consisted of shares.

(ii) *Income.* Where the consideration is other than cash, it is normally necessary to ensure that existing income is at least maintained. A drop may, however, be accepted if it is compensated for by a suitable capital gain or by reasonable expectations of future growth.

(iii) *Future investments.* Shareholders in the target company might want to retain a stake in the business after the takeover, and so would prefer the offer of shares in the bidding company, rather than a cash offer.

Mezzanine finance and takeover bids

2.24 When the purchase consideration in a takeover bid is cash, the cash must be obtained somehow by the bidding company, in order to pay for the shares that it buys.

(a) Occasionally, the company will have sufficient cash in hand to pay for the target company's shares.

(b) More frequently, the cash will have to be raised:
(i) possibly from existing shareholders, by means of a rights issue;
(ii) more probably, by borrowing from banks or other financial institutions.

2.25 When cash for a takeover is raised by borrowing, the loans would normally be medium-term and secured.

2.26 Recently, however, there have been several takeover bids, with a cash purchase option for the target company's shareholders, where the bidding company has arranged loans that:

(i) are short-to-medium term;
(ii) are unsecured (that is, are 'junior' debt, low in the priority list for repayment in the event of liquidation of the borrower);
(iii) because they are unsecured, attract a much higher rate of interest than secured debt;
(iv) often, give the lender the option to exchange the loan for shares after the takeover.

This type of borrowing has been called 'mezzanine finance'.

3. THE POSITION OF SHAREHOLDERS

The market values of the companies' shares during a takeover bid

3.1 Market share prices can be very important during a takeover bid. Suppose that Velvet plc decides to make a takeover bid for the shares of Noggin plc. Noggin plc shares are currently quoted on the market at £2 each. Velvet shares are quoted at £4.50 and Velvet offers one of its shares for every two shares in Noggin, thus making an offer at current market values worth £2.25 per share in Noggin. This is only the value of the bid so long as Velvet's shares remain valued at £4.50. If their value falls, the bid will become less attractive.

This is why companies that make takeover bids with a share exchange offer are always concerned that the market value of their shares should not fall during the takeover negotiations, before the target company's shareholders have decided whether to accept the bid.

3.2 If the market price of the target company's share rises *above* the offer price during the course of a takeover bid, the bid price will seem too low, and the takeover is then likely to fail, with shareholders in the target company refusing to sell their shares to the bidder.

EPS before and after a takeover

3.3 If one company acquires another by issuing shares, its EPS will go up or down according to the P/E ratio at which the target company has been bought.

(a) If the target company's shares are bought at a higher P/E ratio than the predator company's shares, the predator company's shareholders will suffer a fall in EPS.
(b) If the target company's shares are valued at a lower P/E ratio, the predator company's shareholders will benefit from a rise in EPS.

Example

3.4 Giant plc takes over Tiddler Ltd by offering two shares in Giant for one share in Tiddler. Details about each company are as follows.

	Giant plc	*Tiddler Ltd*
Number of shares	2,800,000	100,000
Market value per share	£4	-
Annual earnings	£560,000	£50,000
EPS	20p	50p
P/E ratio	20	

By offering two shares in Giant worth £4 each for one share in Tiddler, the valuation placed on each Tiddler share is £8, and with Tiddler's EPS of 50p, this implies that Tiddler would be acquired on a P/E ratio of 16. This is lower than the P/E ratio of Giant, which is 20.

3.5 If the acquisition produces no synergy, and there is no growth in the earnings of either Giant or its new subsidiary Tiddler, then the EPS of Giant would still be higher than before, because Tiddler was bought on a lower P/E ratio. The combined group's results would be as follows.

	Giant group
Number of shares (2,800,000 + 200,000)	3,000,000
Annual earnings (560,000 + 50,000)	610,000
EPS	20.33p

If the P/E ratio is still 20, the market value per share would be £4.07, which is 7p more than the pre-takeover price.

Example

3.6 Redwood plc agrees to acquire the shares of Hawthorn Ltd in a share exchange arrangement. The agreed P/E ratio for Hawthorn's shares is 15.

	Redwood plc	*Hawthorn Ltd*
Number of shares	3,000,000	100,000
Market price per share	£2	-
Earnings	£600,000	£120,000
P/E ratio	10	

3.7 The EPS of Hawthorn Ltd is £1.20, and so the agreed price per share will be £1.20 × 15 = £18. In a share exchange agreement, Redwood would have to issue nine new shares (valued at £2 each) to acquire each share in Hawthorn, and so a total of 900,000 new shares must be issued to complete the takeover.

3.8 After the takeover, the enlarged company would have 3,900,000 shares in issue and, assuming no earnings growth, total earnings of £720,000. This would give an EPS of

$$\frac{£720,000}{£3,900,000} = 18.5p$$

The pre-takeover EPS of Redwood was 20p, and so the EPS would fall. This is because Hawthorne has been bought on a higher P/E ratio (15 compared with Redwood's 10).

Buying companies on a higher P/E ratio, but with profit growth

3.9 Buying companies on a higher P/E ratio will result in a fall in EPS unless there is profit growth to offset this fall. For example, suppose that Starving plc acquires Bigmeal plc, by offering two shares in Starving for three shares in Bigmeal. Details of each company are as follows.

	Starving plc	*Bigmeal plc*
Number of shares	5,000,000	3,000,000
Value per share	£6	£4
Annual earnings		
Current	£2,000,000	£600,000
Next year	£2,200,000	£950,000
EPS	40p	20p
P/E ratio	15	20

3.10 Starving plc is acquiring Bigmeal plc on a higher P/E ratio, and it is only the profit growth in the acquired subsidiary that gives the enlarged Starving group its growth in EPS.

		Starving group
Number of shares	(5,000,000 + 2,000,000)	7,000,000
Earnings		
If no profit growth	(2,000,000 + 600,000) £2,600,000	EPS would have been 37.24p
With profit growth	(2,200,000 + 950,000) £3,150,000	EPS will be 45p

If an acquisition strategy involves buying companies on a higher P/E ratio, it is therefore essential for continuing EPS growth that the acquired companies offer prospects of strong profit growth.

Reverse takeovers

3.11 A reverse takeover occurs when the smaller company takes over the larger one, so that the 'predator' company has to increase its voting equity by over 100% to complete the takeover.

Further points to consider: net assets per share and the quality of earnings

3.12 It might be concluded from what has been said above that dilution of earnings must be avoided at all cost. However, there are three cases where a dilution of earnings might be accepted on an acquisition if there were other advantages to be gained.

(a) Earnings growth may hide the dilution in EPS as above.

(b) A company might be willing to accept earnings dilution if the quality of the acquired company's earnings is superior to that of the acquiring company.

(c) A trading company with high earnings, but with few assets, may want to increase its asset base by acquiring a company which is strong in assets but weak in earnings so that assets and earnings get more into line with each other. In this case, dilution in earnings is compensated for by an increase in net asset backing.

Example

3.13 Intangible plc has an issued capital of 2,000,000 £1 ordinary shares. Net assets (excluding goodwill) are £2,500,000 and annual earnings average £1,500,000. The company is valued by the stock market on a P/E ratio of 8. Tangible Ltd has an issued capital of 1,000,000 ordinary shares. Net assets (excluding goodwill) are £3,500,000 and annual earnings average £400,000. The shareholders of Tangible Ltd accept an all-equity offer from Intangible plc valuing each share in Tangible Ltd at £4. Calculate Intangible plc's earnings and assets per share before and after the acquisition of Tangible Ltd.

Solution

3.14 (a) Before the acquisition of Tangible Ltd, the position is as follows.

$$\text{Earnings per share (EPS)} = \frac{£1,500,000}{2,000,000} = 75\text{p}$$

$$\text{Assets per share (APS)} = \frac{£2,500,000}{2,000,000} = £1.25$$

(b) Tangible Ltd's EPS figure is 40p (£400,000 ÷ 1,000,000), and the company is being bought on a multiple of 10 at £4 per share. As the takeover consideration is being satisfied by shares, Intangible plc's earnings will be diluted because Intangible plc is valuing Tangible Ltd on a higher multiple of earnings than itself. Intangible plc will have to issue 666,667 shares valued at £6 each (earnings of 75p per share at a multiple of 8) to satisfy the £4,000,000 consideration. The results for Intangible plc will be as follows.

$$\text{EPS} = \frac{£1,900,000}{2,666,667} = 71.25\text{p (3.75p lower than the previous 75p)}$$

$$\text{APS} = \frac{£6,000,000}{2,666,667} = £2.25\text{ (£1 higher than the previous £1.25)}$$

If Intangible plc is still valued on the stock market on a P/E ratio of 8, the share price should fall by approximately 30p (8 × 3.75p, the fall in EPS) but because the asset backing has been increased substantially the company will probably now be valued on a higher P/E ratio than 8.

3.15 The shareholders in Tangible Ltd would receive 666,667 shares in Intangible plc in exchange for their current 1,000,000 shares, that is, two shares in Intangible for every three shares currently held.

(a) Earnings

	£
Three shares in Tangible earn (3 × 40p)	1.200
Two shares in Intangible will earn (2 × 71.25p)	1.425
Increase in earnings, per three shares held in Tangible	0.225

(b) Assets

	£
Three shares in Tangible have an asset backing of (3 × £3.5)	10.50
Two shares in Intangible will have an asset backing of (2 × £2.25)	4.50
Loss in asset backing, per three shares held in Tangible	6.00

The shareholders in Tangible Ltd would be trading asset backing for an increase in earnings.

Dividends and dividend cover

3.16 A further issue which may create some difficulties before a merger or takeover can be agreed is the level of dividends and dividend cover expected by shareholders in each of the companies concerned. Once the companies merge, a single dividend policy will be applied.

4. OTHER MATTERS IN TAKEOVERS

Service contracts for key personnel

4.1 When the target company employs certain key personnel, on whom the success of the company has been based, the predator company might want to ensure that these key people do not leave as soon as the takeover occurs. To do this, it might be necessary to insist as a condition of the offer that the key people should agree to sign service contracts, tying them to the company for a certain time (perhaps three years). Service contracts would have to be attractive to the employees concerned, perhaps through offering a high salary or other benefits such as share options in the predator company.

The Takeover Panel and the City code on takeovers and mergers

4.2 The City code is a code of behaviour which companies are expected to follow during a takeover or merger, as a measure of self-discipline. The code has no legal backing, although it is administered and enforced by the Takeover Panel.

4.3 The nature and purpose of the City code is described within the code itself as follows.

> 'The code represents the collective opinion of those professionally involved in the field of takeovers on a range of business standards. It is not concerned with the financial or commercial advantages or disadvantages of a takeover, which are matters for the company and its shareholders, or with those wider questions which are the responsibility of the government, advised by the Monopolies and Mergers Commission.
>
> The code has not, and does not seek to have, the force of law, but those who wish to take advantage of the facilities of the securities markets in the United Kingdom should conduct themselves in matters relating to takeovers according to the code. Those who do not so conduct themselves cannot expect to enjoy those facilities and may find that they are withheld.'

4.4 Companies subject to the code include all public companies (listed or unlisted) and also some classes of private company.

The City code: general principles

4.5 The City code is divided into general principles and detailed rules which must be observed by persons involved in a merger or takeover transaction. The general principles include the following.

(a) 'All shareholders of the same class of an offeree company must be treated similarly by an offeror.' In other words, a company making a takeover bid cannot offer one set of purchase terms to some shareholders in the target company, and a different set of terms to other shareholders holding shares of the same class in that company.

(b) 'During the course of a takeover, or when such is in contemplation, neither the offeror nor the offeree company ...may furnish information to some shareholders which is not made available to all shareholders.'

(c) 'Shareholders must be given sufficient information and advice to enable them to reach a properly informed decision and must have sufficient time to do so. No relevant information should be withheld from them.'

(d) 'At no time after a *bona fide* offer has been communicated to the board of an offeree company ... may any action be taken by the board of the offeree company in relation to the affairs of the company, without the approval of the shareholders in general meeting, which could effectively result in any *bona fide* offer being frustrated or in the shareholders being denied an opportunity to decide on its merits.'

In other words, directors of a target company are not permitted to frustrate a takeover bid, nor to prevent the shareholders from having a chance to decide for themselves.

(e) 'Rights of control must be exercised in good faith and the oppression of a minority is wholly unacceptable.'

For example, a holding company cannot take decisions about a takeover bid for one of its subsidiaries in such a way that minority shareholders would be unfairly treated.

(f) 'Where control of a company is acquired ... a general offer to all other shareholders is normally required.'

Control is defined as a 'holding , or aggregate holdings, of shares carrying 30% of the voting rights of a company, irrespective of whether that holding or holdings gives *de facto* control.'

The City code: rules

4.6 In addition to its general principles, the City code also contains a number of detailed rules, which are intended to govern the conduct of the parties in a takeover bid. These rules relate to matters such as:

(a) how the approach to the target company should be made by the predator company;
(b) the announcement of a takeover bid;
(c) the obligation of the board of a target company to seek independent advice (for example from a merchant bank);
(d) conduct during the offer.

5. DEMERGERS

5.1 Mergers and takeovers are not inevitably good strategy for a business. In some circumstances, strategies of internal growth, no growth or even demerger might be preferable.

5.2 A demerger is the opposite of a merger. It is the splitting up of a corporate body into two or more separate and independent bodies. For example, the ABC Group plc might demerge by selling its 100% shareholding in a subsidiary, C plc, to an outside buyer, who will then run C plc as an independent company. This would be a case of *disinvestment* by the group, withdrawing from its investment in C plc.

5.3 The reasons for demergers could be any of the following.

(a) An unprofitable subsidiary could be sold. The buyer might perhaps be a group of the subsidiary's managers, with the management buyout team being backed by venture capital finance.

(b) Subsidiaries which are not 'core businesses' and do not fit in with the group's strategic plans could be sold.

(c) A subsidiary with high risk in its operating cash flows could be sold, so as to reduce the business risk of the group as a whole.

(d) A subsidiary could be sold at a profit. Some companies have specialised in taking over large groups of companies, and then selling off parts of the newly-acquired groups, so that the proceeds of sales more than pay for the original takeovers.

5.4 The potential disadvantages with demergers are as follows.

(a) Economies of scale may be lost, where the demerged parts of the business had operations in common to which economies of scale applied.

(b) The smaller companies which result from the demerger will have lower turnover, profits and status than the group before the demerger.

(c) There may be higher overhead costs as a percentage of turnover, resulting from (b).

(d) The ability to raise extra finance, especially debt finance, to support new investments and expansion may be reduced.

6. MANAGEMENT BUYOUTS

6.1 A management buyout is the purchase of all or part of a business from its owners by its managers. For example, the directors of a subsidiary company in a group might buy the company from the holding company, with the intention of running it as proprietors of a separate business entity.

6.2 To the managers, the buyout would be a method of setting up in business for themselves. To the group, the buyout would be a method of disinvestment, selling off the subsidiary as a going concern.

6.3 When a firm decides to divest itself of a part of its operations, it will try to get what it can by selling off the business as a unit, or by selling individual assets. Usually, a better price can be obtained by selling the business as a unit, and there might well be many other firms interested in buying it. In recent years, however, there have been a large number of management buyouts, whereby the subsidiary is sold off to its managers. The managers put in some of their own capital, but obtain the rest from venture capital organisations, and hope to make a bigger success of the business than the company which is selling it.

6.4 Management buyouts might easily be thought of as attempts by a company to sell loss-making subsidiaries. In fact, management buyouts more commonly involve the sale of *profitable* subsidiaries, which are being sold simply because they do not fit in well with the group's strategic plans.

The parties to a buyout

6.5 There are usually three parties to a management buyout.

(a) There is a management team wanting to make a buyout. This team ought to have the skills and ability to convince financial backers that it is worth supporting.

(b) There are the directors of a group of companies, who make the disinvestment decision.

(c) There are financial backers of the buyout team, who will usually want an equity stake in the bought-out business, because of the venture capital risk they are taking. Often, several financial backers provide the venture capital for a single buyout.

6.6 The management team making the buyout would probably have the aims of:
(a) setting up in business themselves, being owners rather than mere employees; or
(b) avoiding redundancy, when the subsidiary is threatened with closure.

6.7 A large organisation's board of directors may agree to a management buyout of a subsidiary for any of a member of different reasons.

(a) The subsidiary may be peripheral to the group's mainstream activities, and no longer fit in with the group's overall strategy.

(b) The group may wish to sell off a loss-making subsidiary, and a management team may think that it can restore the subsidiary's fortunes.

(c) The parent company may need to raise cash quickly.

(d) The subsidiary may be part of a group that has just been taken over and the new parent company may wish to sell off parts of the group it has just acquired.

(e) The best offer price might come from a small management group wanting to arrange a buyout.

(f) When a group has taken the decision to sell a subsidiary, it will probably get better co-operation from the management and employees of the subsidiary if the sale is a management buyout.

6.8 A private company's shareholders might agree to sell to a management team because:
(a) they need cash;
(b) they want to retire;
(c) the business is not profitable enough for them.

6.9 The buyout team will have to find willing financial backers, and so it must convince them that it can run the business successfully. To help with the task of convincing the bank or other institution, the management team should prepare:
(a) a business plan;
(b) estimates of sales, costs, profits and cash flows, in reasonable detail.

6.10 If the parent company's existing shareholders have already indicated their willingness to sell, the management team should have reasonably free access to the sort of figures they need about revenues, costs, areas for improved efficiency and cost savings, and so on.

The appraisal of proposed buyouts

How likely is a management buyout to succeed?

6.11 So far, management-owned companies seem to get better performance out of their company, probably because of:

(a) personal motivation and determination;
(b) quicker decision making and so more flexibility;
(c) keener decisions and action on pricing and debt collection;
(d) savings in overheads, for example avoiding the need to make contributions to a large head office.

However, many management buyouts, once they occur, begin with some redundancies to cut running costs.

6.12 The prospects of success for a management buyout ought to be evaluated:

(a) by the managers who are thinking of making the buyout;
(b) by the institutional investors who are being asked to put in venture capital to finance the buyout.

How should an institutional investor evaluate a buyout?

6.13 An institutional investor should evaluate a buyout before deciding whether or not to finance it. Aspects of any buyout that ought to be checked are as follows.

(a) Does the management team have the full range of management skills that are needed (for example a technical expert and a finance director)? Does it have the right blend of experience? Does it have the commitment?

(b) Why is the company for sale? The possible reasons for buyouts have already been listed. If the reason is that the parent company wants to get rid of a loss-making subsidiary, what evidence is there to suggest that the company can be made profitable after a buyout?

(c) What are the projected profits and cash flows of the business? The prospective returns must justify the risks involved.

(d) What is being bought? The buyout team might be buying
(i) the shares of the company; or
(ii) only selected assets of the company.

Are the assets that are being acquired sufficient for the task? Will more assets have to be bought? When will the existing assets need replacing? How much extra finance would be needed for these asset purchases? Can the company be operated profitably?

(e) What is the price? Is the price right or is it too high?

(f) What financial contribution can be made by members of the management team themselves?

The financial arrangements in a typical buyout

6.14 Typically, the buyout team will have a minority of the equity in the bought-out company, with the financial backers holding a majority of the shares between them. A buyout might have several financial backers, each providing finance in exchange for some equity.

6.15 The financial institutions will regard their investment as a fairly long-term one, but they might hope that if the company is successful, it will eventually be floated on a stock market, perhaps the USM, thus giving a market value to their equity, and the option to sell their shares if they wish to realise their investment.

6.16 Investors of venture capital usually want the managers to be financially committed. Individual managers could borrow personally from a bank, say £20,000 to £50,000. This should be enough to commit them without hurting them too much.

6.17 The suppliers of equity finance might insist on investing part of their capital in the form of redeemable convertible preference shares. These often have voting rights should the preference dividend fall in arrears, giving increased influence over the company's affairs. They are issued in a redeemable form to give some hope of taking out part of the investment if it does not develop satisfactorily, and in convertible form for the opposite reason: to allow an increased stake in the equity of a successful company.

6.18 Some buyouts are very largely financed with debt, rather than equity, lent by external investors. Such buyouts are often referred to as *leveraged buyouts*.

Possible problems with buyouts

6.19 A common problem with management buyouts is that the managers have little or no experience in financial management or financial accounting.

Other problems are:

(a) tax and legal complications;
(b) difficulties in deciding on a fair price to be paid;
(c) convincing employees of the need to change working practices;
(d) inadequate cash flow to finance the maintenance and replacement of tangible fixed assets;
(e) the maintenance of previous employees' pension rights;
(f) accepting the board representation requirement that many sources of funds will insist upon;
(g) the loss of key employees if the company moves geographically, or wage rates are decreased too far, or employment conditions are unacceptable in other ways.

7. BUY-INS

7.1 A management buy-in occurs when a team of *outside* managers, as opposed to managers who are already running the business, mount a takeover bid and then run the business themselves.

7.2 A buy-in might occur when a business venture is running into trouble, and a group of outside managers see an opportunity to take over the business and restore its profitability.

8. CONCLUSION

8.1 Buying another company is a substantial undertaking for a company. The target company's shareholders must be persuaded of the benefits of the takeover. Takeover bids are not infrequent, and it is worth following one or two in the financial press, so as to see how the considerations set out in this chapter translate into practice.

8.2 Management buyouts are a special sort of transaction, involving several parties. A buyout cannot go ahead unless all the parties are satisfied with the arrangements.

TEST YOUR KNOWLEDGE

The numbers in brackets refer to paragraphs of this chapter

1. What might be the reasons for an amalgamation or takeover? (1.4)
2. List the factors in a takeover decision for the bidding company. (1.6)
3. Why might the shareholders of the bidding company disapprove of a bid for a target company by their board of directors? (2.3)
4. What defensive tactics might a company's board of directors adopt to resist an unwelcome takeover bid? (2.9)
5. What factors might affect the choice between a cash offer and a paper offer in a takeover bid? (2.23)
6. What is mezzanine finance? (2.26)
7. If a bidding company issues shares to buy a target company on a *lower* P/E ratio than the bidding company shares are valued at, what will happen to the bidding company's own EPS after the takeover? (3.3)
8. How is dividend policy affected by a takeover bid? (3.16)
9. What are the reasons for demergers? (5.3)
10. Why do management buyouts occur? (6.4)
11. How should an institutional investor evaluate a management buyout? (6.13)
12. Why might an investor in a management buyout ask for redeemable convertible preference shares in return for his investment? (6.17)

Now try question 23 at the end of the text

Chapter 18

THE VALUATION OF LISTED AND UNLISTED COMPANIES

This chapter covers the following topics.

1. Reasons for share valuations
2. Methods of valuing shares

1. REASONS FOR SHARE VALUATIONS

1.1 It may be wondered why, given quoted share prices on the Stock Exchange, there is any need to devise techniques for estimating the value of a share. A share valuation will be necessary:

(a) *for quoted companies*, when there is a takeover bid and the offer price is an estimated 'fair value' in excess of the current market price of the shares;

(b) *for unquoted companies*, when:
   (i) the company wishes to 'go public' and must fix an issue price for its shares;
   (ii) there is a scheme of merger, and a value of shares for each company involved in the merger must be assessed;
   (iii) shares are sold;
   (iv) shares need to be valued for the purposes of taxation;
   (v) shares are pledged as collateral for a loan;

(c) *for subsidiary companies*, when the group's holding company is negotiating the sale of the subsidiary to a management buyout team or to an external buyer.

1.2 Our main interest in this chapter is with methods of valuing the entire equity in a company, perhaps for the purpose of making a takeover bid, rather than with the value of small blocks of shares which an investor might choose to buy or sell on the stock market.

2. METHODS OF VALUING SHARES

2.1 The most common methods of valuing shares for the reasons listed in Paragraph 1.1 are:

(a) the earnings method (P/E ratio method);
(b) the accounting rate of return method;
(c) the net assets method;
(d) the dividend yield method;
(e) use of the CAPM;

(f) the super-profits method;
(g) DCF-based valuations.

Each method will give a different share valuation.

2.2 It is unlikely that one method would be used in isolation. Several valuations might be made, each using a different technique or different assumptions. The valuations could then be compared, and a final price reached as a compromise between the different values.

The P/E ratio (earnings) method of valuation

2.3 This is a common method of valuing a *controlling interest* in a company, where the owner can decide on dividend and retentions policy. The P/E ratio relates earnings per share to a share's value.

$$\text{Since P/E ratio} = \frac{\text{Market value}}{\text{EPS}}$$

$$\text{Market value} = \text{EPS} \times \text{P/E ratio}$$

2.4. The concept of the P/E ratio can be used to make an earnings-based valuation of shares. This is done by deciding a suitable P/E ratio and multiplying this by the EPS for the shares which are being valued. The EPS could be a historical EPS or a prospective future EPS.

2.5 For a given EPS figure, a higher P/E ratio will result in a higher price. A high P/E ratio may indicate:

(a) expectations that the EPS will grow rapidly in the years to come, so that a high price is being paid for future profit prospects. Many small, but successful and fast-growing companies are valued on the stock market on a high P/E ratio;

(b) security of earnings. A well-established low-risk company would be valued on a higher P/E ratio than a similar company whose earnings are subject to greater uncertainty;

(c) status. If a quoted company made a share-for-share takeover bid for an unquoted company, it would normally expect its own shares to be valued on a higher P/E ratio than the target company's shares. This is because a quoted company ought to be a lower-risk company; but in addition, there is a clear advantage in having shares which are quoted on a stock market: the shares can be readily sold. As a general guideline, the P/E ratio of an unquoted company's shares might be around 50% to 60% of the P/E ratio of a similar public company with a full Stock Exchange listing (and perhaps 70% of that of a company whose shares are traded on the USM).

Example

2.6 Spider plc is considering the takeover of an unquoted company, Fly Ltd. Spider's shares are quoted on the Stock Exchange at a price of £3.20 and since the most recent published EPS of the company is 20p, the company's P/E ratio is 16. Fly Ltd is a company with 100,000 shares and current earnings of £50,000, 50p per share. How might Spider plc decide on an offer price?

Solution

2.7 The decision about the offer price is likely to be based on deciding first of all what a reasonable P/E ratio would be.

(a) If Fly Ltd is in the same industry as Spider plc, its P/E ratio ought to be lower, because of its lower status as an unquoted company.

(b) If Fly Ltd is in a different industry, a suitable P/E ratio might be based on the P/E ratio that is typical for quoted companies in that industry.

(c) If Fly Ltd is thought to be growing fast, so that its EPS will rise rapidly in the years to come, the P/E ratio that should be used for the share valuation will be higher than if only small EPS growth is expected.

(d) If the acquisition of Fly Ltd would contribute substantially to Spider's own profitability and growth, or to any other strategic objective that Spider has, then Spider should be willing to offer a higher P/E ratio valuation, in order to secure acceptance of the offer by Fly's shareholders.

Of course, the P/E ratio on which Spider bases its offer will probably be lower than the P/E ratio that Fly's shareholders think their shares ought to be valued on. Some haggling over the price might be necessary.

2.8 Spider might decide that Fly's shares ought to be valued on a P/E ratio of 60% × 16 = 9.6, that is, at 9.6 × 50p = £4.80 each.

Fly's shareholders might reject this offer, and suggest a valuation based on a P/E ratio of, say, 12.5, that is, 12.5 × 50p = £6.25.

Spider's management might then come back with a revised offer, say valuation on a P/E ratio of 10.5, that is, 10.5 × 50p = £5.25.

The haggling will go on until the negotiations either break down, or succeed in arriving at an agreed price.

General guidelines for a P/E ratio-based valuation

2.9 When a company is thinking of acquiring an *unquoted* company in a takeover, the final offer price will be agreed by negotiation, but a list of some of the factors affecting the valuer's choice of P/E ratio is given below.

(a) General economic and financial conditions.

(b) The type of industry and the prospects of that industry.

(c) The size of the undertaking and its status within its industry. If an unquoted company's earnings are growing annually and are currently around £300,000 or so, then it could probably get a quote in its own right on the USM and a higher P/E ratio should therefore be used when valuing its shares.

(d) Marketability. The market in shares which do not have a Stock Exchange quotation is always a restricted one and a higher yield is therefore required. Because of restrictions on transfer given in their Articles, any 'private' market in the shares of private companies is likely to be particularly small. It is not uncommon for a quoted company to have a P/E ratio twice the size of that attributed to a private company in the same industry. For examination purposes, you should normally take a figure around one half to two thirds of the industry average when valuing an unquoted company.

(e) The diversity of shareholdings and the financial status of any principal shareholders.

(f) The reliability of profit estimates and the past profit record.

(g) Asset backing and liquidity.

(h) The nature of the assets, for example whether some of the fixed assets are of a highly specialised nature, and so have only a small break-up value.

(i) Gearing. A relatively high gearing ratio will generally mean greater financial risk for ordinary shareholders and call for a higher rate of return on equity.

(j) The extent to which the business is dependent on the technical skills of one or more individuals.

Exercise

Flycatcher Ltd wishes to make a takeover bid for the shares of an unquoted company, Mayfly Ltd. The earnings of Mayfly Ltd over the past five years have been as follows.

19X0	£50,000	19X3	£71,000
19X1	£72,000	19X4	£75,000
19X2	£68,000		

The average P/E ratio of quoted companies in the industry in which Mayfly Ltd operates is 10. Quoted companies which are similar in many respects to Mayfly Ltd are:

(a) Bumblebee plc, which has a P/E ratio of 15, but is a company with very good growth prospects;

(b) Wasp plc, which has had a poor profit record for several years, and has a P/E ratio of 7.

What would be a suitable range of valuations for the shares of Mayfly Ltd?

Solution

(a) *Earnings*. Average earnings over the last five years have been £67,200, and over the last four years £71,500. There might appear to be some growth prospects, but estimates of future earnings are uncertain.

A low estimate of earnings in 19X5 would be, perhaps, £71,500.

A high estimate of earnings might be £75,000 or more. This solution will use the most recent earnings figure of £75,000 as the high estimate.

(b) *P/E ratio.* A P/E ratio of 15 (Bumblebee's) would be much too high for Mayfly Ltd, because the growth of Mayfly Ltd earnings is not as certain, and Mayfly Ltd is an unquoted company.

On the other hand, Mayfly Ltd's expectations of earnings are probably better than those of Wasp plc. A suitable P/E ratio might be based on the industry's average, 10; but since Mayfly is an unquoted company and therefore more risky, a lower P/E ratio might be more appropriate: perhaps 60% to 70% of 10 = 6 or 7, or conceivably even as low as 50% of 10 = 5.

The valuation of Mayfly Ltd's shares might therefore range between:

high P/E ratio and high earnings: 7 × £75,000 = £525,000; and

low P/E ratio and low earnings: 5 × £71,500 = £357,500.

Forecast growth in earnings

2.10 When one company is thinking about taking over another, it should look at the target company's forecast earnings, not just its historical results.

Forecasts of the future earnings of a target company might be attempted by managers in the company which is planning to make the takeover bid. Quite commonly, however, the management of the predator company will make an initial approach to the board of directors of the target company, to sound them out about a possible takeover bid. If the target company's directors are amenable to a bid, they might agree to produce forecasts of their company's future earnings and growth. These forecasts (for the next year and possibly even further ahead) might then be used by the predator company in choosing an offer price.

2.11 Forecasts of earnings growth should only be used if:

(a) there are good reasons to believe that earnings growth will be achieved;
(b) a reasonable estimate of growth can be made;
(c) any forecasts supplied by the target company's board of directors are made in good faith.

The accounting rate of return (ARR) method of share valuation

2.12 This method considers the accounting rate of return which will be required from the company whose shares are to be valued. It is therefore distinct from the P/E ratio method, which is concerned with the market rate of return required.

The following formula should be used.

$$\text{Value} = \frac{\text{Estimated future profits}}{\text{Required return on capital employed}}$$

2.13 For a takeover bid valuation, it will often be necessary to adjust the profits figure to allow for expected changes after the takeover. Those arising in an examination question might include:

(a) new levels of directors' remuneration;

(b) new levels of interest charges (perhaps because the predator company will be able to replace existing loans with new loans at a lower rate of interest, or because the previous owners had lent the company money at non-commercial rates);

(c) a charge for notional rent where it is intended to sell existing properties or where the rate of return used is based on the results of similar companies that do not own their own properties;

(d) the effects of product rationalisation and improved management.

Example

2.14 Chambers Ltd is considering acquiring Hall Ltd. At present Hall Ltd is earning, on average, £480,000 after tax. The directors of Chambers Ltd feel that after reorganisation, this figure could be increased to £600,000. All the companies in the Chambers group are expected to yield a post-tax accounting return of 15% on capital employed. What should Hall Ltd be valued at?

Solution

2.15 Valuation $= \frac{£600,000}{15\%} = £4,000,000$

This figure is the maximum that Chambers should be prepared to pay. The first offer would probably be much lower.

2.16 An ARR valuation might be used in a takeover when the acquiring company is trying to assess the maximum amount it can afford to pay. This is because it is a measure of management efficiency and the rate used can be selected to reflect (among other things) the return which the acquiring company thinks should be obtainable after any post-acquisition reorganisation has been completed. A valuation on this basis should then be compared with the Stock Exchange price (for quoted companies) or a price arrived at using the P/E ratio of similar quoted companies.

The net assets method of share valuation

2.17 Using this method of valuation, the value of a share in a particular class is equal to the net tangible assets attributable to that class, divided by the number of shares in the class. Intangible assets (including goodwill) should be excluded, unless they have a market value (for example patents and copyrights, which could be sold).

(a) Goodwill, if shown in the accounts, is unlikely to be shown at a true figure for purposes of valuation, and the value of goodwill should be reflected in another method of valuation (for example the earnings basis, the dividend yield basis or the super-profits method).

(b) Development expenditure, if shown in the accounts, would also have a value which is related to future profits rather than to the worth of the company's physical assets.

Example

2.18 The summary balance sheet of Cactus Ltd is as follows.

Fixed assets		£	£
Land and buildings			160,000
Plant and machinery			80,000
Motor vehicles			20,000
			260,000
Goodwill			20,000
Current assets			
Stocks		80,000	
Debtors		60,000	
Short-term investments		15,000	
Cash		5,000	
		160,000	
Current liabilities	£		
Creditors	60,000		
Taxation	20,000		
Proposed ordinary dividend	20,000		
		100,000	
			60,000
			340,000
12% debentures			(60,000)
Deferred taxation			(10,000)
			270,000
			£
Ordinary shares of £1			80,000
Reserves			140,000
			220,000
4.9% preference shares of £1			50,000
			270,000

What is the value of an ordinary share using the net assets basis of valuation?

Solution

2.19 If the figures given for asset values are not questioned, the valuation would be as follows.

	£	£
Total value of net assets		340,000
Less intangible asset (goodwill)		20,000
Total value of tangible assets(net)		320,000
Less: preference shares	50,000	
debentures	60,000	
deferred taxation	10,000	
		120,000
Net asset value of equity		200,000
Number of ordinary shares		80,000
Value per share		£2.50

2.20 The difficulty in an asset valuation method is establishing the asset values to use. Values ought to be realistic.

The figure attached to an individual asset may vary considerably depending on whether it is valued on a going concern or a break-up basis.

2.21 The following list should give you some idea of the factors that must be considered.

(a) Do the assets need professional valuation? If so, how much will this cost?

(b) Have the liabilities been accurately quantified, for example deferred taxation? Are there any contingent liabilities? Will any balancing tax charges arise on disposal?

(c) How have the current assets been valued?

(i) Are all debtors collectable?
(ii) Is all stock realisable?

Can all the assets be physically located and brought into a saleable condition? This may be difficult in certain circumstances where the assets are situated abroad.

(d) Can any hidden liabilities be accurately assessed? Would there be redundancy payments and closure costs?

(e) Is there an available market in which the assets can be realised (on a break-up basis)? If so, do the balance sheet values truly reflect these break-up values?

(f) Are there any prior charges on the assets?

When is the net assets basis of valuation used?

2.22 The net assets basis of valuation should be used:

(a) *as a measure of the 'security' in a share value.* A share might be valued using the earnings basis, and this valuation might be:

(i) higher than the net asset value per share. If the company went into liquidation, the investor could not expect to receive the full value of his shares when the underlying assets were realised;

(ii) lower than the net asset value per share. If the company went into liquidation, the investor might expect to receive the full value of his shares (perhaps much more) when the underlying assets were realised.

The asset backing for shares thus provides a measure of the possible loss if the company fails to make the expected earnings or dividend payments. It is often thought to be a good thing to acquire a company with valuable tangible assets, especially freehold property which might be expected to increase in value over time;

(b) *as a measure of comparison in a scheme of merger*. For example, if company A, which has a low asset backing, is planning a merger with company B, which has a high asset backing, the shareholders of B might consider that their shares' value ought to reflect this. It might therefore be agreed that a something should be added to the value of the company B shares to allow for this difference in asset backing.

For these reasons, it is always advisable to calculate the net assets per share.

The dividend yield method of share valuation

2.23 The dividend yield method of share valuation is suitable for the valuation of small shareholdings in unquoted companies. It is based on the principle that small shareholders are mainly interested in dividends, since they cannot control decisions affecting the company's profits and earnings. A suitable offer price would therefore be one which compensates them for the future dividends they will be giving up if they sell their shares.

2.24 We have already come across the dividend yield model of share valuation. You might be expected to value shares using gross dividend yield rather than net dividend yield. Read any examination question carefully.

2.25 The simplest dividend capitalisation technique is based on the assumption that the level of dividends in the future will be *constant*. A dividend yield valuation would be:

$$\text{Value} = \frac{\text{Dividend in pence}}{\text{Expected dividend yield \%}}$$

2.26 It may be possible to use expected *future* dividends for a share valuation and to predict dividend growth. For this purpose, it is first necessary to predict future earnings and then to decide how changes in earnings will be reflected in the company's dividend policy.

2.27 The dividend growth model for share valuation, you may recall, is as follows.

$$MV = \frac{d_0(1 + g)}{(r - g)}$$

where MV is the current market value ex dividend
d_0 is the current dividend
g is the expected annual growth in dividend, so d_0 (1 + g) is the expected dividend next year
r is the return required.

The CAPM and share price valuations

2.28 The CAPM might be used to value shares, particularly when pricing shares for a stock market listing. The CAPM would be used to establish a required equity yield.

Example

2.29 Suppose that Mackerel plc is planning to obtain a Stock Exchange listing by offering 40% of its existing shares to the public. No new shares will be issued. Its most recent summarised results are as follows.

	£
Turnover	120,000,000
Earnings	1,500,000
Number of shares	3,000,000

The company has low gearing.

It regularly pays 50% of earnings as dividends, and with reinvested earnings is expected to achieve 5% dividend growth each year.

Summarised details of two listed companies in the same industry as Mackerel plc are as follows.

	Salmon plc	*Trout plc*
Gearing (total debt/total equity)	45%	10%
Equity beta	1.50	1.05

The current Treasury bill yield is 7% a year. The average market return is estimated to be 12%.

The new shares will be issued at a discount of 15% to the estimated post-issue market price, in order to increase the prospects of success for the share issue.

What will the issue price be?

Solution

2.30 Using the CAPM, we begin by deciding on a suitable β value for Mackerel's equity. We shall assume that since Mackerel's gearing is close to Trout's, a β of 1.05 is appropriate.

The cost of Mackerel equity is 7% + 1.05 (12 - 7)% = 12.25%

2.31 This can now be used in the dividend growth model. The dividend this year is 50% of £1,500,000 = £750,000.

The total value of Mackerel's equity is $\frac{£750,000\ (1.05)}{(0.1225-0.05)}$ = £10,862,068

There are 3,000,000 shares, giving a market value per share of £3.62.

2.32 Since the shares that are offered to the public will be offered at a discount of about 15% to this value, the share price for the market launch should be about 85% of £3.62 = £3.08.

The super-profits method of share valuation

2.33 This method, which is rather out of fashion at present, starts by applying a 'fair return' to the net tangible assets and comparing the result with the expected profits. Any excess of profits (the super-profits) is used to calculate goodwill.

The goodwill is normally taken as a fixed number of years super-profits. The goodwill is then added to the value of the target company's tangible assets to arrive at a value for the business.

Example

2.34 Light Ltd has net tangible assets of £120,000 and present earnings of £20,000. Doppler Ltd wants to take over Light Ltd and considers that a fair return for this type of industry is 12%, and decides to value Light Ltd taking goodwill at three years super-profits.

	£
Actual profits	20,000
Less fair return on net tangible assets: 12% × £120,000	14,400
Super-profits	5,600
Goodwill: 3 × £5,600	£16,800
Value of Light Ltd: £120,000 + £16,800	£136,800

2.35 The principal drawbacks to this valuation method are as follows.

(a) The rate of return required is chosen subjectively.

(b) The number of years purchase of super-profits is arbitrary. In the example above, goodwill was valued at three years of super-profits, but it could have been, for example, two years or four years of super-profits.

The discounted future profits method of share valuation

2.36 This method of share valuation may be appropriate when one company intends to buy the assets of another company and to make further investments in order to improve profits in the future.

Example

2.37 Diversification Ltd wishes to make a bid for Tadpole Ltd. Tadpole Ltd makes after-tax profits of £40,000 a year. Diversification Ltd believes that if further money is spent on additional investments, the after-tax cash flows (ignoring the purchase consideration) could be as follows.

Year	*Cash flow (net of tax)*
	£
0	(100,000)
1	(80,000)
2	60,000
3	100,000
4	150,000
5	150,000

The after-tax cost of capital of Diversification Ltd is 15% and the company expects all its investments to pay back, in discounted terms, within five years.

What is the maximum price that the company should be willing to pay for the shares of Tadpole Ltd?

Solution

2.38 The maximum price is one which would make the return from the total investment exactly 15% over five years, so that the NPV at 15% would be 0.

Year	*Cash flows ignoring purchase consideration*	*Discount factor at 15%*	*Present value*
	£		£
0	(100,000)	1.000	(100,000)
1	(80,000)	0.870	(69,600)
2	60,000	0.756	45,360
3	100,000	0.658	65,800
4	150,000	0.572	85,800
5	150,000	0.497	74,550
Maximum purchase price			101,910

3. CONCLUSION

3.1 There are a number of different ways of putting a value on a business, or on shares in an unquoted company. It makes sense to use several methods of valuation, and to compare the values they produce. At the end of the day, however, what really matters is the final price that the buyer and the seller agree. The purchase price for a company will usually be discussed mainly in terms of:

(a) P/E ratios, when a large block of shares, or a whole business is being valued;
(b) alternatively, a DCF valuation;
(c) to a lesser extent, the net assets per share.

The dividend yield method is more relevant to small shareholdings.

TEST YOUR KNOWLEDGE

The numbers in brackets refer to paragraphs of this chapter

1. Why are valuations of companies sometimes necessary? (1.1)

2. What guidelines should help to determine the P/E ratio on which to base an offer price for shares in a target company? (2.9)

3. How should the net assets of a company be valued, for a net assets method valuation? (2.17 - 2.21) Why is the net assets method of valuation used as a reference value? (2.22)

4. A company expects to pay no dividends in years 1, 2 or 3, but a dividend of 7.8p per share each year from year 4 in perpetuity. Value its shares on a dividend yield basis, assuming a required yield of 12%. (See below)

Now try question 24 at the end of the text

Solution

4.

$$\frac{7.8p}{(1.12)^4} + \frac{7.8p}{(1.12)^5} + \dots\dots\dots$$

$$= \frac{7.8p}{0.12} \times \frac{1}{(1.12)^3}$$

$$= \frac{65p}{(1.12)^3} = 46.26p, \text{ say } 46p$$

PART E

FINANCIAL STRUCTURING AND CONTROL AND REPORTING

Chapter 19

GROUPS OF COMPANIES

This chapter covers the following topics.

1. Sources of funds and investment decisions
2. Ratio analysis

1. SOURCES OF FUNDS AND INVESTMENT DECISIONS

1.1. The financial management of groups of companies is similar in most respects to the financial management of single companies. The activities of the group need financing; capital investment projects will be required to achieve a minimum return; the group will aim for maximisation of shareholder wealth; and working capital within the group must be managed and controlled.

Sources of funds

1.2 Some subsidiaries may be allowed to raise funds themselves. They cannot do this by issuing new shares (unless the holding company decides to reduce its percentage stake in the subsidiary), and so they must rely on:

(a) loans;
(b) retained profits;
(c) new funds from the holding company.

1.3 If a subsidiary raises funds by borrowing, there are implications for the gearing (and financial risk) of the group as a whole.

If a subsidiary raises funds from retained profits or obtains new funds from the holding company, this affects the group's overall dividend and retentions policy.

Decisions about where funds should be raised, and in what form, will therefore be taken principally by the holding company.

1.4 There might be *capital rationing*, with the holding company having to decide how the limited total funds of the group should be allocated between the subsidiaries.

Investment decisions

1.5 Even where subsidiary companies make most of their own project investment decisions, subject to the availability of capital, the holding company is likely to exercise some control.

(a) The holding company will probably put a limit on each subsidiary's capital budget.

(b) Holding company approval will be required for projects above a certain value.

(c) Some subsidiaries will have a higher business risk than others, and the holding company might therefore establish a cost of equity and so a discount rate for each subsidiary. For example, one might be required to earn 15% on its investments, whereas a riskier subsidiary might be required to earn 20%.

Example

1.6 A group of companies consists of a holding company and three subsidiaries, each operating in a different industry with different business risk characteristics.

The holding company tries to maintain a debt: equity ratio of 1:2 for the group as a whole. The risk-free cost of debt is 6%, but the group is able to borrow at 9%.

The average equity return for the market as a whole is 12%, but within the group, subsidiary A is in an industry which has a beta factor of 1.10, subsidiary B's industry has a beta factor of 0.95 and subsidiary C's industry has a beta factor of 1.40.

What cost of capital should each subsidiary be required to apply to its investments?

Assume a corporation tax rate of 33%.

Solution

1.7

	Cost of equity (Weighting = 2)	*After- tax cost of debt (Weighting = 1)*	*Weighted average cost of capital*
A	6% + 1.10 (12-6)% = 12.6%	(67% of 9) 6.03%	10.41%
B	6% + 0.95 (12-6)% = 11.7%	6.03%	9.81%
C	6% + 1.40 (12-6)% = 14.4%	6.03%	11.61%

Rounding up in each case, the cost of capital for each subsidiary might be set at 11% for A, 10% for B and 12% for C.

2. RATIO ANALYSIS

2.1 Subsidiary companies will be expected to report on their performance to the holding company.

(a) A group's performance can be measured in terms of growth in EPS or growth in dividend per share.

(b) A subsidiary's performance cannot be measured in the same way, because its financial environment is artificial (funds are obtained from the holding company, not from the market) and dividends are decided on by the holding company.

Financial reporting systems are therefore likely to be based on an analysis of financial ratios.

The categories of ratios

2.2 Ratios can be grouped into the following four categories.
(a) Profitability and return
(b) Debt and gearing
(c) Liquidity
(d) Shareholders' investment ratios.

2.3 The key to obtaining meaningful information from ratio analysis is comparison: comparing ratios over time within the same business to establish whether the business is improving or declining, and comparing ratios between similar businesses to see whether the company you are analysing is better or worse than average within its own business sector.

2.4 Ratio analysis on its own is not sufficient for interpreting company accounts, and there are other items of information which should be looked at. These include the following.

(a) Comments in the Chairman's report and the directors' report
(b) The age and nature of the company's assets
(c) Current and future developments in the company's markets, at home and overseas
(d) Recent acquisitions or disposals of a subsidiary by the company
(e) Extraordinary items in the profit and loss account
(f) The statement of source and application of funds
(g) Other features of the report and accounts, such as post balance sheet events, contingent liabilities, a qualified auditors' report and the company's taxation position.

Profitability

2.5 A company ought of course to be profitable, and obvious checks on profitability are:
(a) whether the company has made a profit or a loss on its ordinary activities;
(b) by how much this year's profit or loss is bigger or smaller than last year's profit or loss.

It is probably better to consider separately the profits or losses on extraordinary items if there are any. An extraordinary gain would obviously be a good bonus and an extraordinary loss might cause concern. However, such gains or losses should not be expected to occur again, unlike profits or losses on normal trading.

2.6 Profit on ordinary activities *before* taxation is generally thought to be a better figure to use than profit after taxation, because there might be unusual variations in the tax charge from year to year which would not affect the underlying profitability of the company's operations.

2.7 Another profit figure that should be considered is PBIT, the profit before interest and tax. This is the amount of profit which the company earned before having to pay interest to the providers of loan capital. Short-term borrowing (for example on overdrafts) is usually not treated as loan capital for this purpose, so overdraft interest is deducted in arriving at PBIT.

The return on investment (ROI)

2.8 It is impossible to assess profits or profit growth properly without relating them to the amount of funds (the capital) employed in making the profits.

2.9 The most important profitability ratio is therefore return on investment (ROI), also called return on capital employed (ROCE), which states the profit as a percentage of the amount of capital employed.

2.10 Profit is usually taken as PBIT, and capital employed is shareholders' capital plus long-term liabilities and debt capital. This is the same as total assets less current liabilities. The underlying principle is that we must compare like with like, and so if capital means share capital and reserves plus long-term liabilities and debt capital, profit must mean the profit earned by all this capital together. This is PBIT, since interest is the return for loan capital.

$$\text{Thus ROI} = \frac{\text{Profit on ordinary activities before interest and taxation (PBIT)}}{\text{Capital employed}}$$

Evaluating the ROI

2.11 What does a company's ROI tell us? What should we be looking for?

There are three comparisons that can be made.

(a) The change in ROI from one year to the next.

(b) The ROI being earned by other companies, if this information is available.

(c) A comparison of the ROI with current market borrowing rates.
  (i) What would be the cost of extra borrowing to the company if it needed more loans, and is it earning an ROI that suggests it could make high enough profits to make such borrowing worthwhile?
  (ii) Is the company earning an ROI which suggests that it is making profitable use of its current borrowing?

The return on equity

2.12 A company's management is primarily responsible to the ordinary shareholders. Rather than taking the ROI as the primary financial ratio, it could be argued that a more significant ratio is the return on equity.

$$\text{Return on equity} = \frac{\text{Profit attributable to ordinary shareholders}}{\text{Ordinary share capital + reserves}}$$

2.13 However, although this may be used for the holding company of the group, each subsidiary's primary financial ratio will be the ROI.

Analysing profitability and return in more detail: the secondary ratios

2.14 We can analyse the ROI, to find out why it is high or low, or better or worse than last year.

2.15 There are two factors that contribute towards the ROI, both related to turnover.

(a) *Profit margin.* A company might make a high or a low profit margin on its sales. For example, a company that makes a profit of 25p per £1 of sales is making a bigger return on its turnover than another company making a profit of only 10p per £1 of sales.

(b) *Asset turnover.* Asset turnover is a measure of how well the assets of a business are being used to generate sales. For example, if two companies each have capital employed of £100,000, and company A makes sales of £400,000 a year whereas company B makes sales of only £200,000 a year, company A is making a higher turnover from the same amount of assets and this will help company A to make a higher return on investment than company B. Asset turnover is expressed as 'x times' so that assets generate x times their value in annual turnover. Here, company A's asset turnover is 4 times and company B's is 2 times.

2.16 Profit margin and asset turnover together explain the ROI, and if the ROI is the primary profitability ratio, these other two are the secondary ratios. The relationship between the three ratios is as follows.

Profit margin × Asset turnover = ROI

$$\frac{\text{PBIT}}{\text{Sales}} \times \frac{\text{Sales}}{\text{Capital employed}} = \frac{\text{PBIT}}{\text{Capital employed}}$$

The gross profit margin, the net profit margin and profit analysis

2.17 Depending on the format of the profit and loss account, you may be able to calculate the gross profit margin as well as the net profit margin. Looking at the two together can be quite informative.

Example

2.18 A company has the following summarised profit and loss accounts for two consecutive years.

	Year 1	*Year 2*
	£	£
Turnover	70,000	100,000
Less cost of sales	42,000	55,000
Gross profit	28,000	45,000
Less expenses	21,000	35,000
Net profit	7,000	10,000

Although the net profit margin is the same for both years at 10%, the gross profit margin is not.

In year 1 it is: $\frac{28,000}{70,000}$ = 40%

and in year 2 it is: $\frac{45,000}{100,000}$ = 45%

2.19 Is this good or bad for the business? An increased profit margin must be good because this indicates a wider gap between selling price and cost of sales. However, given that the net profit ratio has stayed the same in the second year, expenses must be rising. In year 1 expenses were 30% of turnover, whereas in year 2 they were 35% of turnover. This indicates that administration or selling and distribution expenses require tight control.

Debt and gearing ratios

2.20 Debt ratios are concerned with how much the company owes in relation to its size and whether it is getting into heavier debt or improving its situation.

(a) When a company is heavily in debt, and seems to be getting even more heavily into debt, the thought that should occur to you is that this cannot continue. If the company carries on wanting to borrow more, banks and other would-be lenders are very soon likely to refuse further borrowing and the company might well find itself in trouble.

(b) When a company is earning only a modest profit before interest and tax, and has a heavy debt burden, there will be very little profit left over for shareholders after the interest charges have been paid. And so if interest rates were to go up or the company were to borrow even more, it might soon be incurring interest charges in excess of PBIT. This might eventually lead to the liquidation of the company.

2.21 These are the two main reasons why companies should keep their debt burden under control. There are four ratios that are particularly worth looking at.
(a) The gearing ratio
(b) Interest cover
(c) The debt ratio
(d) The cash flow ratio.

The first three of these were described in Chapter 6. We will now look at the cash flow ratio.

The cash flow ratio

2.22 The cash flow ratio is the ratio of a company's net annual cash inflow to its total debts:

$$\frac{\text{Net annual cash inflow}}{\text{Total debts}}$$

(a) The net annual cash inflow is the amount of cash which the company has coming into the business each year from its operations. A suitable figure for the net annual cash inflow is the 'funds provided by (or generated by) operations' shown in the statement of source and application of funds.

(b) Total debts are short-term and long-term creditors, together with provisions for liabilities and charges.

2.23 Obviously, a company needs to earn enough cash from operations to be able to meet its foreseeable debts and future commitments, and the cash flow ratio, and changes in the cash flow ratio from one year to the next, provides a useful indicator of a company's cash position.

Liquidity ratios

2.24 Profitability is of course an important aspect of a company's performance, and debt or gearing is another. Neither, however, addresses directly the key issue of liquidity. A company needs liquid assets so that it can meet its debts when they fall due.

2.25 Some assets are more liquid than others. In some businesses stocks of goods are fairly liquid. Stocks of finished production goods might be sold quickly, and a supermarket will hold consumer goods for resale that could well be sold for cash very soon.

2.26 Other stocks are not so liquid. Raw materials and components in a manufacturing company have to be used to make a finished product before they can be sold to realise cash, and so they are less liquid than finished goods. Just how liquid they are depends on the speed of stock turnover and the length of the production cycle.

2.27 The main source of liquid assets for a trading company is sales. A company can obtain cash from sources other than sales, such as the issue of shares for cash, a new loan or the sale of fixed assets. But a company cannot rely on these at all times, and in general, obtaining liquid funds depends on making sales and profits.

2.28 A company must be able to pay its debts when they fall due, and in the balance sheet, foreseeable creditors to be paid are represented by current liabilities, that is, amounts falling due within one year.

2.29 There are other payments that a company might want to make, such as the purchase of a new fixed asset for cash.

The current ratio and the quick ratio

2.30 The standard test of liquidity is the *current ratio*. It can be obtained from the balance sheet, and is

$$\frac{\text{current assets}}{\text{current liabilities}}$$

A company should have enough current assets that give a promise of 'cash to come' to meet its commitments to pay off its current liabilities. Obviously, a ratio in excess of 1 should normally be expected. Otherwise, there would be the prospect that the company might be unable to pay its debts on time. In practice, a ratio comfortably in excess of 1 should normally be expected, but what is 'comfortable' varies between different types of businesses.

2.31 Companies are not able to convert all their current assets into cash very quickly. In particular, some manufacturing companies might hold large quantities of raw material stocks, which must be used in production to create finished goods. Finished goods might be warehoused for a long time, or sold on lengthy credit. In such businesses, where stock turnover is slow, most stocks are not very liquid assets, because the cash cycle is so long. For these reasons, we calculate an additional liquidity ratio, known as the quick ratio or acid test ratio.

2.32 The *quick ratio*, or *acid test ratio*, is $\frac{\text{current assets less stocks}}{\text{current liabilities}}$

This ratio should ideally be at least 1 for companies with a slow stock turnover. For companies with a fast stock turnover, a quick ratio can be less than 1 without suggesting that the company is in cash flow difficulties.

The debtors' payment period

2.33 A rough measure of the average length of time it takes for a company's debtors to pay what they owe is the 'debtor days' ratio, or average debtors' payment period. It is

$$\frac{\text{trade debtors}}{\text{sales}} \times 365 \text{ days}$$

2.34 The figure for sales should be the turnover figure in the profit and loss account. The trade debtors are not the *total* figure for debtors in the balance sheet, which includes prepayments and non-trade debtors. The trade debtors figure will be given in an analysis of the total debtors, in a note to the accounts.

2.35 The estimate of debtor days is only approximate.

(a) The balance sheet value of debtors might be abnormally high or low compared with the level the company usually has.

(b) Turnover in the profit and loss account excludes VAT, but debtors in the balance sheet include VAT. We are not strictly comparing like with like.

2.36 Sales are often made on terms of payment within 30 days, or at the end of the month following the month in which the invoice is sent out. Debtor days *significantly* in excess of this might indicate poor management of the funds of a business. However, some companies must allow generous credit terms to win customers. Exporting companies in particular may have to carry large amounts of debtors, and so their average collection period might be well in excess of 30 days.

2.37 The *trend* of the collection period (debtor days) over time is probably the best guide. If debtor days are increasing, this indicates a poorly managed credit control function. Liquidity problems could then arise, because debtors would not be generating cash fast enough to pay creditors on time.

The stock turnover period

2.38 Another ratio worth calculating is the stock turnover period, or stock days. This is another estimated figure, obtainable from published accounts, which indicates the average number of days that items of stock are held for. As with the average debt collection period, however, it is only an approximate figure, but one which should be reliable enough for finding changes over time.

2.39 The number of stock days is $\frac{\text{stock}}{\text{cost of sales}} \times 365$

2.40 The ratio $\frac{\text{cost of sales}}{\text{stock}}$

is called the *stock turnover*, and is another measure of how vigorously a business is trading. A lengthening stock turnover period indicates:

(a) a slowdown in trading; or
(b) a build-up in stock levels, perhaps suggesting that the investment in stocks is becoming excessive.

2.41 If we add together the stock days and the debtor days, this should give us an indication of how soon stock is convertible into cash, thereby giving a further indication of the company's liquidity.

Shareholders' investment ratios

2.42 The final set of ratios we must consider are the ratios which help equity shareholders and other investors to assess the value and quality of an investment in the ordinary shares of a company. These ratios were described in Chapter 6. They are:

(a) the dividend yield;
(b) earnings per share;
(c) the price/earnings ratio;
(d) the dividend cover;
(e) the earnings yield.

Comparisons of accounting figures

2.43 Useful information is obtained from ratio analysis largely by means of comparisons. Comparisons that might be made are:

(a) between the company's results in the most recent year and its results in previous years;

(b) between the company's results and the results of other companies in the same industry;

(c) between the company's results and the results of other companies in other industries.

Results of the same company over successive accounting periods

2.44 Although a company might present useful information in its five year or ten year summary, it is quite likely that the only detailed comparison you will be able to make is between the current year's and the previous year's result. The comparison should give you some idea of whether the company's situation has improved, worsened or stayed much the same between one year and the next.

2.45 Useful comparisons over time include:

(a) the percentage growth in profit (before and after tax) and the percentage growth in turnover;
(b) increases or decreases in the debt ratio and the gearing ratio;
(c) changes in the current ratio, the stock turnover period and the debtors' payment period;
(d) increases in the EPS, the dividend per share and the market price.

2.46 The principal advantage of making comparisons over time are that they give some indication of progress: are things getting better or worse? However, there are some weaknesses in such comparisons.

(a) The effect of *inflation* should not be forgotten.
(b) The progress a company has made needs to be set in the context of:
    (i) what other companies have done;
    (ii) whether there have been any special 'environmental' or economic influences on the company's performance.

Problems with financial control through ratios

2.47 Ratio analysis does not provide a wholly satisfactory solution to financial control within a group of companies, because the results of one subsidiary will not be readily comparable with the results of another.

(a) Different subsidiaries within the group will have assets of different ages. This will influence the performance of each company as measured by the return on investment.

(b) Transfer prices which are used for sales within the group might have a major effect on the profits. Transfer prices are not necessarily market prices.

(c) The way in which overheads are allocated between subsidiaries will also influence reported profits.

(d) Long-term investments may not provide a good return for several years. If subsidiaries are evaluated using short term financial ratios for the current year, this may deter profitable long-term investments.

(e) Subsidiaries might attempt some 'window dressing' of their accounts in order to make their results look better.

Predicting business failure

2.48. The analysis of financial ratios is largely concerned with the efficiency and effectiveness of the use of resources by a company's management, and also with the financial stability of the company. Investors, including holding companies, will wish to know:

(a) whether additional funds could be lent to the company with reasonable safety;
(b) whether the company would fail without additional funds.

2.49 E I Altman researched into the simultaneous analysis of several financial ratios as a combined predictor of business failure. Altman analysed 22 accounting and non-accounting variables for a selection of failed and non-failed firms in the USA, and from these five key indicators emerged. These five indicators were then used to derive a *Z score*. Firms with a Z score above a certain level would be predicted to be financially sound, and firms with a Z score below a certain level would be expected to fail. Altman also identified a range of Z scores in between the non-failure and failure categories in which eventual failure or non-failure was uncertain.

2.50 Altman's Z score model (derived in 1968) emerged as:

$$Z = 1.2X_1 + 1.4X_2 + 3.3X_3 + 0.6X_4 + 1.0X_5$$

where

X_1 = working capital/total assets
X_2 = retained earnings/total assets
X_3 = earnings before interest and tax/total assets
X_4 = market value of equity/book value of total debt (a form of gearing ratio)
X_5 = sales/total assets.

2.51 In Altman's model, a Z score of 2.7 or more indicated non-failure, and a Z score of 1.8 or less indicated failure.

2.52 Altman's sample size was small, and related to US firms. Subsequent research based on the similar principle of identifying a Z score predictor of business failure has produced different prediction models, using a variety of financial ratios and different Z score values as predictors of failure. It could be argued, for example, that different ratios and Z score values would be appropriate for conditions in the UK.

The value of Z scores

2.53 A current view of the link between financial ratios and business failure would appear to be that:

(a) the financial ratios of firms which fail can be seen in retrospect to have deteriorated significantly prior to failure, and to have been worse than the ratios of non-failed firms. In retrospect, financial ratios can be used to suggest why a firm has failed;

(b) no fully accepted model for *predicting* future business failures has yet been established, although some form of Z score analysis would appear to be the most promising avenue for progress. In the UK, several Z score-type failure prediction models exist, and are used by consultancy firms to assist clients (such as banks).

2.54 Because of the use of X_4: market value of equity/book value of debt, Z score models cannot be used for unquoted companies which lack a market value of equity. Alternative *K score* models which are not limited in this way have been developed.

Other indicators of financial difficulties

2.55 You should not think that ratio analysis of published accounts and Z score analysis are the only ways of spotting that a company might be running into financial difficulties. There are other possible indicators too.

(a) *Other information in the published accounts*
Some information in the published accounts might not lend itself readily to ratio analysis, but can still be an indicator of financial difficulties, for example:

(i) very large increases in intangible fixed assets;
(ii) a worsening net liquid funds position, as shown by the funds flow statement;
(iii) very large contingent liabilities;
(iv) important post balance sheet events.

(b) *Information in the chairman's report and the directors' report*
The report of the chairman or chief executive that accompanies the published accounts might be very revealing. Although this report is not audited, and will no doubt try to paint a rosy picture of the company's affairs, any difficulties the company has had and not yet overcome will probably be discussed in it. There might also be warnings of problems to come in the future.

The directors' report is usually restricted to the minimum information required by law, but it might be interesting to check whether there have been any changes in the composition of the board since last year. Have many of last year's directors gone? Are there many new directors, and if so, what are their qualifications?

(c) *Published information in the press*
Newspapers and financial journals are a source of information about companies, and the difficulties or successes they are having. There may be reports of strikes, redundancies and closures.

There are often articles in newspapers which focus on particular companies. If a company is in financial difficulty, adverse comments might well appear in one of these articles.

(d) *Published information about environmental or external matters*
There will also be published information about matters that will have a direct influence on a company's future, although the connection may not be obvious. Examples of external matters that may affect a company adversely are:

(i) new legislation, for example on product safety standards or pollution controls, which affect a company's main products;

(ii) international events, for example political disagreements with a foreign country, leading to a restriction on trade between the countries. The foreign country concerned might be a major importer of a company's products;

(iii) new and better products being launched on to the market by a competitor;

(iv) a big rise in interest rates, which might affect a highly-geared company seriously;

(v) a big change in foreign exchange rates, which might affect a major importer or exporter seriously.

3. CONCLUSION

3.1 The techniques of ratio analysis have been covered here in the context of control over subsidiaries, in accordance with the syllabus for the 3.2 examination. You should, however, remember that they can also be used to appraise the financial management of independent companies.

TEST YOUR KNOWLEDGE

The numbers in brackets refer to paragraphs of this chapter

1. What sources of finance are available to a subsidiary? (1.2)
2. What are the main categories of ratios? (2.2)
3. Define return on investment. (2.10)
4. How may return on investment be analysed? (2.16)
5. Define the cash flow ratio. (2.22)
6. How does the current ratio differ from the quick ratio? (2.30 - 2.32)
7. Define the stock turnover period. (2.38, 2.39)
8. How may ratios be used in making comparisons? (2.43 - 2.46)

Now try question 25 at the end of the text

Chapter 20

SCHEMES OF CAPITALISATION. FINANCING OVERSEAS OPERATIONS

This chapter covers the following topics.

1. Schemes of capitalisation
2. Scrip dividends, scrip issues and stock splits
3. Financing overseas operations

1. SCHEMES OF CAPITALISATION

1.1 A scheme of capitalisation is a scheme to finance a company or a substantial project with a source of finance or a mixture of sources. Possible sources are:

(a) long-term and medium-term loans, including debentures and bank loans;

(b) equity: retained profits or a new share issue;

(c) short-term borrowing;

(d) borrowing in a foreign currency.

1.2 The choice of financing method must take into account:

(a) the cost of the capital;
(b) the impact on the existing capital structure, gearing and financial risk;
(c) the duration of the investment: long-term projects should be matched by long-term finance;
(d) the business risk: risky ventures are more suited to equity finance;
(e) prospects for investors and investors' attitudes;
(f) foreign currency risk, in the case of overseas investments or foreign currency loans.

Example

1.3 Mungle plc's financial results for the four years to the end of 19X4 are summarised below.

	19X1	*19X2*	*19X3*	*19X4*
	£m	£m	£m	£m
Net fixed assets	178	190	189	195
Stocks	140	155	168	200
Debtors	100	120	152	175
Cash	35	25	3	15
Total current assets	275	300	323	390
Bank overdraft	56	59	38	60
Creditors	107	107	127	132
Taxation	11	12	9	15
Dividends	5	6	6	6
Total current liabilities	179	184	180	213
Net current assets	96	116	143	177
Total assets less current liabilities	274	306	332	372
Loan capital	65	79	91	116
	209	227	241	256
Ordinary share capital (50p shares)	80	80	80	80
Reserves	129	147	161	176
	209	227	241	256

Loan capital as at 31 December 19X4

	£m
Unsecured 14% loan 19X6/X7	40
12% debenture 19X5	51
Variable rate loan 19X9	25
	116

		Year to 31 December		
	19X1	*19X2*	*19X3*	*19X4*
	£m	£m	£m	£m
Turnover	425	470	510	530
Operating profit	48	48	56	62
Less interest (net)	10	10	12	21
Profit before tax	38	38	44	41
Less tax	12	9	15	14
	26	29	29	27
Extraordinary items	0	1	(3)	0
	26	30	26	27
Less dividends	10	12	12	12
	16	18	14	15

	19X1	*19X2*	*19X3*	*19X4*
Average share price of Mungle plc (pence)	160	180	181	135
Average P/E ratio for Mungle's industry	9.8	10.0	12.0	9.5

The company wishes to spend £60,000,000 on a new long-term investment in the USA during 19X5.

The FT Ordinary Share Index has fallen 100 points during the past three months, and is near a two-year low.

Assess Mungle's current financial position, and suggest a strategy for future financing in 19X5.

Solution

1.4 The key trends and ratios are as follows.

	19X1	*19X2*	*19X3*	*19X4*
(a) *Sales growth %*		10.6%	8.5%	3.9%
(b) *Operating profit growth %*		0	15.8%	-6.8%
(c) *Gearing*	65/209	79/227	91/241	116/256
	31%	35%	38%	45%
(d) *Debt ratio*				
(Current liabilities + loans / Current assets + net fixed assets)	244/453	263/490	271/512	329/585
	54%	54%	53%	56%
(e) *Liquidity ratio* (Current assets: current liabilities)	275:179 = 1.5:1	300:184 = 1.6:1	323:180 = 1.8:1	390:213 = 1.8:1
(f) *EPS*	26/160 = 16.25p	29/160 = 18.13p	29/160 = 18.13p	27/160 = 16.88p
(g) *Average P/E ratio*	9.8	9.9	10.0	8.0
(h) *Dividend per share*	6.25p	7.5p	7.5p	7.5p

1.5 These figures suggest that the company is falling into an increasingly difficult financial position.

(a) Its rate of sales growth is falling.
(b) Its operating profits fell in 19X4.

1.6 The company needs some long-term finance next year, partly to finance the investment in the USA (£60,000,000) and partly to repay the debenture (£51,000,000).

(a) Retained profits will be inadequate for this. The company needs finance from other sources.

(b) A little of the finance might be generated by reducing the investment in current assets, although the large bank overdraft suggests that the company's liquidity position would still be precarious.

(c) Raising new equity finance on the stock market might be possible, to finance the overseas investment. However, Mungle's share price fell quite sharply in 19X4, and stock market prices in general are falling. The company's P/E ratio is now less than that of other companies in the industry. Even so, a rights issue for about £60,000,000 might be necessary if the US investment is to go ahead.

(d) The US investment could be financed with a long-term US dollar loan. However, borrowing to finance the US investment would increase the company's debt ratio and gearing.

(e) The company's debt ratio and gearing ratio are both high, and have been getting higher during 19X4. It is uncertain whether investors would be willing to lend more, nor whether Mungle has satisfactory security to offer.

The debenture loan maturing in 19X5 may be a secured loan. It might be possible to redeem the loan by raising another loan on the same security.

(f) *Conclusion and suggestion.* Mungle plc does not seem to be a particularly attractive company for investors as at the end of 19X4. It should try to improve profitability so as to create more earnings, from which investment finance can be obtained. Until this happens, a rights issue of shares and a new loan to replace the maturing loan might be needed.

Loans in foreign currencies

1.7 A UK company could borrow in a foreign currency to finance an investment in sterling. For example, a company could finance a project in the UK by borrowing in US dollars. The loan could be raised:

(a) as a eurocurrency loan from a bank;
(b) in the case of very large companies, as a eurobond issue.

1.8 The *reason* for financing a project in a foreign currency would be the availability of a lower interest rate than the current market rate for sterling loans.

1.9 However, it is easy to be deceived by lower interest rates on eurocurrency loans, and foreign currency loans at a low interest rate could prove more expensive than a loan in domestic currency at a higher interest rate. Companies should beware of this 'interest rate trap.' The project will pay back returns in sterling, but the loan, and interest on the loan, must be paid in the foreign currency. If the currency of the loan strengthens against sterling, the *sterling cost* of the loan interest and the loan repayment will increase.

1.10 For example, suppose that a UK company borrows $6,000,000 at an interest rate of 7%, when the exchange rate is $2 = £1. The loan would finance a UK investment costing £3,000,000. Annual interest on the loan would be $420,000, which would cost £210,000 if the exchange rate does not change. But if sterling falls in value against the dollar, to say $1.50 = £1, the loan interest will cost £280,000 a year, and the capital sum needed to repay the loan at the end of its term will be £4,000,000.

1.11 The foreign exchange risk cannot be predicted accurately, because exchange rates vary in response to market supply and demand. However, as a general guide:

(a) when interest rates on a foreign currency are lower than sterling interest rates, the value of sterling will fall against the foreign currency;

(b) the amount by which sterling will fall in value can be estimated as the interest rate differential on forward exchange contracts in that foreign currency.

2. SCRIP DIVIDENDS, SCRIP ISSUES AND STOCK SPLITS

2.1 Scrip dividends, scrip issues and stock splits are *not* methods of raising new equity funds, but they *are* methods of

(a) altering the share capital structure of a company;
(b) in the case of scrip dividends and scrip issues, increasing the issued share capital of the company.

2.2 A *scrip dividend* is a dividend payment which takes the form of new shares instead of cash. Effectively, it converts profit and loss reserves into issued share capital. When the directors of a company would prefer to retain funds within the business but consider that they must pay at least a certain amount of dividend, they might offer equity shareholders the choice of:

(a) a cash dividend;
(b) a scrip dividend.

Each shareholder would decide separately which to take. There is no need for shareholders to agree on whether to have a cash dividend or a scrip dividend.

2.3 A *scrip issue* (also known as a *bonus issue*) is an issue of new shares to existing shareholders, by converting equity reserves into issued share capital. For example, if a company with issued share capital of 100,000 ordinary shares of £1 each makes a one for five scrip issue, 20,000 new shares would be issued to existing shareholders, one new share for every five old shares held. Issued share capital would be increased by £20,000, and reserves (probably the share premium account, if there is one) would be reduced by this amount.

2.4 By creating more shares in this way, a scrip issue does not raise new funds, but it does have the advantage of making shares cheaper and therefore (perhaps) more easily marketable on the Stock Exchange. For example, if a company's shares are priced at £6 on the Stock Exchange, and the company makes a one for two scrip issue, we should expect the share price after the issue to fall to £4. Shares at £4 might be more easily marketable than shares at £6.

2.5 This advantage of a scrip issue is also attributable to a *stock split*. A stock split occurs where, for example, each ordinary share of £1 each is split into two shares of £0.50 each, thus creating cheaper shares with greater marketability. There is an added psychological advantage, in that investors should expect a company which splits its shares in this way to be planning for substantial earnings growth and dividend growth in the future. As a consequence, the market price of shares may benefit. For example, if one share of £1 has a market value of £6, and it is then split into two shares of £0.50 each, the market value of the new shares might settle at, say, £3.10 instead of the expected £3, in anticipation of strong future growth in earnings and dividends.

2.6 The difference between a stock split and a scrip issue is that a scrip issue converts equity reserves into share capital, whereas a stock split leaves reserves unaffected.

3. FINANCING OVERSEAS OPERATIONS

3.1 When a UK company wishes to finance operations overseas, there may be a foreign exchange risk arising from the method of financing used. For example, if a UK company decides on an investment in the USA, to be financed with a sterling loan:

(a) the investment will provide returns in US dollars;
(b) the investors (the lenders) will want returns paid in sterling.

If the US dollar falls in value against sterling, the sterling value of the project's returns will also fall.

3.2 To reduce or eliminate the foreign exchange risk of an overseas investment, a company might finance it with funds raised in the same currency as the investment.

3.3 The advantages of borrowing in the same currency as an investment are as follows.

(a) Assets and liabilities in the same currency can be matched, thus avoiding exchange losses on conversion in the group's annual accounts.

(b) Revenues in the foreign currency can be used to repay borrowings in the same currency, thus eliminating losses due to fluctuating exchange rates.

3.4 Additional factors to be taken into account when appraising overseas investments are as follows.

(a) Remittances from the foreign subsidiary may be required. It may be unwise to rely totally on dividends in case restrictions on dividend payments are imposed. Some combination of interest, royalty fees, management charges and dividends could be preferable.

(b) Political interference by overseas governments, including exchange controls, extra charges on the profits of overseas companies and employment legislation could be a danger.

(c) Differences in tax systems (and accounting practices) may be significant.

(d) The investor should allow for the extra risk associated with overseas investments, largely as a result of (a), (b) and (c), as well as any foreign exchange risk through not matching foreign currency assets and liabilities, or not matching revenues and finance payments in the foreign currency.

(e) Some countries offer special finance incentives for investment in that country.

(f) It might be better to export than to set up a foreign subsidiary.

4. CONCLUSION

4.1 This chapter has shown how schemes to finance operations involve the comparison of options, with (a) risk and returns varying between options; and (b) foreign exchange risk featuring in options involving foreign currency loans to finance domestic investments or the financing of overseas investments with domestic currency.

TEST YOUR KNOWLEDGE

The numbers in brackets refer to paragraphs of this chapter

1. What factors should be considered in deciding on a scheme of capitalisation? (1.2)
2. What is the interest rate trap in borrowing foreign currency? (1.9)
3. How does a stock split differ from a scrip issue? (2.6)
4. What are the advantages of borrowing in the same currency as an investment? (3.3)

Now try question 26 at the end of the text

PART F

THE MANAGEMENT OF WORKING CAPITAL

Chapter 21

AN INTRODUCTION TO WORKING CAPITAL

This chapter covers the following topics.

1. The need for funds for investment in current assets
2. The control of cash flow

1. THE NEED FOR FUNDS FOR INVESTMENT IN CURRENT ASSETS

1.1 Current assets may be financed either by long-term funds or by current liabilities.

The 'ideal' current ratio (current assets: current liabilities) is generally accepted to be 2:1 (half of current assets should be financed by long-term funds), but this proportion can obviously be varied in practice, depending on the circumstances of an individual company. Similarly, the 'ideal' quick ratio or acid test ratio (current assets minus stocks: current liabilities) is 1:1, although in practice, companies often have much lower quick ratios than this.

1.2 These liquidity ratios are a guide to the risk of cash flow problems and insolvency.

If a company suddenly finds that it is unable to renew its short-term liabilities (for example, if the bank suspends its overdraft facilities, or creditors start to demand earlier payment), there will be a danger of insolvency unless the company is able to turn enough of its current assets into cash quickly. A current ratio of 2:1 and a quick ratio of 1:1 are thought to indicate that a company is reasonably well protected against the danger of insolvency.

1.3 Current liabilities are often a cheap method of finance (trade creditors do not usually carry an interest cost) and companies may therefore consider that in the interest of higher profits, it is worth accepting some risk of insolvency by increasing current liabilities, taking the maximum credit possible from suppliers.

1.4 Management must balance the desire for a higher return (obtained by increasing short-term debts to finance current assets) against the risk of insolvency. The decision as to how working capital should be financed is therefore likely to depend on management's attitude towards risk.

The volume of current assets required

1.5 The volume of current assets required will depend on the nature of the company's business. For example, a manufacturing company may require more stocks than a company in a service industry. As the volume of output by a company increases, the volume of current assets required will also increase.

1.6 Even assuming efficient stock holding, debt collection procedures and cash management, there is still a certain degree of choice in the total volume of current assets required to meet output requirements. Policies of low stock-holding levels, tight credit and minimum cash holdings may be contrasted with policies of high stocks (to allow for safety or buffer stocks) easier credit and sizeable cash holdings (for precautionary reasons).

Over-capitalisation and working capital

1.7 If a company manages its working capital inefficiently, so that there are excessive stocks, debtors and cash, and very few creditors, there will be an over-investment by the company in current assets. Working capital will be excessive and the company will be in this respect over-capitalised. The return on investment will be lower than it should be, and long-term funds will be unnecessarily tied up when they could be invested elsewhere to earn profits.

1.8 Over-capitalisation with respect to working capital should not exist if there is good management, but the warning signs of excessive working capital would be poor accounting ratios. The ratios which can assist in judging whether the investment in working capital is reasonable include the following.

(a) *Sales/working capital.* The volume of sales as a multiple of the working capital investment should indicate whether, in comparison with previous years or with similar companies, the total volume of working capital is too high.

(b) *Liquidity ratios.* A current ratio in excess of 2:1 or a quick ratio in excess of 1:1 may indicate over-investment in working capital.

(c) *Turnover periods.* Excessive turnover periods for stocks and debtors, or a short period of credit taken from suppliers, might indicate that the volume of stocks or debtors is unnecessarily high, or the volume of creditors too low.

Overtrading

1.9 In contrast with over-capitalisation, overtrading happens when a business tries to do too much too quickly with *too little* long-term capital, so that it is trying to support too large a volume of trade with the capital resources at its disposal.

Even if an overtrading business operates at a profit, it could easily run into serious trouble because it is short of money. Such liquidity troubles stem from the fact that it does not have enough capital to provide the cash to pay its debts as they fall due.

Example

1.10 Great Ambition Ltd appoints a new managing director who has great plans to expand the company. He wants to increase turnover by 100% within two years, and to do this he employs extra sales staff. He recognises that customers do not want to have to wait for deliveries, and so he decides that the company must build up its stock levels. There is a substantial increase in the company's stocks. These are held in additional warehouse space which is now rented. The company also buys new cars for its extra sales representatives.

The managing director's policies are immediately successful in boosting sales, which double in just over one year. Stock levels are now much higher, but the company takes longer credit from its suppliers, even though some suppliers have expressed their annoyance at the length of time they must wait for payment. Credit terms for debtors are unchanged, and so the volume of debtors, like the volume of sales, rises by 100%.

In spite of taking longer credit, the company still needs to increase its overdraft facilities with the bank, which are raised from a limit of £40,000 to one of £80,000. The company is profitable, and retains some profits in the business, but profit margins have fallen.

(a) Gross profit margins are lower because some prices have been reduced to obtain extra sales.

(b) Net profit margins are lower because overhead costs are higher. These include sales representatives' wages, car expenses and depreciation on cars, warehouse rent and additional losses from having to write off out-of-date and slow-moving stock items.

1.11 The balance sheet of the company might change over time from (A) to (B).

		Balance sheet (A)			*Balance sheet (B)*	
	£	£	£	£	£	£
Fixed assets			160,000			210,000
Current assets						
Stock		60,000			150,000	
Debtors		64,000			135,000	
Cash		1,000			0	
		125,000			285,000	
Current liabilities						
Bank	25,000			80,000		
Creditors	50,000			200,000		
		75,000			280,000	
			50,000			5,000
			210,000			215,000
Share capital			10,000			10,000
Profit and loss account			200,000			205,000
			210,000			215,000
Sales			£1,000,000			£2,000,000
Gross profit			£200,000			£300,000
Net profit			£50,000			£20,000

In situation (B), the company has reached its overdraft limit and has four times as many creditors as in situation (A) but with only twice the sales turnover. Stock levels are much higher, and stock turnover is lower.

The company is overtrading. If it had to pay its next trade creditor, or salaries and wages, before it received any income, it could not do so without the bank allowing it to exceed its overdraft limit. The company is profitable, although profit margins have fallen, and it ought to expect a prosperous future. But if it does not sort out its cash flow and liquidity, it will not survive to enjoy future profits.

1.12 Suitable solutions to the problem would be measures to reduce the degree of overtrading.

(a) New capital from the shareholders could be injected.

(b) Better control could be applied to stocks and debtors.

(c) The company could abandon ambitious plans for increased sales and more fixed asset purchases until the business has had time to consolidate its position, and build up its capital base with retained profits.

The causes of overtrading

1.13 Emphasis has been given so far to the danger of overtrading when a business seeks to increase its turnover too rapidly without an adequate capital base. In other words, overtrading is brought upon the business by the ambition of management. This is not the only cause of overtrading, however. Other causes are as follows.

(a) When a business repays a loan, it often replaces the old loan with a new one. However a business might repay a loan without replacing it, with the consequence that it has less long-term capital to finance its current level of operations.

(b) A business might be profitable, but in a period of inflation, its retained profits might be insufficient to pay for replacement fixed assets and stocks, which now cost more because of inflation. The business would then rely increasingly on credit, and find itself eventually unable to support its current volume of trading with a capital base that has fallen in real terms.

1.14 Symptoms of overtrading are as follows.

(a) There is a rapid increase in turnover.

(b) There is a rapid increase in the volume of current assets and possibly also fixed assets. Stock turnover and debtors turnover might slow down, in which case the rate of increase in stocks and debtors would be even greater than the rate of increase in sales.

(c) There is only a small increase in proprietors' capital (perhaps through retained profits). Most of the increase in assets is financed by credit, especially:

(i) trade creditors. The payment period to creditors is likely to lengthen;

(ii) a bank overdraft, which often reaches or even exceeds the limit of the facilities agreed by the bank.

(d) Some debt ratios and liquidity ratios alter dramatically.

(i) The proportion of total assets financed by proprietors' capital falls, and the proportion financed by credit rises.

(ii) The current ratio and the quick ratio fall.

(iii) The business might have a liquid deficit, that is, an excess of current liabilities over current assets.

2. THE CONTROL OF CASH FLOW

2.1 The amount tied up in working capital is equal to the value of raw materials, work-in-progress, finished stocks and debtors less creditors. The size of this net figure has a direct effect on the liquidity of an organisation.

The connection between investment in working capital and cash flow may be illustrated by means of the 'cash cycle', 'operating cycle' or 'trading cycle'.

2.2 The operating cycle may be expressed as a period of time.

(a) Raw material stocks are obtained from suppliers.

(b) The trade creditors are paid and cash is therefore paid out.

(c) Raw materials are held in stock until they are issued to production (work-in-progress). At this time, additional liabilities (for labour and other expenses) may be incurred.

(d) On completion of production, the finished goods are held in stock until sold, perhaps on credit.

(e) Cash is received when the debt is collected.

(f) The operating cycle is the period between the payment of cash to creditors (cash out) and the receipt of cash from debtors (cash in).

2.3 If the turnover periods for stocks and debtors lengthen, or the payment period to creditors shortens:

(a) the operating cycle will lengthen;
(b) the investment in working capital will increase.

Example

2.4 The following data relate to Corn Ltd, a manufacturing company.

Turnover for the year	£1,500,000
Costs as percentages of sales	%
Direct materials	30
Direct labour	25
Variable overheads	10
Fixed overheads	15
Selling and distribution	5

On average:

(a) debtors take 2.5 months before payment;
(b) raw materials are in stock for three months;
(c) work-in-progress represents two months worth of half produced goods;
(d) finished goods represents one month's production;
(e) credit is taken as follows.

(i)	Direct materials	2 months
(ii)	Direct labour	1 week
(iii)	Variable overheads	1 month
(iv)	Fixed overheads	1 month
(v)	Selling and distribution	0.5 months

Work-in-progress and finished goods are valued at material, labour and variable expense cost.

Compute the working capital requirement of Corn Ltd assuming the labour force is paid for 50 working weeks a year.

Solution

2.5 (a) The annual costs incurred will be as follows.

		£
Direct materials	30% of £1,500,000	450,000
Direct labour	25% of £1,500,000	375,000
Variable overheads	10% of £1,500,000	150,000
Fixed overheads	15% of £1,500,000	225,000
Selling and distribution	5% of £1,500,000	75,000

(b) The average value of current assets will be as follows.

		£	£
Raw materials	3/12 × 450,000		112,500
Work-in-progress			
Materials (100% complete)	2/12 × 450,000	75,000	
Labour (50% complete)	1/12 × 375,000	31,250	
Variable overheads (50% complete)	1/12 × 150,000	12,500	
			118,750
Finished goods			
Materials	1/12 × 450,000	37,500	
Labour	1/12 × 375,000	31,250	
Variable overheads	1/12 × 150,000	12,500	
			81,250
Debtors	2.5/12 × 150,000		312,500
			625,000

(c) The average value of current liabilities will be as follows.

Materials	2/12 × 450,000	75,000	
Labour	1/50 × 375,000	7,500	
Variable overheads	1/12 × 150,000	12,500	
Fixed overheads	1/12 × 225,000	18,750	
Selling and distribution	1/12 × 75,000	3,125	
			116,875
(d) Working capital required			508,125

It has been assumed that all the direct materials are allocated to work-in-progress when production starts.

Discounted cash flow in working capital problems

2.6 A change in turnover periods will affect the cash flows of a company, perhaps over a long period of time. It follows that decisions by management about stock control, or credit allowed and received, may need to be evaluated using DCF techniques. This is especially the case where the volume of working capital required is expected to increase annually. An example will illustrate the point.

Example

2.7 Humerus Ltd currently expects all debtors to pay at the end of the month following the month of sale. It has been estimated that if, from the beginning of January 19X1, all debtors are allowed a further month's credit, the company would save £1,500 a month (in perpetuity from January 19X1 onwards) in fixed administration costs. The cost of capital is 1% a month. Credit sales in January 19X1 are expected to be £100,000, and a monthly growth of $\frac{1}{2}$% is expected to continue into the indefinite future thereafter. Evaluate the proposed change of working capital policy.

Solution

2.8 DCF techniques are useful because of the growth in working capital requirements.

(a) If the existing credit policy were to be maintained, the cash flows of the company would be as follows, beginning with sales in January 19X1.

End of February 19X1 (receipts from January sales)	£100,000
End of March 19X1	£100,000 $\times$ 1.005
End of April 19X1	£100,000 $\times$ 1.005^2
and so on.	

Taking the beginning of January 19X1 as 'Year 0', the present value of these cash flows is calculated as follows.

(i) The growth model (which was used as a dividend growth model in previous chapters) may also be used to calculate a present value where cash flows are increasing at a constant growth rate, g.

$$PV = \frac{a(1 + g)}{(r - g)}$$

where a is the cash flow in the first period (the equivalent in the dividend growth model would be the dividend in year 0).
g is the growth rate
r is the cost of capital.

(ii) The present value as at end of February 19X1 is as follows.

Month	*Cash flow*	*Discount factor*	*Present value*
	£		£
February	100,000	1.0	100,000
March onwards	Increasing by ½% per month	$\frac{100,000\ (1.005)}{(0.01 - 0.005)}$	20,100,000
Total PV			20,200,000

(iii) This is a present value as at the end of February. To convert this value into a present value as at the beginning of January 19X1, we must discount from month 2 to month 0.

PV at the beginning of January 19X1 $= £20,200,000 \times \frac{1}{1.01^2}$

$= £19,801,980.$

(b) If the proposed credit policy is introduced, the present value of receipts from debtors will be as follows.

End of March 19X1 (receipts from January sales)	£100,000
End of April 19X1	£100,000 $\times$ 1.005
End of May 19X1	£100,000 $\times$ 1.005^2
and so on.	

The present value of these cash flows as at the *end of March* is £20,200,000 (see (a)(ii) above) and the present value as at 1 January 19X1 is

$$£20,200,000 \times \frac{1}{1.01^3} = £19,605,921.$$

The saving in administration costs from January is £1,500 a month, which has a present value of £1,500 ÷ 0.01 = £150,000.

(c) *A comparison of the alternatives*

	£m	£m
Current credit policy		
PV of future receipts		19.80
Proposed credit policy		
PV of future receipts	19.61	
PV of future savings	0.15	
		19.76
Net benefit of maintaining the existing policy		0.04

The existing policy has a higher present value of benefits by £40,000.

3. CONCLUSION

3.1 In this chapter, working capital management has been described in general terms.

In the next chapter we shall look at the control of cash, stocks, debtors and creditors in more detail.

TEST YOUR KNOWLEDGE

The numbers in brackets refer to paragraphs of this chapter

1. What is over-capitalisation? (1.7)
2. What are the causes of overtrading? (1.13)
3. What is the operating cycle? (2.2)
4. Why might DCF techniques be needed in making decisions about working capital? (2.6)

Now try question 27 at the end of the text

Chapter 22

THE MANAGEMENT OF CASH, STOCKS, DEBTORS AND CREDITORS

This chapter covers the following topics.

1. The management of cash
2. The management of stocks
3. The management of debtors
4. The management of creditors

1. THE MANAGEMENT OF CASH

1.1 Cash flow problems can arise in several ways.

(a) *Making losses.* If a business is continually making losses, it will eventually have cash flow problems. Just how long it will take before a loss-making business runs into cash flow trouble will depend on:

(i) how big the losses are;

(ii) whether the depreciation charge is big enough to create a loss despite a cash flow surplus. In such a situation, the cash flow troubles might only begin when the business needs to replace fixed assets.

(b) *Inflation.* In a period of inflation, a business needs ever-increasing amounts of cash just to replace used-up and worn-out assets. A business can be making a profit in historical cost accounting terms, but still not be receiving enough cash to buy the replacement assets it needs.

(c) *Growth.* When a business is growing, it needs to acquire more fixed assets, and to support higher amounts of stocks and debtors. These additional assets must be paid for somehow (or financed by creditors).

(d) *Seasonal business.* When a business has seasonal or cyclical sales, it may have cash flow difficulties at certain times of the year, when (i) cash inflows are low, but (ii) cash outflows are high, perhaps because the business is building up its stocks for the next period of high sales.

(e) *One-off items of expenditure.* There might occasionally be a single non-recurring item of expenditure that creates a cash flow problem, such as:

(i) the repayment of loan capital on maturity of the debt. Businesses often try to finance such loan repayments by borrowing again;

(ii) the purchase of an exceptionally expensive item. For example, a small or medium-sized business might decide to buy a freehold property which then stretches its cash resources for several months or even years.

Four methods of easing cash shortages

1.2 The steps that are usually taken by a company when a need for cash arises, and when it cannot obtain resources from any other source such as a loan or an increased overdraft, are as follows.

(a) *Postponing capital expenditure*

Some capital expenditure items are more important and urgent than others.

(i) It might be imprudent to postpone expenditure on fixed assets which are needed for the development and growth of the business.

(ii) On the other hand, some capital expenditures are routine and might be postponable without serious consequences. The routine replacement of motor vehicles is an example. If a company's policy is to replace company cars every two years, but the company is facing a cash shortage, it might decide to replace cars every three years.

(b) *Accelerating cash inflows which would otherwise be expected in a later period*

The most obvious way of bringing forward cash inflows would be to press debtors for earlier payment.

Often, this policy will result in a loss of goodwill and problems with customers. There will also be very little scope for speeding up payments when the credit period currently allowed to debtors is no more than the norm for the industry.

It might be possible to encourage debtors to pay more quickly by offering discounts for earlier payment.

(c) *Reversing past investment decisions by selling assets previously acquired*

Some assets are less crucial to a business than others and so if cash flow problems are severe, the option of selling investments or property might have to be considered.

(d) *Negotiating a reduction in cash outflows, so as to postpone or even reduce payments*

There are several ways in which this could be done.

(i) Longer credit might be taken from suppliers.
However, if the credit period allowed is already generous, creditors might be very reluctant to extend credit even further and any such extension of credit would have to be negotiated carefully. There would be a serious risk of having further supplies refused.

(ii) Loan repayments could be rescheduled by agreement with a bank.

(iii) A deferral of the payment of corporation tax could be agreed with the Inland Revenue. Corporation tax is payable nine months after a company's year end, but it might be possible to arrange a postponement by a few months. When this happens, the Inland Revenue will charge interest on the outstanding amount of tax.

(iv) Dividend payments could be reduced. Dividend payments are discretionary cash outflows, although a company's directors might be constrained by shareholders' expectations, so that they feel obliged to pay dividends even when there is a cash shortage.

Deviations from expected cash flows

1.3 Cash budgets, whether prepared on an annual, monthly, weekly or even a daily basis, can only be *estimates* of cash flows. Even the best estimates will not be exactly correct, so deviations from the cash budget are inevitable.

1.4 This uncertainty about actual cash flows ought to be considered when the cash budget is prepared. It is desirable to prepare additional cash budgets based on different assumptions about sales levels, costs, collection periods, bad debts and so on.

A cash budget model could be constructed, using a microcomputer and a spreadsheet package, and the sensitivity of cash flow forecasts to changes in estimates of sales, costs and so on could be analysed.

1.5 By planning for different eventualities, management should be able to prepare contingency measures in advance and also appreciate the key factors in the cash budget.

1.6 A knowledge of the probability distribution of possible outcomes for the cash position will allow a more accurate estimate to be made of the minimum cash balances, or the borrowing power necessary, to provide a satisfactory *margin of safety*. Unforeseen deficits can be hard to finance at short notice, and advance planning is desirable.

Cash management services: computerised cash management

1.7 A recent development in banking services is a cash management service for corporate customers. A company with many different bank accounts can obtain information about the cash balance in each account through a computer terminal in the company's treasury department linked to the bank's computer. The company can then arrange to move cash from one account to another and so manage its cash position more efficiently and make optimal use of its funds deposited with banks or in various money market investments. A cash management service can be provided to a company with several bank accounts in the UK, or, through an international network of banks, to a multinational company with accounts in different currencies in various countries.

1.8 The cash management services provided by the banks offer three basic services.

(a) *Account reporting*

(i) Information is given about the balances on sterling or currency accounts whether held in the UK or overseas, including details of the cleared balance for the previous day and any uncleared items.

(ii) Forecast balance reports, which take into account uncleared items and automated entries (BACS credits and debits, standing orders and direct debits) can be obtained.

(iii) Reports giving details of individual transactions can be obtained.

(b) *Funds transfer*
The customer can initiate sterling and currency payments through his terminal. Banks will also give customers with substantial cash floats the opportunity to get in touch with money market dealers directly and deposit funds in the money markets.

(c) *Decision support services*
A rates information service, giving information on foreign exchange rates and money market (sterling deposit) interest rates, can be used.

Float

1.9 The term 'float' is sometimes used to describe the amount of money tied up between:

(a) the time when a payment is initiated (for example when a debtor sends a cheque in payment, probably by post); and
(b) the time when the funds become available for use in the recipient's bank account.

1.10 There are three reasons why there might be a lengthy float.

(a) *Transmission delay*. When payment is sent through the post, it will take a day or longer for the payment to reach the payee.

(b) *Delay in banking the payments received (lodgment delay).* The payee, on receipt of a cheque or cash, might delay presenting the cheque or the cash to his bank. The length of this delay will depend on administrative procedures in the payee's organisation.

(c) *The time needed for a bank to clear a cheque (clearance delay).* A payment is not available for use in the payee's bank account until the cheque has been cleared. This will usually take two or three days for cheques payable in the UK. For cheques payable abroad, the delay is much longer.

1.11 There are several measures that could be taken to reduce the float.

(a) The payee should ensure that the lodgment delay is kept to a minimum. Cheques received should be presented to the bank on the day of receipt.

(b) The payee might, in some cases, arrange to collect cheques from the payer's premises. This would only be practicable, however, if the payer is local. The payment would have to be large to make the extra effort worthwhile.

(c) The payer might be asked to pay through his own branch of a bank. The payer can give his bank detailed payment instructions, and use the credit clearing system of the Bank Giro. The *Bank Giro* is a means of making credit transfers for customers of other banks and other branches. The payee might even include a Bank Giro credit slip on the bottom of his invoice, to help with this method of payment.

(d) *BACS* (Bankers' Automated Clearing Services Ltd) is a banking system which provides for the computerised transfer of funds between banks. In addition, BACS is available to corporate customers of banks for making payments. The customer must supply a magnetic tape or disk to BACS, which contains details of payments, and payment will be made in two days. BACS is now commonly used by companies for salary payments.

(e) For regular payments *standing orders* or *direct debits* might be used.

(f) *CHAPS* (Clearing House Automated Payments System) is a computerised system for banks to make same-day clearances (that is, immediate payment) between each other. Each member bank of CHAPS can allow its own corporate customers to make immediate transfers of funds through CHAPS. However, there is a large minimum size for payments using CHAPS.

Inefficient cash management

1.12 A lengthy float suggests inefficient cash management. But there are other types of delay in receiving payment from debtors, which might also suggest inefficient cash management.

(a) There is the delay created by the length of credit given to customers. There is often a 'normal' credit period for an industry, and companies might be unable to grant less time for payment than this.

(b) There are avoidable delays caused by poor administration (in addition to lodgment delay), such as:

(i) failure to notify the invoicing department that goods have been despatched, so that invoices are not sent promptly;
(ii) cheques from debtors being made out incorrectly, to the wrong company perhaps, because invoices do not contain clear instructions.

Example

1.13 Ryan Coates owns a chain of seven clothes shops in the London area. Takings at each shop are remitted once a week on Thursday evening to the head office, and are then banked at the start of business on Friday morning. As business is expanding, Ryan Coates has hired an accountant to help him. The accountant gave him the following advice.

'Turnover at the seven shops totalled £1,950,000 last year, at a constant daily rate, but you were paying bank overdraft charges at a rate of 11%. You could have reduced your overdraft costs by banking the shop takings each day, except on Saturdays. Saturday takings could have been banked on Mondays.'

Comment on the significance of this statement, stating your assumptions. The shops are closed on Sundays.

Solution

1.14 (a) A bank overdraft rate of 11% a year is approximately 11/365 = 0.03% a day

(b) Annual takings of £1,950,000 would be an average of £1,950,000/312 = £6,250 a day for the seven shops in total, on the assumption that they opened for a 52 week year of six days a week (312 days).

(c) Using the approximate overdraft cost of 0.03% a day, the cost of holding £6,250 for one day instead of banking it is 0.03% × £6,250 = £1.875.

(d) Banking all takings up to Thursday evening of each week on Friday morning involves an unnecessary delay in paying cash into the bank. The cost of this delay would be either:
(i) the opportunity cost of investment capital for the business; or
(ii) the cost of avoidable bank overdraft charges.

It is assumed here that the overdraft cost is higher and is therefore more appropriate.

Takings on	*Could be banked on*	*Number of days delay incurred by Friday banking*
Monday	Tuesday	3
Tuesday	Wednesday	2
Wednesday	Thursday	1
Thursday	Friday	0
Friday	Monday	4
Saturday	Monday	4
		14

In one week, the total number of days delay incurred by Friday banking is 14. At a cost of £1.875 a day, the weekly cost of Friday banking was £1.875 × 14 = £26.25, and the annual cost of Friday banking was £26.25 × 52 = £1,365.

(e) *Conclusion.* The company could have saved about £1,365 a year in bank overdraft charges last year. If the overdraft rate remains at 11% and turnover continues to increase, the saving from daily banking would be even higher next year.

2. THE MANAGEMENT OF STOCKS

2.1 Some businesses attempt to control stocks on a scientific basis by balancing the costs of stock shortages against those of stock holding.

The 'scientific' control of stocks may be analysed into three parts.

(a) The economic order quantity (EOQ) model can be used to decide the optimum order size for stocks which will minimise the costs of ordering stocks plus stockholding costs.

(b) If discounts for bulk purchases are available, it may be cheaper to buy stocks in large order sizes so as to obtain the discounts.

(c) Uncertainty in the demand for stocks and/or the supply lead time may lead a company to decide to hold buffer stocks (thereby increasing its investment in working capital) in order to reduce or eliminate the risk of 'stock-outs' (running out of stock).

Stock costs

2.2 Stock costs can be conveniently classified into four groups.

(a) *Holding costs* comprise the cost of capital tied up, warehousing and handling costs, deterioration, obsolescence, insurance and pilferage.

(b) *Procuring costs* depend on how the stock is obtained but will consist of *ordering costs* for goods purchased externally, such as clerical costs, telephone charges and delivery costs.

(c) *Shortage costs* may be:

(i) the loss of a sale and the contribution which could have been earned from the sale;
(ii) the extra cost of having to buy an emergency supply of stocks at a high price;
(iii) the cost of lost production and sales, where the stock-out brings an entire process to a halt.

(d) *The cost of the stock itself*, the supplier's price or the direct cost per unit of production, will also need to be considered when the supplier offers a discount on orders for purchases in bulk.

Stock models

2.3 There are several different types of stock model, and these can be classified under the following headings.

(a) *Deterministic stock models*

A deterministic model is one in which all the 'parameters' are known with certainty. In particular, the rate of demand and the supply lead time are known.

(b) *Stochastic stock models*

A stochastic model is one in which the supply lead time or the rate of demand for an item is not known with certainty. However, the demand or the lead time follows a known probability distribution (probably constructed from a historical analysis of demand or lead time in the past).

In a deterministic system, since the demand and the lead time are known with certainty, there is no need for a safety stock. However, in a stochastic model, it may be necessary to have a buffer stock to limit the number of stock-outs or to avoid stock-outs completely.

2.4 Stochastic models are sometimes classified as follows.

(a) *A P system* is a *periodic review system* in which the requirement for stock is reviewed at fixed time intervals, and varying quantities are ordered on each occasion, according to the current level of stocks remaining.

(b) *A Q system* is a *re-order level system* in which a fixed quantity is ordered at irregular intervals, when stock levels have fallen to a re-order level specified on the store-keeper's records or 'bin card'.

A deterministic model: the basic EOQ formula

2.5 The economic order quantity (EOQ) is the optimal ordering quantity for an item of stock which will minimise costs.

Let d = the usage in units for one year (the demand)
c = the cost of making one order
h = the holding cost per unit of stock for one year
Q = the re-order quantity

(c and h: relevant costs only)

The total annual cost of having stock (T) is

Holding costs + Ordering costs

$$\frac{Qh}{2} + \frac{cd}{Q}$$

The objective is to minimise $T = \frac{Qh}{2} + \frac{cd}{Q}$

2.6 The order quantity, Q, which will minimise these total costs, assuming no bulk purchase discounts is

$$Q = \sqrt{\frac{2cd}{h}}$$

Example

2.7 The demand for a commodity is 40,000 units a year, at a steady rate. It costs £20 to place an order, and 40p to hold a unit for a year. Find the order size to minimise stock costs, the number of orders placed each year, and the length of the stock cycle.

Solution

2.8
$$Q = \sqrt{\frac{2cd}{h}} = \sqrt{\frac{2 \times 20 \times 40,000}{0.4}}$$

$$= 2,000 \text{ units}$$

This means that there will be

$\frac{40,000}{2,000}$ = 20 orders placed each year, so that the stock cycle is once every $52 \div 20 = 2.6$ weeks.

Total costs will be $(20 \times £20) + (\frac{2000}{2} \times 40p)$

= £800 a year.

Uncertainties in demand and lead times: a re-order level system

2.9 When the volume of demand is uncertain, or the supply lead time is variable, there are problems in deciding what the re-order level should be. By holding a 'safety stock', a company can reduce the likelihood that stocks run out during the re-order period (due to high demand or a long lead time before the new supply is delivered). The average annual cost of such a safety stock would be

Quantity of safety stock (in units)	×	Stock holding cost per unit per annum

2.10 The behaviour of the system would appear in a diagram as follows.

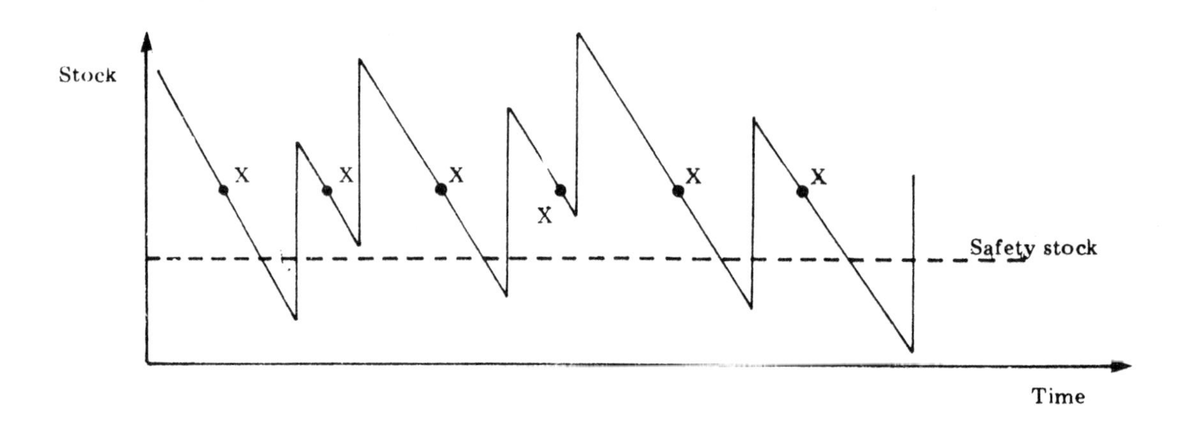

Points marked 'X' show the re-order level at which a new order is placed. The number of units ordered each time is the EOQ. Actual stock levels sometimes fall below the safety stock level, and sometimes the re-supply arrives before stocks have fallen to the safety level, but on average, extra stock holding amounts to the volume of safety stock.

The size of the safety stock will depend on whether stock-outs are allowed.

3. THE MANAGEMENT OF DEBTORS

3.1 Several factors should be considered by management when a policy for credit control is formulated. These include:

(a) the administrative costs of debt collection;

(b) the procedures for controlling credit to individual customers and for debt collection;

(c) the amount of extra capital required to finance an extension of total credit. There might be an increase in debtors, stocks and creditors, and the net increase in working capital must be financed;

(d) the cost of the additional finance required for any increase in the volume of debtors (or the savings from a reduction in debtors). This cost might be bank overdraft interest, or the cost of long-term funds (such as loan stock or equity);

(e) any savings or additional expenses in operating the credit policy (for example the extra work involved in pursuing slow payers);

(f) the ways in which the credit policy could be implemented. For example:

(i) credit could be eased by giving debtors a longer period in which to settle their accounts. The cost would be the resulting increase in debtors;

(ii) a discount could be offered for early payment. The cost would be the amount of the discounts taken;

(g) the effects of easing credit which might be:

(i) to encourage a higher proportion of bad debts;

(ii) an increase in sales volume.

Provided that the extra gross contribution from the increase in sales exceeds the increase in fixed cost expenses, bad debts, discounts and the finance cost of an increase in working capital, a policy to relax credit terms would be profitable.

Some of these factors involved in credit policy decisions will now be considered in more detail.

The debt collection policy

3.2 The overall debt collection policy of the firm should be such that the administrative costs and other costs incurred in debt collection do not exceed the benefits from incurring those costs.

Some extra spending on debt collection procedures might:

(a) reduce bad debt losses;
(b) reduce the average collection period, and therefore the cost of the investment in debtors.

Beyond a certain level of spending, however, additional expenditure on debt collection would not have enough effect on bad debts or on the average collection period to justify the extra administrative costs.

Example

3.3 Couttes Purse Ltd requires advice on its debt collection policy. Should the current policy be discarded in favour of Option 1 or Option 2?

	Current policy	*Option 1*	*Option 2*
Annual expenditure on debt collection procedures	£240,000	£300,000	£400,000
Bad debt losses (% of sales)	3%	2%	1%
Average collection period	2 months	$1\frac{1}{2}$ months	1 month

Current sales are £4,800,000 a year, and the company requires a 15% return on its investments.

Solution

3.4

		Current policy	*Option 1*	*Option 2*
		£	£	£
	Average debtors	800,000	600,000	400,000
	Reduction in working capital	-	200,000	400,000
(a)	Interest saving (15% of reduction)		30,000	60,000
	Bad debt losses (sales value)	144,000	96,000	48,000
(b)	Reduction in losses	-	48,000	96,000
	Benefits of each option (a) + (b)	-	78,000	156,000
	Extra costs of debt collection	-	60,000	160,000
	Benefit/(loss) from option		18,000	(4,000)

Option 1 is preferable to the current policy, but Option 2 is worse than the current policy.

Credit control: individual accounts

3.5 Credit control involves the initial investigation of potential credit customers and the continuing control of outstanding accounts.

The main points to note are as follows.

(a) New customers should give two good references, including one from a bank, before being granted credit.

(b) Credit ratings might be checked through a credit rating agency.

(c) A new customer's credit limit should be fixed at a low level and only increased if his payment record subsequently warrants it.

(d) For large value customers, a file should be maintained of any available financial information about the customer. This file should be reviewed regularly. Information is available from:

- (i) an analysis of the company's annual report and accounts;
- (ii) Extel cards (sheets of accounting information about public companies in the UK, and also major overseas companies, produced by Extel).

(e) The Department of Trade and Industry and the Export Credit Guarantee Department will both be able to advise on overseas companies.

(f) Press comments may give information about what a company is currently doing (as opposed to the historical results in Extel cards or published accounts which only show what the company has done in the past).

(g) The company could send a member of staff to visit the company concerned, to get a first-hand impression of the company and its prospects. This would be advisable in the case of a prospective major customer.

(h) Aged lists of debts should be produced and reviewed at regular intervals.

(i) The credit limit for an existing customer should be periodically reviewed, but it should only be raised if the customer's credit standing is good.

(j) It is essential to have procedures which ensure that further orders are not accepted from nor goods sent to a customer who is in difficulties. If a customer has exceeded his credit limit, or has not paid debts despite several reminders, or is otherwise known to be in difficulties, sales staff and warehouse staff must be notified immediately (and not, for example, at the end of the week, by which time more goods might have been supplied).

3.6 An organisation might devise a credit-rating system for new individual customers that is based on characteristics of the customer (such as whether the customer is a home owner, and the customer's age and occupation). Points would be awarded according to the characteristics of the customer, and the amount of credit that is offered would depend on his or her credit score.

Debt collection procedures

3.7 The three main areas which ought to be considered in connection with the control of debtors are:

(a) paperwork;
(b) debt collection;
(c) credit control.

3.8 Sales paperwork should be dealt with promptly and accurately.

(a) Invoices should be sent out immediately after delivery.

(b) Checks should be carried out to ensure that invoices are accurate.

(c) The investigation of queries and complaints and, if appropriate, the issue of credit notes should be carried out promptly.

(d) If practical, monthly statements should be issued early so that all items on the statement might then be included in customers' monthly settlements of bills.

Total credit

3.9 To determine whether it would be profitable to extend the level of total credit, it is necessary to assess:
(a) the extra sales that a more generous credit policy would stimulate;
(b) the profitability of the extra sales;
(c) the extra length of the average debt collection period;
(d) the required rate of return on the investment in additional debtors.

Example

3.10 Russian Beard Ltd is considering a change of credit policy which will result in an increase in the average collection period from one to two months. The relaxation in credit is expected to produce an increase in sales in each year amounting to 25% of the current sales volume.

Selling price per unit	£10
Variable cost per unit	£8.50
Current annual sales	£2,400,000.

The required rate of return on investments is 20%.

Assume that the 25% increase in sales would result in additional stocks of £100,000 and additional creditors of £20,000.

Advise the company on whether or not to extend the credit period offered to customers, if:

(a) all customers take the longer credit of two months;
(b) existing customers do not change their payment habits, and only the new customers take a full two months credit.

Solution

3.11 The change in credit policy is justifiable if the rate of return on the additional investment in working capital would exceed 20%.

Extra profit	
Contribution/sales ratio	15%
Increase in sales revenue	£600,000
Increase in contribution and profit	£90,000

(a) Extra investment, if all debtors take two months credit

	£
Average debtors after the sales increase (2/12 × £3,000,000)	500,000
Less current average debtors (1/12 × £2,400,000)	200,000
Increase in debtors	300,000
Increase in stocks	100,000
	400,000
Less increase in creditors	20,000
Net increase in working capital investment	380,000

Return on extra investment $\frac{£90,000}{£380,000}$ = 23.7%

(b) Extra investment, if only the new debtors take two months credit

	£
Increase in debtors (2/12 of £600,000)	100,000
Increase in stocks	100,000
	200,000
Less increase in creditors	20,000
Net increase in working capital investment	180,000

Return on extra investment $\frac{£90,000}{£180,000}$ = 50%

In both case (a) and case (b) the new credit policy appears to be worthwhile.

Discount policies

3.12 Varying the discount allowed for early payment of debts:

(a) affects the average collection period;
(b) affects the volume of demand (and possibly, therefore, indirectly affects bad debt losses).

To see whether the offer of a discount for early payment is financially worthwhile we must compare the cost of the discount with the benefit of a reduced investment in debtors.

We shall begin with examples where the offer of a discount for early payment does not affect the volume of demand.

Example

3.13 Lowe and Price Ltd has annual credit sales of £12,000,000, and three months are allowed for payment. The company decides to offer a 2% discount for payments made within ten days of the invoice being sent, and to reduce the maximum time allowed for payment to two months. It is estimated that 50% of customers will take the discount. If the company requires a 20% return on investments, what will be the effect of the discount if the cost per unit is £9 and the selling price is £10? Assume that the volume of sales will be unaffected by the discount.

Solution: first method

3.14 This method is to calculate:

(a) the profits forgone by offering the discount;
(b) the interest charges saved or incurred as a result of the changes in the cash flows of the company.

3.15 (a) The volume of debtors, if the company policy remains unchanged, would be

$3/12 \times £12,000,000 = £3,000,000.$

(b) If the policy is changed the volume of debtors would be

$$\left(\frac{10}{360} \times 50\% \times £12,000,000\right) + \left(\frac{2}{12} \times 50\% \times £12,000,000\right)$$

$$= £166,667 + £1,000,000 = £1,166,667.$$

(c) There will be a reduction in debtors of £1,833,333.

(d) Since the company can invest at 20% a year, the value of a reduction in debtors (a source of funds) is 20% of £1,833,333 each year in perpetuity, that is, £366,667 a year.

(e) *Summary*

	£
Value of reduction in debtors each year	366,667
Less discounts allowed each year (2% × 50% × £12,000,000)	120,000
Net benefit of new discount policy each year	246,667

Solution: second method, using DCF

3.16 Another approach is to calculate the cash flows in perpetuity by either discount policy, and to calculate a present value of the future cash flows. An annual cost of capital of 20% is approximately equivalent to a monthly cost of $1\frac{1}{2}$%, or 0.015.

(a) If the present discount policy is maintained, the present value of future receipts from debtors for sales from January 19X0 would be as follows.

(i) Cash flows would be £1,000,000 a month in perpetuity from April 19X0.

(ii) The present value of these cash flows, as at the end of March 19X0, would be $\frac{£1,000,000}{0.015}$

(iii) The present value these cash flows, as at beginning of January 19X0, would be

$$= \frac{£1,000,000}{0.015} \times \frac{1}{(1.015)^3}$$

= £63,754,466.

(b) If the proposed discount policy is introduced, the cash flows would be as follows, assuming as an approximation that $\frac{2}{3}$ of debtors taking the discount will pay in the month of sale.

January 19X0 cash flow	$\frac{2}{3}$ × 50% × £1,000,000 × 98% = £326,667
February 19X0	($\frac{1}{3}$ × 50% × £1,000,000 × 98%) + ($\frac{2}{3}$ × 50% × £1,000,000 × 98%) = £490,000
March 19X0	(50% × £1,000,000 × 98%) + (50% × £1,000,000) = £990,000
April 19X0 onwards	£990,000 a month in perpetuity

The PV of these cash flows as at January 19X0 is as follows.

Month	*Cash flow* £'000	*Discount factor*	*PV* £'000
Jan 19X0	327	$\frac{1}{(1.015)}$	322.2
Feb 19X0	490	$\frac{1}{(1.015)^2}$	475.6
March 19X0 onwards	990 per month	$\frac{1}{0.015} \times \frac{1}{(1.015)^2}$	64,063.7
			64,861.5

(c) The proposed discount policy therefore offers a higher PV of receipts by £(64,861,500 - 63,754,466) = £1,107,034.

A comparison of the two solutions

3.17 It is useful to review the two different solutions to the same problem.

Because of the variations in the assumptions and approximations employed, the methods produce different numerical solutions (although both agree that the discount is worthwhile). The conclusions to be drawn are these.

(a) Since different approaches can be used, you should adopt an approach which seems suitable to the information provided in the question.

(b) Solutions can only give approximations to the financial advantages and disadvantages of offering discounts. You should therefore treat your solution with some caution.

3.18 An extension of the payment period allowed to debtors may be introduced in order to increase sales volume.

Example

3.19 Enticement Ltd currently expects sales of £50,000 a month. Variable costs of sales are £40,000 a month (all payable in the month of sale). It is estimated that if the credit period allowed to debtors were to be increased from 30 days to 60 days, sales volume would increase by 20%. All customers would be expected to take advantage of the extended credit. If the cost of capital is 12½% a year (or approximately 1% a month), is the extension of the credit period justifiable in financial terms?

Solution: method 1

3.20

	£
Current debtors (1 month)	50,000
Debtors after implementing the proposal (2 months)	120,000
Increase in debtors	70,000

	£
Financing cost (× 12½%)	8,750
Annual contribution from additional sales (12 months × 20% × £10,000)	24,000
Annual net benefit from extending credit period	15,250

Solution: method 2 (the DCF method)

3.21

		PV £
Current contribution per month, from month 1 in perpetuity (£10,000 a month)	$\frac{10,000}{0.01}$	1,000,000
New policy: contribution per month from month 2 in perpetuity (£12,000 a month)	$\frac{12,000}{0.01} \times \frac{1}{1.01}$	1,188,119
NPV of changing to the new policy		188,119

Bad debt risk

3.22 Different credit policies are likely to have differing levels of bad debt risk. The higher turnover resulting from easier credit terms should be sufficiently profitable to exceed the cost of:
(a) bad debts; and
(b) the additional investment necessary to achieve the higher sales.

Example

3.23 Grabbit Quick Ltd achieves current annual sales of £1,800,000. The cost of sales is 80% of this amount, but bad debts average 1% of total sales, and the annual profit is as follows.

	£
Sales	1,800,000
Less cost of sales	1,440,000
	360,000
Less bad debts	18,000
Profit	342,000

The current debt collection period is one month, and the management consider that if credit terms were eased (option A), the effects would be as follows.

	Present policy	*Option A*
Additional sales (%)	-	25%
Average collection period	1 month	2 months
Bad debts (% of sales)	1%	3%

The company requires a 20% return on its investments. If the costs of sales are 75% variable and 25% fixed, and on the assumptions that:

(a) there would be no increase in fixed costs from the extra turnover;
(b) there would be no increase in average stocks or creditors;

what is the preferable policy, Option A or the present one?

Solution

3.24 The increase in profit before the cost of additional finance for Option A can be found as follows.

	£
(a) Increase in contribution from additional sales	
25% × £1,800,000 × 40%*	180,000
Less increase in bad debts	
(3% × £2,250,000) - £18,000	49,500
Increase in annual profit	130,500

* The C/S ratio is (100% - 75%) × 80% = 40%

(b)

	£
Proposed investment in debtors	
£2,250,000 × 1/6	375,000
Less current investment in debtors	
£1,800,000 × 1/12	150,000
Additional investment required	225,000
Cost of additional finance at 20%	£45,000

(c) As the increase in profit exceeds the cost of additional finance Option A should be adopted.

Credit insurance

3.25 Companies might be able to obtain credit insurance against certain approved debts going bad through a specialist credit insurance firm. A company cannot insure against all its bad debt losses, but may be able to insure against losses above the normal level.

3.26 When a company arranges credit insurance, it must submit specific proposals for credit to the insurance company, stating the name of each customer to which it wants to give credit and the amount of credit it wants to give. The insurance company will accept, amend or refuse these proposals, depending on its assessment of each of these customers.

3.27 Credit insurance is normally available for only up to about 75% of a company's potential bad debt loss. The remaining 25% of any bad debt costs are borne by the company itself. This is to ensure that the company does not become slack with its credit control and debt collection procedures, for example by indulging in overtrading and not chasing slow payers hard enough.

4. THE MANAGEMENT OF CREDITORS

4.1 The management of creditors consists of:

(a) attempting to obtain satisfactory credit from suppliers;
(b) attempting to extend credit during periods of cash shortage;
(c) maintaining good relations with regular and important suppliers.

4.2 If a supplier offers a discount for the early payment of debts, the evaluation of the decision whether or not to accept the discount is similar to the evaluation of the decision whether or not to *offer* a discount. One problem is the mirror image of the other. The methods of evaluating the offer of a discount to customers were described in the previous section of this chapter.

5. CONCLUSION

5.1 In contrast to theories of capital structure, the management of working capital gets right down to the day-to-day practicalities of running a business. In answering questions on working capital management, you should always consider whether any proposed course of action really makes business sense.

TEST YOUR KNOWLEDGE

The numbers in brackets refer to paragraphs of this chapter

1. How do cash flow problems arise? (1.1)
2. When a company is faced with a cash flow problem, what steps might it take to overcome the problem? (1.2)
3. What are cash management services? (1.7, 1.8)
4. What factors should be considered by management in the formulation of a policy for credit control? (3.1)
5. How might the credit-worthiness of a potential new customer be checked? (3.5, 3.6)
6. What is credit insurance? (3.25 - 3.27)

Now try questions 28 and 29 at the end of the text

Chapter 23

OTHER ASPECTS OF WORKING CAPITAL MANAGEMENT

This chapter covers the following topics.

1. Factoring
2. Short-term investments
3. Foreign trade and debt management
4. Risk management

1. FACTORING

1.1 Factoring is a service that does not have a concise definition. A factor is defined as 'a doer or transactor of business for another', but a factoring organisation specialises in trade debts, and manages the debts owed to a client (a business customer) on the client's behalf.

1.2 The main aspects of factoring are:

(a) administration of the client's invoicing, sales accounting and debt collection service;

(b) credit protection for the client's debts, whereby the factor takes over the risk of loss from bad debts and so 'insures' the client against such losses. This service is also referred to as 'debt underwriting' or the 'purchase of a client's debts'. The factor usually purchases these debts 'without recourse' to the client, which means that if the client's debtors do not pay what they owe, the factor will not ask for his money back from the client.

(c) making payments to the client in advance of collecting the debts. This is sometimes referred to as 'factor finance' because the factor is providing cash to the client against outstanding debts.

The debts administration service of factoring companies

1.3 A company might be struggling just to do the administrative tasks of recording credit sales, sending out invoices, sending out monthly statements and reminders, and collecting and recording payments from customers. If the company's turnover is growing rapidly, or if its sales are changing from largely cash sales to largely credit sales, the accounting administration might be unable to cope with the extra work. A factoring organisation can help.

1.4 The administration of a client's debts by the factor covers:

(a) keeping the books of account for sales;
(b) sending out invoices to customers;
(c) collecting the debts;
(d) credit control (ensuring that customers pay on time) and chasing late payers.

1.5 For the client the advantages are that:

(a) the factor takes on a job of administration which saves staff costs for the client;

(b) the factor performs the service economically, by taking advantage of economies of scale for a large debts administration organisation. This enables the factor to price his services reasonably.

1.6 The factor's service fee for debt administration varies according to the size of the client's operation, but it is typically between 0.75% and 2% of the book value of the client's debts. A business might be considered too small for factoring if its annual turnover were less than £250,000.

1.7 A factor is unlikely to agree to provide a service to small firms, firms which have only recently been established, firms in a high-risk market or with a history of bad debts, or businesses selling small value items to the general public (such as mail order firms).

Credit protection (debt underwriting) and factoring

1.8 Another problem that a company might have with its debtors is credit control and bad debts. If a company grants credit, how should it decide how much credit to give to each customer, and which customers should not be given any credit at all? The problem of bad debts can be controlled by exercising careful management over granting credit in the first place.

1.9 Many companies do not have the information or the capability to assess credit risks properly. Factors, however, do have this capability, and can therefore carry out the credit control function for a client, vetting individual customers and deciding whether to grant credit and how much credit to allow. Because they control credit in this way, they will also underwrite their client's debts.

1.10 Most factors provide a debts administration service in which credit protection is an integral part. This is because the service is usually without recourse to the client in the event of non-payment by the customer. Without recourse factoring or non-recourse factoring effectively means that the factor buys the client's debts from him and so the client is guaranteed protection against bad debts.

1.11 It is important to realise, however, that a factor is not a debt collection agency in the sense that he can be relied on to get money out of customers when no one else can. Factors are involved in normal debtors administration (bookkeeping, invoicing and credit management as well as collecting money) and do not want to get involved with problem customers.

1.12 Under a without recourse arrangement, the factor assumes full responsibility for credit control, because he now bears the credit risk.

(a) The factors will approve the amount of credit to be allowed to individual customers by the client.

(b) The factor will keep a continuous watch over customers' accounts.

(c) If a payment becomes overdue, the factor will consult the client. The client may decide to take over the bad debt risk from the factor, rather than incur badwill from the customer if the factor were to take legal action to recover the debt. Otherwise the factor is free to take non-payers to court to obtain payment.

1.13 Not every factoring organisation will purchase approved debts without recourse and 'with recourse' factoring might be provided, for example for very large debts.

Making advances on debts (factor finance)

1.14 Some companies have difficulty in financing their debtors. There are two main reasons for this.

(a) If a company's turnover is rising rapidly, its total debtors will rise quickly too. Selling more on credit will put a strain on the company's cash flow. The company, although making profits, might find itself in difficulties because it has too many debtors and not enough cash.

(b) If a company grants long credit to its customers, it might run into cash flow difficulties for much the same reason. Exporting companies must often allow long periods of credit to foreign buyers.

1.15 Factors offer their clients a debt financing service to overcome these problems, and will be prepared to advance cash to the client against the security of the client's debtors. The client will assign his debtors to the factor.

1.16 A factoring organisation might be asked by a client to advance funds to the client against the debts which the factor has purchased, up to 80% of the value of the debts. For example, if a client makes credit sales of £100,000 a month, the factor might be willing to advance up to 80% of the invoice value (here £80,000) in return for a commission charge, and interest will be charged on the amount of funds advanced.

The rate of interest will be tied to bank base rate, and may be a little higher than the client would pay a bank for an overdraft. The balance of the money will be paid to the client when the customers have paid the factor, or after an agreed period.

1.17 Advances from factors should be used in order to finance the extra stock and debtors required for growth. The funds should not be used to finance fixed assets, and should not be a long-term source of funds. Factor financing might help a company to adjust to growth, but growth does not continue indefinitely, and when business settles down at a steady level, the need for money in advance ought to disappear.

The advantages of factoring

1.18 The benefits of factoring for a business customer include the following.

(a) The business can pay its suppliers promptly, and so be able to take advantage of any early payment discounts that are available.

(b) Optimum stock levels can be maintained, because the business will have enough cash to pay for the stocks it needs.

(c) Growth can be financed through sales rather than by injecting fresh external capital.

(d) The business gets finance linked to its volume of sales. In contrast, overdraft limits tend to be determined by historical balance sheets.

(e) The managers of the business do not have to spend their time on the problems of slow paying debtors.

(f) The business does not incur the costs of running its own sales ledger department.

Factoring and bank finance

1.19 If a company arranges with a factor for advances to be made against its debts, the debts will become the security for the advance. If the same company already has a bank overdraft facility, the bank may be relying on the debts as a form of security (perhaps not legal security, in the form of a floating charge over stocks and debtors, but as an element in the decision about how much overdraft to allow the company). The bank may therefore wish to reduce the company's overdraft limit.

1.20 Certainly, a company should inform its bank when it makes an agreement with a factor for advances against debts.

Example

1.21 A company makes annual credit sales of £1,500,000. Credit terms are 30 days, but its debt administration has been poor and the average collection period has been 45 days with 0.5% of sales resulting in bad debts which are written off.

A factor would take on the task of debt administration and credit checking, at an annual fee of 2.5% of credit sales. The company would save £30,000 a year in administration costs. The payment period would be 30 days.

The factor would also provide an advance of 80% of invoiced debts at an interest rate of 14% (3% over the current base rate). The company can obtain an overdraft facility to finance its debtors at a rate of 2.5% over base rate.

Should the factor's services be accepted? Assume a constant monthly turnover.

Solution

1.22 It is assumed that the factor would advance an amount equal to 80% of the invoiced debts, and the balance 30 days later.

(a) The current situation is as follows, using the company's debt collection staff and a bank overdraft to finance all debts.

Credit sales	£1,500,000 pa
Average credit period	45 days

The annual cost is as follows.	£
$\frac{45}{365}$ × £1,500,000 × 13.5%	24,966
Bad debts: 0.5% × £1,500,000	7,500
Total cost	32,466

(b) *The cost of the factor*
80% of credit sales financed by the factor would be 80% of £1,500,000 = £1,200,000. For a consistent comparison, we must assume that 20% of credit sales would be financed by a bank overdraft.

The average credit period would be only 30 days.

The annual cost would be as follows.

		£
Factor's finance	$\frac{30}{365}$ × £1,200,000 × 14%	13,808
Overdraft	$\frac{30}{365}$ × £300,000 × 13.5%	3,329
		17,137
Cost of factor's services: 2.5% × £1,500,000		37,500
Less savings in company's administration costs		(30,000)
Net cost of the factor		24,637

(c) *Conclusion*
The factor is cheaper. In this case, the factor's fees exactly equal the savings in bad debts (£7,500) and administration costs (£30,000). The factor is then cheaper overall because it will be more efficient at collecting debts. The advance of 80% of debts is not needed, however, if the company has sufficient overdraft facility because the factor's finance charge of 14% is higher than the company's overdraft rate of 13.5%.

Invoice discounting

1.23 Invoice discounting is related to factoring and many factors will provide an invoice discounting service. It is the purchase of a selection of invoices, at a discount. The invoice discounter does not take over the administration of the client's sales ledger, and the arrangement is purely for the advance of cash. A client should only want to have some invoices discounted when he has a temporary cash shortage, and so invoice discounting tends to consist of one-off deals.

1.24 Confidential invoice discounting is an arrangement whereby a debt is confidentially assigned to the factor, and the client's customer will only become aware of the arrangement if he does not pay his debt to the client.

1.25 If a client needs to generate cash, he can approach a factor or invoice discounter, who will offer to purchase selected invoices and advance up to 75% of their value. At the end of each month, the factor will pay over the balance of the purchase price, less charges, on the invoices that have been settled in the month. (Receipts from the paid invoices belong to the invoice discounter or factor).

1.26 There is an element of credit protection in the invoice discounting service, but its real purpose is to improve the client's cash flow. Since the invoice discounter does not control debt administration, and relies on the client to collect the debts for him, it is a more risky operation than 'factoring proper' and so a factor might only agree to offer an invoice discounting service to reliable, well-established companies.

2. SHORT-TERM INVESTMENTS

2.1 Companies and other organisations sometimes have a surplus of cash and become 'cash rich'. A cash surplus is likely to be temporary, but while it exists the company should seek to obtain a good return by investing or depositing the cash, without the risk of a capital loss (or at least, without the risk of an excessive capital loss).

2.2 Three possible reasons for a cash surplus are:

(a) profitability from trading operations;

(b) low capital expenditure, perhaps because of an absence of profitable new investment opportunities;

(c) receipts from selling parts of the business.

The board of directors might keep the surplus in liquid form:

(a) to benefit from high interest rates that might be available from bank deposits, when returns on re-investment in the company appear to be lower;
(b) to have cash available should a strategic opportunity arise, perhaps for the takeover of another company for which a cash consideration might be needed;
(c) to buy back shares from shareholders in the near future;
(d) to pay an increased dividend to shareholders.

Short-term investments

2.3 Temporary cash surpluses are likely to be:

(a) deposited with a bank or similar financial institution;

(b) invested in short-term debt instruments. Debt instruments are debt securities which can be traded;

(c) invested in longer term debt instruments, which can be sold on the stock market when the company eventually needs the cash;

(d) invested in shares of listed companies, which can be sold on the stock market when the company eventually needs the cash.

2.4 The problem with (c) and (d) is the risk of capital losses due to a fall in the market value of the securities. With short-term debt instruments (item (b)) any capital losses should not be large, because of the short term to maturity. With bank deposits (item (a)) the risk of capital losses is minimal.

Short-term deposits

2.5 Cash can of course be put into a bank deposit to earn interest. The rate of interest obtainable depends on the size of the deposit, and varies from bank to bank.

2.6 There are other types of deposit.

(a) *Money market lending*. There is a very large money market in the UK for inter-bank lending, with banks lending to each other and borrowing from each other for short terms ranging from as little as overnight up to terms of a year or more.

The interest rates in the market are related to the London Interbank Offer Rate (LIBOR) and the London Interbank Bid Rate (LIBID).

(i) A large company will be able to lend surplus cash directly to a borrowing bank in the market.

(ii) A smaller company with a fairly large cash surplus will usually be able to arrange to lend money on the interbank market, but through its bank, and possibly on condition that the money can only be withdrawn at three months notice.

(b) *Local authority deposits*. Local authorities often need short-term cash, and investors can deposit funds with them for periods ranging from overnight up to one year or more.

(c) *Finance house deposits*. These are time deposits with finance houses (usually subsidiaries of banks).

2.7 Deposits with banks, local authorities and finance houses are non-negotiable, which means that the investor who deposits funds cannot sell the deposit to another investor, should an unexpected need for cash arise. The deposit will only be released back to the investor when its term ends.

Short-term debt instruments

2.8 There are a number of short-term debt instruments which an investor can re-sell before the debt matures and is repaid.

2.9 These debt instruments include:

(a) certificates of deposit (CDs);
(b) Treasury bills;
(c) bank bills, also called sterling bankers' acceptances;
(d) trade bills;
(e) sterling commercial paper;
(f) US commercial paper;
(g) Eurocommercial paper (ECP).

Items (c) to (g) are normally purchased initially by banks, and are ways for companies to *raise* short term funds other than to invest surplus cash.

Certificates of deposit (CDs)

2.10 A CD is a security that is issued by a bank, acknowledging that a certain amount of money has been deposited with it for a certain period of time (usually, a short term). The CD is issued to the depositor, and attracts a stated amount of interest. The depositor will be another bank or a large commercial organisation. CDs are negotiable and traded on the CD market (a money market), so if a CD holder wishes to obtain immediate cash, he can sell the CD on the market at any time. This secondhand market in CDs makes them attractive, flexible investments for organisations with excess cash.

2.11 A company with surplus cash can:

(a) deposit a certain amount of cash with a bank for a fixed period, and receive a certificate of deposit from the bank; or

(b). buy an existing CD, which may have a much shorter period to maturity, on the CD market.

2.12 CDs are mainly denominated in sterling, but there is a growing market in US dollar CDs, and in deposits linked to the value of the European currency unit (ecu).

Treasury bills

2.13 *Treasury bills* are issued weekly by the government to finance short-term cash deficiencies in the government's expenditure programme. They are IOUs issued by the government, giving a promise to pay a certain amount to their holder on maturity. Treasury bills have a term of 91 days to maturity, after which the holder is paid the full value of the bill. Most Treasury bills are denominated in sterling, but some are in ecus.

2.14 Treasury bills do not pay interest, but the purchase price of a Treasury bill is less than its face value, the amount that the government will eventually pay on maturity. There is thus an implied rate of interest in the price at which the bills are traded. The secondhand value of Treasury bills in the discount market (the money market in which they are traded) varies with current interest rates but will never exceed their face value.

2.15 A company can arrange through its bank to invest in Treasury bills. Since they are negotiable, they can be re-sold, if required, on the discount market before their maturity date.

Eligible bank bills (sterling bankers' acceptances)

2.16 Bank bills are IOUs issued by a bank. Eligible bank bills are bills issued by 'eligible' banks: top-rated banks whose bills the Bank of England will agree to buy on the money market. They are denominated in sterling and are short-term.

Like Treasury bills, they are negotiable and traded on the discount market. Most purchasers of bank bills are other banks, including the Bank of England.

Local authority bonds

2.17 These are short-term securities issued by local authorities to raise cash. They carry interest, and are repayable on maturity. They are traded secondhand in the money market, and so, like CDs, are a flexible investment for organisations with excess cash. They are not always available, however.

3. FOREIGN TRADE AND DEBT MANAGEMENT

3.1 Foreign debts raise the following special problems.

(a) When goods are sold abroad, the customer might ask for credit. The period of credit might be 30 days or 60 days, say, after receipt of the goods; or perhaps 90 days after shipment.

Exports take time to arrange, and there might be complex paperwork. Transporting the goods can be slow, if they are sent by sea.

These delays in foreign trade mean that exporters often build up large investments in stocks and debtors. These working capital investments have to be financed somehow.

(b) The risk of bad debts can be greater with foreign trade than with domestic trade. If a foreign debtor refuses to pay a debt, the exporter must pursue the debt in the debtor's own country, where procedures will be subject to the laws of that country.

There are several measures available to exporters to overcome these problems.

Reducing the investment in foreign debtors

3.2 A company can reduce its investment in foreign debtors by insisting on earlier payment for goods.

3.3 Another approach is for an exporter to arrange for a bank to give cash for a foreign debt, sooner than the exporter would receive payment in the normal course of events. There are several ways in which this might be done.

(a) *Advances against collections*

Where the exporter asks his bank to handle the collection of payment (of a bill of exchange or a cheque) on his behalf, the bank may be prepared to make an advance to the exporter against the collection. The amount of the advance might be 80% to 90% of the value of the collection. The bank will expect repayment of the advance from the proceeds of the bill or the cheque.

Advances against collections would be arranged where the bill or cheque is payable in the exporter's own country.

(b) *Negotiation of bills or cheques*. This is similar to an advance against collection, but would be used where the bill or cheque is payable outside the exporter's country (for example in the foreign buyer's country).

(c) *Documentary credits*. These are described below.

Reducing the bad debt risk

3.4 Methods of minimising bad debt risks are broadly similar to those for domestic trade. An exporting company should vet the creditworthiness of each customer, and grant credit terms accordingly.

3.5 Three important methods of reducing the risks of bad debts in foreign trade are:
(a) export factoring;
(b) use of the Export Credit Guarantee Department (ECGD);
(c) documentary credits.

Export factoring

3.6 Export factoring is the same as factoring domestic trade debts, which was described earlier.

The Export Credit Guarantee Department (ECGD)

3.7 The Export Credit Guarantee Department (ECGD) is a department of the government which assists exporters in two ways.

(a) It sells credit insurance to exporters, to protect them from the risk of non-payment by an overseas buyer.

(b) It provides guarantees to banks on behalf of exporters, so that banks will be prepared to lend money either to the exporter or to the exporter's overseas customers.

At the time of writing, a bill to privatise most of the ECGD (by selling it to financial institutions) is going through Parliament.

Documentary credits

3.8 Documentary credits provide a method of payment in international trade, which gives the exporter a risk-free method of obtaining payment.

3.9 At the same time, documentary credits are a method of obtaining short-term finance from a bank, for working capital. This is because a bank might agree to discount or negotiate a bill of exchange, and so:

(a) the exporter receives immediate payment of the amount due to him, less the discount, instead of having to wait for payment until the end of the credit period allowed to the buyer;

(b) the buyer is able to get a period of credit before having to pay for the imports.

3.10 The buyer (a foreign buyer, or a UK importer) and the seller (a UK exporter or a foreign supplier) first of all agree a contract for the sale of the goods, which provides for payment through a documentary credit.

The *buyer* then requests a bank in his country to issue a *letter of credit* in favour of the exporter. This bank which issues the letter of credit is known as the *issuing bank*. The buyer is known as the *applicant* for the credit and the exporter is known as the *beneficiary* (because he receives the benefits).

3.11 The issuing bank, by issuing its letter of credit, guarantees payment to the beneficiary.

3.12 The issuing bank asks a bank in the exporter's country to advise the credit to the exporter. This bank is known as the *advising bank*. The advising bank agrees to handle the credit (on terms arranged with the issuing bank) but does not normally make any commitment itself to guarantee payment to the exporter.

3.13 The advising bank (in the exporter's country) might be required by the issuing bank to add its own 'confirmation' to the credit. The advising bank would then be adding its own guarantee of payment to the guarantee already provided by the issuing bank. If it does confirm the credit, it is then known and the *confirming bank*. Thus, a *confirmed* letter of credit carries the guarantees of two banks, usually one in the exporter's country (the confirming bank) and one in the buyer's country (the issuing bank).

The cost of issuing a letter of credit is usually borne by the buyer.

3.14 A documentary credit arrangement must be made between the exporter, the buyer and participating banks *before the export sale takes place*. Documentary credits are slow to arrange, and administratively cumbersome; however, they might be considered essential where the risk of non-payment is high.

4. RISK MANAGEMENT

4.1 Management involves taking risks. Business risks are risks associated with the success or failure of business operations, such as launching a new product that might or might not be profitable. Financial risks are risks associated with the way in which a business conducts its financial affairs, and the possibility of making losses (or even going into liquidation) as a result.

4.2 One aspect of financial risk is gearing. A highly geared company is more at risk than a company with low gearing in periods when profits before interest and tax are low.

Other aspects of financial risk involve:
(a) interest rates on borrowing;
(b) foreign exchange.

One of the tasks of a treasurer or financial manager is to reduce these risks to an acceptable level.

Exposure and hedging

4.3 *Exposure* means vulnerability to risk.

(a) *Interest rate exposure* arises when a company's borrowing is such that a change in interest rates might expose it to interest charges that are unacceptably high. For example, if a company's debt capital is all at fixed rates of interest and due for repayment within the next few months, and all the loans are to be replaced or renegotiated, the company would be vulnerable to a sudden increase in market interest rates.

(b) *Foreign exchange exposure* arises when exporting or importing companies wish to exchange sterling into foreign currency or vice versa. Exposure arises because the exporter or importer is vulnerable to adverse movements in foreign exchange rates when there is a period of credit involved (as there almost always is). For example, if an exporter sells goods to the USA for US $57,600 when the exchange rate is US $1.60 to £1, he would expect to earn £36,000 from the sale. However, if the customer is allowed credit of three months and the exchange rate alters to US $1.80 to £1 in this time, the eventual income would be only £32,000, which is £4,000 less than expected.

4.4 *Hedging* means taking action to reduce or 'cover' an exposure: hedging is the process of financial risk management. Hedging has a cost, either a fee to a financial institution or a reduction in profit, but companies might well consider the costs to be justified by the reduction in financial risks that the hedging achieves.

Managing a debt portfolio

4.5 There are three important considerations for corporate treasurers in managing a debt portfolio, that is, in deciding how a company should obtain its short-term funds so as to be able to repay debts as they mature and to minimise any inherent risks, notably foreign exchange risk, in the debts the company owes and is owed. These three considerations are as follows.

(a) *Maturity mix.* The treasurer must avoid having too much debt becoming repayable within a short period.

(b) *Currency mix.* Foreign currency debts create a risk of losses through adverse movements in foreign exchange rates before the debt falls due for payment. Foreign currency management involves hedging against foreign currency risks, for example by means of forward exchange contracts, or having debts in several currencies, some of which will strengthen and some of which will weaken over time.

(c) *The mix of fixed interest and floating rate debts*

(i) Too much fixed interest rate debt creates an unnecessary cost when market interest rates fall. A company might find itself committed to high interest costs that it could have avoided.

(ii) Too much borrowing at a variable rate of interest (such as bank overdrafts and medium-term bank lending) leads to high costs when interest rates go up.

Interest rate risk management

4.6 Methods of reducing interest rate risk include interest rate swaps, forward rate interest agreements (FRAs), interest rate futures and interest rate guarantees (IRGs).

Interest rate swaps

4.7 These are transactions that exploit different interest rates in different markets for borrowing, to reduce interest costs for either fixed or floating rate loans. They are most commonly used by banks, but can be used by companies.

4.8 Interest rate swaps are arrangements whereby two companies swap interest rate commitments with each other, with the following effects.

(a) A company which has debt at a fixed rate of interest can make a swap so that it ends up paying interest at a variable rate.

(b) A company which has debt at a variable rate of interest (floating rate debt) ends up paying a fixed rate of interest.

Example

4.9 Goodcredit plc has been given a high credit rating. It can borrow at a fixed rate of 11%, or at a variable interest rate equal to LIBOR, which also happens to be 11% at the moment. It would like to borrow at a variable rate.

Secondtier plc is a company with a lower credit rating, which can borrow at a fixed rate of 12.5% or at a variable rate of LIBOR plus 0.5%. It would like to borrow at a fixed rate.

(a) Without a swap, Goodcredit would borrow at LIBOR which is currently 11%, and Secondtier would borrow at 12.5% fixed.

(b) With a swap,

(i) Goodcredit would borrow at a fixed rate (11%);
(ii) Secondtier would borrow at a variable rate (LIBOR plus 0.5%), currently 11.5%;
(iii) They would then agree a rate for swapping interest, perhaps with:

(1) Goodcredit paying Secondtier variable rate interest, at LIBOR;
(2) Secondtier paying Goodcredit fixed rate interest, say at 11.5%.

4.10 The net result is as follows.

Goodcredit plc		*Secondtier plc*	
Pays		Pays	
to bank	(11%)	to bank	(LIBOR plus 0.5%)
in swap	(LIBOR)	in swap	(11.5%)
Receives		Receives	
in swap	11.5%	in swap	LIBOR
Net interest cost	LIBOR less 0.5%	Net interest cost	12%

4.11 The results of the swap are that Goodcredit ends up paying variable rate interest, but at a lower cost than it could get from a bank, and Secondtier ends up paying fixed rate interest, also at a lower cost than it could get from investors or a bank.

Other advantages of swaps

4.12 Interest rate swaps have several further attractions.

(a) They are easy to arrange.

(b) They are flexible. They can be arranged in any size and, if required, reversed.

(c) The transaction costs are low, limited to legal fees.

Forward interest rate agreements (FRAs)

4.13 These are agreements between a company and a bank about the interest rate on *future* borrowing or bank deposits.

For example, a company can enter into a FRA with a bank that fixes the rate of interest for borrowing at a certain time in the future. If the actual interest rate proves to be higher than the rate agreed, the bank pays the company the difference. If the actual interest rate is lower than the rate agreed, the company pays the bank the difference.

Interest rate futures

4.14 Interest rate futures are similar to FRAs, except that the terms, the amounts and the periods are standardised.

Interest rate guarantees (IRGs)

4.15 These are more expensive for a company to obtain than FRAs. They are agreements with a bank on the maximum borrowing rate that will apply at a certain time in the future. For example, a company might obtain an IRG from its bank that the interest rate will not exceed 14%. If it does, the bank must pay the company the difference. If market interest rates turn out to be lower, the company is not bound to accept 14%. Instead, it can abandon the guarantee and borrow at the lower existing market rate. IRGs are sometimes referred to as interest rate options or interest rate caps.

Methods of hedging against foreign currency risk

4.16 There are a number of ways of hedging against foreign currency risk. We shall look at foreign exchange management in some detail in the next chapter.

5. CONCLUSION

5.1 Factoring is a possibility which any company of sufficient size should consider, though if it is used purely as a means of obtaining finance it can be expensive. The other topics covered in this chapter relate to special circumstances: cash surpluses, foreign trade and the management of interest rate risk. Small companies may find they have no choice but to accept what their bank managers or overseas customers offer them, but larger companies should actively manage their deposits, borrowings and foreign debtors.

TEST YOUR KNOWLEDGE

The numbers in brackets refer to paragraphs of this chapter

1. What services do factors provide? (1.2)
2. What is invoice discounting? (1.23)
3. What short-term debt instruments are available for the investment of surplus cash? (2.9)
4. How are documentary credits used? (3.8 - 3.13)
5. What is an interest rate swap? (4.8)

Now try questions 30 and 31 at the end of the text

Chapter 24

FOREIGN EXCHANGE RISK MANAGEMENT

This chapter covers the following topics.

1. Selling and buying currency
2. Forward exchange contracts
3. Other risk management techniques

1. SELLING AND BUYING CURRENCY

1.1 If an importer has to pay a foreign supplier in a foreign currency, he might ask his bank to sell him the required amount of the currency. For example, suppose that a bank's customer, a trading company, has imported goods for which it must now pay US$10,000.

(a) The company will ask the bank to sell it $10,000. If the company is buying currency, the bank is selling it.

(b) When the bank agrees to sell US$10,000 to the company, it will tell the company what the range of exchange will be for the transaction. If the bank's selling rate is, say $1.7935, the bank will charge the company

$$\frac{\$10,000}{\$1.7935 \text{ per } £1} = £5,579.69 \text{ for the currency.}$$

1.2 Similarly, if an exporter is paid, say, US$10,000 by a customer in the USA, he may wish to exchange the dollars to obtain sterling. He will therefore ask his bank to buy the dollars from him. Since the exporter is selling currency to the bank, the bank is buying the currency.

If the bank quotes a buying rate of, say $1.8075, the bank will pay the exporter

$$\frac{\$10,000}{\$1.8075 \text{ per } £1} = £5,532.50 \text{ for the currency.}$$

1.3 A bank expects to make a profit from selling and buying currency, and it does so by offering a rate for selling a currency which is different from the rate for buying the currency.

1.4 If a bank were to buy a quantity of foreign currency from a customer, and then were to re-sell it to another customer, it would charge the second customer more (in sterling) for the currency than it would pay the first customer. The difference would be profit. For example, the figures used for illustration in the previous paragraphs show a bank selling some US dollars for £5,575.69 and buying the same quantity of dollars for £5,532.50, at selling and buying rates that might be in use at the same time. The bank would make a profit of £43.19.

Bank commission

1.5 In addition, a bank will charge a customer commission on a foreign exchange transaction. A UK bank buying currency from or selling currency to a customer will charge commission in sterling.

If you are told that commission is, say, 1 per mille, this would be one-thousandth of the sterling value of the transaction. Just as one per cent (1%) is one-hundredth, one per mille (0.1%) is one thousandth, and 2 per mille (0.2%) is two thousandths.

Spot rates

1.6 A spot rate is the rate of exchange which is used for currency dealing without any advance arrangement for the purchase or sale having been made. A spot rate is a rate quoted immediately, for delivery of the currency to the buyer two working days later. The 'spot date' is when the currency is delivered and settlement is made. All the rates so far mentioned in this chapter have been spot rates.

Exercise

Calculate how much sterling exporters would receive or how much sterling importers would pay, ignoring the bank's commission, in each of the following situations, if they were to exchange currency and sterling at the spot rate.

(a) A UK exporter receives a payment from a French customer of FF 150,000.

(b) A UK importer buys goods from a Japanese supplier and pays 1 million yen.

(c) A UK exporter receives a payment of 80,000 guilders from a Dutch customer.

(d) A UK importer pays a German consultancy firm DM 120,000 for services provided by the firm.

Spot rates are as follows.

France	10.73	-	10.76
Japan	233½	-	235½
Netherlands	3.55	-	3.57
Germany	3.1725	-	3.1775

Solution

(a) The bank is being asked to buy the French francs and will give the exporter

$$\frac{150,000}{10.76} = £13,940.52 \text{ in exchange.}$$

(b) The bank is being asked to sell the yen to the importer and will charge

$$\frac{1,000,000}{233\frac{1}{2}} = £4,282.66$$

(c) The bank is being asked to buy the guilders from the exporter and will pay

$$\frac{80,000}{3.57} = £22,408.96$$

(d) The bank is being asked to sell the DM, and will charge

$$\frac{120,000}{3.1725} = £37,825.06$$

Foreknowledge of foreign currency receipts and payments: exposure and foreign exchange risk

1.7 Much international trade involves credit. An importer will take credit often for several months and sometimes longer, and an exporter will grant credit. One consequence of taking and granting credit is that international traders will know in advance about the receipts and payments arising from their trade. They will know:

(a) what foreign currency they will receive or pay;
(b) when the receipt or payment will occur;
(c) how much of the currency will be received or paid.

1.8 Importers and exporters alike will be concerned about the profit they can expect to make from trade. An exporter who invoices a foreign buyer in the buyer's currency will expect to be able to exchange his foreign currency proceeds from the buyer for his domestic currency and earn enough domestic currency to cover his costs and make a profit. Similarly, an importer might buy goods from abroad for which he is invoiced in foreign currency. If he plans to sell the imports, he will produce a price list for his customers, or agree prices with his customers, so as to earn enough domestic currency from selling the goods to pay the foreign supplier in foreign currency, and make a profit.

1.9 The great danger to profit margins is the movement in exchange rates. The risk faces (i) exporters who invoice in a foreign currency and (ii) importers who pay in a foreign currency.

This risk arises even when the foreign currency concerned is in the European exchange rate mechanism (ERM), as sterling can move by up to 6% either side of its central value within the ERM.

Exercise

Bulldog Ltd, a UK company, buys goods from Redland which cost 100,000 Reds (the local currency). The goods are re-sold in the UK for £32,000. At the time of the import purchase the exchange rate for Reds against sterling is 3.5650 - 3.5800.

Bulldog Ltd sells its foreign currency income as soon as it is received, at the spot rate. The overseas buyer is given three months credit.

Required

(a) What is the expected profit on the re-sale?

(b) What would the actual profit be if the spot rate at the time when the currency is received has moved to:

(i) 3.0800 - 3.0950
(ii) 4.0650 - 4.0800?

Ignore bank commission charges.

Solution

(a) Bulldog must buy Reds to pay the supplier, and so the bank is selling Reds. The expected profit is as follows.

	£
Revenue from re-sale of goods	32,000.00
Less cost of 100,000 Reds in sterling (÷ 3.5650)	28,050.49
Expected profit	3,949.51

(b) (i) If the actual spot rate for Bulldog to buy and the bank to sell the Reds is 3.0800, the result is as follows.

	£
Revenue from re-sale	32,000.00
Less cost (100,000 ÷ 3.0800)	32,467.53
Loss	(467.53)

(ii) If the actual spot rate for Bulldog to buy and the bank to sell the currency is 4.0650, the result is as follows.

	£
Revenue from re-sale	32,000.00
Less cost (100,000 ÷ 4.0650)	24,600.25
Profit	7,399.75

---

2. FORWARD EXCHANGE CONTRACTS

2.1 Foreign exchange risk can be overcome by means of a forward exchange contract, whereby the importer or exporter arranges for a bank to sell or buy a quantity of foreign currency at a future date, at a rate of exchange that is determined when the forward contract is made.

2.2 Forward exchange contracts allow a trader who knows that he will have to buy or sell foreign currency at a date in the future, to make the purchase or sale at a predetermined rate of exchange. The trader will therefore know in advance either how much local currency he will receive (if he is selling foreign currency to the bank) or how much local currency he must pay (if he is buying foreign currency from the bank).

Example

2.3 A UK importer knows on 1 April that he must pay a foreign seller 26,500 Swiss francs in one month's time, on 1 May. He can arrange a forward exchange contract with his bank on 1 April, whereby the bank undertakes to sell the importer 26,500 Swiss francs on 1 May, at a fixed rate of say 2.64.

The UK importer can be certain that whatever the spot rate is between Swiss francs and sterling on 1 May, he will have to pay on that date, at this forward rate,

$$\frac{26.500}{2.64} = £10,037.88.$$

(a) If the spot rate is lower than 2.64, the importer would have successfully protected himself against a weakening of sterling, and would have avoided paying more sterling to obtain the Swiss francs.

(b) If the spot rate is higher than 2.64, sterling's value against the Swiss franc would mean that the importer would pay more under the forward exchange contract than he would have had to pay if he had obtained the francs at the spot rate on 1 May. He cannot avoid this extra cost, because a forward contract is binding.

Forward rates and future exchange rate movements

2.4 A forward price is the spot price ruling on the day a forward exchange contract is made plus or minus the interest differential for the period of the contract. It is wrong to think of a forward rate as a forecast of what the spot rate will be on a given date in the future, and it will be a coincidence if the forward rate turns out to be the same as the spot rate on that future date.

2.5 It is however likely that the spot rate will move in the direction indicated by the forward rate.

For example, suppose that a spot rate on 1 June is US$1.7430 - 1.7440 to £1, and the three months forward rate (for 1 September) is US$1.7380 - 1.7395 to £1. It is likely that between 1 June and 1 September, sterling will weaken slightly against the dollar. In this example, interest rates in the UK on 1 June would be higher than interest rates in the USA, which accounts for the forward rates for dollars against sterling being lower than the spot rates on 1 June.

Currencies with high interest rates are likely to depreciate in value against currencies with lower interest rates: it is only the attraction of higher interest that persuades an investor to hold amounts of a currency that is expected to depreciate. Indeed, if the difference between spot and forward rates did not reflect differences in interest rates in this way, investors holding the currency with the lower interest rates would switch to the other currency for (say) three months, ensuring that they would not lose on returning to the original currency by fixing the exchange rate in advance at the forward rate. If enough investors acted in this way (known as *arbitrage*), forces of supply and demand would lead to a change in the forward rate to prevent such risk-free profit making.

Forward exchange contracts: a definition

2.6 A forward exchange contract is:

(a) an immediately firm and binding contract between a bank and its customer;

(b) for the purchase or sale of a specified quantity of a stated foreign currency;

(c) at a rate of exchange fixed at the time the contract is made;

(d) for performance (delivery of the currency and payment for it) at a future time which is agreed upon when making the contract. This future time will be either a specified date, or any time between two specified dates.

Fixed and option contracts

2.7 A forward exchange contract may be either *fixed* or *option*.

(a) 'Fixed' means that performance of the contract will take place on a specified date in the future. For example, a two months forward *fixed* contract taken out on 1 September will require performance on 1 November.

(b) 'Option' means that performance of the contract may take place, at the option of the customer, either

(i) at any date from the contract being made up to and including a specified final date for performance; or
(ii) at any date between two specified dates.

Premiums and discounts: quoting a forward rate

2.8 A forward exchange rate might be higher or lower than the spot rate.

2.9 If it is higher, the quoted currency will be cheaper forward than spot. For example, if in the case of Italian lire against sterling (i) the spot rate is 2,156 - 2,166 and (ii) the three months forward rate is 2,207 - 2,222:

(a) a bank would sell 2,000,000 lire

(i) at the spot rate, now, for £927.64 $\left(\frac{2,000,000}{2,156}\right)$

(ii) in three months time, under a forward contract, for £906.21 $\left(\frac{2,000,000}{2,207}\right)$

(b) a bank would buy 2,000,000 lire

(i)	at the spot rate, now, for	£923.36	$\left(\frac{2,000,000}{2,166}\right)$
(ii)	in three months time, under a forward contract, for	£900.09	$\left(\frac{2,000,000}{2,222}\right)$

2.10 In both cases, the quoted currency (lire) would be worth less against sterling in a forward contract than at the current spot rate. This is because it is quoted forward cheaper, or 'at a discount', against sterling.

2.11 If the forward exchange rate is lower than the spot rate, the quoted currency will be more expensive forward than spot. For example,

(a) if the spot rate for DM against sterling is 3.05 - 3.06, and
(b) the one month forward rate is 3.03 - 3.04½,

then DM are more expensive (quoted 'at a premium') forward than spot.

2.12 Forward rates are not quoted independently, but are quoted as adjustments to the spot rates.

(a) If the forward rate for a currency is cheaper than the spot rate, it is quoted as a *discount* to the spot rate. The forward rate will be higher than the spot rate by the amount of the discount.

(b) If the forward rate for a currency is more expensive than the spot rate, it is quoted as a *premium* to the spot rate. The forward rate will be lower than the spot rate by the amount of the premium.

The rule for adding or subtracting discounts and premiums

2.13 A *discount* is therefore *added* to the spot rate, and a *premium* is therefore *subtracted* from the spot rate.

2.14 It might help you to think of 'lavatory brush rule': ADDIS.

The rule derives from the well-known brand name of the lavatory brush manufacturer, and may help you to remember that we ADD DIScounts and so subtract premiums.

2.15 The longer the duration of a forward contract, the larger will be the quoted premium or discount. Thus premiums or discounts will be larger three months forward than one month forward.

Exercise

You are given the following information about currency rates for sterling spot and forward.

	Spot	*One month forward*	*Three months forward*
US (dollar)	1.5200 - 1.5210	0.32 - 0.27c pm	0.89 - 0.84 pm
Canada (dollar)	1.8630 - 1.8640	0.30 - 0.20c pm	0.90 - 0.80 pm
Netherland (guilder)	4.05¼ - 4.06¼	2⅜ - 1⅞c pm	6¾ - 6¼ pm
Belgium (franc)	72.20 - 72.30	10 - 20c dis	45 - 55 dis
Denmark (krone)	13.01 - 13.02	4¼ - 5⅝ ore dis	18⅜ - 19¾ dis
Germany (DM)	3.06½ - 3.07½	2 - 1½pf pm	5½ - 5 pm

Calculate the cost or value in sterling to a customer who wishes to

(a) buy US$14,000 one month forward from his bank;
(b) buy Canadian $25,000 spot;
(c) buy Belgian francs 75,000 three months forward;
(d) sell guilders 28,000 one month forward;
(e) sell Danish kroner 20,000 three months forward;
(f) sell DM 6,000 one month forward.

Solution

(a), (b) and (c). When the customer buys, the bank sells.

	US$ 1 month forward	*Can $ spot*	*Belg Fr 3 months forward*
Spot rate	1.5200	1.8630	72.20
Subtract premium (1 month)	0.0032c		
Add discount (3 months)			0.45c
Bank's selling rate	1.5168	1.8630	72.65
Currency required by customer	US$14,000	Can$25,000	BelgFr74,000
Cost in sterling	£9,229.96	£13,419.22	£1,032.35

(d), (e) and (f). When the customer sells, the bank buys.

	Guilder 1 month forward	*Kroner 3 months forward*	*DM 1 month forward*
Spot rate	4.06¼	13.02	3.07½
Subtract premium	0.01⅞		0.01½
Add discount		0 19¾	
Bank's buying rate	4.04⅜	13.21¾	3.06
Currency for sale by customer	Guilders28,000	Kroner20,000	DM6,000
Value in sterling	£6,924.27	£1,513.15	£1,960.78

Option forward exchange contracts

2.16 Option contracts are forward exchange contracts where the customer has the option to call for performance of the contract:

(a) at any date from the contract being made up to a specified date in the future; or
(b) at any date between two dates both in the future.

The contract must be performed at some time: the customer cannot avoid performance altogether.

2.17 Option contracts are normally used to cover whole months straddling the likely payment date, where the customer is not sure of the exact date on which he will want to buy or sell currency. (The purpose of an option contract is to avoid having to renew a forward exchange contract and extend it by a few days, because extending a forward contract can be expensive.)

2.18 Option contracts can also be used bit by bit. For example, if a customer makes an option forward contract to sell DM 100,000 at any time between 3 July and 3 August, he might sell DM 20,000 on 5 July, DM 50,000 on 15 July and DM 30,000 on 1 August.

2.19 When a customer makes an option forward exchange contract with his bank, the bank will quote. The bank will quote the rate which is most favourable to itself out of the forward rates for all dates within the option period. This is because the customer has the option to call for performance of the contract on any date within the period, and the bank will try to ensure that the customer does not obtain a favourable rate at the bank's expense.

What happens if a customer cannot satisfy a forward contract?

2.20 A customer might be unable to satisfy a forward contract for any one of a number of reasons.

(a) An importer might find that:

(i) his supplier fails to deliver the goods as specified, so the importer will not accept the goods delivered and will not agree to pay for them;

(ii) the supplier sends fewer goods than expected, perhaps because of supply shortages, and so the importer has less to pay for;

(iii) the supplier is late with the delivery, and so the importer does not have to pay for the goods until later than expected.

(b) An exporter might find the same types of situation, but in reverse, so that he does not receive any payment at all, or he receives more or less than originally expected, or he receives the expected amount, but only after some delay.

Close-out of forward contracts

2.21 If a customer cannot satisfy a forward exchange contract, the bank will make the customer fulfil the contract.

(a) If the customer has arranged for the bank to buy currency but then cannot deliver the currency for the bank to buy, the bank will:
   (i) sell currency to the customer at the spot rate (when the contract falls due for performance);
   (ii) buy the currency back, under the terms of the forward exchange contract.

(b) If the customer has contracted for the bank to sell him currency, the bank will:
   (i) sell the customer the specified amount of currency at the forward exchange rate;
   (ii) buy back the unwanted currency at the spot rate.

2.22 Thus, the bank arranges for the customer to perform his part of the forward exchange contract by either selling or buying the 'missing' currency at the spot rate.

These arrangements are known as *closing out* a forward exchange contract.

Example

2.23 Shutter Ltd arranges on 1 January with a US supplier for the delivery of a consignment of goods costing US$96,000. Shutter Ltd will have to pay for the goods in six months time, on 1 July. The company therefore arranges a forward exchange contract for its bank to sell it US$96,000 six months hence.

In the event, the size of the consignment is reduced, and on 1 July, Shutter Ltd only needs US$50,000 to pay its supplier. The bank will therefore arrange to close out the forward exchange contract for the US$46,000 which Shutter Ltd does not need. This is called a partial close-out.

Exchange rates between the US dollar and sterling are as follows.

1 January	
Spot	$1.5145 - 1.5155
6 months forward	0.95 - 0.85c pm
1 July Spot	$1.5100 - 1.5110

Compute the cost to Shutter Ltd of the whole transaction, ignoring commission.

Solution

2.24 (a) The bank will sell Shutter Ltd US$96,000, to fulfil the original forward contract. The six months forward rate on 1 January was as follows.

Spot rate	1.5145
Less premium	0.0095
Forward rate	1.5050

(b) The bank will buy back the unwanted US$46,000 at the spot rate on 1 July, thus closing out the contract.

	£
Sale of US$96,000 at $1.5050	63,787.38
Purchase of US$46,000 at $1.5110	30,443.41
Cost to Shutter Ltd	33,343.97

Extensions of forward contracts

2.25 When a forward exchange contract reaches the end of its period, a customer might find that he has not yet received the expected currency from an overseas buyer, or does not yet have to pay an overseas seller. The customer still wants to buy or sell the agreed amount of currency in the forward exchange contract, but he wants to defer the delivery date for the currency under the contract.

2.26 The customer has two choices available to him.

(a) He can ask the bank to close out the old contract at the appropriate spot rate, and ask for a new contract for the extra period, with the rate being calculated in the usual way.

(b) He can ask the bank to extend the contract, by changing the bank's selling or buying rate in the contract. The bank will then arrange a new forward exchange contract with the customer at a rate that is slightly more favourable to the customer than for an ordinary forward exchange contract.

The cost of forward exchange cover

2.27 There is an implied interest rate in the cost of forward cover. The approximate cost (as an interest percentage) of forward exchange cover is

$$\frac{\text{Premium or discount} \times 12 \text{ months} \times 100}{\text{Number of months forward cover is taken} \times \text{the forward rate}}$$

Example

2.28 The bank's quoted prices for US dollars against sterling are as follows.

Spot	1.6365 - 1.6385
One month forward	0.50 - 0.47 cents pm

What is the approximate cost of forward cover?

Solution

2.29 (a) For a customer buying dollars one month forward,

$$\frac{0.005 \times 12 \text{ months} \times 100\%}{1 \text{ month} \times (1.6365 - 0.0050)} = 3.68\%$$

(b) For a customer selling dollars one month forward,

$$\frac{0.0047 \times 12 \text{ months} \times 100\%}{1 \text{ month} \times (1.6385 - 0.0047)} = 3.45\%$$

The average of these two rates is 3.57%, which is the rate that would be shown in the financial press.

2.30 The relevance of implied interest rates in forward exchange rates is that the cost of forward cover can be compared with the cost of foreign currency borrowing, as an alternative method of obtaining cover against foreign exchange risk.

3. OTHER RISK MANAGEMENT TECHNIQUES

Matching receipts and payments

3.1 A company can reduce or eliminate its foreign exchange exposure by matching receipts and payments. Wherever possible, a UK company that expects to make payments and have receipts in the same foreign currency should plan to offset its payments against its receipts in the currency.

This process of matching is easier if the company maintains a bank account in the foreign currency in question with an overdraft facility.

3.2 Since the company will be setting off foreign currency receipts against foreign currency payments, it does not matter whether the currency strengthens or weakens against the company's domestic currency because there will be no purchase or sale of the currency.

3.3 Foreign exchange exposure can be reduced in this way at relatively little cost, but it is only practicable, of course, to the extent that a company can match currency receipts and payments.

Leads and lags

3.4 Companies might try to use:
(a) lead payments: payments in advance; or
(b) lagged payments: delaying payments beyond their due date

in order to speculate on foreign exchange rate movements.

With a lead payment, paying in advance of the due date, there is a finance cost to consider. This is the interest cost on the money used to make the payment.

Example

3.5 A company owes $30,000 to a US supplier, payable in 90 days. It might suspect that the US dollar will strengthen against sterling over the next three months, because the US dollar is quoted forward at a premium against sterling on the foreign exchange market. The spot exchange rate is $1.50 = £1.

(a) The company could pay the $30,000 now, instead of in 90 days time. This would cost £20,000 now, which is a payment that could have been delayed by 90 days.

(b) The cost of this lead payment would be interest on £20,000 for 90 days, at the company's borrowing rate or its opportunity cost of capital.

Using the currency market

3.6 An exporter who invoices foreign customers in a foreign currency can hedge against the exchange risk by:

(a) borrowing an amount in the foreign currency immediately;
(b) converting the foreign currency into domestic currency at the spot rate;
(c) repaying the loan with interest out of the eventual foreign currency receipts.

3.7 Similarly, if a company has to make a foreign currency payment in the future, it can buy the currency now at the spot rate and put it on deposit, using the principal and the interest earned to make the currency payment when it falls due.

Choosing between the forward exchange market and the currency market

3.8 When a company expects to receive or pay a sum of foreign currency in the next few months, it can choose between using the forward exchange market and the currency market to hedge against the foreign exchange risk. The cheaper option available is the one that ought to be chosen.

Example

3.9 Trumpton plc has bought goods from a US supplier, and must pay $4,000,000 for them in three months time. The company's finance director wishes to hedge against the foreign exchange risk, and the three methods which the company usually considers are:

(a) using forward exchange contracts;
(b) using currency borrowing or lending;
(c) making lead payments.

The following annual interest rates and exchange rates are currently available.

	US Dollar		*Sterling*	
	Deposit rate	*Borrowing rate*	*Deposit rate*	*Borrowing rate*
	%	%	%	%
1 month	7	10.25	10.75	14.00
3 months	7	10.75	11.00	14.25

	\$/£ exchange rate (\$ = £1)
Spot	1.8625 - 1.8635
1 month forward	0.60c - 0.58c pm
3 months forward	1.80c - 1.75c pm

Which is the cheapest method for Trumpton plc? Ignore commission costs (the bank charges for arranging a forward contract or a loan).

Solution

3.10 The three choices must be compared on a similar basis, which means working out the cost of each to Trumpton either now or in three months time. Here the cost to Trumpton now will be determined.

Choice 1: the forward exchange market

3.11 Trumpton must buy dollars in order to pay the US supplier. The exchange rate in a forward exchange contract to buy $4,000,000 in three months time (bank sells) is:

	$
Spot rate	1.8625
Less 3 months premium	0.0180
Forward rate	1.8445

The cost of the $4,000,000 to Trumpton in three months time will be

$$\frac{\$4,000,000}{\$1.8445} = £2,168,609.38$$

3.12 This is the cost in three months. To work out the cost now, we could say that by deferring payment for three months, the company is:

(a) saving having to borrow money now at 14.25% a year to make the payment now; or
(b) avoiding the loss of interest on cash on deposit, earning 11% a year.

The choice between (a) and (b) depends on whether Trumpton plc needs to borrow to make any current payment (a) or is cash rich (b). Here, assumption (a) is selected, but (b) might in fact apply.

3.13 At an annual interest rate of 14.25% the rate for three months is approximately 14.25/4 = 3.5625%. The 'present cost' of £2,168,609.38 in three months time is

$$\frac{£2,168,609.38}{1.035625} = £2,094,010.27$$

Choice 2: the currency markets

3.14 Using the currency markets involves:

(a) borrowing in the foreign currency, if the company will eventually receive the currency;

(b) lending in the foreign currency, if the company will eventually pay the currency.

Here, Trumpton will pay $4,000,000 and so it would lend US dollars.

3.15 It would lend enough US dollars for three months, so that the principal repaid in three months time plus interest will amount to the payment due of $4,000,000.

(a) Since the US dollar deposit rate is 7%, the rate for three months is approximately 7/4 = 1.75%.

(b) To earn $4,000,000 in three months time at 1.75% interest, Trumpton would have to lend now

$$\frac{\$4,000,000}{1.0175} = \$3,931,203.93$$

3.16 These dollars would have to be purchased now at the spot rate of (bank sells) $1.8625. The cost would be

$$\frac{\$3,931,203.93}{\$1.8625} = £2,110,713.52$$

By lending US dollars for three months, Trumpton is matching eventual receipts and payments in US dollars, and so has hedged against foreign exchange risk.

3.17 *Choice 3: lead payments.* Lead payments should be considered when the currency of payment is expected to strengthen over time, and is quoted forward at a premium on the foreign exchange market.

Here, the cost of a lead payment (paying $4,000,000 now) would be $4,000,000 ÷ $1.8625 = £2,147,651.01.

3.18 In this example, the costs are as follows.

	£
Forward exchange contract	2,094,010.27 (cheapest)
Currency lending	2,110,713.52
Lead payment	2,147,651.01

Currency options

3.19 Currency options are not the same as forward exchange option contracts.

3.20 A currency option is similar to a share option. It is an agreement whereby a company buys an option to buy or sell a certain quantity of currency at a stated rate of exchange at some time in the future. The company can avoid going through with the deal simply by abandoning the option.

3.21 The purpose of currency options is to reduce or eliminate exposure to currency risks, and they are particularly useful for companies which must:

(a) make a tender for an overseas contract, priced in a foreign currency;

(b) publish price lists for their goods in a foreign currency.

In both situations (a) and (b), a company would not know when fixing its prices whether it would have any foreign currency income. It could not therefore risk making a binding forward exchange contract to sell foreign currency.

Example

3.22 Tartan plc has been invited to tender for a contract in Blueland with the bid priced in Blues (the local currency). Tartan thinks that the contract would cost £1,850,000. Because of the fierce competition for the bid, Tartan is prepared to price the contract at £2,000,000, and since the exchange rate is currently B2.80 = £1, it puts in a bid of B5,600,000.

The contract will not be awarded until after six months.

3.23 What can happen to Tartan with the contract? There are two 'worst possible' outcomes.

(a) Tartan plc decides to hedge against the currency risk, and on the assumption that it will be awarded the contract in six months time, it enters into a forward exchange contract to sell B5,600,000 in six months time at a rate of B2.8 = £1.

As it turns out, the company fails to win the contract and so it must buy B5,600,000 spot to meet its obligation under the forward contract. The exchange rate has changed, say, to B2.5 = £1.

	£
At the outset:	
Tartan sells B5,600,000 forward at B2.8 to £1	2,000,000
Six months later	
Tartan buys B5,600,000 spot to cover the hedge, at B2.5 to £1	(2,240,000)
Loss	(240,000)

(b) Alternatively, Tartan plc might decide not to make a forward exchange contract at all, but to wait and see what happens. As it turns out, Tartan is awarded the contract six months later, but by this time, the value of the Blue has fallen, say, to B3.2 = £1.

	£
Tartan wins the contract for B5,600,000, which has a sterling value of (B3.2 = £1)	1,750,000
Cost of the contract	(1,850,000)
Loss	(100,000)

3.24 A currency option would, for a fixed cost, eliminate these risks for Tartan plc. When it makes its tender for the contract, Tartan might purchase a currency option to sell B5,600,000 in six months time at B2.8 to £1, at a cost of £40,000.

3.25 The worst possible outcome for Tartan plc is now a loss of £40,000.

(a) If the company fails to win the contract, Tartan will abandon the option (unless the exchange rate has moved in Tartan's favour and the Blue has weakened against sterling so that the company can make a profit by buying B5,600,000 at the spot rate and selling it at B2.8 = £1).

(b) If the company wins the contract and the exchange rate of the Blue has weakened against sterling, Tartan will exercise the option and sell the Blues at 2.80.

	£	£
Proceeds from selling B5,600,000		2,000,000
Cost of contract	1,850,000	
Cost of currency option	40,000	
		1,890,000
Net profit		110,000

If the Blue has strengthened against sterling, Tartan will abandon the option. For example, if Tartan wins the contract and the exchange rate has moved to B2.5 = £1, Tartan will sell the B5,600,000 at this rate to earn £2,240,000, and will incur costs, including the abandoned currency option, of £1,890,000.

Currency options: terminology

3.26 (a) (i) A call option is an option to buy currency.
(ii) A put option is an option to sell currency.

(b) The exercise price may be the *same* as the current spot rate, or it may be *more favourable* or *less favourable* to the option holder than the current spot rate. Options are 'at-the-money' 'in-the-money' or 'out-of-the-money' accordingly.

(c) An American option is an option that can be exercised at any time during the option period. A European option can only be exercised at the end of the option period.

(d) Companies can choose whether to buy:
(i) a tailor-made currency option from a bank, suited to the company's specific needs. These are *over-the-counter* (OTC) options;
(ii) a standard option, in certain currencies only, from an options exchange. Such options are known as *exchange-traded* options.

The drawbacks of currency options

3.27 The major drawbacks of currency options are as follows.

(a) The cost is about 5% of the total amount of foreign exchange covered, although the exact amount depends on the expected volatility of the exchange rate.

(b) Options must be paid for as soon as they are bought.

(c) Tailor-made options lack negotiability.

(d) Traded options are not available in every currency.

Futures: the London International Financial Futures Exchange (LIFFE)

3.28 LIFFE is a London exchange for trading financial futures. Futures are a form of forward contract, which give a fixed rate for security prices, or exchange rates, or interest rates, at a future date. A futures contract can be defined as 'a standardised contract covering the sale or purchase at a future date of a set quantity of a commodity, financial investments or cash'.

LIFFE had intended to merge with the London Traded Options Market (LTOM) to form the London Derivatives Exchange (LDE) early in 1991. At the time of writing, this merger had not taken place, but it may do so shortly.

3.29 LIFFE allows investors to use financial futures to hedge against risks of adverse movements in:
(a) gilt prices;
(b) interest rates;
(c) foreign currency exchange rates;
(d) share prices;
(e) bond prices (such as Japanese, US and UK government bonds).

Examples of LIFFE transactions will illustrate how they work. We shall begin with share price futures, before going on to look at LIFFE sterling futures.

Hedging against adverse share price movements: LIFFE futures

3.30 One contract bought and sold on LIFFE is the Financial Times Stock Exchange 100 Index future. The FT-SE 100 index is a share price index for 100 different shares quoted on the Stock Exchange, with the shares intended to be a sufficiently broad cross section so that movements in the index of share prices would be typical of movements in the value of the portfolio of shares of an average investor.

Example

3.31 An investor holds a portfolio of shares with a value of £1,000,000 in June. He is worried that by the end of September when he wants to sell the shares to raise cash, their value will have fallen. He decides to hedge by:

(a) selling some FT-SE 100 futures contracts, for delivery three months later in September. If the Index value for contracts to be completed in September stands at 100, the value of a contract would be £25,000 and so he would sell 40 contracts (40 × £25,000 = £1,000,000, the value of his portfolio);

(b) in September, reversing this deal by buying back 40 FT-SE contracts 'spot', that is, for immediate delivery.

3.32 If the index has fallen to 90 by the end of September, the value of his actual portfolio of shares will have dropped to about £900,000. But so too would the price of 40 FT-SE 100 contracts. The results would be as follows.

June:	Holds portfolio of shares, value	£1,000,000
	Sells FT-SE 100 contracts at September index value (index = 100) 40 × £25,000	£1,000,000
Sept:	Holds portfolio of shares, value	£900,000
	Buys back 40 FT-SE 100 contracts at spot value (index = 90) 40 × 90% × £25,000	£900,000

	£
Loss on holding portfolio of shares	100,000
Profit on selling and buying futures	100,000
Net gain/(loss)	0

The investor could sell his portfolio and take the profit on his futures trading, to obtain the £1,000,000 cash he planned to have.

3.33 We will now consider currency futures.

Example

3.34 A UK importer buys goods from a US supplier for US$320,000. The purchase takes place on 21 March but the goods do not have to be paid for until 21 April. The spot rate of exchange on 21 March between sterling and the US dollar is £1 = $1.60.

3.35 The UK importer can hedge against the currency risk (the risk of a fall in the value of sterling against the dollar in the credit period) with currency futures. The expected cost of the purchase in sterling on 21 March is 320,000/1.60 = £200,000.

3.36 Sterling futures must be bought and sold in blocks of £25,000 and so the UK importer could sell eight sterling futures contracts at the current rate of US$1.60 = £1. To do this, the importer must deposit £1,000 per contract, or £8,000 in total.

3.37 Suppose that on 21 April, when the UK importer must pay the $320,000:

(a) the spot rate of exchange is £1 = $1.50;
(b) the rate at which sterling futures can be closed out is £1 = $1.51.

3.38 On 21 April, the importer will:

(a) buy US$320,000 spot for $1.5000, at a cost of $\frac{320,000}{1.50}$ = £213,333.33.

This is £13,333.33 more than was expected on 21 March;

(b) close out the futures contract at £1 = $1.5100. The value is £211,920.52 giving a realised profit of £11,920.52.

3.39 The importer's net position is as follows.

	£
Loss on fall in value of sterling from $1.60 to $1.50	(13,333.33)
Profit on futures	11,920.52
Net loss	(1,412.81)

The importer has therefore been able to hedge his position with futures for only a small net cost, which might be less than the cost of hedging with a forward exchange contract.

4. CONCLUSION

4.1 There are a number of techniques for risk management, particularly when the risk is over a period of less than a year (as, for example, with foreign trade debtors and creditors). Examination questions could well focus on the selection of the cheapest *appropriate* technique, so it is important to grasp not only the mathematics of these techniques but also what financial commitments are necessary to use each one.

TEST YOUR KNOWLEDGE

The numbers in brackets refer to paragraphs of this chapter

1. Define a forward exchange contract. (2.6)
2. Is a forward rate premium added to the spot rate, or subtracted? (2.13)
3. What happens if a company cannot satisfy a forward exchange contract? (2.21, 2.25, 2.26)
4. What does matching mean? (3.1)
5. What are currency options? How do they differ from forward exchange contracts? (3.20)
6. What are futures? (3.28)

Now try questions 32 and 33 at the end of the text

ILLUSTRATIVE QUESTIONS AND SUGGESTED SOLUTIONS

1 FINANCIAL OBJECTIVE (25 marks)

The primary objective in financial management is usually assumed to be the maximisation (or improvement) of the wealth of ordinary shareholders. One way this can be achieved is to obtain a consistent rate of growth in the earnings per share.

The ability of a company to achieve such consistent growth depends to some extent on:
(a) the external environment of the company;
(b) the company's operating cost structure;
(c) the company's capital gearing and the cost of debt capital.

Required

(a) Show how these factors are relevant to a consistent growth in earnings per share, using the information provided below about two companies, X Ltd and Y Ltd. (8 marks)

(b) Discuss the financial management of both companies, insofar as the information provided allows. (17 marks)

Note. Earnings per share (EPS) are the profits distributable to ordinary shareholders (after interest, tax and preference dividend) divided by the number of ordinary shares in issue.

	X Ltd				*Y Ltd*			
Year	*19X1*	*19X2*	*19X3*	*19X4*	*19X1*	*19X2*	*19X3*	*19X4*
	£'000	£'000	£'000	£'000	£'000	£'000	£'000	£'000
Profit & loss account								
Turnover	100	124	175	254	400	448	582	728
Variable costs	60	77	112	165	120	140	192	286
Fixed costs	26	31	42	58	180	196	230	256
Total costs	86	108	154	223	300	336	422	542
Earnings before interest and tax	14	16	21	31	100	112	160	186
Less interest	4	4	7	8	10	16	19	19
Earnings before tax	10	12	14	23	90	96	141	167
Less tax	4	5	6	11	40	44	70	83
Distributable profits	6	7	8	12	50	52	71	84
Less dividends	3	3	4	4	18	18	30	40
Retained earnings	3	4	4	8	32	34	41	44
Balance sheet								
Fixed assets	29	42	56	64	300	318	400	425
Net current assets	31	34	49	72	80	153	207	232
	60	76	105	136	380	471	607	657
Ordinary shares of £1	20	20	20	25	200	200	250	250
Asset revaluation reserve	0	12	16	20	0	0	0	0
Reserves	15	19	23	31	100	134	175	225
Equity funds	35	51	59	76	300	334	425	475
Loans	25	25	46	60	80	137	182	182
	60	76	105	136	380	471	607	657
EPS (pence)	30.0	35.0	40.0	48.0	25.0	26.0	28.4	33.6

2 GROWTH PLC (20 marks)

Growth plc, a company in the leisure industry with turnover of £20,000,000 in the year just ended, was formed six years ago. So far, the company has been financed by wealthy individual shareholders and by bank loans, but it is now clear that a wider range of investors will be needed to fund further expansion. Furthermore, some of the existing shareholders would like there to be a market for shares in the company, so that they could sell some shares.

Turnover and earnings have grown steadily since the company's formation, but it is recognised that the leisure industry is vulnerable to fluctuations in individuals' real earnings.

Required

Suggest a capital market to meet the requirements of the company and its shareholders, and discuss the advantages and disadvantages of your suggestion.

3 SHARE VALUES (20 marks)

(a) Outline the fundamental analysis theory of share values, giving numerical examples. (10 marks)

(b) To what extent is the validity of the fundamental analysis theory affected by the efficiency of the stock market? (10 marks)

4 RYOTT TISSUES PLC (20 marks)

(a) For what purposes might a company consider making a rights issue of ordinary shares?

Why under particular circumstances might this be preferable to other means of raising long-term capital? (5 marks)

(b) Do you consider that a dilution in net earnings per share as the result of a rights issue would ever be acceptable to shareholders? (5 marks)

(c) Ryott Tissues plc has 10,000,000 ordinary shares issued and fully paid, and these are currently quoted on the stock exchange at £1.60. Earnings are relatively stable and, as reported in the most recent annual accounts, were equivalent to 40p a share.

The company wishes to redeem £3,000,000 10% loan stock by making a rights issue of ordinary shares, but does not want to dilute the earnings per share by more than 10%. The rights issue is to be priced approximately 20% below the market price at the time of issue.

There is a general upward movement in share prices, and you are asked:

(i) how many shares would be required and what is the lowest market price at which the company would consider making the issue?
(ii) in theory what would be the resultant ex rights price of the shares, and the corresponding P/E ratio?

The rate of corporation tax is to be taken as 33%. (10 marks)

5 LOGJAM PLC (25 marks)

Logjam plc has decided to undertake a major new investment project, to develop a new product. The project will be a high risk undertaking, and the company's earnings might increase substantially as a result, but they might also fall.

Estimates of the likely change in the company's total earnings before interest and tax (EBIT) in year 2 of the project are as follows.

Success of project	*Growth in total EBIT in year 2 over year 1*	*Probability*
Failure	- 10%	0.1
Moderate	+ 5%	0.2
Average	+ 10%	0.3
Good	+ 30%	0.3
Very good	+ 50%	0.1

EBIT in year 1 of the project are expected to be 5% higher than those achieved in the year just ended, and the impact of the new project will not be known until year 2.

The directors of Logjam plc are now trying to decide how to raise the finance for the project. There are no internally-generated funds available, although dividends in year 1 could be reduced to make some equity funds available.

There are two financing alternatives under consideration.

(1) A one for four rights issue at a 20% discount to the current market price, plus a £25,000,000 debenture issue at par. The debentures would carry a 13% fixed rate of interest.

(2) An issue of £40,000,000 of convertible debentures. The debentures would carry an 11% rate of interest, and each £100 of stock would be convertible into 30 ordinary shares between four and six years in the future. In addition, in year 1 only, the company's dividend to ordinary shareholders would be reduced by £29,000,000.

The company has recently reached its accounting year end, and balance sheet and profit and loss account details are as follows.

BALANCE SHEET

	£'000	£'000
Land and buildings (at cost)		84,210
Plant and machinery		72,180
		156,390
Stock	76,840	
Debtors	66,290	
Marketable investments	4,500	
Bank	1,500	
		149,130
Bank overdraft	46,320	
Creditors	26,270	
Taxation	22,000	
Proposed dividend	29,500	
		(124,090)
		181,430

	£'000
Ordinary shares (50p nominal value)	40,000
Reserves	86,430
8% Preference shares (£1 nominal value)	20,000
12% Debenture (redeemable in ten years time)	25,000
Floating rate loan (maturing in four years time)	10,000
	181,430

PROFIT AND LOSS ACCOUNT

	£'000
Turnover	330,530
Earnings before interest and tax	91,535
Less interest	10,840
Taxable earnings	80,695
Less tax (33%)	26,629
Earnings after tax	54,066
Less preference dividend	(1,600)
Less ordinary dividend	(29,500)
Retained earnings	22,966

The current market price of Logjam's ordinary shares is 276p. The preference shares are quoted at 59p and the debentures at £94 per cent.

Required

Discuss the merits and/or disadvantages of each of the proposed financing packages, supporting your comments with calculations where appropriate. State clearly any assumptions that you make.

6 BABINGTON LTD (15 marks)

Babington Ltd, an owner-managed company, has developed a radically new item of sports equipment and has financed the development and prototype stages from its own resources. Market research indicates the possibility of a large volume of demand and a significant amount of additional capital will be needed to finance production.

Required

Advise Babington Ltd on:

(a) the advantages and disadvantages of loan or equity capital; (5 marks)

(b) the various types of capital likely to be available and the sources from which they might be obtained; (5 marks)

(c) the method(s) of finance likely to be most satisfactory to both Babington Ltd and the supplier of funds. (5 marks)

7 KNIGHT PLC (25 marks)

Knight plc is an investment company whose investments in other companies range from small holdings of shares or loan capital to complete holdings. As a senior manager in Knight plc you have been asked to study the following most recent published financial statements of Etna plc with a view to deciding whether to invest in any of its securities.

ETNA PLC
PROFIT AND LOSS ACCOUNT FOR THE YEAR ENDED 31 DECEMBER 19X2

	£
Profit before tax	1,660,000
Less corporation tax	547,800
Profit after tax	1,112,200
Less preference dividend	35,000
	1,077,200
Less proposed ordinary dividend	700,000
Retained profits	377,200

BALANCE SHEET AS AT 31 DECEMBER 19X2

	£
Net fixed assets	11,500,000
Net current assets	1,200,000
	12,700,000
	£
Authorised, issued and fully paid shares	
7,000,000 ordinary £1 shares	7,000,000
500,000 7% cumulative £1 preference shares	500,000
	7,500,000
Reserves	700,000
	8,200,000
Loan stock	
£3,000,000 7% unsecured loan stock	3,000,000
£1,500,000 9% convertible unsecured loan stock (12 years to redemption)	1,500,000
	12,700,000

Notes

1. At the balance sheet date, the market value of the securities of Etna plc were as follows.
   (a) £1 ordinary shares £1.50 each ex div.
   (b) 7% preference shares 96p each ex div.
   (c) 7% unsecured loan stock £57 per cent ex interest.
   (d) 9% convertible unsecured loan stock £82 per cent ex interest.

2. The conversion terms for the convertible unsecured loan stock are four ordinary shares per £10 of stock.

3. The forecast pre-tax profits for the next 12 months will be 7% higher than in the previous year.

4. The fixed assets are estimated to be worth £13,000,000.

5. Corporation tax is at 33% and the basic rate of income tax is 25%.

Required

Analyse the significant financial features which should be considered before any decision is taken by Knight plc to invest in all or any of Etna's share and loan capital.

8 P/E RATIOS (10 marks)

List and discuss briefly five reasons why companies in the same type of business might have different P/E ratios.

Comment on the view that the P/E ratio is 'an attempt to value a company in terms of its earnings'.

9 CRYSTAL PLC (25 marks)

The following figures have been extracted from the most recent accounts of Crystal plc.

BALANCE SHEET AS ON 30 JUNE 19X9

	£'000	£'000
Fixed assets		10,115
Investments		821
Current assets	3,658	
Less current liabilities	1,735	1,923
		12,859
Ordinary share capital		
Authorised: 4,000,000 shares of £1		
Issued: 3,000,000 shares of £1		3,000
Reserves		6,542
Shareholders' funds		9,542
7% Debentures		1,300
Deferred taxation		583
Corporation tax		1,434
		12,859

Summary of Profits and Dividends

Year ended 30 June:	*19X5*	*19X6*	*19X7*	*19X8*	*19X9*
	£'000	£'000	£'000	£'000	£'000
Profit after interest and before tax	1,737	2,090	1,940	1,866	2,179
Less tax	573	690	640	616	719
Profit after interest and tax	1,164	1,400	1,300	1,250	1,460
Less dividends	620	680	740	740	810
Added to reserves	544	720	560	510	650

The current (1 July 19X9) market value of Crystal plc's ordinary shares is £3.27 per share cum div. An annual dividend of £810,000 is due for payment shortly. The debentures are redeemable at par in ten years time. Their current market value is £77.10 per cent. Annual interest has just been paid on the debentures. There have been no issues or redemptions of ordinary shares or debentures during the past five years.

The current rate of corporation tax is 33%, and the current basic rate of income tax is 25%. Assume that there have been no changes in the system or rates of taxation during the last five years.

Required

(a) Estimate the cost of capital which Crystal plc should use as a discount rate when appraising new investment opportunities. (20 marks)

(b) Discuss any difficulties and uncertainties in your estimates. (5 marks)

10 BUTLER PLC (20 marks)

Butler plc has issued £500,000 of 12% convertible loan stock which is due for redemption on 31 January 19X8. Assume that it is now ten years before this date.

The issue was made to the general public at a price of £105 per £100 of stock. Its current market price is £134 per cent (interest having just been paid).

Non-convertible loan stock of a similar risk class currently yields 14% per annum.

The option to convert loan stock into shares can be taken by the security holders at any time up to 31 January 19X2 (four years from now). If the options are not taken up by this date, they will lapse. The rate of conversion is 20 shares per £100 of stock.

Ordinary shares of the company have a current market value of £5.70 (ex div), and the dividend paid recently was 57 pence per share (net).

You are the holder of £50,000 of the stock, and you wish to decide whether to:

(a) hold on to the stock until it matures;
(b) convert the stock into shares;
(c) sell the stock.

Ignore taxation.

Required

(a) What would be the value of the stock you hold, if it could not be converted into shares? (5 marks)

(b) What would be the expected minimum annual growth rate in the market price of ordinary shares of the company to justify a decision to hold on to the stock for the moment with the intention of converting it into shares before the option period expires? (7 marks)

(c) What would be your best investment decision? Explain your reasons, making whatever assumptions you think are necessary. (8 marks)

11 EMMA PLC (20 marks)

Emma plc is currently financed by 3,000,000 £1 ordinary shares, which have a market value ex div of £3.20 each. The company has always been an all equity company, but is now considering raising some debt finance for a new project.

The after tax operating cash flows of the project would be as follows.

Cost	£3,600,000
Benefit	£500,000 a year in perpetuity

The project would be financed by the issue at par of £3,600,000 of 10% debt capital. The very large increase in gearing that this would involve is thought to be feasible. Indeed, it has been suggested that the resulting gearing (measured in market value rather than book value terms) and weighted average cost of capital would be at the optimum level.

Emma plc's current after tax cost of equity is 16% and the new project would have the same operating risk characteristics as the company's existing projects. The company pays out all its after tax earnings as dividends.

The tax rate is 33% and there is no delay in receiving the benefit of tax relief.

Ignore issue costs.

Required

(a) The company's objective is to maximise the wealth of its shareholders. Apply Modigliani and Miller's propositions to calculate whether the project would be worthwhile:

(i) if it were all-equity financed;

(ii) if it were financed by the proposed issue of debt capital;

(iii) if Emma plc had already been a geared company with its weighted average cost of capital at the optimum level, and if the project had been financed in such a way as to leave this weighted average cost of capital unchanged. (13 marks)

(b) Assuming that the project is financed by the issue of debt capital:

(i) calculate the weighted average cost of capital after undertaking the project;

(ii) calculate the incremental cost of capital when compared with the company's previous all equity state. The incremental cost of capital is found by relating the incremental after tax benefits of the project to the increase in the market value of the company as a consequence of the project.

(iii) Use the results in (b)(i) and (b)(ii) to support your conclusions in (a)(ii) and (a)(iii) above. (7 marks)

12 PORTFOLIO (15 marks)

You are considering making an investment in one or both of two securities, X and Y, and you are given the following information.

Security	*Possible rates of return %*	*Probability of occurrence*
X	30	0.3
	25	0.4
	20	0.3
Y	50	0.2
	30	0.6
	10	0.2

Required

(a) Calculate the expected return for each security separately and for a portfolio comprising 60% X and 40% Y, assuming no correlation between the possible rates of return from the shares comprising the portfolio. (4 marks)

(b) Calculate the risk of each security separately and of the portfolio as defined above. Measure risk by the standard deviation of returns from the expected rate of return. (6 marks)

(c) Outline the objectives of portfolio diversification, and explain in general terms why the risk of individual securities may differ from that of a portfolio as a whole. (5 marks)

13 MOODY AND HART (12 marks)

Moody plc has an opportunity to invest in a project lasting one year.

Hart plc has three projects, each lasting one year, but in different industries.

The net cash flows (arising at the end of the year) and the beta factors for each of the projects are as follows.

	£'000	β
Moody plc	500	1.20
Hart plc	200	1.25
	100	0.80
	200	1.35

The market return is 12% and the risk-free rate of interest is 7%.

Required

(a) Calculate the total present value of the projects that can be undertaken by
 (i) Moody plc;
 (ii) Hart plc. (4 marks)

(b) Calculate the overall beta factor for Hart plc's projects, assuming that all three are undertaken. (3 marks)

(c) Using this information, discuss which company is likely to be valued more highly by investors, and suggest how portfolio diversification *by a company* can reduce the risk experienced by an investor. (5 marks)

14 BETTALUCK PLC (15 marks)

Bettaluck plc has been enjoying a substantial net cash inflow, and until the surplus funds are needed to meet tax and dividend payments, and to finance further capital expenditure in several months time, they have been invested in a small portfolio of short-term equity investments.

Details of the portfolio, which consists of shares in four UK listed companies, are as follows.

Company	*Number of shares held*	*Beta equity coefficient*	*Market price per share*	*Latest dividend yield*	*Expected return on equity in the next year*
				%	%
Dashing plc	60,000	1.16	£4.29	6.1	19.5
Elegant plc	80,000	1.28	£2.92	3.4	24.0
Fantastic plc	100,000	0.90	£2.17	5.7	17.5
Gaudy plc	125,000	1.50	£3.14	3.3	23.0

The current market return is 19% a year and the Treasury bill yield is 11% a year.

Required

(a) On the basis of the data given, calculate the risk of Bettaluck plc's short-term investment portfolio relative to that of the market. (5 marks)

(b) Recommend, with reasons, whether Bettaluck plc should change the composition of its portfolio. (10 marks)

15 THREE DECISIONS (15 marks)

For the purpose of achieving the long-term financial objectives of a company, the financial manager will be faced with decisions on investment policy, on financing policy and on dividend policy.

Required

(a) Explain the nature of these three types of decision and the extent to which they are inter-related. (7 marks)

(b) List the types of current and forecast information which might be relevant to each decision. (8 marks)

16 KNUCKLE DOWN LTD (25 marks)

The management of Knuckle Down Ltd are reviewing the company's capital investment options for the coming year, and are considering six projects.

Project A would cost £29,000 now, and would earn the following cash profits.

1st year	£ 8,000	3rd year	£10,000
2nd year	£12,000	4th year	£ 6,000

The capital equipment purchased at the start of the project could be resold for £5,000 at the start of the fifth year.

Project B would involve a current outlay of £44,000 on capital equipment and £20,000 on working capital. The profits from the project would be as follows.

Year	*Sales*	*Variable costs*	*Contribution*	*Fixed costs*	*Profit*
	£	£	£	£	£
1	75,000	50,000	25,000	10,000	15,000
2	90,000	60,000	30,000	10,000	20,000
3	42,000	28,000	14,000	8,000	6,000

Fixed costs include an annual charge of £4,000 for depreciation. At the end of the third year the working capital investment would be recovered and the equipment would be sold for £5,000.

Project C would involve a current outlay of £50,000 on equipment and £15,000 on working capital. The investment in working capital would be increased to £21,000 at the end of the first year. Annual cash profits would be £18,000 for five years, at the end of which the investment in working capital would be recovered.

Project D would involve an outlay of £20,000 now and a further outlay of £20,000 after one year. Cash profits thereafter would be as follows.

2nd year £15,000 3rd year £12,000 4th to 8th years £8,000 pa

Project E is a long-term project, involving an immediate outlay of £32,000 and annual cash profits of £4,500 in perpetuity.

Project F is another long-term project, involving an immediately outlay of £20,000 and annual cash profits as follows.

1st to 5th years £5,000 6th to 10th years £4,000 11th year onwards for ever £3,000

The company discounts all projects of ten years duration or less at a cost of capital of 12%, and all other projects at a cost of 15%.

Ignore taxation.

Required

(a) Calculate the NPV of each project, and determine which should be undertaken by the company. (17 marks)

(b) Calculate the IRR of projects A, C and E. (8 marks)

17 NEWBEGIN ENTERPRISES LTD (25 marks)

Newbegin Enterprises Ltd is considering whether to invest in a project which would entail immediate expenditure on capital equipment of £40,000.

Expected sales from the project are as follows.

Probability	*Sales volume*
	Units
0.10	2,000
0.25	6,000
0.40	8,000
0.15	10,000
0.10	14,000

Once sales are established at a certain volume in the first year, they will continue at that same volume in later years. The unit price will be £10, the unit variable cost will be £6 and additional fixed costs will be £20,000.

The project would have a life of six years, after which the equipment would be sold for scrap to earn £3,000.

The company's cost of capital is 10%.

Required

(a) What is the expected value of the NPV of the project? (5 marks)

(b) What is the minimum annual volume of sales required to justify the project? (5 marks)

(c) Making whatever assumptions you consider necessary, describe several different methods of analysing the risk or uncertainty in the project. Support your descriptions with calculations. (15 marks)

18 MUGGINS PLC (15 marks)

Muggins plc is evaluating a project to produce a new product. The product has an expected life of four years. Costs associated with the product are expected to be as follows.

Variable costs per unit
Labour: £30
Materials:
6 kg of material X at £1.64 per kg
3 units of component Y at £4.20 per unit
Other variable costs: £4.40

Indirect costs each year
Apportionment of head office salaries £118,000
Apportionment of general building occupancy £168,000
Other overheads £80,000, of which £60,000 represent additional cash expenditures (including rent of machinery)

To manufacture the product, a product manager will have to be recruited at an annual gross cost of £34,000, and one assistant manager whose current annual salary is £30,000 will be transferred from another department, where he will be replaced by a new appointee at a cost of £27,000 a year.

The necessary machinery will be rented. It will be installed in the company's factory. This will take up space that would otherwise be rented to another local company for £135,000 a year. This rent (for the factory space) is not subject to any uncertainty, as a binding four year lease would be created.

60,000 kg of material X are already in stock, at a purchase value of £98,400. They have no use other than the manufacture of the new product. Their disposal value is £50,000.

Expected sales volumes of the product, at the proposed selling price of £125 a unit, are as follows.

Year	*Expected sales*
	Units
1	10,000
2	18,000
3	18,000
4	19,000

All sales and costs will be on a cash basis and should be assumed to occur at the end of the year. Ignore taxation.

The company requires that certainty equivalent cash flows have a positive NPV at a discount rate of 14%. Adjustment factors to arrive at certainty equivalent amounts are as follows.

Year	*Costs*	*Benefits*
1	1.1	0.9
2	1.3	0.8
3	1.4	0.7
4	1.5	0.6

Required

Is the project acceptable?

19 BRIDGEFORD PLC (15 marks)

Bridgeford plc is considering whether or not to invest in the development of a new product, which would have an expected market life of five years. Estimates for the project are as follows.

Year	*0*	*1*	*2*	*3*	*4*	*5*
	£'000	£'000	£'000	£'000	£'000	£'000
Cost of equipment	2,000					
Total investment in working capital	200	250	300	350	350	300
Sales		2,500	3,000	3,500	3,500	3,000
Materials costs		500	600	700	700	600
Labour costs		750	900	1,100	1,100	1,000
Overhead costs		300	350	350	350	350
Interest		240	240	240	240	240
Depreciation		400	400	400	400	400
Total costs		2,190	2,490	2,790	2,790	2,590
Profit		310	510	710	710	410

These figures are based on year 0 prices. They ignore both inflation and capital allowances on the equipment, and you are to prepare an amended assessment of the project with the following data.

(a) Selling prices and overhead expenses will increase with inflation by 5% a year.

(b) Materials costs, labour costs and the working capital requirements, will increase by 10% a year.

(c) For taxation purposes, capital allowances will be available against the taxable profits of the project, at 25% a year on a reducing balance basis.

(d) The rate of corporation tax on taxable profits is 33%, payable one year in arrears.

(e) The equipment will have a zero salvage value at the end of the project's life.

(f) The company's real after-tax weighted average cost of capital is estimated to be 7%, and its nominal after-tax weighted average cost of capital is 12%.

Required

Estimate the net present value of the project, and recommend, on the basis of the NPV, whether or not the project should be undertaken.

20 SHORT O'FUNDS LTD (15 marks)

(a) Short O'Funds Ltd has capital of £130,000 available for investment in the forthcoming period, at a cost of capital of 20%. Capital will be freely available thereafter. Details of six projects under consideration are as follows.

Project	*Investment required*	*Net present value at 20%*
	£'000	£'000
P	40	16.5
Q	50	17.0
R	30	18.8
S	45	14.0
T	15	7.4
U	20	10.8

All projects are independent and divisible.

Required

Which projects should be undertaken and what total NPV will result? (7 marks)

(b) X Ltd has the following six investment opportunities open to it, with the cash flows shown.

Project	Year *0*	*1*	*2*	*3*	*4*	*5*	*NPV at 15%*
	£'000	£'000	£'000	£'000	£'000	£'000	£'000
A	-200	-100	-50	+200	+200	+200	20.53
B	-60	-80	+110	+110	0	0	25.94
C	0	-120	-50	+170	+210	0	89.69
D	0	0	-250	+240	+120	+110	92.07
E	-80	-100	+100	+150	+150	-100	43.33
F	-150	-150	+200	+180	+50	0	17.73

The company wishes to place a limit of £300,000 on the amount invested in projects in any one year. The investment limit cannot be supplemented with income from the projects. Projects are divisible but cannot be repeated more than once. Project timings cannot be advanced or delayed.

Required

Formulate a linear programming problem to determine the optimum choice of projects. (8 marks)

21 REPLACER LTD (15 marks)

Replacer Ltd uses a machine in its business. The machine is nearing the end of its life, and its maintenance costs are increasing. The company must decide when to replace it with a new type of machine (which has the same capacity but is cheaper to run), and how often to replace the new type of machine. Relevant data are as follows.

The existing machine

Replace at year	*Resale value*	*Extra expenditure from keeping during the year*
	£	£
0	25,000	0
1	12,000	15,000
2	0	18,000

The new type of machine

Purchase cost £30,000

	Year 1	*Year 2*	*Year 3*
	£	£	£
Running costs (cash expenses)	3,000	4,000	5,000
Resale value (end of year)	10,000	7,000	4,000

The company's cost of capital is 15%, and the equivalent annual cost method is to be used.

Required

Determine the optimum replacement cycle for the new type of machine, and the best time to replace the existing machine. Ignore inflation and taxation.

22 FLOCKS LTD (20 marks)

The management of Flocks Ltd is trying to decide which of two machines to purchase, to help with production. Only one of the two machines will be purchased.

Machine X costs £63,000 and machine Y costs £110,000. Both machines would require a working capital investment of £12,500 throughout their operational life, which is four years for machine X and six years for machine Y. The expected scrap value of either machine would be zero.

The estimated pre-tax operating net cash inflows with each machine are as follows.

Year	*Machine X*	*Machine Y*
	£	£
1	25,900	40,300
2	28,800	32,900
3	30,500	32,000
4	29,500	32,700
5	-	48,500
6	-	44,200

With machine Y, there is some doubt about its design features, and consequently there is some risk that it might prove unsuitable. Because of the higher business risk with machine Y, the machine Y project cash flows should be discounted at 15%, whereas machine X cash flows should be discounted at only 13%.

Flocks Ltd intends to finance the machine it eventually selects, X or Y, by borrowing at 11%.

Tax is payable at 33% on operating cash flows one year in arrears. Capital allowances are available at 25% a year on a reducing balance basis.

Required

(a) For both machine X and machine Y, calculate:

   (i) the (undiscounted) payback period;
   (ii) the net present value;

   and recommend which of the two machines Flocks Ltd should purchase. (13 marks)

(b) Suppose that Flocks Ltd has the opportunity to lease machine X under a finance lease arrangement, at an annual rent of £20,000 for four years, payable at the end of each year. Should the company lease or buy the machine, assuming it chooses machine X? (7 marks)

23 BANBURY AND COVENTRY (25 marks)

Two relatively small companies, Banbury Ltd and Coventry Ltd, have decided in principle to merge so that they can compete more effectively with larger companies. It has been decided that a scheme of amalgamation should be drawn up based on the following agreed figures.

	Banbury Ltd	*Coventry Ltd*
Net assets	£2,900,000	£2,750,000
	£	£
Share capital		
(ordinary £1 shares; no variation for seven years)	900,000	500,000
4% preference shares	0	100,000
Reserves	2,000,000	1,500,000
7% loan stock	0	650,000
	2,900,000	2,750,000
Forecast maintainable equity earnings (earnings available for ordinary shareholders after tax, interest and preference dividends)	£337,500	£200,000

	Banbury Ltd		*Coventry Ltd*	
	Equity earnings	*Dividends*	*Equity earnings*	*Dividends*
	£	%	£	%
Historical equity earnings and dividends				
1 year previous	300,000	10	190,000	15
2 years previous	270,000	10	90,000	10
3 years previous	190,000	5	80,000	10
4 years previous	120,000	5	130,000	12.5
5 years previous	100,000	5	70,000	10
Agreed P/E ratio for amalgamation	20		15	

Required

(a) Comment on the values which have been placed on the ordinary shares for the purpose of the amalgamation. (10 marks)

(b) Suggest and comment on a scheme of amalgamation drawing attention to matters which you think might require special consideration by the shareholders of Banbury Ltd and/or Coventry Ltd. Assume a corporation tax rate of 33%. (15 marks)

24 BLACK RAVEN LTD (25 marks)

Black Raven Ltd is a prosperous private company, whose owners are also the directors. The directors have decided to sell their business, and have begun a search for organisations interested in its purchase. They have asked for your assessment of the price per ordinary share a purchaser might be expected to offer.

Relevant information is as follows.

THE MOST RECENT BALANCE SHEET

	£'000	£'000	£'000
Fixed assets (net book value)			
Land and buildings			800
Plant and equipment			450
Motor vehicles			55
Patents			2
			1,307
Current assets			
Stock		250	
Debtors		125	
Cash		8	
		383	
Current liabilities			
Creditors	180		
Taxation	50		
		230	
			153
			1,460
Long-term liability			
Loan secured on property			400
			1,060
Share capital (300,000 ordinary shares of £1)			300
Reserves			760
			1,060

The profits after tax and interest but before dividends over the last five years have been as follows.

Year		£
	1	90,000
	2	80,000
	3	105,000
	4	90,000
	5 (most recent)	100,000

The annual dividend has been £45,000 (gross) for the last six years.

The company's five year plan forecasts an after-tax profit of £100,000 for the next 12 months, with an increase of 4% a year over each of the next four years.

As part of their preparations to sell the company, the directors of Black Raven Ltd have had the fixed assets and revalued by an independent expert, with the following results.

	£
Land and buildings	1,075,000
Plant and equipment	480,000
Motor vehicles	45,000

The dividend yields and P/E ratios of three quoted companies in the same industry as Black Raven Ltd over the last three years have been as follows.

	Aardvark plc		*Bullfinch plc*		*Crow plc*	
	Div. yield	*P/E ratio*	*Div. yield*	*P/E ratio*	*Div. yield*	*P/E ratio*
	%		%		%	
Recent year	12	8.5	11.0	9.0	13.0	10.0
Previous year	12	8.0	10.6	8.5	12.6	9.5
Three years ago	12	8.5	9.3	8.0	12.4	9.0
Average	12	8.33	10.3	8.5	12.7	9.5

Large companies in the industry apply an after-tax cost of capital of about 18% to acquisition proposals when the investment is not backed by tangible assets, as opposed to a rate of only 14% on the net tangible assets.

Your assessment of the net cash flows which would accrue to a purchasing company, allowing for taxation and the capital expenditure required after the acquisition to achieve the company's target five year plan, is as follows.

	£
Year 1	120,000
Year 2	120,000
Year 3	140,000
Year 4	70,000
Year 5	120,000

Required

Use the information provided to suggest seven valuations which prospective purchasers might make.

25 SUBSIDIARIES (20 marks)

Your company has two subsidiaries, X Ltd and Y Ltd, both providing computer services, notably software development and implementation. The United Kingdom market for such services is said to be growing at about 20% a year. The business is seasonal, peaking between September and March.

You have available the comparative data shown in the Appendix to this question. The holding company's policy is to leave the financing and management of subsidiaries entirely to the subsidiaries' directors.

Required

In the light of this information, compare the performance of the two subsidiaries.

It may be assumed that the difference in size of the two companies does not invalidate a comparison of the ratios provided.

Appendix

	X Ltd	Y Ltd
Turnover in most recent year (£'000)		
Home	2,856	6,080
Export	2,080	1,084
Total	4,936	7,164
Index of turnover 19X9 (19X6 = 100)		
Home	190%	235%
Export	220%	150%
Total	200%	220%
Operating profit 19X9 (£'000)	840	720
Operating capital employed 19X9 (£'000)	625	1,895

Ratio analysis		*X Ltd*			*Y Ltd*		
		19X9	*19X8*	*19X7*	*19X9*	*19X8*	*19X7*
Return on operating capital employed	%	134	142	47	38	40	52
Operating profit: Sales	%	17	16	6	10	8	5
Sales: Operating capital employed	×	8	9	8	4	5	10
Percentages to sales value:							
Cost of sales	%	65	67	71	49	49	51
Selling and distribution costs	%	12	11	15	15	16	19
Administration expenses	%	6	6	8	26	27	25
Number of employees		123	127	88	123	114	91
Sales per employee	£'000	40	37	31	58	52	47
Average remuneration per employee	£'000	13	13	12	16	14	13
Tangible fixed assets							
Turnover rate	×	20	21	14	9	11	14
Additions, at cost	%	57	47	58	303	9	124
Percentage depreciated	%	45	36	20	41	60	72
Product development costs carried forward as a percentage of turnover	%	0	0	0	10	8	6
Debtors : Sales	%	18	18	22	61	41	39
Stocks : Sales	%	0	1	0	2	2	1
Cash : Sales	%	7	9	2	1	1	0
Trade creditors : Sales	%	2	2	3	32	21	24
Trade creditors : Debtors	%	11	14	15	53	50	62
Current ratio (:1)		1.5	1.3	1.2	1.1	1.1	0.9
Liquid ratio (:1)		1.5	1.3	1.2	1.0	1.0	0.9
Liquid ratio excluding bank overdraft		0	0	0	1.4	1.5	1.2
Total debt : Total assets	%	61	71	109	75	72	84

Data in this Appendix should be accepted as correct. Any apparent internal inconsistencies are due to rounding of the figures.

26 VEREY PLC (20 marks)

Verey plc is a quoted manufacturing company trading solely in the UK. It has the following capital structure.

	Book value £'000	*Market value* £'000
£1 ordinary shares	2,500	4,000
10% secured debentures	1,000	980
14% unsecured loan stock	800	795
	4,300	5,775

The secured debentures were issued ten years ago and will not be redeemed for another 20 years, but the unsecured loan stock must be redeemed at par in six months time. All market values are ex div or ex int, a final dividend and half a year's interest being payable next week. Interest is covered four times.

The company has no cash available in excess of what it needs for working capital. It is contemplating an investment in a factory in Redland which would cost R$800,000 (R$ is the local currency), and which would yield a steady annual operating income of R$90,000. The present exchange rate is R$2 = £1, but this rate could fluctuate. There are no exchange controls.

Required

Comment on the company's existing capital structure, and on how it might finance the redemption of the loan stock and the investment in Redland. Make any assumptions you need to, but state them clearly. Ignore taxation.

27 WORKING CAPITAL (20 marks)

(a) In an article dealing with company liquidity, the statement was made that 'it is widely accepted that stronger and more profitable companies have a higher proportion of working capital'.

Set out and comment on the various circumstances under which this belief might or might not be true. (10 marks)

(b) Discuss whether long-term or short-term sources of funds should be used to finance trade debtors and stocks. (10 marks)

28 RASCAL PLC (18 marks)

Rascal plc sells its products in two distinct markets, the industrial and commercial markets. Sales next year are expected to be £3,600,000, divided 30%: 70% between the industrial and commercial markets respectively. All sales are on credit, and the variable cost of sales is 60% of the selling price. The company suffers no bad debts, although industrial customers take on average 90 days credit and commercial customers take 50 days credit.

Rascal is now considering an advertising campaign, which it is hoped would boost total sales by 25%, although most new customers would be industrial, and the ratio of industrial: commercial sales would change to 40%: 60%. The increase in sales would not affect the volume of stocks or creditors.

The directors of Rascal plc are also giving some thought to offering a discount of 3% for payment of debts within 30 days, with net terms for payment within 60 days. The discount will not be introduced unless the advertising campaign takes place.

If the advertising campaign is undertaken, and sales increase, there will be some bad debts, and there will also be a change in the pattern of payments from debtors. The following estimate of payments has been made.

Number of days	*No cash discounts*		*Cash discounts*	
credit taken	*Industrial*	*Commercial*	*Industrial*	*Commercial*
	%	%	%	%
30 days	10	10	40	50
50 days	20	10	18	25
60 days	0	79	20	14
90 days	67	0	20	10
Bad debts	3	1	2	1

Short-term finance is readily available at 10% a year.

Assume a 360 day year.

Required

(a) Ignoring the option to introduce cash discounts, determine:

(i) the anticipated effect of the advertising campaign on Rascal's debtors position, net of bad debts;

(ii) the maximum amount it would be worth paying at the end of the year for the advertising campaign. (11 marks)

(b) Assuming that the advertising campaign is undertaken, determine the annual benefit from the application of the cash discount terms to sales to each of two markets. Is it worthwhile introducing the cash discount terms if they must apply to all Rascal's sales without differentiating between markets? (7 marks)

29 BLEARY HYDE LTD (20 marks)

Bleary Hyde Ltd has just received an order from a customer in Country X for 6,000 widgets at a unit price of £2.50, payable in sterling. Bleary Hyde's terms of sale for export orders are:

(a) 10% payment with order; and
(b) the balance payable within 180 days of shipment.

The customer has sent a 10% deposit with his order.

It has been the experience of Bleary Hyde that customers from Country X have been slow payers, usually taking one year's credit before paying invoices, and several have defaulted on payment. The company estimates that for any new customer from Country X there would be:

(a) a 30% chance of the customer defaulting;
(b) only a 40% chance of receiving payment within one year.

The contribution that can be earned on selling widgets is £0.75 per unit, after deducting shipping costs. However, there is an estimated cost of £800 to collect an overdue debt, the cost being incurred one year after the sale is made. If, after this action, the debt remains unpaid, it is written off. There is only a 50% chance that such action will get the customer to pay what he owes.

The company considers that granting export credit is a form of investment decision, with a suitable discount rate to apply being 15%.

Required

Assess whether Bleary Hyde Ltd should accept the order from the new customer:

(a) on the basis of the above information; (8 marks)

(b) if there is a 50% chance that the customer will send in a repeat order after 12 months. Following payment for the first order, the probability of default for repeat orders is 10%, but no attempt would be made to collect any overdue debt a year after a repeat order is placed; (8 marks)

(c) if the customer states his definite intention of repeating his order after 12 months. (4 marks)

State any assumptions that you make.

30 KNOSSOS LTD (20 marks)

It is now the end of 19X0. Knossos Ltd is a small manufacturing company which is experiencing a short-term liquidity crisis. The company accountant has estimated that by the end of February 19X1, a further £200,000 of funds will be required. Since the company already has a large overdraft, its banker will not advance any more funds. Three solutions to the problem have been put forward.

(a) *Option 1.* A short-term loan of £200,000 could be raised for six months from 1 January 19X1 at an annual interest rate of 18%. This would be obtained through a finance company, but there would be no costs involved in raising the funds.

(b) *Option 2.* The company could forgo cash discounts of 2% which are obtained from suppliers of raw materials for payment within 30 days. The maximum credit which could safely be taken is 90 days. Monthly purchases of raw materials amount to £100,000, before discounts. Knossos Ltd would forgo the discount for six months before reviewing the position again.

(c) *Option 3.* The company could factor its trade debtors. A factor has been found who would be prepared, for a period of six months from 1 January 19X1, to advance Knossos Ltd 75% of the value of its invoices less factoring charges, immediately on receipt of the invoices. (You may assume that all invoices are sent out at the end of the month of sale). The factoring charges would be:

   (i) an interest charge of 15% a year on the amount of money advanced, calculated on a day-to-day basis, and estimated and deducted in advance;
   (ii) a fee for taking on the task of collecting Knossos Ltd's debts, amounting to 2% of the total invoiced and deducted in advance.

Monthly sales are expected to be £300,000. The factor would pay the balance owing on the invoices to Knossos on receipt of the money from the debtors. On average, debtors pay at the end of the month following the month of sale. As a result of using the factor, Knossos Ltd estimates that there would be savings in administration costs of £4,000 a month.

Any surplus funds in excess of the £200,000 required would be used to reduce the bank overdraft, which costs 1% a month.

Required

(a) Show which of the three options is cheapest. (13 marks)
(b) If the factoring arrangement is the option preferred, what would be the cash receipts for the first eight months of 19X1? (4 marks)
(c) Briefly describe the other considerations which should be taken into account when choosing between the three options. (3 marks)

Ignore taxation.

31 AARDVARK LTD (12 marks)

Aardvark Ltd has been having some difficulty with the collection of debts from export customers. At present the company makes no special arrangements for export sales.

As a result the company is considering either:

(a) employing the services of a non-recourse export factoring company; or

(b) insuring its exports against non-payment through the ECGD.

The two alternatives also provide possible ways of financing sales.

An export factor will, if required, provide immediate finance of 80% of export credit sales at an interest rate of 2% above bank base rate (the base rate is 8%). The service fee for debt collection is 3% of credit sales. If the factor is used, administrative savings of £35,000 a year should be possible.

An ECGD comprehensive insurance policy costs 35 pence per £100 insured and covers 90% of the risk of non-payment for exports. The ECGD will probably allow Aardvark Ltd to assign its rights to a bank, in return for which the bank will provide an advance of 70% of the sales value of insured debts, at a cost of 1.5% above base rate.

Aardvark's annual exports total £1,000,000. Export sales are on open account terms of 60 days credit, but on average payments have been 30 days late. Approximately 0.5%, by value, of credit sales result in bad debts which have to be written off.

The company is able to borrow on overdraft from its bank, unsecured, at 2.5% above base rate. Assume a 360 day year.

Required

Determine which combination of export administration and financing Aardvark Ltd should use.

32 IMPORT-EXPORT MERCHANT (15 marks)

An import-export merchant contracts on 31 December to buy 1,500 tonnes of a certain product from a supplier in country X at a price of X$ 11,820 per tonne. Shipment will be made direct to a customer in country Y to whom he has sold the product at Y$ 462 per tonne. Of the total quantity, 500 tonnes will be shipped during January and the balance by the end of February. Payment to the suppliers is to be made immediately on shipment, whilst one month's credit from the date of shipment is allowed to the country Y customer.

The merchant arranges with his bank to cover these transactions in sterling on the forward exchange market, the exchange rates at 31 December being those given below.

	X$	Y$
Spot	107.45 - 107.75	3.84 - 3.88
1 month forward	55 - 105 c dis	$2\frac{1}{2}$ - $1\frac{1}{2}$ c premium
2 months forward	75 - 175 c dis	4 - 3 c premium
3 months forward	106 - 250 c dis	$6\frac{1}{2}$ - $5\frac{1}{2}$ c premium

Exchange commission is 1 per mille (maximum £10) on each transaction.

Required

(a) Calculate (to the nearest pound) the profit the merchant will make on the transaction. (8 marks)

(b) Explain how calculations of further exchange profit or loss would be made if:
  (i) the February shipment were cancelled;
  (ii) the February shipment were delayed until April. (7 marks)

33 BRINGASOCK LTD (12 marks)

Bringasock Ltd sells shoes to Italy. A shipment has just been made to a major Italian customer, who has been invoiced in Italian lire, payable in three months time. The amount due is 56,000,000 lire.

Bringasock's financial director has the following information about foreign exchange rates and interest rates.

Exchange rate, lire/£

Spot	2,320 - 2,322
3 months forward	15 - 23 dis

Interest rates	*Sterling*		*Lire*	
	Deposit	*Borrowing*	*Deposit*	*Borrowing*
	6%	8%	10%	12%

Required

(a) What course of action would you recommend to the finance director for converting the lire into sterling, so as to maximise sterling receipts from the shipment? (9 marks)

(b) How would your advice differ, if at all, were Bringasock Ltd also due to make a payment of 30,000,000 lire to an Italian supplier in three months time? (3 marks)

1 FINANCIAL OBJECTIVE

(a) In the last three years, each company has achieved a reasonably consistent increase in growth in EPS, with Y Ltd's growth rate doubling in each of these years. The ability of the companies to do this depends partly on:

(i) the external environment. This includes market demand and inflation. The large increase in turnover of both companies, because of price or sales volume increases, has contributed to the increase in EBIT, and therefore to the increase in distributable earnings. The rate of taxation as a percentage of EBIT appears to have risen slightly between 19X1 and 19X4; this had the effect of reducing the rate of growth in EPS;

(ii) the companies' operating cost structures. Although variable costs as a percentage of sales rose in both companies between 19X1 and 19X4, there was a reduction in the ratio of fixed cost to sales, so that the operating profit to sales ratio remained fairly constant over this period. This meant that EBIT increased at about the same rate as the rate of increase in sales. However, since X Ltd operates with a lower contribution/sales ratio than Y Ltd, an increase in turnover will have a much greater effect on the EBIT (and therefore the EPS) of Y Ltd than of X Ltd. In 19X4, each extra pound of sales earned X Ltd 35p contribution before tax, compared with 61p for Y Ltd;

(iii) gearing. X Ltd is more highly geared than Y Ltd. This might explain X Ltd's stronger earnings growth. The gearing ratio of X Ltd remained fairly constant in the period, although it would have been much higher but for the asset revaluation reserve. Y Ltd increased its gearing ratio substantially in 19X2. Interest rates appear to have fallen during the period, so both companies financed their expansion to a considerable extent by acquiring relatively cheap loans.

(b) The financial management of X Ltd shows some cause for concern in spite of the increase in turnover, profits and EPS.

(i) The gearing of the company is rather high. In 19X4 it is 44%, and if the asset revaluation reserve is removed, the gearing ratio is 60/116 = 52%. Although we do not know the working capital structure, the debt ratio is probably in excess of 50%, and it is surprising that the company was able to raise an extra £14,000 in loans in 19X4 (£60,000 - £46,000). The higher rates of interest paid by X Ltd (compared to Y Ltd) probably reflect the higher risk of investing in X Ltd.

(ii) The revaluation of assets (by £12,000 out of £42,000 in 19X2) seems surprisingly high.

(iii) The need for additional sources of funds to finance the growth in sales has meant that earnings have had to be retained. It is perhaps significant that in 19X4 dividends were only a third of distributable profits, whereas in earlier years the fraction was about half.

(iv) It would appear, from results in 19X4 when a high proportion of earnings were retained and a new issue of shares was made, that the company is reaching the limit of its ability to borrow without first reducing its gearing and debt ratios. It should be expected, however, that in view of the increasing profitability, the company should be able to restore itself to a position of financial strength with prudent financial management.

Even so, ROI is quite high, and the company might therefore be attractive to investors.

Y Ltd has lower gearing than X Ltd, and there has been no revaluation of assets. Any such revaluation would reduce the gearing ratio considerably. The interest cover in Y Ltd is very high, and this too suggests good security for lenders.

The company's rate of growth in EPS is high, and if the company wishes to continue to expand rapidly, it appears to be in a sound financial position to do so.

(i) Retained earnings are high.

(ii) At the same time, dividends have risen more quickly than earnings, and shareholders are receiving the benefit of the growth in profits. This is likely to increase the value of Y Ltd's shares.

(iii) The company was able to raise an extra £50,000 in new shares in 19X3, and loan capital has more than doubled. There would appear to be scope for further borrowing if required.

(iv) ROI is about 28% in 19X4, rather higher than for X Ltd.

Y Ltd offers security to lenders, safe gearing, and a fast growth in profits and dividends. In these respects, its financial management appears to be very sound. Some thought should be given, however, to a revaluation of the company's fixed assets, if this seems appropriate.

Workings

	X Ltd				*Y Ltd*			
	19X1	*19X2*	*19X3*	*19X4*	*19X1*	*19X2*	*19X3*	*19X4*
Growth in EBIT (%)		14.3%	31.2%	47.6%		12.0%	42.9%	16.2%
Growth in EPS (%)		16.7%	14.3%	20.0%		4.0%	9.2%	18.3%
Growth in EPS (pence)		5	5	8		1	2.4	5.2
Cost structure	%	%	%	%	%	%	%	%
Variable cost/sales ratio	60	62	64	65	30	31	33	39
Fixed cost/sales ratio	26	25	24	23	45	44	40	35
EBIT/sales ratio	14	13	12	12	25	25	27	26
	100	100	100	100	100	100	100	100
Gearing ratio (Loans/capital employed)	42%	33%	44%	44%	21%	29%	30%	28%
Interest cover (EBIT/interest)	3.5×	4.0×	3.0×	3.9×	10.0×	7.0×	8.4×	9.8×
Average cost of interest (Interest/loan capital)	16%	16%	15%	13%	12.5%	12%	10%	10%

Financing of increases in assets								
		£'000	£'000	£'000		£'000	£'000	£'000
Extra shares		0	0	5		0	50	0
Revaluation		12	4	4		0	0	0
Retained profits		4	4	8		34	41	50
Equity		16	8	17		34	91	50
Loans		0	21	14		57	45	0
Increase in assets		16	29	31		91	136	50
ROI								
(i) EBIT/capital employed	23%	21%	20%	23%	26%	24%	26%	28%
(ii) Earnings before tax/ equity capital	29%	24%	24%	30%	30%	29%	33%	35%

2 GROWTH PLC

The capital market

The company is a substantial one, with a reasonably long trading record over which steady growth has been achieved. It should therefore apply for a full listing on the Stock Exchange. There seems to be little point in joining the Unlisted Securities Market first, as the company would very soon want to move on to a full listing. The over-the-counter markets are too small, too illiquid and too poorly regulated to be of any use to Growth plc.

Advantages to the company

The company will probably raise equity funds on joining the market, through an issue of new shares. Some shares will have to be issued in any case, so that at least 25% of the company's shares become available to the market, unless some existing shareholders wish to sell large parts of their holdings immediately.

Future equity issues will be easier if the company is listed than if it is not. It may also be easier to raise debt capital, because listed companies are generally thought of as less risky than unlisted companies.

The company may find it easier to take over other companies, because listed shares are often acceptable as consideration in a takeover.

Share option schemes as incentives to senior employees are more feasible for listed than for unlisted companies.

Advantages to the existing shareholders

When a company has a full listing, its shares are likely to be fairly readily marketable (although shares in some listed companies are not much traded). Shareholders wishing to sell shares should be able to do so, and shareholders needing a market value for their shares (perhaps for tax purposes) will be able to obtain one.

The status attached to being a listed company may itself lead to a rise in the value of the shares.

Disadvantages for the company

Joining the stock market can be expensive. Fees must be paid to professional advisers and to the Stock Exchange.

Once the company has obtained a listing, there will be further costs of compliance with Stock Exchange disclosure requirements, and also the Stock Exchange annual fee. Expenditure on public relations for the company as a whole (as opposed to the advertising of specific products) may also be needed.

The company will be expected to show reasonable results each year. If results are poor and it is suspected that bad management is to blame (rather than a general downturn in the leisure market), the company could become vulnerable to a hostile takeover bid. Because demand for the company's products is sensitive to individuals' real incomes, there is a serious risk of fluctuations in performance.

The company could become the victim of a 'bear raid', a campaign to drive the share price down by selling shares.

Disadvantages for the existing shareholders

The shareholders will ultimately bear the costs of being listed which the company must pay.

Control of the company will be diluted, as shares must be made available to the market. A new investor, such as an insurance company, might build up a substantial stake by buying shares in the market. Such a shareholder could achieve effective control over the company even with a minority holding, if other large shareholders do not act in unison.

As mentioned above, the share price could be driven down in a bear raid; it could also fluctuate sharply on the publication of the company's results or other news relating to the company or its markets.

3 SHARE VALUES

(a) The fundamental analysis theory of share values states that the value of a share is the present value of the expected future dividends. No buyer would pay more for the share than this amount, because he would only have to invest this amount elsewhere to obtain the same income stream; and no seller would accept less than this amount, as to do so would involve an avoidable loss of wealth.

The theory assumes that there is a single discount rate applicable to all investors and potential investors in the shares (of one class) in a given company. This rate is applied to the expected future dividends to obtain a present value.

Examples

(i) X plc is expected to pay a dividend of 30p a share each year for ever, starting one year from now. An appropriate discount rate is 25%. The current market value per share (ex div) should be 30p/0.25 = £1.20.

(ii) Y plc is expected to pay a dividend of 21p a share one year from now. Thereafter, dividends are expected to rise by 3% a year. An appropriate discount rate is 15%. The current market value (taking into account the expected dividend growth) is

$$\frac{21}{1.15} + \frac{21 \times 1.03}{1.15^2} + \frac{21 \times 1.03^2}{1.15^3} + \ldots = \frac{21}{0.15 - 0.03} = 175\text{p} = £1.75.$$

The theory can be applied to the valuation of interest-bearing securities. The income stream from such securities is usually known with certainty, whereas future dividends from shares can only be estimated. With redeemable securities, not only the interest but also the amount due on maturity must be discounted in arriving at a present value.

(b) In an efficient stock market, no one investor dominates the market, transaction costs are not a significant deterrent to dealing and the prices at which shares are bought and sold reflect all available relevant information. Share prices will therefore be set in a rational way, taking account of the prospects for companies, and one would expect the fundamental analysis theory to apply. Exactly how it would apply would depend on the level of efficiency of the stock market, which is considered below.

If the stock market is inefficient, share prices may differ significantly and permanently from what the fundamental analysis theory would lead one to expect. A dominant investor or high dealing costs may distort prices; and if share prices do not reflect all available relevant information about companies, they may come to bear little relation to likely future dividends.

The level of efficiency of a stock market depends on the extent to which market prices reflect relevant information. Under weak form efficiency, only information about past price movements and their implications is reflected in current market prices; under semi-strong form efficiency, all publicly available information is reflected in current market prices; and under strong form efficiency, even confidential information (such as secret plans for new investments) is reflected in current market prices.

Information about a company, such as recent results or a proposed new investment, is normally known to only a few people at first. It is published, and after a while several investors will have dealt in the company's shares, at prices which reflect the information. Thus whatever the level of efficiency of the stock market, if it is efficient at all then share prices will eventually reflect each item of relevant information about the company. Share prices should therefore be determined according to the principles of the fundamental analysis theory, although perhaps after some delay, even if the stock market shows only weak form efficiency.

4 RYOTT TISSUES PLC

(a) (i) A rights issue of ordinary shares would be made to raise a substantial amount of new long-term capital.

(ii) If an issue of shares to outsiders is chosen as an alternative to a rights issue, it is a Stock Exchange requirement that prior approval must have been obtained within the past 12 months, from the shareholders in a general meeting, for the issue of shares for cash other than as a rights issue. A rights issue could also be more likely to be successful than a public issue, because:

(1) the offer is to existing investors who are familiar with the company;

(2) existing shareholders may wish to take up the rights offer in order to preserve their relative shareholdings in the company;

(3) the offer price, below the current market price, would be set in such a way as to attract shareholders into acceptance. The cost of a rights issue would also be less than that of an offer for sale.

(iii) The main drawback of a rights issue is its cost. Placings are cheaper, and would probably be preferred for smaller issues.

(iv) A rights issue would be preferable to raising long-term loan capital:

(1) where the interest rate on the loan capital which must be offered to attract investors is unacceptably high;

(2) where the company's level of gearing would become unacceptably high, possibly causing a reduction in the market value of the ordinary shares as a result of the extra financial risk to shareholders;

(3) where the company wishes to reduce its level of gearing.

(b) A dilution in net earnings per share would generally be expected as a result of a rights issue, at least in the short term. This should be acceptable to shareholders provided that the return obtained on their total investment is at least as high as it was before the rights issue.

Example

A company which has in issue 3,000,000 ordinary shares with a market value of £3,000,000 and current annual earnings of £300,000 or 10p per share, decides to make a one for three rights issue to finance new investment. The offer price is 80p per share.

The current P/E ratio is 10 (market value = £1 per share, EPS = 10p).

The theoretical market value of the 4,000,000 shares in issue after the rights issue is £3,800,000. If the P/E ratio of 10 is maintained, the market value of the 4,000,000 shares must be sustained by annual earnings of £380,000, or 9.5p per share.

Provided that the company pursues a consistent dividend policy (that is, that the dividend cover is held constant) shareholders would be satisfied by their return, in spite of a lower EPS.

(c) The requirements of the company are incompatible.

(i) Total earnings after the redemption of the loan stock would be £4,201,000.

	£	£
Current earnings (10,000,000 × 40p)		4,000,000
Additional earnings after redemption		
Interest saved £3,000,000 × 10%	300,000	
Less tax on extra profits (33%)	99,000	
		201,000
Earnings after redemption		4,201,000

If the EPS is to be diluted by no more than 10%, that is, it is to be no less than 36p, the number of shares in issue must be

$$\frac{\text{Total earnings}}{\text{EPS}} = \frac{4{,}201{,}000}{0.36} = 11{,}669{,}444$$

The additional number of shares issued could not exceed 1,669,444, requiring a rights issue price of:

$$\frac{£3{,}000{,}000}{1{,}669{,}444} = £1.80$$

As this is above the current market value of £1.60 per share, there must be a larger issue of shares, and an EPS lower than 36p.

(ii) A rights issue price 20% below the current market price would be £1.60 × 80% = £1.28. To raise £3,000,000, 2,343,750 shares would need to be issued, and the EPS would be

$$\frac{£4{,}201{,}000}{12{,}343{,}750} = 34.03\text{p}$$

This is $\frac{5.97}{40}$ = 15% below the current EPS.

(iii) Since a rights issue usually involves an 'administratively convenient' number of shares, the company would probably make a one for four issue. The issue price per share would be:

$$\frac{£3{,}000{,}000}{2{,}500{,}000} = £1.20$$

which is 25% below the current market value. (It is assumed that any upward movement in the share price before the announcement of the rights issue would be negligible).

Although a 6 for 25 rights issue, to raise £3,000,000 from 2,400,000 shares at £1.25 per share might seem preferable (resulting in a diluted EPS of 33.88p), the one for four issue is probably the one which would be considered: the EPS would be 33.61p.

(iv) The theoretical ex rights price of the shares would be as follows.

	£
Market value cum rights of four shares	6.40
Rights issue price of one share	1.20
Theoretical value of five shares	7.60

The theoretical ex rights price would be £1.52 per share.

The P/E ratio would be $\frac{£1.52}{0.3361} = 4.5$

5 LOGJAM PLC

Tutorial note. The sight of a probability distribution in the question might have tempted you to conclude that expected values should be a feature of a solution. In this case, however, an expected value of year 2 earnings would not really tell us much. It is more useful to produce (for each method of financing) five separate earnings forecasts, one for each of the five possible outcomes.

Suggested solution

Each method of raising finance will be considered in turn. The costs of raising the finance are ignored.

Alternative (1)

Ordinary shares currently in issue	80,000,000
Current market price	276p
Rights issue price (20% discount)	220.8p, say 221p

A one for four rights issue would result in the creation of 20,000,000 new shares, and it would raise (× 221p per share) £44,200,000.

With the debenture issue, the total amount of funds raised would be £69,200,000.

The theoretical ex rights price of the shares would be as follows.

	Pence
Four shares, value (× 276p)	1,104
One share, value (× 221p)	221
Theoretical value of five shares	1,325
Theoretical ex rights price	265 pence

If we assume that the debentures are issued at par and that the post-rights issue market price of the shares is 265p, we can calculate the book value-based and market value-based gearing ratios of the company, using the balance sheet as a base for our calculations. (The bank overdraft is included in prior charge capital.)

	Book values		*Market values*
	£'000		£'000
Bank overdraft	46,320		46,320
Preference shares	20,000	(× 0.59)	11,800
12% Debenture	25,000	(× 0.94)	23,500
Floating rate loan	10,000	(at par)	10,000
	101,320		91,620
13% Debenture	25,000		25,000
Prior charge capital	126,320		116,620
Ordinary shares pre-rights issue	40,000	(80m × 276p)	220,800
Reserves pre-rights issue	86,430		0
	126,430		220,800
Rights issue (20m × 221p)	44,200		44,200
Equity	170,630		265,000
Gearing ratio	74%		44%

This compares with a current gearing ratio of (101,320 ÷ 126,430) 80% based on book values and (91,620 ÷ 220,800) 41.5% based on market values. These changes in gearing would not appear to be significant, and so this method of raising funds should not create problems for the company's debt management, subject to interest cover remaining satisfactory.

The EPS in the year just ended was $\frac{54{,}066 - 1{,}600}{80{,}000}$ = 65.6p and the dividend per ordinary share was (29,500 ÷ 80,000) 36.9p.

If this method of finance is used, the future EPS in years 1 and 2 will be as follows.

	Year 1			*Year 2*		
		Failure	*Moderate*	*Average*	*Good*	*Very good*
	£'000	£'000	£'000	£'000	£'000	£'000
EBIT	96,112	86,501	100,918	105,723	124,946	144,168
Less interest						
Existing debt	(10,840)	(10,840)	(10,840)	(10,840)	(10,840)	(10,840)
New debentures (13% × £25m)	(3,250)	(3,250)	(3,250)	(3,250)	(3,250)	(3,250)
Taxable profits	82,022	72,411	86,828	91,633	110,856	130,078
Less tax (33%)	(27,067)	(23,896)	(28,653)	(30,239)	(36,582)	(42,926)
	54,955	48,515	58,175	61,394	74,274	87,152
Less preference dividend	(1,600)	(1,600)	(1,600)	(1,600)	(1,600)	(1,600)
Earnings	53,355	46,915	56,575	59,794	72,674	85,552
EPS	53.4p	46.9p	56.6p	59.8p	72.7p	85.6p
Probability		0.1	0.2	0.3	0.3	0.1

There would be a dilution in EPS in year 1, but this is to be expected to some extent because of the rights issue. However, total earnings in year 1 would be only 1.7% higher than in the year just ended, because of the higher interest costs, and with 25% more equity in issue, the fall in EPS would be 18.6%.

Expected year 2 earnings are therefore important. There is a 0.1 probability of a further fall in EPS, which would probably cause a fall in the share price. If the product has moderate or average success, EPS would rise in year 2 compared with year 1, and allowing for the dilution caused by the rights issue, would amount to growth in EPS compared with the current year. If the product has good or very good success, (combined probability 0.4) the EPS will be higher in year 2 than in the current year, in spite of the rights issue. The share price would presumably rise if this were to happen.

It would obviously be helpful, however, to have estimates of earnings growth (if any) in year 3 and subsequent years.

Alternative (2)

The total amount of finance raised will be £69,000,000, including the increase in retained earnings. The company's gearing ratio will worsen, because of the issue of the convertible debentures. Assuming that the dividend reduction will affect year 1 dividends, the company's gearing after the stock issue would be as follows.

Book values	*Market values*
$\frac{101,320 + 40,000}{126,430}$	$\frac{91,620 + 40,000}{220,800}$
= 112%	= 60%

(It is assumed that the issue of the convertible stock will not affect the market price of the ordinary shares.)

Gearing would therefore be substantially higher and with the reduced dividend in year 1, the share price could well fall. When the stockholders eventually obtain their right to convert their stock into shares, in four to six years time, gearing would fall substantially. However, the rate of conversion seems favourable to the convertible stockholders. £100 of stock can be converted into 30 ordinary shares. 30 shares have a current market value of (× 276p) £82.80, and so the shares would need to increase in value by just £17.20 or about 21% in four to six years before stock could be converted at no profit or loss. Any greater increase in share price in the four to six year period, which is likely, would benefit the loan stockholders. Any excessive benefits for loan stockholders would be at the expense of existing ordinary shareholders. This suggests that the conversion terms of 30 shares for £100 of stock might be too generous.

If this method of finance is used, the estimated future EPS in years 1 and 2 will be as follows.

	Year 1			*Year 2*		
		Failure	*Moderate*	*Average*	*Good*	*Very good*
	£'000	£'000	£'000	£'000	£'000	£'000
EBIT	96,112	86,501	100,918	105,723	124,946	144,168
Less interest						
Existing debt	(10,840)	(10,840)	(10,840)	(10,840)	(10,840)	(10,840)
Convertibles						
(40m × 11%)	(4,400)	(4,400)	(4,400)	(4,400)	(4,400)	(4,400)
Taxable profits	80,872	71,261	85,678	90,483	109,706	128,928
Less tax (33%)	(26,688)	(23,516)	(28,274)	(29,859)	(36,203)	(42,546)
	54,184	47,745	57,404	60,624	73,503	86,382
Less preference dividend	(1,600)	(1,600)	(1,600)	(1,600)	(1,600)	(1,600)
Earnings	52,584	46,145	55,804	59,024	71,903	84,782
EPS	65.7p	57.7p	69.8p	73.8p	89.9p	106.0p

	£'000	£'000	£'000	£'000	£'000	£'000
Earnings	52,584	46,145	55,804	59,024	71,903	84,782
Add back convertible debenture interest, less tax at 33% (67% of £4.4m)	2,948	2,948	2,948	2,948	2,948	2,948
Adjusted earnings	55,532	49,093	58,752	61,972	74,851	87,730

The maximum number of shares on conversion is (80 + 40 × 30/100) 92,000,000.

Fully diluted EPS	60.4p	53.4p	63.9p	67.4p	81.4p	95.4p
Probability		0.1	0.2	0.3	0.3	0.1

These EPS figures show that compared with the current EPS of 65.6p, this method of financing would result in a slightly higher EPS in year 1, and a higher EPS in year 2, *unless* the new product performs poorly (probability 0.1). There is a 0.7 probability that the fully diluted EPS in year 2 will be higher than in the current year.

Significantly, however, this method of financing will involve a very low dividend in year 1, and perhaps no dividend at all, since the proposed dividend reduction in year 1 is nearly the same amount as the dividend paid in the current year (just ended).

The attractiveness of this method of financing lies in the prospects for EPS growth in year 2, but the drawbacks are the potential effects on the share price of higher gearing and a very low year 1 dividend.

As with alternative (1), it would be useful to have data about expected earnings from year 3 onwards, and not just data for years 1 and 2.

6 BABINGTON LTD

(a) *Loan capital*

The advantages of loan capital are as follows.

(i) In the case of a new business with no record of profitability it is likely to be easier to attract than risk capital, at least if Babington Ltd is able to offer some security.

(ii) The existing shareholders are likely to be able to retain greater control of the business if loan finance is used rather than equity finance. However, potential lenders will seek to exercise at least some control over the business.

(iii) In times of inflation, borrowing is advantageous in that the monetary liability remains fixed and the real rate of interest is low or even negative.

Equity capital

The advantages of equity capital are as follows.

(i) The pattern of earnings for a new enterprise such as this is frequently erratic, possibly with significant losses in opening years. This might make regular loan repayments difficult to cope with.

(ii) Equity providers might be more willing to take a risk on an investment offering little security if they have the chance of a high return later.

The advantages of each type of finance correspond to disadvantages of the other type.

(b) The various sources of finance include:

(i) clearing banks. If the amount of capital required is small a bank might be willing to consider an overdraft or a loan;

(ii) special financial institutions, such as Investors in Industry;

(iii) venture capital. Various government incentives have been introduced in recent years to encourage private investment in industry. Some financial institutions have set up machinery to bring together potential investors with businesses looking for finance. This is particularly so with the Business Expansion Scheme and Babington Ltd might be able to obtain finance from a business expansion fund.

(c) The considerations which are relevant here are substantially those set out in part (a) above. An additional factor is the type of contribution which a supplier of capital might wish to make to the business. This might go so far as to constitute a joint venture arrangement if the supplier of capital had technical or managerial expertise and Babington Ltd's existing owner-managers were willing to relinquish a share in the running of the business.

7 KNIGHT PLC

We should consider the significant features of both the individual types of security of Etna plc and the company as a whole.

Ordinary shares

(a) The EPS in 19X2 was $\frac{£1,077,200}{7,000,000} = 15.39p$

Given a market value of £1.50 per share, the P/E ratio was therefore 9.75. This should be compared with the P/E ratio of similar quoted companies, since a high P/E ratio reflects market confidence in the quality of earnings and the future earnings potential of a company.

(b) Although we are not certain of the reliability of the profit forecast for the next year, it is worth considering the expected results.

	£
Profit before tax (7% higher)	1,776,200
Less corporation tax (33%)	586,146
Profit after tax	1,190,054
Less preference dividend	35,000
Earnings available for equity	1,155,054

EPS = $\frac{£1,155,054}{7,000,000} = 16.50p$

If the P/E ratio remained at 9.75, the market value would increase to £1.61.

(c) We should also consider the effect of the conversion of the convertible loan stock, by calculating an EPS based on fully diluted earnings.

	£	*Earnings in previous year* £	*Forecast earnings* £
Earnings before dilution available to equity		1,077,200	1,155,054
Add interest paid on convertible loan stock	135,000		
Less tax at 33%	44,550		
		90,450	90,450
Earnings after dilution available to equity		1,167,650	1,245,504
Number of shares			
Existing	7,000,000		
Extra on conversion	600,000		
		7,600,000	7,600,000
EPS		15.36p	16.39p

If the P/E ratio remained at 9.75, and the level of earnings remained at current or forecast levels, the market value of ordinary shares after conversion would be expected to be in the region of only £1.50 to £1.60.

(d) The dividend on ordinary shares in 19X2 was 10p per share net, which is 13.33p gross, giving a dividend yield of 8.9%.

Net dividend proposed	£700,000
Gross dividend ($\times \frac{100}{75}$)	£933,333
Gross dividend per share	13.33p
Market value per share	£1.50
Dividend yield	8.9%

This should be compared with the dividend yield from equity shares in other companies. This comparison may be of significance in deciding whether to acquire a small ordinary shareholding.

(e) The asset value per ordinary share was £1.31, based on realisable values of fixed assets and balance sheet values of net current assets.

	£
Value of assets	14,200,000
Less book value of preference shares and loan stock	5,000,000
Asset value of equity	9,200,000
Number of shares	7,000,000
Asset value per ordinary share	£1.31

This is below the market value per share, which suggests that the company is not worth acquiring in order to break it up and sell off its assets.

(f) The dividend cover is 1.54 times.

$$\frac{\text{Earnings}}{\text{Dividend}} = \frac{£1,077,200}{£700,000} = 1.54$$

This may be rather low compared to similar quoted companies.

Preference shares

The (gross) dividend yield on preference shares is currently 9.7%.

Gross dividend $(7p \times \frac{100}{75})$	9.33p
Market value per share	96p
Dividend yield	9.7%

This should be compared with the yield from preference shares in similar companies and with the yield from ordinary shares and loan stock in Etna plc.

Unsecured loan stock

The yield from the 7% unsecured loan stock is 12.3%.

Interest	7%
Market value	£57 per cent
Yield	12.3%

Convertible loan stock

The yield from the 9% convertible loan stock is 11%.

Interest	9%
Market value	£82 per cent
Yield	11.0%

Comparison of the yields from different securities	*Yield* %
Ordinary shares (ignoring capital growth)	8.9
Preference shares	9.7
Unsecured loan stock	12.3
Convertible loan stock	11.0

Because the different securities have differing degrees of financial risk associated with them, we should expect the yields to differ. In selecting which security or securities are preferable to the others, the investment company's decision must be based on the expected returns it requires for differing degrees of risk.

A further comparison of convertible loan stock with ordinary shares	£
Market price per £10 of 9% convertible loan stock	8.20
Convertible into four ordinary shares, market value	6.00
Premium over ordinary share value	2.20
	= 36.7%

The equivalent value of the convertible loan stock is currently 36.7% higher than the value of ordinary shares, reflecting investors' expectations of an increase in the share price before the date when conversion rights can be exercised. However, the stock currently yields 11%, compared with a dividend yield of just 8.9% on equity.

Summary

The calculations above show significant features of the results of Etna plc. Before a final decision can be made about investing in its securities, more information is required about:

(a) the future earnings of Etna plc;
(b) the attitude of Knight plc towards the return required for varying levels of financial risk associated with different types of investment;
(c) alternative investments in other companies' securities;
(d) the desirability of acquiring a significant shareholding in Etna plc (or in any other company).

8 P/E RATIOS

(a) A well-established company is likely to have a higher P/E ratio than a company which is newly quoted on the Stock Exchange.

(b) A large company with a high asset backing is likely to have a higher P/E ratio than a small company with a smaller asset base, because assets are regarded as a last resort security in the event of a winding up.

(c) A company may suffer a temporary fall in profits, and if investors expect profits to recover, they may be prepared to pay more for a share than current performance would justify. The P/E ratio may then be temporarily high.

(d) Investors may expect a company to grow considerably in the next few years, and in anticipation of growth, will pay a high price for shares now. A company with growth prospects should therefore have a higher P/E ratio than companies where little or no growth is expected.

(e) Dividend policies affect share prices as much as, if not more than, earnings. A company which pays high dividends and has a low earnings retention rate may therefore have a higher P/E ratio than a company with the same volume of earnings but which pays a lower dividend. Dividend cover may therefore influence the P/E ratio.

A P/E ratio is the ratio of the market value of a share to the earnings per share. It is often described as the number of years earnings required before an investor recovers the purchase price of a share (on the assumption that annual earnings are constant). The earnings of a company with a high P/E ratio are therefore valued more by investors because they are prepared to wait longer to recover their investment. A high P/E ratio therefore tends to indicate that a company is more secure.

A P/E ratio may be estimated and used as a method of valuing the shares of an unquoted company, but it is wrong to attach too much significance to the P/E ratios of quoted companies. The EPS is determined by the success (or otherwise) of a company's management, and the share price on the market is determined by many factors (dividends, growth prospects, government policy, the economic situation and so on), of which the EPS is only one.

9 CRYSTAL PLC

(a) The post-tax weighted average cost of capital should first be calculated.

(i) *Ordinary shares*

	£
Market value of shares cum div.	3.27
Less dividend per share (810 ÷ 3,000)	0.27
Market value of shares ex div.	3.00

The formula for calculating the cost of equity when there is dividend growth is

$$r = \frac{d(1 + g)}{v} + g$$

where r = cost of equity
d = current dividend
g = rate of growth
v = current ex div market value.

In this case we shall estimate the future rate of growth (g) from the average growth in dividends over the past four years.

$$810 = 620\,(1 + g)^4$$

$$(1 + g)^4 = \frac{810}{620}$$

$$= 1.3065$$

$$(1 + g) = 1.069$$

$$g = 0.069 = 6.9\%$$

$$r = \frac{0.27 \times 1.069}{3} + 0.069 = 16.5\%$$

(ii) *7% Debentures*

In order to find the post-tax cost of the debentures, which are redeemable in ten years time, it is necessary to find the discount rate (IRR) which will give the future post-tax cash flows a present value of £77.10.

The relevant cash flows are:

(1) annual interest payments, net of tax, which are £1,300 × 7% × 67% = £60.97 (for ten years);

(2) a capital repayment of £1,300 (in ten years time).

It is assumed that tax relief on the debenture interest arises at the same time as the interest payment. In practice the cash flow effect is unlikely to be felt for about a year, but this will have no significant effect on the calculations.

	Present value
Try 8%	£'000
Current market value of debentures	
(1,300 at £77.10 per cent)	(1,002.3)
Annual interest payments net of tax	
60.97 × 6.710 (8% for ten years)	409.1
Capital repayment	
1,300 × 0.463 (8% in ten years time)	601.9
	8.7

Try 9%		£'000
Current market value of debentures		(1,002.3)
Annual interest payments net of tax		
60.97 × 6.418		391.3
Capital repayment		
1,300 × 0.422		548.6
	NPV	(62.4)

$$\text{IRR} = 8\% + \left[\frac{8.7}{8.7 - -62.4} \times (9 - 8) \right] \%$$

$$= 8.12\%$$

(iii) *The weighted average cost of capital*

	Market value £'000	*Cost* %	*Product*
Equity	9,000	16.50	1,485
7% Debentures	1,002	8.12	81
	10,002		1,566

$$\frac{1,566}{10,002} \times 100 = 15.7\%$$

The above calculations suggest that a discount rate in the region of 16% might be appropriate for the appraisal of new investment opportunities.

(b) Difficulties and uncertainties in the above estimates arise in a number of areas.

(i) *The cost of equity*. The above calculation assumes that all shareholders have the same marginal cost of capital and the same dividend expectations, which is unrealistic. In addition, it is assumed that dividend growth has been and will be at a constant rate of 7%. In fact, actual growth in the years 19X5/6 and 19X8/9 was in excess of 9%, while in the year 19X7/8 there was negative dividend growth. 7% is merely the average rate of growth for the past four years. The rate of future growth will depend more on the return from future projects undertaken than on the past dividend record.

(ii) *The use of the weighted average cost of capital*. Use of the weighted average cost of capital as a discount rate is only justified where the company in question has achieved what it believes to be the optimal capital structure (the mix of debt and equity) and where it intends to maintain this structure in the long term.

(iii) *The projects themselves*. The weighted average cost of capital makes no allowance for the business risk of individual projects. In practice some companies, having calculated the WACC, then add a premium for risk. In this case, for example, if one used a risk premium of 5% the final discount rate would be 21%. Ideally the risk premium should vary from project to project, since not all projects are equally risky. In general, the riskier the project the higher the discount rate which should be used.

10 BUTLER PLC

(a) The value of the stock, as simple unconvertible loan stock with a redemption date at the end of ten years, would be established by expected rates of return on the market. Since a return of 14% seems to be expected by investors in stocks of a similar risk class, we would predict that the market value would be the future cash flows from the £50,000 of stock, discounted at 14%.

Year	*Item*	*Cash flow*	*Discount factor*	*PV of cash flow*
		£	14%	£
1 - 10	Interest	6,000 pa	5.216	31,296
10	Redemption of capital	50,000	0.270	13,500
				44,796

The value of the stock would be approximately £44,800 or £89.60 per cent.

(b) The stock could now be sold for £134 per cent, and re-invested to earn 14% per annum. To justify holding on to the stock in order to exercise the option to convert into shares, the value of the shares must have risen, by the end of four years, to an amount where:

(i) the interest on the stock, plus
(ii) the value of the shares at the time of conversion;

give an annual return of at least 14% on the investment.

Let the annual growth rate in the share price be g. After four years, the £50,000 of stock can be converted into 10,000 shares, which will have a market value of £5.70 $(1 + g)^4$ each.

The £50,000 of stock could be sold now for £67,000, and so the minimum g is given by the following equation.

$$67{,}000 = (6{,}000 \times 2.914^*) + 57{,}000\,(1 + g)^4 \times 0.592$$

$$67{,}000 = 17{,}484 + 33{,}744\,(1 + g)^4$$

$$\frac{49{,}516}{33{,}744} = (1 + g)^4$$

$$1.4674 = (1 + g)^4$$

$$1.10 = 1 + g$$

$$g = 0.10 = 10\%$$

* Discount factor of £1 pa for four years at 14%.

The minimum annual growth rate in the share price to justify retention of the stock with a view to conversion into shares before 31 January 19X2 is 10%.

(c) If the loan stock did not have the conversion rights, they would have a market value of only £89.60 per cent, instead of the existing £134.0 per cent. Holding on to the stock until it is redeemed in 19X8 would be unprofitable, because a bigger return would be earned by selling the stock now (for £67,000) and investing elsewhere at 14%.

The choice is between selling the stock and investing at 14%, or exercising the option to convert (or selling part of the stock, and converting the remainder into shares). Holding on to the stock, to convert it before 31 January 19X2, would be more profitable if the annual growth in the value of shares is at least 10%.

The investing public obviously regards the eventual growth in share price as a distinct possibility; otherwise stock would not be as highly valued on the market. Capital growth might even exceed 10% per annum, in which case the return from the option to convert would exceed 14%.

The choice is between:

(a) a certain return of 14% per annum;
(b) the chance of a return of over 14%, but with the risk of a lower return.

A 10% annual growth in value (on the assumption that this is not already reflected in the current share price) would mean an increase in the share price to £5.70 × 1.10^4 = £8.35, an increase of £2.65 per share over four years.

The choice does depend very much on the preferences and expectations of the investor. Some information might be obtainable about the profitability, earnings, dividends and growth of the company in recent years. Information might be available about future prospects.

11 EMMA PLC

(a) (i)

Year	*Cash flow*	*Discount factor*	*Present value*
	£m	16%	£m
0	(3.6)	1.0	(3.600)
In perpetuity	0.5	1 ÷ 0.16	3.125
		NPV =	(0.475)

The NPV is negative and the project should not be undertaken.

(ii) We can use the formula $V_g = V_u + Dt$

D = £3,600,000

t = 0.33

	£m
Current value of Emma plc (3,000,000 × £3.20)	9.600
Additional present value of project benefits, if the project were all equity financed (see (a)(i))	3.125
V_u	12.725

V_g = £12,725,000 + £3,600,000 × 0.33

= £13,913,000

	£m
Total value of geared company	13.913
Less value of debt	3.600
Value of equity	10.313

This shows an increase in the value of equity of £10,313,000 - £9,600,000 = £713,000. The project is therefore worthwhile if it is financed by debt.

(iii) The gearing of the company after the project is undertaken in (a)(ii) would be

$$\frac{D}{D + V_{eg}} = \frac{3.6}{(3.6 + 10.313)} = 0.2587508$$

Again, using the formula

$$V_g = V_u + Dt$$

but applying it only to the incremental project, we get

$$V_g = 3.125m^* + (0.33 \times 0.2587508V_g)$$

$$0.9146\ V_g = 3.125m$$
$$V_g = 3.417m$$

($^*V_u$ is the value of benefits calculated in (a)(i)).

	£m
Project benefits	3.417
Project cost	3.600
Loss in value due to project	0.183

Again, as in (a)(i), the project would not be worthwhile.

(b) (i) $$WACC_g = K_u \times (1 - \frac{tD}{D + V_{eg}})$$

$$WACC_g = 0.16 \times [1 - \frac{0.33\ (3.6)}{(3.6 + 10.313)}]$$

$$= 0.14634, \text{ which is just over } 14.6\%$$

(ii) The incremental cost of capital is

$$\frac{\text{incremental after-tax annual cash benefits in perpetuity}}{\text{incremental value of the company}}$$

$$= \frac{£500,000}{£13,913,000 - £9,600,000} \times 100\%$$

$$= \frac{£500,000}{£4,313,000} \times 100\% = 11.5929\%$$

(iii) The figures in (b)(i) and (b)(ii) can be used to support the solutions in (a)(ii) and (a)(iii) as follows.

(1) WACC

	£m
PV of cost	(3.600)
PV of benefits £500,000 ÷ 0.14634	3.417
NPV	(0.183)

This supports the solution in (a)(iii).

(2) Incremental WACC

	£m
PV of cost	(3.600)
PV of benefits £500,000 ÷ 0.115929	4.313
Increase in equity value from incremental investment	0.713

This supports the solution in (a)(ii).

12 PORTFOLIO

(a)

		Return %	*Probability*	*EV* %
(i)	Security X	30	0.3	9
		25	0.4	10
		20	0.3	6
	Expected return, security X			25
(ii)	Security Y	50	0.2	10
		30	0.6	18
		10	0.2	2
	Expected return, security Y			30

(iii) Portfolio of 60% X and 40% Y
The expected return is (60% of 25%) + (40% of 30%) = 15% + 12% = 27%

(b) (i) Security X. The average return, $\bar{x}$, is 25%.

Return x	$(x - \bar{x})$	*Probability* p	$p(x - \bar{x})^2$
30	5	0.3	7.5
25	0	0.4	0
20	(5)	0.3	7.5
			15.0

Risk = standard deviation = $\sqrt{15}$ = 3.87%

(ii) Security Y: The average return, $\bar{x}$, is 30%.

Return x	$(x - \bar{x})$	*Probability* p	$p(x - \bar{x})^2$
50	20	0.2	80
30	0	0.6	0
10	(20)	0.2	80
			160

Risk = standard deviation = $\sqrt{160}$ = 12.65%

(iii)

$$\sigma_p = \sqrt{(W_x)^2(\sigma_x)^2 + (W_y)^2(\sigma_y)^2 + 2(W_x)(W_y)(r)(\sigma_x)(\sigma_y)}$$

The correlation coefficient r is 0

$$\sigma_p = \sqrt{(0.6)^2(15) + (0.4)^2(160)}$$

$$= \sqrt{5.4 + 25.6} = \sqrt{31} = 5.6\%$$

(c) The objectives of portfolio diversification are to achieve a satisfactory rate of return at a minimum risk for that return. This return will be equal to a risk-free rate of return, when the portfolio consists entirely of risk-free securities. Since most portfolios include some risky securities, the expected return should exceed the risk-free rate as a reward for accepting risk. There is an 'efficient frontier' of portfolios which have either:
(i) a higher expected return; or
(ii) a lower risk
than any other portfolio. An investor should select a portfolio on this frontier, although the actual portfolio he prefers will depend on his attitude to risk.

A portfolio is preferable to holding individual securities because it reduces risk whilst still offering a satisfactory rate of return. This is because it is very unlikely that all the investments in a diverse portfolio will simultaneously perform badly.

13 MOODY AND HART

(a) Project discount rates are as follows.

Moody plc		7% + 1.2(12 - 7)%	=	13%
Hart plc	(i)	7% + 1.25(12 - 7)%	=	13.25%
	(ii)	7% + 0.8(12 - 7)%	=	11%
	(iii)	7% + 1.35(12 - 7)%	=	13.75%

The net present values are as follows.

Moody plc		$\frac{500}{1.13}$	=	(in £'000) 442.48
				£'000
Hart plc	(i)	$\frac{200}{1.1325}$	=	176.60
	(ii)	$\frac{100}{1.11}$	=	90.09
	(iii)	$\frac{200}{1.1375}$	=	175.82
				442.51

Allowing for rounding errors, the present values of the three projects of Hart add up to the same amount as the present value of the project of Moody.

(b) Hart's overall beta factor is a weighted average of the beta factors of the three projects.

Project	*Value*	*β*	*Product*
(i)	200	1.25	250
(ii)	100	0.80	80
(iii)	200	1.35	270
	500		600

Overall beta factor = $\frac{600}{500}$ = 1.2

This is the same as Moody plc's project beta factor.

(c) Considering only the projects under review both companies have the same present value and the same systematic risk (the same beta factor). It follows that on the basis of these projects alone, both companies should be valued equally by investors.

It might be tempting to assume that since Hart plc is diversifying into three separate projects, whereas Moody is investing in only one project, investors should prefer the lower-risk Hart plc because Moody's unsystematic risk will be higher. But with CAPM theory, it is assumed that investors can eliminate unsystematic risk by diversifying their own investment portfolios, and do not have to rely on companies to diversify on their behalf.

Portfolio diversification reduces risk because the returns from projects will not be perfectly positively correlated, and diversification reduces risk more when project returns show little or no positive correlation (or even better, negative correlation). However, diversification by a company reduces the risk of insolvency for the company itself. But if corporate insolvency brings no added costs to the investor, CAPM theory states that diversification by a company should have no effect on the risks experienced by a well-diversified investor.

14 BETTALUCK PLC

(a) The risk of the portfolio can be measured by the weighted average beta factor for the shares in the portfolio. The weights should be the market prices of the shares.

Shares	*Number*	*Market price*	*Total market value*	*Beta factor*	*MV × β*
		£	£		
Dashing plc	60,000	4.29	257,400	1.16	298,584
Elegant plc	80,000	2.92	233,600	1.28	299,008
Fantastic plc	100,000	2.17	217,000	0.90	195,300
Gaudy plc	125,000	3.14	392,500	1.50	588,750
			1,100,500		1,381,642

The estimated beta factor for the portfolio as a whole is

$$\frac{1,381,642}{1,100,500} = 1.26$$

Since the beta factor is over 1, we can conclude that the risk of the portfolio is higher than the risk of the market as a whole.

(b) The composition of the portfolio should be considered in two ways.

(i) Are the individual shares in the portfolio performing well enough, and should an investor sell, hold or buy more of the shares?

(ii) Is the composition of the portfolio as a whole satisfactory, bearing in mind that it is intended as a portfolio of short-term rather than long-term investments?

Individual shares in the portfolio

We can assess whether each individual share is expected to yield a return which is satisfactory for the amount of systematic risk involved. The required return for each share can be calculated from the formula $R_f + \beta(R_m - R_f)$.

Share	*Expected return*	*Required return*	*Difference*	*Conclusion*
Dashing	19.5%	11% + 1.16 (19-11)% = 20.28%	- 0.78%	Sell shares
Elegant	24.0%	11% + 1.28 (19-11)% = 21.24%	+ 2.76%	Buy more shares
Fantastic	17.5%	11% + 0.90 (19-11)% = 18.20%	- 0.70%	Sell shares
Gaudy	23.0%	11% + 1.50 (19-11)% = 23.00%	0	Hold

These figures suggest that shares in Dashing and Fantastic are not expected to give a satisfactory return relative to their systematic risk, and so should be sold. In contrast, shares in Elegant are expected to yield a high return relative to their systematic risk, so that an investor should buy more of them. Shares in Gaudy, where expected and required returns are the same, should be held.

However, with Dashing and Fantastic, the difference between required and expected returns is less than 1%, and so given the uncertainty about future returns, and the probability of *abnormal returns* affecting the actual outcome, a financial manager might decide to hold the shares in these companies. Transaction costs are a further deterrent to selling shares unless the investor can obtain substantially better returns by doing so.

The portfolio as a whole

(i) The portfolio consists of shares in only four companies, and so it is not well diversified. This means that the actual risk for the investor will be much higher than the systematic risk would suggest. Bettaluck plc faces abnormal, non-systematic risks in addition to the systematic risk.

(ii) A company's short-term investment portfolio is usually intended to provide a temporary use for a short-term cash surplus, which can be realised by the company when it eventually needs the cash. The portfolio should yield a good return, but companies are usually reluctant to avoid the risks of sharp falls in share prices, and so a big loss in capital value on the portfolio. Some risk of capital loss will often be acceptable, but companies will usually prefer to invest short- term in interest-bearing marketable securities, where the risks of capital losses are smaller.

Recommendation

Bettaluck plc should change the composition of its portfolio, because it is a risky portfolio (beta factor 1.26) measured by systematic risk and because since it consists of just four different shares, the non-systematic risk will be very high. The portfolio could yield very high returns, but it might also yield poor returns or even a capital loss.

Since there is only about £1,000,000 invested in the portfolio, it would not be appropriate to alter the portfolio by including many more different shares in it: transaction costs and portfolio management costs would become too high. It is therefore recommended that a new portfolio consisting of interest-bearing securities (either marketable securities or short-term securities) should be built up.

15 THREE DECISIONS

(a) *Investment decisions*
These decisions involve the selection of new projects, or of companies or other securities to invest in. Such decisions will be taken in the light of required rates of return and estimated risks. Financial managers should also consider the effect on cash flows, and the ease with which investments can be withdrawn from should it be necessary.

Financing decisions
Once investments have been identified as possibly suitable for the company, methods of financing them must be selected. Possibilities include new share issues, loans, the retention of profits and sales of assets. The costs of different sources of finance will be relevant here.

Dividend decisions
When a company makes profits, they may be distributed to shareholders or retained in the business. The directors must decide how much to distribute, taking into account the needs of the business and the preferences of shareholders for current income or future capital gains.

These three types of decision all interact. The acceptability of an investment depends on the cost of the chosen method of finance. One possible source of finance is the retention of profits, and hence the restriction of dividends. A company's dividend policy may well affect its share price, and hence the scope for financing investments by share issues. Loans for investments may be made conditional on a certain dividend policy. Finally, the selection of profitable investments should give scope for increased dividends in the future.

(b) *Relevant information*

(i) *Investment decisions: new projects*

Estimated amounts and timings of cash flows
The level of uncertainty of those estimates
An appropriate discount rate, and the net present value at that rate
The internal rate of return
The impact on accounting profit
Details of alternative projects

(ii) *Investment decisions: investment in other companies and securities*

Amounts available to invest
Current and forecast returns
Market rates of return
Prospects for capital growth
Levels of risk involved

(iii) *Financing decisions*

Possible sources of finance
The current share price
The current state of the stock market
Current and forecast interest rates
The company's level of gearing
Cash flow projections

(iv) *Dividend decisions*

Profits available for distribution
Market expectations
The need to maintain a high share price
Cash flow projections
Opportunities for internal use of retained profits

16 KNUCKLE DOWN LTD

(a) (i) Project A

Year	*Cash flow*	*Discount factor*	*Present value*
	£	12%	£
0	(29,000)	1.000	(29,000)
1	8,000	0.893	7,144
2	12,000	0.797	9,566
3	10,000	0.712	7,120
4	11,000	0.636	6,996
		Net present value +	1,826

(ii) Project B

Year	*Equipment*	*Working capital*	*Cash profit*	*Net cash flow*	*Discount factor*	*Present value*
	£	£	£	£	12%	£
0	(44,000)	(20,000)		(64,000)	1.000	(64,000)
1			19,000	19,000	0.893	16,967
2			24,000	24,000	0.797	19,128
3	5,000	20,000	10,000	35,000	0.712	24,920
				Net present value		(2,985)

(iii) Project C

Year	Equipment	Working capital	Cash profit	Net cash flow	Discount factor	Present value
	£	£	£	£	12%	£
0	(50,000)	(15,000)		(65,000)	1.000	(65,000)
1		(6,000)		(6,000)	0.893	(5,358)
1-5			18,000	18,000	3.605	64,890
5		21,000		21,000	0.567	11,907
				Net present value	+	6,439

(iv) Project D

Year	Net cash flow	Discount factor	Present value
	£	12%	£
0	(20,000)	1.000	(20,000)
1	(20,000)	0.893	(17,860)
2	15,000	0.797	11,958
3	12,000	0.712	8,544
4-8	8,000	2.566	20,528
		Net present value +	3,170

Discount factor at 12%, years 1 to 8	4.968
Less discount factor at 12%, years 1 to 3	2.402
Discount factor at 12%, years 4 to 8	2.566

(v) Project E

The cumulative discount factor for a perpetuity at 15% is 1/0.15 = 6.667.

Year	Net cash flow	Discount factor	Present value
	£	15%	£
0	(32,000)	1.000	(32,000)
1 - ∞	4,500	6.667	30,000
		Net present value	(2,000)

(vi) Project F

	£
1. Present value (at 15%) of £3,000 a year from year 1 in perpetuity	20,000
Less present value of £3,000 a year for years 1 to 10 (× 5.019)	15,057
Present value of £3,000 a year from year 11 in perpetuity	4,943

2. Discount factor at 15%, years 1 to 10	5.019
Less discount factor at 15%, years 1 to 5	3.352
Discount factor at 15%, years 6 to 10	1.667

3.

Year	Net cash flow	Discount factor	Present value
	£	15%	£
0	(20,000)	1.000	(20,000)
1-5	5,000	3.352	16,760
6-10	4,000	1.667	6,668
11-∞	3,000	see above	4,940
		Net present value +	8,368

(vii) Projects A, C, D and F have positive net present values and should be undertaken. Projects B and E should not be undertaken.

(b) (i) The IRR of project A is above 12% (where the NPV is £1,826). We will calculate the NPV at 15%.

Year	*Cash flow*	*Discount factor*	*Present value*
	£	15%	£
0	(29,000)	1.000	(29,000)
1	8,000	0.870	6,960
2	12,000	0.756	9,072
3	10,000	0.658	6,580
4	11,000	0.572	6,292
		NPV	(96)

The IRR is between 12% and 15%. By interpolation, we can estimate the IRR as about

$$12\% + \left[\frac{1{,}826}{(1{,}826 - - 96)} \times (15 - 12) \right]\%$$

$$= 14.85\%$$

(ii) The IRR of project C is above 12%, where the NPV is £6,439. Try 20%.

Year	*Net cash flow*	*Discount factor*	*Present value*
	£	20%	£
0	(65,000)	1.000	(65,000)
1	(6,000)	0.833	(4,998)
1-5	18,000	2.991	53,838
5	21,000	0.402	8,442
		NPV	(7,718)

The IRR is approximately $12\% + \left[\frac{6{,}439}{(6{,}439 - - 7{,}718)} \times (20 - 12) \right]\% = 15.6\%$

(iii) The IRR, r, of project E is found as follows.

PV of cost = PV of benefits

$$(32{,}000) = \frac{4{,}500}{r}$$

$$r = \frac{4{,}500}{32{,}000} = 0.140625$$

IRR = 14.0625%.

17 NEWBEGIN ENTERPRISES LTD

(a) The EV of annual sales volume is as follows.

Probability	*Sales volume*	*Expected value*
	Units	Units
0.10	2,000	200
0.25	6,000	1,500
0.40	8,000	3,200
0.15	10,000	1,500
0.10	14,000	1,400
		7,800

The EV of contribution will be 7,800 × £(10 - 6) = £31,200. The EV of additional cash profits each year will be £31,200 - £20,000 = £11,200.

Year	*Cash flow*	*Discount factor* 10%	*Present value of cash flow*
	£		£
0	(40,000)	1.000	(40,000)
1-6	11,200	4.355	48,776
6	3,000	0.564	1,692
			10,468

The expected value of the NPV of the project is £10,468.

(b) To justify the project the NPV must be at least zero. Assuming that the cost of the equipment and its residual value are known with certainty, we can calculate the minimum required PV of annual cash profits, as follows.

	Present value
	£
PV of capital outlay	40,000
Less PV of residual value	1,692
PV of annual cash profits required for NPV of zero	38,308

Discount factor of £1 pa for six years at 10% — 4.355

Annual cash profit required for NPV of zero = $\frac{£38,308}{4.355}$ = £8,796

Annual fixed costs	£20,000
Annual contribution required for NPV of zero	£28,796
Contribution per unit	£4

Annual sales required are $\frac{£28,796}{£4}$ = 7,199 units

say 7,200 units

(c) Risk and uncertainty analysis can be carried out in several ways.

(i) Sensitivity analysis could be used to measure the percentage adverse change in estimates of cost or revenues which would make the NPV of the project negative.

The sales volume

Since the breakeven annual sales volume is about 7,200 units and expected sales are 7,800 units, the EV of sales volume could fall by 600 units or about 7.7% before the project ceases to be viable.

The price and fixed and variable costs

	£
EV of annual sales revenue (7,800 × £10)	78,000
EV of annual variable costs (7,800 × £6)	46,800
Annual fixed costs	20,000
PV of sales revenue over six years (× 4.355)	339,690
PV of variable costs over six years (× 4.355)	203,814
PV of fixed costs over six years (× 4.355)	87,100

A fall in NPV of £10,468 to £0 would occur, at an annual sales volume of 7,800 units, if:

(1) the sales price were $\frac{10,468}{339,690}$ = 3.1% lower

(that is, 31 pence less per unit, a price of £9.69 per unit)

(2) the variable costs were $\frac{10,468}{203,814}$ = 5.1% higher

(that is, 31 pence per unit higher, at £6.31 per unit)

(3) annual fixed costs were $\frac{10,468}{87,100}$ = 12% higher

(that is, £2,240 higher, at £22,400).

The capital cost of equipment

If the residual value is certain to be £3,000, the project would cease to be viable if the cost of the equipment were more than

$\frac{10,468}{40,000}$ or about 26.2% above the estimated cost.

(ii) To allow for risk, we could raise the discount rate from 10% to, say, 15%. If the NPV is still positive at 15%, we might then assume that the project is both viable and reasonably safe.

Year	*Cash flow*	*Discount factor* 15%	*Present value of cash flow*
	£		£
0	(40,000)	1.000	(40,000)
1-6	11,200	3.784	42,381
6	3,000	0.432	1,296
			3,677

(iii) To allow for the uncertainty of cash flows in the distant future, the cash flow each year could be adjusted to a 'certainty equivalent' and an NPV could be calculated on these adjusted cash flows.

(iv) Risk can be assessed by considering the worst (or best) possible outcome, and estimating the probability that this might occur.

If annual sales are only 2,000 units, there would be an annual contribution of £8,000 and an annual loss of £12,000. Similarly, if sales are 6,000 or 8,000 units, the annual profit would be £4,000 or £12,000 respectively.

		Sales 2,000		*Sales 6,000*		*Sales 8,000*	
Year	*Discount Factor* 10%	*Cash flow*	*Present value*	*Cash flow*	*Present value*	*Cash flow*	*Present value*
		£	£	£	£	£	£
0	1.000	(40,000)	(40,000)	(40,000)	(40,000)	(40,000)	(40,000)
1-6	4.355	(12,000)	(52,260)	4,000	17,420	12,000	52,260
6	0.564	3,000	1,692	3,000	1,692	3,000	1,692
Net Present Value			(90,568)		(20,888)		13,952
Probability			0.1		0.25		

There is a 35% probability that the NPV will be negative. The worst possible outcome (10% probability) is that the NPV will be £(90,568).

(v) The payback period could be considered. The non-discounted payback period, assuming annual sales of 7,800 units, is $\frac{40,000}{11,200}$ = 3.6 years. The discounted payback period is where the cumulative discount factor of £1 pa at 10% equals $\frac{40,000}{11,200}$ = 3.571.

The cumulative discount factor for four years at 10% is 3.170
The cumulative discount factor for five years at 10% is 3.791

The discounted payback period is between four and five years.

If this payback period is too long, the project should not be undertaken.

(vi) The standard deviation of the expected cash flows each year can be calculated as follows.

Probability	Sales Units	*Profit* * *(x)*	$(x - \bar{x})$	$p(x - \bar{x})^2$
		£	£	
0.10	2,000	(12,000)	(23,200)	53.824
0.25	6,000	4,000	(7,200)	12.960
0.40	8,000	12,000	800	0.256
0.15	10,000	20,000	8,800	11.616
0.10	14,000	36,000	24,800	61.504
EV	7,800	11,200		140.160

* Contribution of £4 per unit minus fixed costs of £20,000.

The standard deviation is $\sqrt{140,160,000}$ = £11,839.

18 MUGGINS PLC

Certainty equivalent cash flows

	Year 1	*Year 2*	*Year 3*	*Year 4*
	£'000	£'000	£'000	£'000
Sales (W1)	1,125	1,800	1,575	1,425
Material X (W2)	50	230	248	280
Other variable costs (W3)	517	1,100	1,184	1,340
Management salaries (W4)	67	79	85	92
Rental: opportunity cost	135	135	135	135
Other overheads (× 1.1, 1.3, 1.4, 1.5)	66	78	84	90
	835	1,622	1,736	1,937
Sales less cash costs	290	178	(161)	(512)
Discount factor at 14%	0.877	0.769	0.675	0.592
Present value	254	137	(109)	(303)

The net present value is -£21,000, so the project is not acceptable.

Workings

1. *Sales*

   Year 1 10,000 × £125 × 0.9
   Year 2 18,000 × £125 × 0.8
   Year 3 18,000 × £125 × 0.7
   Year 4 19,000 × £125 × 0.6

2. *Material X*

   Year 1 £50,000 opportunity cost
   Year 2 18,000 × 6 × £1.64 × 1.3
   Year 3 18,000 × 6 × £1.64 × 1.4
   Year 4 19,000 × 6 × £1.64 × 1.5

3. *Other variable costs*

   Per unit: £30 + 3 × £4.20 + £4.40 = £47
   Year 1 10,000 × £47 × 1.1
   Year 2 18,000 × £47 × 1.3
   Year 3 18,000 × £47 × 1.4
   Year 4 19,000 × £147 × 1.5

4. *Management salaries*

   Year 1 £34,000 + £27,000 = £61,000 × 1.1
   Year 2 £61,000 × 1.3
   Year 3 £61,000 × 1.4
   Year 4 £61,000 × 1.5

5. Apportioned costs are irrelevant because they are not incremental cash flows.

19 BRIDGEFORD PLC

All workings are to the nearest £1,000.

Cash flows at actual prices

	1	*2*	*Year* *3*	*4*	*5*
	£'000	£'000	£'000	£'000	£'000
Total investment in working capital	275	363	466	512	
Cash flow effect of working capital changes	(75)	(88)	(103)	(46)	
Sales	2,625	3,308	4,052	4,254	3,829
Materials costs	550	726	932	1,025	966
Labour costs	825	1,089	1,464	1,611	1,611
Overhead costs*	315	386	405	425	447
Total operating costs: cash outflows	1,690	2,201	2,801	3,061	3,024

* All are assumed to involve cash outflows.

Capital allowances

It is assumed that the capital allowances will be claimed from year 1, and will have an effect on cash flows one year later.

Year of claim		*Allowance*
		£'000
1	(25% of £2,000)	500
2	(75% of £500)	375
3	(75% of £375)	281
4	(75% of £281)	211
		1,367
5	(2,000 - 1,367)	633

Taxation

	1	*2*	*Year* *3*	*4*	*5*
	£'000	£'000	£'000	£'000	£'000
Sales	2,625	3,308	4,052	4,254	3,829
Operating costs	(1,690)	(2,201)	(2,801)	(3,061)	(3,024)
Capital allowances	(500)	(375)	(281)	(211)	(633)
Taxable profits	435	732	970	982	172
Tax at 33% (one year in arrears)	144	242	320	324	57

NPV calculations

Year	*Equipment cost*	*Working capital*	*Sales*	*Operating costs*	*Tax*	*Net cash flow*	*Discount factor*	*Present value*
	£'000	£'000	£'000	£'000	£'000	£'000	12%	£'000
0	(2,000)	(200)				(2,200)	1.000	(2,200)
1		(75)	2,625	(1,690)		860	0.893	768
2		(88)	3,308	(2,201)	(144)	875	0.797	697
3		(103)	4,052	(2,801)	(242)	906	0.712	645
4		(46)	4,254	(3,061)	(320)	827	0.636	526
5		512	3,829	(3,024)	(324)	993	0.567	563
6					(57)	(57)	0.507	(29)
						NPV	=	970

The interest costs of £240,000 a year have been omitted from the cash flows, because the cost of finance is encompassed within the discount rate.

The NPV is positive, + £970,000, and so the project should be undertaken.

20 SHORT O'FUNDS LTD

(a) The first step is to rank the projects according to the return achieved per pound invested.

Project	*NPV*	*Investment*	*NPV per £1 invested*	*Ranking*
	£'000	£'000	£	
P	16.5	40	0.41	4
Q	17.0	50	0.34	5
R	18.8	30	0.63	1
S	14.0	45	0.31	6
T	7.4	15	0.49	3
U	10.8	20	0.54	2

The available funds of £130,000 should be allocated as follows.

Project	*Investment*		*NPV*
	£'000		£'000
R	30		18.8
U	20		10.8
T	15		7.4
P	40		16.5
Q	25		8.5
	130	Maximum NPV =	62.0

Project S should not be undertaken and only half of project Q should be undertaken.

(b) The objective is to maximise the total NPV from the projects.

Objective function

Maximise $20.53A + 25.94B + 89.69C + 92.07D + 43.33E + 17.73F$

where A, B, C, D, E and F are the proportions of each of the projects to be undertaken.

The £300,000 limit on funds does not apply in years 3 and 4 because there are no cash outflows in those years.

Constraints

Year 0:	200A + 60B + 80E + 150F	$\leq$ 300
Year 1:	100A + 80B + 120C + 100E + 150F	$\leq$ 300
Year 2:	50A + 50C + 250D	$\leq$ 300
Year 5:	100E	$\leq$ 300

Non negativity: A $\geq$ 0, B $\geq$ 0, C $\geq$ 0, D $\geq$ 0, E $\geq$ 0, F $\geq$ 0

No repetition: A $\leq$ 1, B $\leq$ 1, C $\leq$ 1, D $\leq$ 1, E $\leq$ 1, F $\leq$ 1

The objective function and the constraints having been established, the problem could be solved using the simplex technique (covered in the ACCA 2.6 examination).

21 REPLACER LTD

The optimum replacement cycle

	Replace every year		*Replace every two years*		*Replace every three years*	
Year	*Cash flow*	*PV at 15%*	*Cash flow*	*PV at 15%*	*Cash flow*	*PV at 15%*
	£	£	£	£	£	£
0	(30,000)	(30,000)	(30,000)	(30,000)	(30,000)	(30,000)
1	7,000	6,090	(3,000)	(2,610)	(3,000)	(2,610)
2			3,000	2,268	(4,000)	(3,024)
3					(1,000)	(658)
		(23,910)		(30,342)		(36,292)

Note. Present values have been computed using the following factors: one year, 0.870; two years, 0.756; three years, 0.658. If you used factors to a different number of decimal places, you would have obtained slightly different figures.

Years between replacements		*Equivalent annual cost*
		£
1	£23,910/0.870 =	27,483
2	£30,324/1.626 =	19,879
3	£36,292/2.283 =	15,897

The new type of machine should be replaced every three years.

The replacement of the existing machine

The present value (as at the time of replacement) of the cost of the succession of machines of the new type is £15,897/0.15 = £105,980.

Years to replacement	*Year of cash flow*	*Cash flow*	*Present value*
		£	£
0	0	(105,980)	
		25,000	
		(80,980)	(80,980)
1	1	(105,980)	
		(15,000)	
		12,000	
		(108,980)	(94,813)
2	1	(15,000)	(13,050)
	2	(105,980)	
		(18,000)	
		(123,980)	(93,729)
			(106,779)

The old machine should be sold immediately.

22 FLOCKS LTD

(a) *Workings*

(i) *Capital allowances*

Year		*Machine X allowance*
		£
1	(25% of £63,000)	15,750
2	(75% of £15,750)	11,813
3	(75% of £11,813)	8,859
		36,422
4	(£63,000 - £36,422)	26,578

Year		*Machine Y allowance*
		£
1	(25% of £110,000)	27,500
2	(75% of £27,500)	20,625
3	(75% of £20,625)	15,469
4	(75% of £15,469)	11,602
5	(75% of £11,602)	8,702
		83,898
6	(£110,000 - £83,898)	26,102

(ii) *Taxable profits and tax liabilities*

Machine X

Year	*Cash profits*	*Allowance*	*Taxable profits*	*Tax at 33% (one year later)*
	£	£	£	£
1	25,900	15,750	10,150	3,350
2	28,800	11,813	16,987	5,606
3	30,500	8,859	21,641	7,142
4	29,500	26,578	2,922	964

Machine Y

Year	*Cash profits*	*Allowance*	*Taxable profits*	*Tax at 33% (one year later)*
	£	£	£	£
1	40,300	27,500	12,800	4,224
2	32,900	20,625	12,275	4,051
3	32,000	15,469	16,531	5,455
4	32,700	11,602	21,098	6,962
5	48,500	8,702	39,798	13,133
6	44,200	26,102	18,098	5,972

NPV and payback calculations

Machine X

Year	*Machine cost*	*Working capital*	*Cash profits*	*Tax*	*Net cash flow*	*Discount factor*	*Present value*	*Cumulative cash flow*
	£	£	£	£	£	13%	£	£
0	(63,000)	(12,500)			(75,500)	1.000	(75,500)	(75,500)
1			25,900		25,900	0.885	22,922	(49,600)
2			28,800	(3,350)	25,450	0.783	19,927	(24,150)
3			30,500	(5,606)	24,894	0.693	17,252	744
4		12,500	29,500	(7,142)	34,858	0.613	21,368	
5				(964)	(964)	0.543	(523)	
							+ 5,446	

The NPV for machine X is + £5,446, and the payback period is about three years.

Machine Y

Year	*Machine cost*	*Working capital*	*Cash profits*	*Tax*	*Net cash flow*	*Discount factor*	*Present value*	*Cumulative cash flow*
	£	£	£	£	£	15%	£	£
0	(110,000)	(12,500)			(122,500)	1.000	(122,500)	(122,500)
1			40,300		40,300	0.870	35,061	(82,200)
2			32,900	(4,224)	28,676	0.756	21,679	(53,524)
3			32,000	(4,051)	27,949	0.658	18,390	(25,575)
4			32,700	(5,455)	27,245	0.572	15,584	1,670
5			48,500	(6,962)	41,538	0.497	20,644	
6		12,500	44,200	(13,133)	43,567	0.432	18,821	
7				(5,972)	(5,972)	0.376	(2,245)	
						NPV +	5,434	

The NPV for machine Y is + £5,434 and the payback period is about four years.

Machine X would appear to be the preferable option.

(b) The financing decision will be appraised by discounting the relevant cash flows at the after-tax cost of borrowing, which is 11% × 67% = 7.37%, say 7%.

(i) *Purchase option*

Year	*Item*	*Cash flow*	*Discount factor*	*Present value*
		£	7%	£
0	Cost of machine	(63,000)	1.000	(63,000)
	Tax saved from capital allowances			
2	33% × £15,750	5,198	0.873	4,538
3	33% × £11,813	3,898	0.816	3,181
4	33% × £8,859	2,923	0.763	2,230
5	33% × £26,578	8,771	0.713	6,254
				(46,797)

(ii) *Leasing option*

Years	*Item*	*Cash flow*	*Discount factor*	*Present value*
		£	7%	£
1 - 4	Lease costs	(20,000)	3.387	(67,740)
2 - 5	Tax savings on lease costs (× 33%)	6,600	3.165	20,889
				(46,851)

The purchase option is marginally cheaper, using a cost of capital based on the after-tax cost of borrowing.

On the assumption that investors would regard borrowing and leasing as equally risky finance options, the purchase option is recommended.

23 BANBURY AND COVENTRY

(a) *The values of shares for amalgamation*
It is assumed that the P/E ratio will be applied to forecast earnings rather than historic earnings.

	P/E ratio		*EPS*		*Valuation per share*
Banbury Ltd	20	×	£337,500 / 900,000	=	£7.50
Coventry Ltd	15	×	£200,000 / 500,000	=	£6.00

The total value of shares in the companies would be as follows.

Banbury Ltd	(900,000 × £7.50)	£6,750,000
Coventry Ltd	(500,000 × £6.00)	£3,000,000

On these valuations the implied net dividend yields would be as follows.

	Banbury Ltd	*Coventry Ltd*
Dividends (net) / Market value	£90,000 / £6,750,000	£75,000 / £3,000,000
	= 1.33%	= 2.5%

Earnings per share based on:	*Banbury Ltd*	*Coventry Ltd*
(i) Last year's earnings	33.3p	38p
(ii) Forecast earnings	37.5p	40p

Despite the higher EPS of Coventry based on forecast earnings, a higher valuate has been placed on each share of Banbury Ltd apparently because of its lower gearing and therefore better borrowing potential, and/or because of its better earnings record in terms of both growth and consistency, and/or the certainty of the forecast earnings for Banbury compared to Coventry in light of past performance.

(b) There are several possible schemes for a merger, but one method commonly used is for the larger company to become a holding and trading company, and to make a bid for the shares of the smaller company. In this example, Banbury Ltd would make a bid for the equity of Coventry Ltd, which would become a subsidiary.

This scheme enables Coventry's cheap preference shares and loan stock to be kept, and avoids the costs of a new holding company being formed.

The purchase consideration might be shares, convertible loan stock, redeemable loan stock, irredeemable loan stock or cash.

If the offer is shares in Banbury Ltd, Banbury must issue $\frac{£3,000,000}{£7.50} = 400,000$ shares to the shareholders of Coventry. The terms of the exchange would therefore be four shares in Banbury for every five shares held in Coventry.

Banbury Ltd shareholders would benefit from the arrangement as follows.

(i) The EPS of the enlarged Banbury (assuming no synergy) would be

$$\frac{(£337,500 + £200,000)}{(900,000 + 400,000) \text{ shares}} = 41.346 \text{ pence}$$

This is an improvement on both the historic and the forecast EPS for Banbury Ltd.

(ii) The net assets per share in the old Banbury were £3.22 and the new Banbury they would be

$$\frac{£(2,900,000 + 2,750,000 - 750,000)}{1,300,000 \text{ shares}} = £3.77$$

This too shows a substantial improvement.

Coventry Ltd shareholders would lose in terms of earnings (because its shares have been valued on a lower P/E ratio) and also in terms of asset backing per share.

		£
(i)	Forecast earnings of five shares in Coventry (5 × 40p)	2.00
	Forecast earnings of four shares in the merged Banbury	1.65
	Loss of earnings per five shares held in Coventry	0.35
(ii)	Asset backing of five shares in Coventry (5 × £4)	20.00
	Asset backing of four shares in the merged Banbury (4 × £3.77)	15.08
	Loss of asset backing per five shares held in Coventry	4.92

The dividend policy of Banbury Ltd might also be unacceptable to shareholders in Coventry Ltd who are used to a higher dividend. If they are to continue to receive a dividend of £75,000 in the new company, the total dividends of Banbury Ltd must be increased to

$$£75{,}000 \times \frac{1{,}300{,}000 \text{ shares}}{400{,}000 \text{ shares}} = £243{,}750$$

Since maintainable earnings are expected to be £537,500, the dividend cover would fall to

$$\frac{£537{,}500}{£243{,}750} = 2.2 \text{ times}$$

This cover might be too low for existing shareholders in Banbury Ltd, who might want higher retention of earnings to secure better long-term growth for the company.

An alternative scheme

An alternative scheme would be to pay some of the purchase consideration to shareholders in Coventry Ltd in loan stock yielding a high rate of interest (or in cash, obtained by means of a new issue of loan stock). Suppose that shareholders in Coventry receive the following.

	£	£
200,000 shares in Banbury (× £7.50)		1,500,000
£1,500,000 in 11% loan stock		1,500,000
Purchase consideration		3,000,000

The EPS of the enlarged Banbury would be as follows.

Forecast total earnings before deducting loan stock interest		537,500
Loan stock interest	165,000	
Less tax relief (33%)	54,450	
		110,550
Earnings		426,950
Number of shares (900,000 + 200,000)		1,100,000
EPS		38.8 pence

This represents an improvement for current Banbury Ltd shareholders. Shareholders in Coventry might also find the scheme acceptable. They would receive two shares in Banbury for every five shares held in Coventry plus £15 of 11% loan stock. The earnings of the shares would be 2 × 38.8p = 77.6p and interest on the loan stock would be £1.65, giving total income of £2.43. This compares to forecast maintainable earnings of £2.00 (5 × 40p) for five shares in Coventry Ltd.

Asset backing per share in the enlarged company would be

$$\frac{£(2{,}900{,}000 + 2{,}750{,}000 - 750{,}000 - 1{,}500{,}000)}{1{,}100{,}000 \text{ shares}} = £3.09$$

This would still represent a fall for shareholders in Coventry Ltd.

24 BLACK RAVEN LTD

(a) *An assets basis valuation*
If we assume that a purchaser would accept the revaluation of assets by the independent valuer, an assets valuation of equity would be as follows.

	£	£
Fixed assets		
(ignore patents, assumed to have no market value)		
Land and buildings		1,075,000
Plant and equipment		480,000
Motor vehicles		45,000
		1,600,000
Current assets		383,000
		1,983,000
Less: current liabilities	230,000	
loan	400,000	
		630,000
Asset value of equity (300,000 shares)		1,353,000

Value per share = £4.51

Unless the purchasing company intends to sell the assets acquired, it is more likely that a valuation would be based on earnings.

(b) *Earnings basis valuations*
If the purchaser believes that earnings over the last five years are an appropriate measure for valuation, we could take average earnings in these years, which were

$$\frac{£465{,}000}{5} = £93{,}000$$

An appropriate P/E ratio for an earnings basis valuation might be the average of the three publicly quoted companies for the recent year. (A trend towards an increase in the P/E ratio over three years is assumed, and even though average earnings have been taken, the most recent year's P/E ratios are considered to be the only figures which are appropriate.)

	P/E ratio
Aardvark plc	8.5
Bullfinch plc	9.0
Crow plc	10.0
Average	9.167 (i)
Reduce by about 40% to allow for unquoted status	5.5 (ii)

Share valuations on a past earnings basis are as follows.

	P/E ratio	*Earnings* £'000	*Valuation* £'000	*Number of shares*	*Value per share*
(i)	9.167	93	852.5	300,000	£2.84
(ii)	5.5	93	511.5	300,000	£1.71

Because of the unquoted status of Black Raven Ltd, purchasers would probably apply a lower P/E ratio, and an offer of about £1.71 per share would be more likely than one of £2.84.

Future earnings might be used. Forecast earnings based on the company's five year plan will be used.

		£
Expected earnings:	Year 1	100,000
	Year 2	104,000
	Year 3	108,160
	Year 4	112,486
	Year 5	116,986
	Average	108,326.4 (say £108,000)

A share valuations on an expected earnings basis would be as follows.

P/E ratio	*Average future earnings*	*Valuation*	*Value per share*
5.5	£108,000	£594,000	£1.98

It is not clear whether the purchasing company would accept Black Raven's own estimates of earnings.

(c) *A dividend yield basis of valuation with no growth*
There seems to have been a general pattern of increase in dividend yields to shareholders in quoted companies, and it is reasonable to suppose that investors in Black Raven would require at least the same yield.

An average yield for the recent year for the three quoted companies will be used. This is 12%. The only reliable dividend figure for Black Raven Ltd is £45,000 a year gross, in spite of the expected increase in future earnings. A yield basis valuation would therefore be

$$\frac{£45,000}{12\%} = £375,000 \text{ or } £1.25 \text{ per share.}$$

A purchasing company would, however, be more concerned with earnings than with dividends if it intended to buy the entire company, and an offer price of £1.25 should be considered too low. On the other hand, since Black Raven Ltd is an unquoted company, a higher yield than 12% might be expected.

(d) *A dividend yield basis of valuation, with growth*
Since earnings are expected to increase by 4% a year, it could be argued that a similar growth rate in dividends would be expected. We shall assume that the required yield is 17%, rather more than the 12% for quoted companies because Black Raven Ltd is unquoted. However, in the absence of information about the expected growth of dividends in the quoted companies, the choice of 12%, 17% or whatever, is not much better than a guess.

$$MV = \frac{d(1+g)}{(r-g)} = \frac{45,000(1.04)}{(0.17-0.04)} = £360,000 \text{ or } £1.20 \text{ per share.}$$

(e) *The discounted value of future cash flows*
The present value of cash inflows from an investment by a purchaser of Black Raven Ltd's shares would be discounted at either 18% or 14%, depending on the view taken of Black Raven Ltd's assets. Although the loan of £400,000 is secured on some of the company's property, there are enough assets against which there is no charge to assume that a purchaser would consider the investment to be backed by tangible assets.

The present value of the benefits from the investment would be as follows.

Year	*Cash flow*	*Discount factor*	*PV of cash flow*
	£'000	14%	£'000
1	120	0.877	105.24
2	120	0.769	92.28
3	140	0.675	94.50
4	70	0.592	41.44
5	120	0.519	62.28
			395.74

A valuation per share of £1.32 might therefore be made. This basis of valuation is one which a purchasing company ought to consider. It might be argued that cash flows beyond year 5 should be considered and a higher valuation could be appropriate, but a figure of less than £2 per share would be offered on a DCF valuation basis.

(f) *The accounting rate of return method*
If a company wishing to take over Black Raven Ltd expects to make an accounting rate of return of, say, 20%, and assuming that a return of £100,000 is assumed for this purpose the valuation of Black Raven Ltd might be

$$\frac{£100,000}{20\%} = £500,000, \text{ or } £1.67 \text{ per share.}$$

(g) *The super-profits method*
If we assume that the normal rate of profit is 5% on net assets, the normal profits might be as follows (although 'net assets' could be defined in other ways).

	£
Asset value of equity (see (a))	1,353,000
Add asset value of loan stock	400,000
Net assets	1,753,000
Actual (current) profit	100,000
Less normal profit after taxation (5%)	87,650
Super-profits	12,350
Goodwill (say two years purchase of super-profits)	£24,700

The total purchase consideration for equity would be £1,353,000 + £24,700 = £1,377,700 or £4.59 per share.

(h) *Summary*
Any of the preceding valuations might be made, but since share valuation is largely a subjective matter, many other prices might be offered. In view of the high asset values of the company an asset stripping purchaser might come forward.

25 SUBSIDIARIES

X Ltd is the more profitable company, both in absolute terms and in proportion to sales and to operating capital employed. This may indicate that X Ltd is much better managed than Y Ltd, but this is not the only possibility, and a study of the other data shows that Y Ltd's profitability, while at present lower, may be more sustainable.

A higher percentage of Y's sales are to the home market, while it has still achieved fairly substantial export sales. This suggests that Y could have done better in exploiting the export market, but also that Y is less exposed than X to exchange rate fluctuations and the possible imposition of trade barriers. The prospects for the home market appear good, and should give scope for adequate growth. Y has achieved higher growth in total turnover than X over the past three years.

While Y appears to be making worse use of its assets than X, with asset turnover ratios lower than X's and falling, this seems to be largely because Y has recently acquired substantial new assets. It may be that within the next few years X will have to undertake a major renewals programme, with consequent adverse effects on its asset turnover ratios.

While X may be making better use of its assets (subject to the reservations set out above), Y is making sales per employee about 50% higher than X, and has consistently done so over the past three years. X shows no sign of catching up, despite the fact that its total number of employees has recently fallen slightly. The modest rises in sales per employee over the past three years in both X and Y may be due largely to inflation.

Y seems to be significantly better than X at controlling the cost of sales (49% of sales in Y, and 65% in X), though X has made improvements over the past three years while there has been little change in Y. On the other hand, X's administration expenses have been only 6% of sales, while Y's have been 26% of sales. This contrast between the two types of cost suggests that different categorisations of costs may have been used. If we combine the cost of sales and administration expenses, then for X they total 71% of sales and for Y they total 75% of sales. There is thus little difference between the companies, though X has shown improved cost control while Y has not. X has also had lower selling and distribution costs. One must however bear in mind that X will have had a lower depreciation element in its costs than Y, because Y has recently invested substantially in fixed assets. Y's costs will also be increased by its higher salaries, which may pay off in better employee motivation and hence higher sales per employee. On the other hand, Y's costs have been kept down by the carrying forward of an increasing amount of product development costs, an accounting policy which may well be imprudent.

In working capital management, X has the edge. Y has very high debtors, and these have recently risen sharply as a proportion of turnover. Y also carries rather more stock than X, and has very little cash. While both companies have tolerable current and liquid ratios, X's are certainly safer. Y achieves a liquid ratio of 1:1 almost entirely by relying on debtors. If it suffers substantial bad debts, or if the bank should become concerned and call in the overdraft, Y could suffer serious liquidity problems. It also depends heavily on trade credit to finance debtors. While it is sensible to take advantage of trade credit offered, Y may depend too much on the continued goodwill of its suppliers. This may indicate the need for a fresh injection of equity.

On balance, X seems to be a sounder company than Y, with better financial management.

26 VEREY PLC

The existing capital structure

The existing capital structure appears to be reasonably safe. Taking market values, gearing is (980 + 795)/4,000 = 44%, which is not high, and interest is covered four times. The one area of concern, on which full information is not given, is the short-term liquidity of the company. Manufacturing companies often have to invest heavily in working capital and have to wait a long time for stocks to be turned into cash. It is stated that the company has no spare cash. Presumably cash has been set aside to make next week's payments of dividend and interest; it is to be hoped that the company plans to accumulate enough cash over the next six months to make the next interest payment on the 10% secured debentures (and perhaps also the final interest payment on the 14% loan stock, unless money is raised for that along with money to redeem the stock).

It is not possible to say whether the company's capital structure is optimal. The market value of the 10% secured debentures is very close to par, suggesting that market interest rates are close to 10%. This makes the 14% loan stock seem a little expensive, and perhaps it is a good thing that it will soon be redeemed. (The fact that the market value of the 14% loan stock is close to par is explained by the fact that it will soon be redeemed at par.) The company could consider higher gearing, perhaps through financing the proposed investment in Redland by borrowing. There is unlikely to be any point in reducing the gearing by replacing the 14% loan stock with equity.

The redemption of the 14% loan stock

It is almost certainly appropriate to redeem the 14% loan stock by the issue of new loan stock. A lower rate of interest than 14% could probably be obtained, particularly if the new loan stock is secured. The existing secured debentures are probably secured on the company's land and buildings. These assets are likely to have increased substantially in value over the ten years since the debentures were issued, giving scope for a further issue secured (as a second charge) on the same property. A rate of interest close to 10% may be achievable.

The financing of the new investment in Redland

At the present rate of exchange, this investment would cost £400,000, and would yield annual income of £45,000, or 11.25% of the cost. This would suggest that the investment could be financed by a sterling loan at about 10% and would still be profitable. However, UK investors in the company might well expect an increased return if the company engaged in substantial overseas operations, because of the perceived higher risk than that of the company's existing UK operations. Furthermore, the company would be exposed to exchange rate fluctuations. If the R$ were to weaken to, say, R$2.5 = £1, the annual sterling income would fall to £36,000, which would be only 9% of the original sterling investment. This could well be less than the interest rate on sterling loan capital raised to finance the investment.

Given the company's low gearing, there is little point in making a rights issue to finance the investment (although with the market value of shares well above par, there is no obvious problem with such an issue). The company should consider raising a loan in R$ to finance the investment, with the income from the investment being used to make interest payments. Exchange rate fluctuations could not then make the investment unprofitable, although they would of course affect the sterling value of the surplus profit after paying the loan interest. The feasibility of this plan does of course depend on R$ loans being available at less than 90/800 = 11.25%, and on lenders in Redland having sufficient confidence in the company's ability and willingness to meet interest payments from its resources in the UK, should the operating income from the Redland factory be lower than expected.

27 WORKING CAPITAL

(a) In order to carry on a business successfully a company cannot just invest in capital projects and fixed assets. It must also invest in and exercise control over working capital: stocks, debtors and creditors. This working capital has an important bearing on a company's cash needs and cash flows, and therefore on its liquidity which is as important as its profitability.

Different companies will have different working capital needs depending on the nature of the company's business. The statement in the question that 'stronger and more profitable companies have a higher proportion of working capital' may well be true for a manufacturing company. A manufacturing company will need substantial levels of stocks and will probably have high levels of debtors and creditors as well. However, an equally profitable service company may have a much lower proportion of working capital as although it may have debtors and some creditors, a service company is unlikely to have large stocks.

Even in manufacturing companies, a decision to use Just in Time techniques of production, if implemented successfully, would result in lower stocks, with smaller batches being produced and so smaller stocks of finished goods.

So a company need not necessarily have a high proportion of working capital in order to be profitable or strong. Conversely companies with high proportions of working capital are not necessarily profitable, well managed companies. It may be that in some companies the reason for high working capital is bad management. Stock control and credit control may be lax whilst not enough advantage is being taken of available trade credit. A much more profitable company may have lower levels of working capital due to an efficient stock-holding policy, tight credit and minimum cash holdings.

(b) There is no rigid rule as to how, ideally, trade debtors and stocks should be financed. Generally current assets are financed by a mixture of short-term and long-term funds.

However, certain values of ratios are accepted as being 'ideal' although these will vary depending upon the circumstances of an individual company. The ratios used to measure the financing of current assets are the liquidity ratios.

(i) The current ratio (current assets:current liabilities) is generally thought to be ideal at a ratio of 2:1. This means that half of current assets should be financed by current liabilities and half by long-term funds.

(ii) The quick ratio (current assets minus stock:current liabilities) is generally thought to be ideal at a ratio of 1:1.

When deciding upon the policy to be adopted by a company in financing its trade debtors and stocks, the management of a company must balance the cost of financing against the risk of insolvency. If the company's creditors suddenly demand immediate payment or the bank demands repayment of the company's overdraft, the company will be in danger of insolvency unless it is able to turn enough of its assets into cash quickly. Trade debtors can be more easily converted into cash than stocks, as stocks must first be sold to generate debtors and the debts must be collected in cash: if the company's current assets were financed wholly by its trade creditors or overdraft (a current ratio of 1:1) then there would be a danger of the company's becoming insolvent.

On the other hand current liabilities are often a much cheaper form of finance than long-term funds. Creditors and amounts owing in taxation rarely carry an interest cost and bank overdraft interest is calculated on the balance borrowed from day to day.

Therefore trade debtors and stocks should be financed by a mixture of long-term and short-term funds but the proportions in which these two sources of finance are used will vary from enterprise to enterprise. Companies have to consider whether in the interest of higher profits it is worth accepting the risk of insolvency by increasing current liabilities. The final decision on how current assets are financed will therefore depend on the management's attitude to this risk.

28 RASCAL PLC

(a) (i)

		Industrial		*Commercial*
If the advertising campaign goes ahead				
		£'000		£'000
Sales £3,600,000 × 1.25 = £4,500,000	(40%)	1,800	(60%)	2,700
Debtors				
30 days 30/360 × 1,800 × 10% =		15.0		
50 days 50/360 × 1,800 × 20% =		50.0		
90 days 90/360 × 1,800 × 67% =		301.5		
30 days 30/360 × 2,700 × 10% =				22.5
50 days 50/360 × 2,700 × 10% =				37.5
60 days 60/360 × 2,700 × 79% =				355.5
		366.5		415.5
If the advertising campaign does not go ahead				
Sales £3,600,000 total				
Industrial (30%) £1,080,000				
Commercial (70%) £2,520,000				
Debtors 90/360 × 1,080		270.0		
50/360 × 2,520				350.0
Increase in debtors		96.5		65.5

Total increase in debtors = £96,500 + £65,500 = £162,200

(ii) Extra sales = 25% × £3,600,000 = £900,000 a year

	£	£
Extra contribution from extra sales (40% × £900,000)		360,000
Less bad debts		
Industrial 3% × £1,800,000	54,000	
Commercial 1% × £2,700,000	27,000	
		(81,000)
Less cost of extra investment in debtors (10% of £162,000) *		(16,200)
Incremental benefit		262,800

* Alternatively, you could take 10% of the *cost* of the higher debtors = 10% of 60% of £162,000 = £9,720.

The maximum amount that should be paid for the advertising campaign is about £260,000.

(b)

	Industrial	Commercial
	£'000	£'000
Debtors, if the advertising campaign goes ahead		
30 days: 30/360 × 1,800 × 40%	60.0	
50 days: 50/360 × 1,800 × 18%	45.0	
60 days: 60/360 × 1,800 × 20%	60.0	
90 days: 90/360 × 1,800 × 20%	90.0	
30 days: 30/360 × 2,700 × 50%		112.50
50 days: 50/360 × 2,700 × 25%		93.75
60 days: 60/360 × 2,700 × 14%		63.00
90 days: 90/360 × 2,700 × 10%		67.50
	255.0	336.75
Debtors with advertising, but no discounts (see (a) (i))	366.5	415.50
Reduction in debtors	111.5	78.75
	£	£
Cost of discounts		
3% of £1,800 × 40%	(21,600)	
3% of £2,700 × 50%		(40,500)
Savings from reduced debtors		
10% of £111,500	11,150	
10% of £78,750		7,875
Savings in bad debts		
(industrial only) 1% of £1,800,000	18,000	0
Benefit/(loss) from discount	7,500	(32,625)

If the discount has to be introduced to both markets, it is not worth offering. The extra profit from the industrial market would be more than offset by the loss of profit from the commercial market.

29 BLEARY HYDE LTD

(a) It is assumed that the normal credit terms will not strictly apply, and that the customer would pay the balance due after one year, or not at all. The three possible outcomes are as follows.

(i) *The customer pays after one year, without a special debt collection effort*

Probability 0.4

Item	*Year*	*Cash flow*	*Discount factor*	*PV*
		£	15%	£
Cost of order (6,000 × (2.5 - 0.75))	0	(10,500)	1.000	(10,500)
Deposit with order (10% of (6,000 × 2.5))	0	1,500	1.000	1,500
Balance of payment (90% of (6,000 × 2.5))	1	13,500	0.870	11,745
			NPV	+ 2,745

(ii) *The customer pays after one year, but with a special debt collection effort needed*

Probability customer does not pay without prompting 0.6
Probability customer pays after prompting (50% × 0.6) 0.3

Item	*Year*	*Cash flow*	*Discount factor*	*PV*
		£	15%	£
Cost of order	0	(10,500)	1.000	(10,500)
Deposit with order	0	1,500	1.000	1,500
Cost of debt collection	1	(800)	0.870	(696)
Balance of payment	1	13,500	0.870	11,745
			NPV	+ 2,049

(iii) *The customer defaults in spite of special debt collection effort*

Probability 0.3

Item	*Year*	*Cash flow*	*Discount factor*	*PV*
		£	15%	£
Cost of order	0	(10,500)	1.000	(10,500)
Initial deposit	0	1,500	1.000	1,500
Cost of debt collection effort	1	(800)	0.870	(696)
			NPV	(9,696)

The expected value of the NPV is (0.4 × £2,745) + (0.3 × 2,049) + (0.3 × - 9,696) = -£1,196.1

The order should be rejected, because the expected value of the NPV is negative.

(b) It is assumed that a repeat order would only be accepted after 12 months if the customer did not default on the first order. This has a 0.7 probability. Since the probability of a repeat order is only 50%, the joint probability of a repeat order which will be accepted is 0.7 × 0.5 = 0.35.

The additional cash flows to consider are those for the second order.

Probability of second order which will be accepted = 0.35
Probability of second order being accepted and payment being received = 0.9 × 0.35 = 0.315
Probability of second order being accepted and customer defaulting = 0.1 × 0.35 = 0.035

Customer pays

Item	*Year*	*Cash flow*	*Discount factor*	*PV*
		£	15%	£
Cost of second order	1	(10,500)	0.870	(9,135)
10% deposit	1	1,500	0.870	1,305
Balance of payment	2	13,500	0.756	10,206
			NPV	+ 2,376

Customer defaults

NPV = - 9,135 + 1,305 = -£7,830

The expected value of the NPV of second year order cash flows is therefore (0.315 × £2,376) + (0.035 × -£7,830) = +£474.39.

Summary

	£
EV of NPV of first year order (as in (a))	(1,196.10)
EV of NPV of second year order	474.39
Total EV of NPV (as at year 0)	(721.71)

The order should not be accepted, because the expected value of the NPV is negative.

(c) The probability of a second order is 100%, but since it will only be accepted if the customer did not default in the first year, we now have the following.

Probability of second order which will be accepted	= 0.7
Probability of second order being accepted and payment being received	= 0.9 × 0.7
	= 0.63
Probability of second order being accepted and customer defaulting	= 0.1 × 0.7
	= 0.07

The expected value of the NPV (as at year 0) of the second year order cash flows will therefore be

(0.63 × £2,376) + (0.07 × -£7,830) = +£948.78.

Summary

	£
EV of NPV of first year order cash flows	(1,196.10)
EV of NPV of second year order cash flows	948.78
Total EV of NPV	(247.32)

The order should still not be accepted.

30 KNOSSOS LTD

(a) (i) Option 1 would cost six months interest: 0.5 × 18% × £200,000 = £18,000. Tax relief on the interest is ignored, as required by the question.

(ii) Option 2 would involve the deferral of payments for material purchases in December and January. Instead of paying at the end of January and February, Knossos Ltd would withhold payment until March and April (taking two months extra credit and thereby reducing expected cash payments by £200,000, before discounts). Monthly payments of £100,000 would resume in March. The cost of this option would be lost discounts: 6 months × 2% × £100,000 = £12,000.

The actual improvement in cash flow would not be £200,000, because discounts of £4,000 (two months) would be forgone; therefore Knossos Ltd would only raise £196,000 in funds this way. It is assumed that the difference of £4,000 is not significant.

Since Knossos Ltd would not require the funds until the end of February 19X1, the £98,000 saved in January would reduce overdraft interest by 1% × £98,000 = £980.

The net cost of forgoing discounts for six months would be as follows.

	£
Lost discounts	12,000
Less saving in overdraft interest	980
Net cost	11,020

(iii) With option 3, the receipts from the factor at the end of January would be as follows.

	£	£
75% of £300,000		225,000
Less fees		
Debt collection charges (2% of £300,000)	6,000	
Interest (1.25% of £225,000)	2,813	
		8,813
		216,187

(An annual interest rate of 15% has been taken as a monthly interest rate of approximately 1.25%.)

There would also be monthly savings in administration costs of £4,000. Surplus funds would therefore consist of:

(1) £216,187 - £200,000 = £16,187 for a six month period from 31 January;
(2) monthly savings of £4,000 for a period of six months.

Interest savings, at a monthly rate of 1%, would be as follows.

	£
1% × £16,187 × 6 months	971
1% × £4,000 × 5 months	200
1% × £4,000 × 4 months	160
1% × £4,000 × 3 months	120
1% × £4,000 × 2 months	80
1% × £4,000 × 1 month	40
	1,571

This figure is an approximation because of the assumptions used.

The net cost of factoring over six months would be as follows.

	£
Monthly fees (6 × £8,813)	52,878
Less savings in administration costs (6 × £4,000)	24,000
	28,878
Less savings in interest	1,571
	27,307

(iv) The cheapest alternative is option 2.

(b) *Receipts with factoring (assuming no bad debts)*

	Debts collected directly	*Advance by factor*	*Balance of debts from factor*	*Total*
	£	£	£	£
January 19X1	300,000	216,187		516,187
February		216,187	*75,000	291,187
March		216,187	75,000	291,187
April		216,187	75,000	291,187
May		216,187	75,000	291,187
June		216,187	75,000	291,187
July			75,000	75,000
August	**300,000			300,000

* January sales
** July sales

(c) *Other considerations*

(i) Would there by any long-term effect on relations with suppliers if extra credit is taken and the discounts forgone?

(ii) What would be the reaction of employees if a factor is used to do debt collection work?

(iii) What might go wrong? For example, if the extra funds were needed for a longer period than six months, or that funds in excess of £200,000 were needed, what would the company then be able to do?

31 AARDVARK LTD

Aardvark Ltd has the following options.

(a) It can continue its existing policy.
(b) It can use the export factor, either in combination with its existing overdraft, or using the 80% finance offered by the factor.
(c) It can use the ECGD, with the assignment of policy rights (since cheaper finance is available at no extra cost.

It is assumed that all export debts will be financed by an overdraft or by special lending arrangements.

(i) *Use of the export factor for debt collection only*

	£
Service fee 3% × £1,000,000	(30,000)
Bad debts saved (by insurance) 0.5% × £1,000,000	5,000
Administration costs saved	35,000
Net saving	10,000

(ii) *Use of the export factor for debt collection and finance*

That there will be a saving in finance charges of 0.5% a year on 80% of the average debtors required.

	£
Service fee for debt collection	(30,000)
Interest costs saved (0.5% × 80% × £1,000,000 × 90/360	1,000
Bad debts saved	5,000
Administrative costs saved	35,000
Net saving	11,000

(iii) *Use of the ECGD*

If the ECGD is used, there will be a saving of 1% on 70% of the finance required, since 70% of finance will be obtained at just 1.5% above base rate, instead of 2.5% above base rate.

	£
Insurance costs 0.35% × £1,000,000	(3,500)
Savings in bank interest 1% × 70% × £1,000,000 × 90/360	1,750
Savings in bad debts 90% × 0.5% × £1,000,000	4,500
Net saving	2,750

Conclusion

Aardvark Ltd should use the services of the export factor, and obtain finance for 80% of export credit sales from the factor.

32 IMPORT-EXPORT MERCHANT

(a) The foreign exchange operations are assumed to occur as follows. On 31 December, the merchant will arrange four foreign exchange transactions. These are:

(i) to obtain sufficient X$ to purchase 500 tonnes in January, at the spot rate;

(ii) to obtain sufficient X$ to purchase 1,000 tonnes in February, at the one month forward rate, that is, at the beginning of February;

(iii) to sell Y$ to be received from the customer (for the first 500 tonnes) in February, at the end of February rate (two months forward);

(iv) to sell Y$ to be received by the end of March on the final 1,000 tonnes at the end of March rate (three months forward).

The bank selling rate (customer buying rate) is the left hand column of figures quoted, and the bank buying rate (customer selling rate) for foreign currency is the right hand column of figures.

Purchase costs			X$	£
(i)	January:	X$11,820 × 500 tonnes	5,910,000	
		Rate of conversion	107.45	
				55,002
(ii)	February	X$11,820 × 1,000 tonnes	11,820,000	
		Rate of conversion (107.45 + 0.55)*	108.00	
				109,444
Purchases				164,446

*add discount

Sales value		Y$	£
(i)	January sales (462 × 500)	231,000	
	Rate of conversion (3.88 - .03)**	3.85	
			60,000
(ii)	February sales (462 × 1,000)	462,000	
	Rate of conversion (3.88 - 0.055)**	3.825	
			120,784
Sales			180,784

**subtract premium

The commission of £1 per mille or 0.001 on each of the four transactions (i) to (iv) would exceed £10 in every case, therefore the total commission is 4 × £10 = £40.

	£
Sales	180,784
Less cost of sales	164,446
Profit on transaction	16,338
Less commission	40
Net profit	16,298

(b) If the February shipment were cancelled after the merchant has entered into the forward exchange contracts, the contracts would still have to be honoured. He would still have to buy X$11,820,000 at a rate of 108.00, and would have to sell Y$462,000 at a rate of 3.825. Without the February shipment, the merchant would be obliged to 'close out' the contracts. He would have to:

(i) sell the X$ he must buy, at the spot rate available at the time;

(ii) buy Y$ at the available spot rate (or at a suitable forward rate) on the foreign exchange market, for resale.

In both (i) and (ii) there would probably be a loss because the resale of the foreign currencies would probably earn less (in pounds) than it would cost the merchant to buy them (depending on how exchange rates have moved since the original forward exchange contracts were entered into).

If the February shipment were delayed for two months until April, the contracts entered into at the end of December would still have to be honoured.

The X$11,820,000 would be obtained too early and it is unlikely that the merchant would have enough funds in his business to hold them for two months. He might sell the X$ he must buy in February, and make a loss on this transaction, and then enter into another forward exchange contract to obtain X$11,820,000 in February.

The merchant would have to sell Y$462,000 in March, so he would have to buy this amount at the spot rate in order to resell it. There would be a loss on this transaction, just as if the February shipment had been cancelled.

The merchant would then probably decide to enter into another forward exchange contract to sell Y$462,000 two months later than originally expected, that is, in May.

The effect of a delay in shipment would then be similar to the effect of a cancellation, with the exception that the merchant would arrange two further foreign exchange contracts, one to buy more X$ and the other to sell forward more Y$.

The merchant would really be trying to extend each of his forward exchange contracts by a further two months. The merchant's bank might offer him slightly better exchange rates to extend the contracts than he would have to use to close out the contracts and make new contracts.

33 BRINGASOCK LTD

(a) The finance director could take a chance on future changes in the lire/sterling exchange rate, and do nothing for three months. When the 56,000,000 lire are received, they could then be exchanged at the spot rate, whatever that happens to be.

However, this is not recommended. The company should have a policy of hedging against foreign exchange risk, in view of its regular export sales. The two principal methods to consider are:

(i) a forward exchange contract;
(ii) the currency market.

A forward exchange contract

The forward exchange rate for Bringasock to sell 56,000,000 lire in three months time is as follows.

Spot rate	2,322
Add discount	23
Forward rate	2,345

The sterling value of the receipts would be

$$\frac{56,000,000}{2,345} = £23,880.60.$$

The currency market

The lire will be received in three months, so Bringasock should borrow lire now. At a borrowing rate of 12% a year or 3% a quarter, the amount to be borrowed so that 56,000,000 lire become payable in three months time is

$$\frac{56,000,000}{1.03} = 54,369,000 \text{ lire.}$$

The borrowed lire would be converted into sterling at the spot rate of 2,322, to yield

$$\frac{54,369,000}{2,322} = £23,414.73.$$

On the assumption that this cash could be invested to earn the deposit rate for sterling (6% a year = $1\frac{1}{2}$% a quarter) this would have a value in three months time of

$$£23,414.73 \times 1.015 = £23,765.95.$$

A forward exchange contract would be more profitable than the use of the currency market, and is therefore recommended.

(b) The receipt of 56,000,000 lire could be partially matched with the payment of 30,000,000 lire, so that the foreign exchange risk is eliminated by using lire receipts to make lire payments. A forward exchange contract should be taken out for the remaining 26,000,000 lire, and the net receipts would be

$$\frac{26,000,000}{2,345} = £11,087.42.$$

INDEX

INDEX

FURTHER READING

For further question practice on Financial Management, BPP publish a companion Practice and Revision Kit. This contains a bank of 70 questions, mostly drawn from past examinations, and each one is accompanied by a fully worked suggested solution. The current (1991) edition is priced at £8.95.

You may also wish to test your grasp of the subject by tackling short questions in multiple choice format. BPP publish the *Password* series of books, each of which incorporates a large collection of multiple choice questions with solutions, comments and marking guides. The Password title relevant to the 3.2 syllabus is *Password: Financial Management*. This is priced at £6.95 and contains about 300 questions.

To order your Practice and Revision Kit and Password book, ring our credit card hotline on 081-740 6808 or tear out this page and send it to our Freepost address.

To: BPP Publishing Ltd, FREEPOST, London W12 8BR Tel: 081-740 6808

Forenames (Mr / Ms) ____________________

Surname: ____________________

Address: ____________________

____

Post code: ____________________

Please send me the following books:	*Quantity*	*Price*	*Total*
ACCA 3.2 Financial Management Kit		£8.95	
Password Financial Management		£6.95	

Please include postage:

UK: £1.50 for first plus 50p for each extra book ....

Overseas: £3 for first plus £1.50 for each extra book ....

I enclose a cheque for £________ or charge to Access/Visa

Card number [| | | | | | | | | | | | | | | |]

Expiry date ____________ Signature ____________________

If you are placing an order, you might like to look at the reverse of this page. It's a Review Form, which you can send in to us with comments and suggestions on the text you've just finished. Your feedback really does make a difference: it helps us to make the next edition that bit better. So if you're posting the coupon, do fill in the Review Form as well.

ACCA - 3.2 FINANCIAL MANAGEMENT TEXT

Name: ______________________________

How have you used this text?

Home study (book only)	☐	With 'correspondence' package	☐
On a course: college ____________	☐	Other ____________	

How did you obtain this text?

From us by mail order	☐	From us by phone	☐
From a bookshop	☐	From your college	☐

Where did you hear about BPP texts?

At bookshop	☐	Recommended by lecturer	☐
Recommended by friend	☐	Mailshot from BPP	☐
Advertisement in ____________	☐	Other ____________	

Have you used the companion kit for this subject? Yes/No

Your comments and suggestions would be appreciated on the following areas.

Syllabus coverage

Illustrative questions

Errors (please specify, and refer to a page number, if you've spotted anything!)

Presentation

Other (index, cross-referencing, price - whatever!)

Notes